Pillars of the NFL

Coaches Who Have Won
Three or More Championships

Patrick McCaskey

Sporting Chance Press™, Inc.
1074 Butler Drive
Crystal Lake, IL 60014
sportingchancepress.com

Nash's "My Colts, verses and reverses Copyright 1968 by Ogden Nash. First Appeared in *Life* Magazine. Reprinted by permission of Curtis Brown, Ltd.

Photographs and illustrations appearing in *Pillars of the NFL: Coaches Who Have Won Three or More Championships* were supplied by the Archives and Special Collections of Fordham University Library, Chicago History Museum, Goal Line Art, Inc., William Potter, Rob Sherwood, the McCaskey family, the Library of Congress, Miami University of Ohio, the Wisconsin Historical Society, Michael Schwartz Library of Cleveland State University, St. Norbert College, Pittsburgh Post-Gazette, San Jose State University Athletics, Keith Allison, and Wikipedia Commons (U.S. Air Force Staff Sgt. D. Myles Cullen). Please see the Photographs and Illustrations Credits Table on page 394 for information.

The opinions and ideas expressed are those of the author who is entirely responsible for its content. The author has composed *Pillars of the NFL* at his own expense, using his own resources and technology.

Table of Contents

Preface

Pillars of the NFL examines the football lives of those coaches who hoisted professional football upon their shoulders and won the most NFL Championships. The Pillars include: George Halas (6 championships), Curly Lambeau (6 championships), Vince Lombardi (5 championships), Guy Chamberlin (4 championships), Chuck Noll (4 championships), Paul Brown (3 championships), Weeb Ewbank (3 championships), Bill Walsh (3 championships), Joe Gibbs (3 championships) and Bill Belichick (3 championships). These ten men are responsible for 40 championships.

The first Super Bowl took place in 1966, but there were NFL champions from 1920 forward. Some "Pillars" toiled in the early days of professional football and some later, but all made vital contributions. Like the pillars of a Cathedral support the weight of its magnificent structure, the NFL Pillars continue to bear the weight of professional football—allowing light to shine on players and fans. These Pillars, their co-workers, and their players created a game of such excellence that it is routinely described in superlatives.

In an effort to establish a historical flow to *Pillars of the NFL*, we present the coaches in order of their first championships. In some ways, the book provides a history of professional football. At the beginning of each chapter, each coach is introduced in a kind of "you are there" present tense event. Often, a little poetic license is at work in this section. For example, the author was neither present in Chuck Noll's house to hear his thinking on retirement as a player nor was the author standing with Guy Chamberlin on his father's farm in Nebraska after he hung up his coach's whistle. However, the author did have the privilege of watching his grandfather, George Halas, express pleasure in the outcome at the 1963 College All Star game as described. For all the Pillars, the introduction in each chapter provides an important point of reference.

In *Pillars of the NFL*, once the reader comes to know each coach's place in the NFL universe, the coach's teams are tracked, championships described, and contributions are examined. The Steelers' fan may come to appreciate how the 49ers won their championships under Walsh and the 49ers' fan may come to appreciate the Steelers' accomplishments under Chuck Noll. Fans will come to a better appreciation of Weeb Ewbank who was able to win three championships with two world class athletes—Johnny Unitas in Baltimore and Joe Namath in New York. Fans will learn how two very different coaches, Curly Lambeau and Vince Lombardi, won a special place of honor for Green Bay, the one small city where a pro football franchise survived many financial challenges to achieve unparalleled success.

Perhaps the story of the least-known Pillar, Guy "the Champ" Chamberlin, will surprise readers the most. This Nebraska native came right off the farm to coach and play football in its most rugged period and won four championships on three different teams. Like Lombardi and Lambeau, he won three championships in a row albeit Chamberlin did so with two different teams. What many fans will appreciate most is that the "Champ" often won his games on the strength of his best player—Chamberlin himself. In Joe Gibbs, fans will see a confident coach who is supremely competitive in everything he does. Gibbs is an evangelist for his faith, who established a winning NASCAR race team as a second career. Bill Belichick is seen as a man who was raised to be an NFL coach who manages the Patriots with an uncompromising team-first mantle that works today.

Paul Brown's body of work cuts across a huge swath of pro football history. Brown combined military precision with a colorblind appreciation for talent and a passion for execution. Most innovations in modern football can be found in some way in Brown's programs.

George Halas was unique and someone the author knew firsthand. Halas's time in the NFL spanned a good part of the tumultuous 20th Century, from the league's first kickoff to the modern age of television. In Halas, there is a pioneer who kept one eye on his team and another on his league.

In *Pillars of the NFL*, the backgrounds, actions and accomplishments of these great coaches are presented without trying to pass judgment or critique them. The Pillars of the NFL were human beings and no doubt each one had his own share of failings and foibles. But here we simply present their football accomplishments for those who love the game.

Patrick McCaskey

Acknowledgments

Larry Norris of Sporting Chance Press sat in my office in Halas Hall a few years ago and spoke to me about my writings. I had developed an outline for a new book called *Sports and Faith: Stories of the Devoted and the Devout* and he wanted to know how much material I had on hand for the project. I smiled as I reached over to a shelf behind me and pulled out a large pile of booklets that I had written and printed over a 30-year period. As a lover of Bears' history and family lore, I made a practice of writing, printing, and distributing a booklet on such things once a year for family and friends. Happily, Norris took those booklets back to his office. He and I worked together to update and expand the materials to create a single logical volume with my stories that flowed into a new sports and faith themed book. It took many months, but *Sports and Faith* was published in 2011. Reactions from readers have been positive and kind.

After *Sports and Faith* was published, Norris and I sat together again to discuss another project. This project we called *Pillars of the NFL*—a book that examines the football lives of the greatest NFL coaches. We believed strongly that a book on this topic would be appreciated by football fans. Pillars would take longer than Sports and Faith and require more new work. I had little to fall back on other than my writing on George Halas. I began a migration of new materials to the publisher, which he has helped me craft into a book.

When you write on sports and sports people who lived many years ago, you are not sitting at a football game watching sports history unfold or roaming the sidelines interviewing people. You are not working with "first source" materials. There are books, newspaper and magazine articles, team source history, postings, and much more that provide the basic source materials. The author and publisher worked more than a year with such histories to carve something geared towards readers who are interested in the men who got the job done—the Pillars of the NFL.

In some ways, writing this book was a little like pitching pennies. The pennies of those before you are out there towards the line and you use them to gauge your own toss. Many publications and other sources are listed to acknowledge the materials that were referenced for Pillars, but it is an imperfect process. Stories are repeated so often in sports literature, it is often impractical if not impossible to know where something appeared originally. If a mistake is made in one place, it is likely to appear in several more.

In the early days of football reporting, the stories were often written by someone who had an interest in promoting the teams and games. My grandfather described his efforts writing and distributing his own "press releases" with newspapers and his unabashed use of superlatives in such reporting. In Green Bay, George Calhoun of the *Press-Gazette* had a long association with the Packers all the while reporting on its seasons. Such efforts were critical to the survival of professional football. Often such newspaper stories are the only record of a game. And we were glad to have them.

Luckily, in *Pillars*, the focus was on telling the story of a coach and a career rather than a technical analysis of the game or its metrics. There are many sources that proved helpful. Pro-Football-Reference.com is a good source to check scores and other facts. NFL Team web sites are often excellent sources of materials, but they vary greatly by team. The Pro Football Hall of Fame offers players biographies and other information. *Wikipedia* is often a good place to look for information at first blush and then move on to other sources for more detail and to ensure accuracy. Some media sources are more user friendly than others. *Sports Illustrated* offers many great articles in their "Vault" site. Pro Football Researchers "Coffin Corner" offers a great deal of information provided by their membership of football historians and buffs. There are dozens of books on the Pillars and we would like to thank all those authors whom you find cited in this book. You might say that the endnotes in this book provide a running tally of those sources we would like to thank. Of course, there are books that offer a certain slant or angle in covering a team, a player, or a coach. A reference to one of those does not denote any special endorsement for that author's opinions and ideas.

Rob Sherwood, the grandson of Guy Chamberlin, was especially kind in sharing his historic information on the "Champ." Of all our Pillars, coverage of Guy Chamberlin was especially scarce since the teams he coached are no longer in existence. Lesa Arteburn, the Gage County (Nebraska) Historical Society Director and Janet Roberts of the Wymore Public Library also provided help and materials on Chamberlin. Lou Ann Moore, the Director of the Indiana Football Hall of Fame Museum; Sue King of the Morrison-Reeves Library; and Carolyn Lafever from the Wayne County Historical Society all helped point to or provide information on Weeb Ewbank.

Our illustrator, Bill Potter, gave us images for each Pillar to help capture our subjects in a way that transcends the written word. Bill provides a historic ray of light that visually displays the personalities of the Pillars. Bill's illustrations are a core part of Pillars of the NFL. Book designer Don Torres did much to make Pillars classically stylish and attractive as he has done with other Sporting Chance Press books.

Our overall ambition in publishing *Pillars of the NFL* is to make the football histories of the top ten coaches come to life for readers in an easily accessible way. If *Pillars* achieves this end for you, it will be a success for us.

The Ten Commandments of Football

I   Football is a wonderful game. There's blocking and tackling and much, much more. Be enthusiastic.

II   Weddings, births, and vacations should take place during the off-seasons.

III   Remember the Hupmobile and the original meeting.

IV   All previous games are preparation for the next one.

V   Obey the personal conduct policy.

VI   Work for the good of the league.

VII   Win championships with sportsmanship.

VIII   You shall not criticize the officials.

IX   You shall not covet other teams' players or coaches.

X   Game times are tentative and subject to flexible scheduling.

—Patrick McCaskey

George Halas

"Who do we play next week?"

George Halas stands up and stretches out in the Soldier Field stands on the evening of August 2, 1963. He is wearing a light grey summer suit and felt fedora. He is also wearing a smile. The College All-Stars have just played the NFL champion Green Bay Packers in the annual charity game. It did not go Green Bay's way. The All-Stars won by a score of 20–17.

Papa Bear stands next to his coaches who have watched the game with him and he looks behind him at a row of seats occupied by family members including several grandchildren. He sees the happy faces and he knows that they are aware of the importance of a Packers' loss, any Packers' loss. Halas rubs his hands together enthusiastically and says in a loud voice:

This is very encouraging.

George (Mugs) Halas, Jr. chuckles in response to his father's comment. He knows it will not be easy to knock the Packers from the NFL championship perch they have held for 2 years, but he also knows that if anyone is up to it, it is his father.

In a few seconds, all the grandkids present are up and hopping about anxious to get back home. Halas's daughter, Virginia McCaskey, and her husband Ed, stand and gather their kids together for the trek to their cars. Football excites the entire family and the McCaskeys love to spend time with their busy grandfather. The 68-year-old Bears' coach and owner carries himself like a much younger man. He has a great attitude for any age. As he walks along, he reaches out to the kids with his big hands and tousles a head of hair here and gives a shoulder a squeeze there.

When the McCaskeys reach the parking area, they wave to Uncle Mugs who gives them a beep of the horn as he pulls away. The grandchildren say their goodbyes to Grandpa before they find their seats in the family cars. Papa Bear jumps into another car that takes him up through the Chicago Loop to his apartment home along Lake Michigan. He reviews the game in his head and thinks about the Bears' prospects for the coming season. He repeats to himself: "This is very encouraging."

Early Life

On February 2, 1895, George Stanley Halas was born to Frank and Barbara Halas on the lower west side of Chicago. George was the youngest of eight children, but of those eight, only four survived to adulthood. He would grow up with his brothers, Walter and Frank, and his sister, Lillian. The Halases owned a three story building. The family lived on the ground floor and rented the upper two. They built a second building on the property to serve in part as Frank Halas's tailor shop—a business that flourished when large clothiers started buying his ready-cut suits. The business grew, employees were added, and Barbara worked in the business as well. When Frank suffered a stroke, he sold his tailor business and built an apartment building with a corner store that Barbara used to open a grocery and dairy. The Halases doubled the size of this second property when they added three more apartments. While George was in high school, his father died. His mother carried on and she managed their properties with plenty of help from her children. The family lived comfortably, and Barbara was determined to see her boys get a college education.[1]

Tall and thin, George Halas was tough and he loved to play rough. Halas played baseball and lightweight football at Crane Tech in Chicago. He also set many records in track and field. After graduating from high school in 1913, he worked for a year at the Hawthorne Works of Western Electric in Cicero, Illinois, before starting college. The Hawthorne Works was the manufacturing arm of the Bell Telephone System, an industrial city in itself, and the site of seminal industrial studies. It was a good workplace for a boy with engineering interests.

University of Illinois

In 1914, George Halas attended the University of Illinois with his older brother Walter, who was the Illini's star pitcher. George enrolled in civil engineering, joined a fraternity, and got a job as a waiter. Although he was a thin underclassman, he started out with designs on playing the halfback position on the football team. He took a terrific beating and was switched to end. After the 1914 football season, George Halas played on the freshman baseball team. When summer came, he returned to Chicago and a summer job at the Western Electric Company.

Summer Break and the S.S. Eastland

Western Electric's fifth annual family picnic to be held in Michigan City, Indiana, was slated for July 24, 1915. Halas and 7,000 other employees purchased tickets for the event that featured a trip on one of five excursion boats hired to take employees and guests to the picnic via Lake Michigan. One of the boats was the S.S. Eastland, known as the "speed queen of the Great Lakes." When George was ready to head out to the picnic, he was stopped by his brother Frank and asked to get on the scale for a weigh-in. The family was working together to see that George gained weight for football. At 163 pounds that day, George set out for the dock a few minutes later than he had planned. Upon arrival, he learned that the Eastland, the boat that he was going to take, had just capsized with 2,500 people on board. When too many passengers had lined up on one side to view the traffic on the Chicago River, the boat tipped over with appalling results. Over 800 people lost their lives, including 22 entire families.[2] It appeared that Frank's weigh-in had delayed George just enough to save his life. Sometimes it's OK to be late. When a list of ticket holders was printed in the newspaper the following day, two of Halas's fraternity brothers, Elmer Strumf and Walter Straub, showed up at the Halas home to extend their condolences. George Halas answered the door to the shock of his friends. Halas said a rosary of gratitude that night. George returned to school after the summer with an even stronger sense of purpose after being spared.

Illini Coaches

At the University of Illinois, George Halas would play under some of the greatest coaches of his day. Coach Robert Zuppke, a legend at the university, won induction into the College Hall of Fame on the strength of a 28-year career for the Illini during which his teams won four national championships in football.[3]

On the basketball court, George Halas played for Ralph Jones, another remarkable coach. Jones was an excellent teacher and very versatile. In addition to basketball, he coached baseball and football. Halas needed great coaching in basketball especially. He had a physical intensity on the court that the coach had to help him control. Halas appreciated the help and he liked Jones so much that he would later ask him to coach the Bears.

Halas played baseball under yet another University of Illinois legend, George Huff, who had also coached football and served as athletic director. Like his brother Walter, George Halas was an excellent college baseball player. Like fellow NFL owner Pittsburgh's Art Rooney, he enjoyed baseball most of all and would be a fan all of his life.

Perhaps because he had played under a virtual who's who of college coaching, Halas would never be entirely satisfied with his own coaching although by all accounts he would turn out to be one of the greats.

Perseverance at Illinois

On the field, Halas would give his all. In his sophomore year, he broke his jaw diving to make a tackle—players wore no facemasks then.[4] In his junior year, Halas broke his leg one day at practice and continued to play, attempting to ignore the pain until the coach criticized his play. After a five-day hospital stay, he was back on the sidelines to cheer his team on in practice.[5] He recovered and resumed his athletic career once again. As an upperclassman, Halas did well in football. The speedy end returned kickoffs and punts. He also performed well on the baseball team, playing outfield and batting about .350. Halas made a name for himself at the university and established friendships there that would last a lifetime. In his senior year in the midst of the basketball season, the United States entered World War I.

World War I Service

Anxious to serve his country, with only six credit hours remaining to graduate, Halas joined the Navy. The University granted him a degree and sent his diploma on to the family after he left for the service. George Stanley Halas entered Officer Candidate School and ended up serving at Great Lakes Naval Station as recreation officer. A far cry from the sea duty he had envisioned, but it was a providential assignment that brought him together with many great college players. His duties involved playing and coaching football as well as playing baseball and basketball. The Great Lakes football team was a powerhouse in 1918. This second "college career" gave Halas another opportunity to shine and play with a terrific group of athletes. It also provided an opportunity to size up the best talent in football for the future.

Rose Bowl MVP

The highlight of his Great Lakes career was playing the Mare Island Marines in the Rose Bowl on January 1, 1919. On that particular day, Halas played exceptionally well on both defense and offense, perhaps the best of his long career. He scored a touchdown on a 45-yard pass from Paddy Driscoll. On defense, he tackled Marines all over the field and he intercepted a pass that he ran back 77 yards. He was named the Rose Bowl's Most Valuable Player; Great Lakes won, 17–0.

New York Yankees

Halas also played baseball at Great Lakes and he made an impression on the diamond. After the war ended, he was invited to the Yankees' spring training. He was an excellent outfielder, but he had difficulty hitting the curve ball—a malady that has ended many a professional baseball career. But because he showed so much promise in the field and he was a switch-hitter, Yankee manager Miller Huggins kept him on.

A hip injury threatened his career early, but his condition improved after treatment by the famous hands of "Doctor" Bonesetter Reese of Youngstown.[6] Unfortunately, he continued to have difficulties hitting and he was sent down to the St. Paul Saints, a minor league team coached by renowned manager Mike Kelley. He was making good progress but not quick enough for his high expectations. The Yankees were acquiring a young man named Babe Ruth and they had plenty of veteran talent on the team. They simply did not have room for a player who needed more time to develop. When Halas was asked to return to the minors for one more season, he declined.

Back to Football

After starting a new engineering job for the Chicago, Burlington, and Quincy Railroad, Halas tried out and made a semipro football team, the Hammond Pros in 1919. In his first game, he saw celebrated athlete Jim Thorpe and Hammond teammate Gil Falcon repeatedly go after each other like a couple of charging bulls. Thorpe ended up winning the game on a touchdown run that was followed by a fine play on defense. Thorpe was impressive in many ways—he was a one-man sports franchise who might play on several different teams in a single week. Halas was awed with how football could attract a crowd, even at a semipro level.[7] He also remembered something Coach Zuppke said to his players:

Just when I teach you fellows how to play football, you graduate, and I lose you.[8]

Halas saw firsthand how men, who were past their college years, could get bigger, stronger, faster, and tougher—taking the sport to a new level.

Professional Football Opportunity

Halas was recruited to work at Staley Starch Company in Decatur in a dual management-training and athletic-director position. Staley had baseball, basketball, and football teams. Halas sharpened his sports management skills by running the Staleys football team. Scheduling games among unaffiliated teams was difficult; Halas sensed an opportunity to organize the teams that had been playing together to form a league. He sent a letter expressing such an interest to Ralph Hay of Canton, Ohio. Hay was working to improve the organization of Ohio teams. In many ways, Canton was the fertile crescent of pro football. Hay's Canton Bulldogs had the 1912 Olympic Athlete Jim Thorpe as its player-coach at the time. Hay invited interested parties to Canton, where they outlined the basic league structure. On paper, the Staleys and 10 other teams pitched in $100 each and made up the new American Professional Football Association that would come to be called the National Football League in 1922. Halas said later that none of those at the meeting actually had $100 so the fee was never collected.[9] Like early professional baseball, professional football would be a precarious business investment. Popularizing professional football was difficult because many Americans thought that college football was the highest form of the game and they believed professional football was a poor imitation of the sport that could have a corrupting influence.

Halas's Players

Halas had seen many of the top players in action himself. He also traveled to see others in whom he was interested. As professional football developed, Halas continued to look out for good recruits. He was drawn to tough competitive men who played aggressively.

Abe Gibron

One of Paul Brown's best guards on the early 1950s Cleveland championship teams, Abe Gibron, was 5-foot-11, but he weighed 250 pounds. He was a force—quick off the ball and a strong blocker who played for the Bears in 1958-1959. He would be hired back to coach the Bears from 1972-1974.

Beattie "Big Chief" Feathers

In his first year with the Bears in 1934, halfback Beattie Feathers became the first player to rush for over 1,000 yards. Feathers injured his shoulder early in his career and some believe that the injury kept him from having a Hall of Fame career.

Bill George

Bill George played the middle guard position when he joined the Bears in 1952. On pass plays, the middle guard would make contact with the offensive center and then drop back and cover. George decided that on a passing play, he would drop back before the play was underway. In this way he was able to fill the space better and disrupt the shortest of passes in the middle. Essentially, George's middle guard position morphed into the middle linebacker position. Hall of Famer George had all the skills to cover a huge part of the field, defend against the pass and the run, pursue plays to the outside, and play with an aggression and force that became the prototype for others who followed him—Butkus, Singletary, and Urlacher. George played for the Bears from 1952-1965.

Bill Hewitt

Bill Hewitt, Hall of Fame end, played for the Bears from 1932-1936. Exceptional on both offense and defense, when the Bears had the ball in critical situations, Hewitt especially enjoyed trick plays that fooled unsuspecting defenders.

Bill Osmanski

Bears' first round draft choice in 1939, Bill Osmanski, was one of the best fullbacks in the league. Off to the war in 1944-1945, Osmanski returned for the 1946-1947 seasons before he retired.

Bill Wade

Bill Wade was the Bears' quarterback during the early to mid 1960s and a team-leader throughout his tenure in Chicago. Although a leading passer in many categories in 1961 and 1962, Wade and the Bears played a very conservative, mistake-averse game in their championship run in 1963.

Bob Wetoska

Bob Wetoska played tackle for the Bears during the 1960s. At 6-foot-3 and 240 pounds, Wetoska was a natural guard, but he played tackle most of the time. He created holes for Gale Sayers and pass blocked for Bill Wade.

Brian Piccolo

Brian Piccolo played for four short seasons, but he left a legacy of courage with the Bears and the NFL. Piccolo played halfback and fullback. He blocked for his superstar teammate Gale Sayers and he filled in for Sayers as well when he was injured. Piccolo was diagnosed with cancer, which ended his career in 1969 and his life in 1970 at age 26. His life and relationship with Sayers and the Bears was presented in the popular 1971 movie "Brian's Song," which was remade in 2001.

Bronislaw "Bronko" Nagurski

Hall of famer Bronko Nagurski was a one-of-a-kind fullback and linebacker who played in the 1930s. "Bronk" had the size, strength, and speed of modern fullbacks coupled with the toughness of a freight train. He also became a professional wrestler and returned to the Bears in 1943.

Clyde "Bulldog" Turner

Bulldog Turner was a Hall of Famer and a Bears' first round draft choice in 1940. The great center and linebacker graced the Bears' roster for 13 seasons. Turner was a gifted athlete and he could fill in at a variety of positions when players were injured.

Danny Fortmann

Danny Fortmann was a Hall of Fame guard and excellent defender for the Bears, who played eight brilliant seasons while earning his medical degree. The Colgate guard was drafted by the Bears in the first college draft in 1936. He began his career as the youngest player in the league at age 20.

Dick Butkus

Hall of Famer Dick Butkus was one of the most intimidating players in the NFL when he played middle linebacker for the Bears from 1965-1973. At the snap of the ball, he attacked the opposing team and clawed at anyone in his way in a frenzied pursuit of running backs and quarterbacks.

Dick Plasman

Dick Plasman was an excellent end who personified toughness and played with reckless abandon. In addition to his "take no prisoners" style of play, Plasman was the last man to play without a football helmet in the NFL. In a Bears-Packers game in Wrigley Field in 1938, he ran into the Wrigley Field wall at the end of the short end zone. Some described the laceration Plasman received as a scalping, but he recovered and continued to play that season. Plasman went into the service during World War II. When Plasman returned to play ball after the war, he donned the newly required, no-exceptions, protective helmet like everyone else.

Doug Atkins

Hall of Famer Doug Atkins was a giant defensive end for his era at 6-foot-8 and 257 pounds—a true Monster of the Midway. Atkins posed the greatest challenge to offensive lines and quarterbacks. Having a track and basketball background, he could leap over blockers, extend his arms to control large swaths of running lanes, and block passes from heights unseen. The toughest of men on the field, Atkins was also tough to coach, but Halas managed the big man very well from 1955-1966.

Dutch Sternaman

Dutch Sternaman was connected to Halas in many ways. He attended the University of Illinois, played with the Staleys and the Bears, and was Halas's business partner. Sternaman could play any position in the backfield and kicked as well. He was co-coach with Halas from 1920-1929.

Ed Healey

Ed Healey, Hall of Fame tackle, played for the Bears from 1922-1927. Healey was a player who seemed to be all over the field. Coach Halas praised him for his versatility and acquired him for his rugged play.

Ed O'Bradovich

Ed O'Bradovich played defensive end from 1962-1971. He was a key player in the Bears' run at the championship in 1963 and had a long productive career with the team. Occasionally, O'Bradovich played offensive end to the delight of Bears' fans who enjoyed seeing an occasional pass to the big man. In a way, O'Bradovich's offensive efforts prefigured the efforts of another big defender, William "the Refrigerator" Perry, who would occasionally be asked to play offense and challenge opposing defenses 20 years later.

Ed Sprinkle

Ed Sprinkle was called by George Halas, "the greatest pass rusher I've ever seen." He played right end and was left handed; this in addition to his quickness, speed off the ball, and his hyper aggressive play made him a difficult adversary for opponents. Once called "the meanest man in football," Sprinkle played defensive end for the Bears from 1944-1955.[10]

Gale Sayers

Hall of Famer Gale Sayers was an exemplary running back with the Bears from 1965-1971. Although his career was cut short from serious knee injuries, Sayers's play entertained football fans with his acrobatic and powerful running style that routinely wowed footballs fans.

George Blanda

George Blanda spent 10 seasons with the Bears from 1949-1958. Blanda played quarterback, kicker, and occasionally linebacker for the Bears. Halas believed Blanda's strength was in kicking. Blanda retired and then restarted his career, playing seven seasons with the newly formed AFL Houston Oilers and an incredible nine more seasons with the Oakland Raiders.

George Connor

Hall of Famer George Connor played tackle and linebacker on the Bears from 1948-1955. The Adonis-like muscleman starred on both offense and defense. According to Coach Halas: "He parlayed leadership and intelligence and fine ability into one of the great careers of our time!"[11]

George McAfee

Hall of Famer George McAfee was an all-around great back who could run as well as receive; pass when called upon; and return kickoffs and punts. As a defensive back, he had 25 interceptions. He was always a threat to score whenever and wherever he got his hands on the ball. No one will know how good McAfee would have been because he served in the military during his prime playing years, age 24-26.

George Musso

George Musso, Hall of Fame lineman, played from 1933 to 1944. At 6-foot-2 and 270 pounds, Musso was one of the most intimidating linemen on the Bears and served as team captain for nine years.

George Trafton

Hall of Famer George Trafton was a 6-foot-2, 230 pound bull who loved to mix it up. Hated by opposing teams for his aggressive play and loved by his teammates for his winning contributions, Trafton played center for the Staleys/Bears right from the start, 1920-1932.

George Wilson

George Wilson played end for the Bears from 1937-1946 and was excellent on offense and defense. After playing on four championship teams with the Bears, he became head coach of the Detroit Lions from 1957-1964 where he won a championship in 1957. After Detroit, he moved on to the Miami Dolphins from 1966-1969.

Guy Chamberlin

Hall of Famer Guy Chamberlin was a peerless defensive end, excellent rusher, and receiver. He played for the Staleys/Bears in 1920 and 1921. His contributions to the 1921 championship were essential to the Bears' success.

Hugh Blacklock

All-American Hugh Blacklock from Michigan State was a contemporary of George Halas. Blacklock was one of the first stars signed by Halas and played tackle on the Staleys/Bears from 1920-1925.

Jim Dooley

Jim Dooley played with the Bears from 1952-1954, served in the Air Force, returned for part of the 1956 season, and continued playing through 1961.

Dooley played defensive back and then mostly receiver. He was fast and he created innovative moves in his passing patterns. He worked in various coaching, scouting, and consulting capacities over several decades.

Joe Marconi

Joe Marconi played fullback for the Bears in the last 5 years of his 11-year career. He was an important contributor to the Bears' championship run in 1963.

Joe Stydahar

Joe Stydahar was a Hall of Fame tackle whom the Bears drafted in the first round of the 1936 draft. The 6-foot-4, 233 pound tackle played 7 years for the Bears, served in the military for 2 years during World War II, and then returned to play 2 more years.

Joey Sternaman

Joey Sternaman was an excellent quarterback who played seven seasons for the Bears in the 1920s. He was the brother of Dutch Sternaman and a gifted athlete although just 5-foot-6 and 152 pounds.

Keith Molesworth

One of the fastest men in the NFL, Keith Molesworth was an elusive back and quarterback for the Bears during the 1930s. "Moley" was a superb athlete who moved from halfback to the Bears' T-Formation quarterback. He was also a superb kick and punt returner. An outstanding all-around athlete, Molesworth played minor league baseball.[12]

Johnny Morris

Johnny Morris was a flanker who played for the Bears from 1958-1967. He also served as the Bears' punt and kick returner for several seasons.

Larry Morris

Larry Morris played linebacker for the Bears from 1959-1965. He was the MVP of the 1963 NFL Championship Game.

Link Lyman

Hall of Famer Link Lyman played in the very earliest days of professional football with fellow University of Nebraska standout, Guy Chamberlin.

Lyman took part in a barnstorming tour that featured Red Grange and served to promote professional football in its earliest days. He played tackle for the Bears from 1926-1928, 1930-1931, and 1933-1934. On defense, he shifted positions to fool blockers.

Luke Johnsos

Luke Johnsos played end for the Bears from 1929-1936. He was an excellent receiver and after his playing career, he returned to the Bears as an assistant coach.

Mike Ditka

Mike Ditka, Hall of Fame tight end, had size, power, skill, and desire. The 6-foot-3, 228 pound Ditka impressed football opponents with excellent receiving skills, the strength of an interior lineman, and the running ability of a halfback. He played for the Bears from 1961-1966 and returned as head coach in 1982 to lead the Bears to their Super Bowl XX championship.

Paddy Driscoll

A contemporary of George Halas, Paddy Driscoll had a knack for playing his best when the two faced off against each other on the field. Hall of Famer Driscoll was an excellent team leader and played in the backfield at quarterback and halfback. He was also one of the best dropkickers and punters in the league when he played in the 1920s. He played the last four seasons of his 10-season career with his friend and adversary, George Halas, and the Chicago Bears.

Ray "Muscles" Bray

Ray Bray played guard for the Bears from 1939-1951, except for the 1943-1945 World War II seasons when he served in the Navy. Bray was rated in a 1987 Chicago Tribune poll of experts to be the most outstanding Bears' guard of all time and he is often mentioned as someone who should be in the Pro Football Hall of Fame. The 6-foot, 235 pound guard was an early advocate of weight training for football players.

Red Grange

Hall of Famer Red Grange was an original football superstar who was in a class by himself for attracting fans and playing winning football when he entered the NFL with the Bears in 1925. He was excitement in motion as a running back in his early career until he injured his knee. After his playing career, Grange served as a Bears' assistant coach and a Bears' broadcaster.

Richie Petitbon

Richie Petitbon was a superb safety who played for the Bears for the first 10 seasons of his career, from 1959-1968. He would also serve as a highly successful defensive coordinator of the Washington Redskins during Joe Gibbs's first term as head coach from 1981-1992. Petitbon would serve as head coach of the Redskins in 1993.

Rosey Taylor

Rosey Taylor played safety for the Bears during the 1960s. He was a leading defensive star for the team and led the league with nine interceptions in 1963.

Sid Luckman

Sid Luckman was the perfect quarterback for George Halas's complex modified T Formation. He was also gifted physically as an excellent passer and runner. The Hall of Famer would play 12 years for the Bears; lead in most every passing category for at least one season; and hold many Bears' passing marks over 60 years after his career ended.

Stan Jones

Hall of Famer Stan Jones was a key lineman who played for the Bears from 1954-1965. Jones played offense and defense and he was an early advocate of weightlifting.

Ted Karras

Ted Karras was a key lineman who played tackle and guard for the Bears from 1958-1964. He served as the starting left guard on the 1963 championship team.

Walter "Sweetness" Payton

Hall of Famer Walter Payton has been described by many as simply the best football player of all time. The outstanding running back played for the Bears from 1975-1987.

Willie Galimore

Often described as one of the most elusive runners in NFL history, Willie Galimore played halfback for the Bears from 1957-1963. He was known for making quick movements in any direction—even backwards—that prevented tacklers from grasping him. Once he had an opening, he would head towards the goal while accelerating at uncatchable speeds.

Halas's Coaches

In his college days and in his time in the service, Halas got to know many coaches that he could tap for help in his early NFL career. His circle of football acquaintances continued to grow throughout the decades.

Clark Shaughnessy

Clark Shaughnessy was a college coach and football genius who helped Halas develop the modified T Formation used by the Bears. He would later serve as head coach of the Los Angeles Rams from 1948-1949. He was also a Bears' assistant coach from 1951-1962.

George Allen

George Allen was hired in 1959 and worked his way up to coordinate the defense as the Bears developed into one of the league's best teams in the early to mid 1960s. Allen was a smart, detail-minded strategist who could motivate his players to achieve his vision. Under Allen, the defense excelled and many consider it to be one of the best in NFL history.

Hunk Anderson

A contemporary of George Halas, Hunk Anderson played guard and center for the Bears from 1922-1925. When his playing days ended, he became one of the most innovative coaches in football. His blocking techniques and schemes helped modernize football and power the modified T formation. He was also creative with defense and an early proponent of the blitz. Halas said, "When it came to line play or defense, Hunk was a genius."[13]

Jack Pardee

Jack Pardee had a remarkable 15-year career as a linebacker in the NFL before he began an 11-year head coaching career. He served as the Bears' head coach from 1975-1977.

Jim Dooley

Former Bears' player, Jim Dooley, served as an assistant coach with the Bears after his playing career and then worked as head coach from 1968-1971.

Luke Johnsos

End Luke Johnsos played for the Bears from 1929-1936 and returned to the Bears as an assistant coach following the 1936 season. He was part of the coaching team that took over when Halas went to serve during World War II.

Paddy Driscoll

Paddy Driscoll, like his old friend George Halas, played in the first decade of the NFL. A leader on the field as a player and a football man all his life, Driscoll served as Bears' head coach in 1956 and 1957. He was also a long-time assistant coach and technical adviser.

Ralph Jones

Halas knew Ralph Jones when they were both at the University of Illinois, Halas as a player and Jones as a coach. Jones coached in the early 1930s and helped revitalize the Bears' offense for a championship run.

Staleys in 1920

Halas had recruited some of the top players in the country for the 1920 Staleys. In addition to Halas himself, the Staleys featured Hall of Famers George Trafton, Jimmy Conzelman, and Guy Chamberlin for starters. Trafton was a 6-foot-2, 230 pound bull who loved to mix it up. He was a tough player who was known around the league for his aggressive style of play. Conzelman was highly intelligent and played quarterback in 1920. Chamberlin was a game changer—a peerless defensive end, and on offense an excellent rusher and receiver. Halas's future Bears' partner Dutch Sternaman, could play any position in the backfield. Among others who joined the team were tackle Hugh Blacklock, back Jake Lanum, center John Mintun, and quarterback Pard Pearce. Several of Halas's recruits were players he knew from his time at Great Lakes and the University of Illinois.

After easily beating two semipro industrial teams, the Staleys traveled to Rock Island to defeat the tough Independents 7–0 in their first league match. The Staleys shut out the Chicago Tigers, 10–0, beat Rockford, 29–0, and then had a rematch with the Rock Island Independents that ended in a 0–0 tie. Halas's men were too much for the Minneapolis Marines, 3–0, and the Hammond Pros, 28–7. Once again they shut out the Chicago Tigers, this time 6–0.

Halas had back-to-back games against another Great Lakes pal, Paddy Driscoll, who was a player-coach with the Chicago Cardinals. In the first game, the Staleys kicked off to the Cardinals and when the ball touched a Cardinal player, fullback Bob Koehler picked it up and ran it in for the Staleys' score. The extra point was missed.[14] Behind 6–0, Leonard Sachs picked up a Staleys' fumble on the 20-yard line and ran it in for the score. The Cardinals' successful extra point gave them a 7–6 win. When the Staleys played the Cardinals the following week, the Staleys won, 10–0.

The final game of the season matched the Decatur Staleys with the Akron Pros. Akron's 7–0–3 record was slightly better than Decatur's 10–1–1 record. It would take a win for the Staleys to become champions. Halas's friend and football adversary from the Cardinals, quarterback Paddy Driscoll, joined the

Staleys for this one game in what was billed the league championship.[15] The Pros had a huge star of their own—Hall of Fame running back, Fritz Pollard. African American Pollard was an excellent runner and dangerous punt and kick returner. When Pollard ran around end, Chamberlin, Halas, and others had their hands full trying to contain him.

Regardless of the offensive talent in the game, defense ruled the day. Two penalties ruined promising Akron drives in the first half. One opportunity for the Staleys came in the third quarter. The Staleys drove down to the 18-yard line and moved a few yards toward center on two more plays for a field goal attempt. The kick was wide and the teams fought the rest of the way to a 0–0 tie. When the team managers got together long after the season had ended, they voted Akron the league champion.[16]

Professional Football Team Owner

In 1921, the economy hit a downturn. The Staley Starch Company determined that it could no longer afford the juggernaut that Halas had assembled. Owner A. E. Staley seeded funds to Halas that allowed the young coach to start up his own team in Chicago.[17] Halas made fellow University of Illinois alum, Edward "Dutch" Sternaman, whom he had recruited in 1920, co-owner. Of the original 11 professional football teams, only two would survive: The Staleys-Bears and the Cardinals. In the 90+ years since the league's founding, the Bears moved from Decatur to Chicago; the Cardinals moved from Chicago to Saint Louis to Arizona.

Halas worked with Chicago Cubs' President William Veeck Sr. to arrange playing time in Cubs Park—later known as Wrigley Field. Halas was a baseball fan. He called his team the Bears given the larger size of football players. Having a great deal of experience with players of the era, Halas had an eye for talent, understood the player's mentality, and worked diligently to establish professional football. For many years, professional football was a financially fragile undertaking. Players were paid on a game-by-game basis and sometimes the money was difficult to find. A poorly attended game could be financially disastrous. Few players thought of professional football providing a long term living.

Chicago Staleys' 1921 Season

In their first game of the season, the "starchworkers" defeated the Rock Island Independents. Former Staleys' quarterback Jimmy Conzelman, now playing for the Independents, drop kicked a field goal in the second quarter for the only score of the first half. In the third quarter, when Independents' end Obe Wenig was sent in to punt the ball from the 10-yard line, his kick went straight up in the air and the Staleys got possession on the 18-yard line. Halfback Chic Harley passed to George Halas who drove down to the 5-yard line. Fullback Ken Huffine "carried the ball over on two smashes."[18] In the fourth quarter, a

Conzelman pass was intercepted by George Trafton at the Rock Island 20 and carried up to the 15-yard line. A short drive was capped off by a Harley pass to Halas for the Staleys' second score. Conzelman came back later in the fourth quarter and drove down the field on a series of passes. A short pass to end Dave Hayes gave the Independents the final score of the game. The Staleys won 14–10.

Halas's squad beat the Rochester Jeffersons, the Dayton Triangles, and the Detroit Tigers. The Staleys had to come from behind to beat the Rochester Jeffersons. The Jeffersons were led by a tremendous athlete named Joe Howard Berry from Penn who won the pentathlon 3 consecutive years at the Penn Relays and played both professional football and baseball.[19] In the first quarter, Berry drop kicked a field goal from the 23-yard line. He intercepted a pass in the second half that he ran back for an 85-yard score and kicked the extra point. The Staleys countered with a Dutch Sternaman field goal from the 30-yard line, a blocked Barry punt recovered for a touchdown, and a run by Huffine for the winning touchdown.

The Staleys one loss came at the hands of the Buffalo All-Stars who beat them 7–6 on November 24. Two weeks later on December 4, the Staleys avenged that loss by beating the All-Stars, 10–7. In that game, Chamberlin intercepted a pass and ran it back 70 yards for the Staleys one touchdown.[20]

A team called the Green Bay Packers that would contend with the best of the NFL and offer Halas a worthy foe for the remainder of his career entered the league that season. The Staleys beat the Packers 20–0 in their 8th contest of the year. Wins against Buffalo and Canton followed. In the last game of the season, the Staleys battled to a 0–0 tie with the Cardinals. The Chicago Staleys captured the APFA championship with a 9–1–1 record. For the season, the Staleys scored 128 points and allowed 53 from their opponents.

Chicago Bears

In two seasons the Staleys proved they had what it takes to win it all and perhaps win for several years. But it was almost impossible for any team to keep all of its top players. Halas would say: "There was no bidding for players in those days, no one had the money." Chicago lost a big star in Guy Chamberlin who left for Canton after the 1921 season. Halas would later say that Guy Chamberlin was one that got away and he regretted it.

Halas however, had plenty of success. In a league that was sometimes bloated with more than 20 teams, his Staleys-Bears of the Roaring 20s managed to win, place, or show every year from 1920-1927. He was also busy in the middle of the decade working hard to recruit, sign, and promote the first superstar of professional football, Red Grange. Halas's efforts would provide sustenance for the Bears and other NFL teams that were trying to survive. Halas's work for the league would not go unnoticed by Guy Chamberlin. Chamberlin would say:

Pro football owes George Halas a great debt. Everything he has fought for over the years has been for the good of the league, not just for his own job.[21]

1922 Season

In the early years, the Bears and professional football struggled in obscurity, but Halas kept faith that the team and the game would prevail. Joining the Bears in 1922, were guard/center/kicker, Hunk Anderson; Hall of Fame lineman Ed Healey; and Dutch Sternaman's gifted brother, Joey. Hunk Anderson played under Knute Rockne at Notre Dame and although he would have a brief playing career, he was a great football man and would have a long coaching career including head coaching duties for the Chicago Bears during the war years. Healey was a remarkable lineman who had speed and extraordinary toughness—the kind the Bears coveted. Halas acquired Healey by forgiving a $100 debt owed by Healey's boss, Rock Island's owner Walter Flanigan. It was one of the first player trades. Joey Sternaman was a quarterback, a playmaker, and a solid defender as well. His talents would help the Bears win many games.

The Bears finished 9–3–0 for second place. For the season, the Bears scored 123 points and allowed 44 from their opponents. After four wins to start the season, they lost to the Canton Bulldogs who would go undefeated and win the championship. The Chicago Cardinals would also beat the Bears that year.

In the tenth game of the 1922 season, the Bears faced the Chicago Cardinals. Paddy Driscoll of Chicago's south side Cardinals was giving the rival north side Bears all they could handle running around end. When Halas and Joey Sternaman tried to give Driscoll a little something extra in a tackle, Driscoll took it personally and threw several punches at Sternaman.[22] Both teams, the crowd, and the Chicago police joined the fracas. Tough Ed Healey, who had not been a Bear for long, was knocking heads pretty well although he would later claim he was on the side line "in prayer." Driscoll was ousted from the game, but Halas tried to intercede on his behalf knowing that perhaps Sternaman deserved everything that Driscoll had dealt. Halas's chatter with the refs only added fuel to the fire and another melee ensued. The refs decided to sort it out this time by sending Sternaman and Halas to join Driscoll in the showers. The Cardinals beat the Bears 6–0, but Halas knew that a winning game was not always dictated by the score. It seemed the entire city of Chicago was now emotionally engaged in the rivalry.

A rematch was scheduled for a few weeks later on December 10. The rematch drew a season high 10,000 fans in attendance. Driscoll's Cardinals beat the Bears again, this time by a score of 9–0. Nevertheless, the contest was a brilliant spectacle that captured the hearts of fans all over the city of Chicago.

1923 Season

In 1923, the Bears played Jim Thorpe's Native American team from LaRue, Ohio. Halas picked up a Thorpe fumble on the 2-yard line and ran it back 98 yards for a touchdown—a record return that would stay in the books for decades. As Halas was running downfield, a thundering, angry Jim Thorpe was in hot pursuit. Halas zigged and zagged and zigged again to avoid the Olympian.[23] When Thorpe finally caught up with Halas and threw himself at him, the collision sent Halas the last few paces into the end zone for the score. Thus Halas could say that he not only recovered a Thorpe fumble and carried it into the end zone on a staggering 98 yard gallop, but he also met up with Thorpe on the back end of the play.

1924 Season

In some ways, it might be said that the 1924 NFL Championship was decided in the first week of the season. Guy Chamberlin's Cleveland Bulldogs beat the Bears in week one, 16–14. The two point difference was enough to earn the 7–1–1 Cleveland team the championship over the 6–1–4 Bears at the end of the season.

In game seven, the Bears took on the Columbus Tigers and disaster was averted by the heads-up play of Ed Healey. Bears' speedster Oscar Knop snagged an interception, but he became disoriented and popped off towards the wrong goal. Healey, who was considered one of the finest tacklers of his day, alertly saw Knop's mistake and raced to stop him. Knop was tackled by his teammate just before he hit the end zone. The Bears prevailed, 12–6, but perhaps more important was Healey's preservation of Knop's dignity. Knop played eight seasons in the National Football League and had five good seasons with the Bears. He was a Chicago local who attended Lane Tech High School and like his coach attended the University of Illinois.

Magnificent Red Grange

As Halas struggled to keep the Bears going, he was contacted by C. C. Pyle who was positioning himself as agent for University of Illinois football sensation Red Grange. Halas had kept an eye on Grange and like several NFL team owners and coaches, he was trying to position himself to hire the greatest football talent of the time.

Jim Thorpe was beyond a doubt the greatest all-around male athlete in the first half of the 20th Century, but Red Grange was unique in football. Grange was not just a great football player; he was the best ever for a short time. Moreover, he was easily the most entertaining sports figure to ever put on a pair of football cleats. For the opposition, he was difficult to tackle. For football fans, he was easy to watch. Chicago sportswriter Warren Brown called him the "Galloping Ghost." Famous for long, fan-pleasing runs for the University of Illinois, in 1924 against a University of Michigan team that had a long winning streak, he ran back the opening kickoff 95 yards. Grange scored five touchdowns for the day and passed for another score. He gained 402 yards in that one contest including 212 yards rushing, 64 yards passing, and 126 yards on kickoffs.

Grantland Rice, a poetic sportswriter for the *New York Herald-Tribune*, was so inspired he penned a famous poem after the game:[24]

A streak of fire, a breath of flame
Eluding all who reach and clutch;
A gray ghost thrown into the game
That rival hands may never touch;
A rubber bounding, blasting soul
Whose destination is the goal.
　　　　　　–Grange of Illinois

Grange was a three-time All American and made the cover of *Time Magazine*. His jersey number 77 at the University of Illinois was retired in 1925. That distinction has only been given to one other player in University of Illinois history: Dick Butkus's number 50 was retired in 1986.

Pyle suggested to Halas that Grange could draw huge crowds for the Bears, but he would need a large stake in the gate receipts in order to play ball. Halas agreed to pay Grange handsomely for his efforts. The Bears went on an exhausting barnstorming tour late in 1925 into early 1926. There is nothing like it in modern sport to compare. The crowds and the gates were large. The tour not only helped improve the Bears' financial footing, it improved team finances in other cities where Grange played. It was never easy to keep the Bears running and it took decades for the franchise to make a consistent and comfortable profit. Halas's persistence and grit made it happen—and so did Red Grange, especially in 1925-1926.

For many Americans, college football was the best kind of football. Some feared professional football would ruin the sport. But Halas and others were convinced that professional football could be more entertaining than the college game because athletes would continue to improve and develop after college. Better players would result in a better game. In early 1926, in order to quell fears in the college ranks and improve the reputation of professional football, Halas and the league established a rule that young men could not be signed to the professional ranks until after their college class had graduated.

After the Bears' barnstorming tour, the ambitious Pyle took Red Grange and started up his own professional football league. His American Football

League folded in a year. His team, the New York Yankees, moved over to the National Football League with Red Grange in tow, but it did not survive. Grange had to sit out all of 1928 with a knee injury. He returned to the Bears in 1929, but his injury had taken its toll. Grange was never the "Galloping Ghost" again, but he was an excellent defensive back for the Bears who would prove his mettle over and over again.

1925-1928 Seasons

Red Grange turned pro on Thanksgiving Day, November 26, 1925. Paddy Driscoll's Chicago Cardinals were on their way to the NFL championship season; the Bears were 6–2–2. The game is remembered for Paddy Driscoll disappointing the crowd by punting away from Red Grange. Games could be awash in punts in those days as the teams scratched and clawed for field position and often quick-kicked when the ball was back in their own territory. Grange was at his most dangerous in the open field and the Cardinals did everything they could to contain him.

The Galloping Ghost did field three punts and ran each of them back for 25 yards. Driscoll himself stopped Grange from a touchdown on one punt and his teammates managed to stop him on the others. The Bears had their opportunities, but they fumbled the ball away twice deep into Cardinals' territory. The Cardinals had missed opportunities themselves. Driscoll missed two dropkick field goal attempts although they were from long distances. On another play, Grange intercepted a Driscoll pass deep in the Bears' territory. The Bears punted the ball away on the next play.[25] The game ended in a 0–0 tie.

The game was also instructive in that it showed the risks involved in the passing game in the early days of pro football. The Bears passed seven times. One completion resulted along with three misses and three interceptions. On the completed pass play the Bears lost 1 yard. The Bears' 9–5–3 season gave them a seventh place finish in a bloated 20-team league for 1925.

The 1926 Bears were one of the best teams in the NFL, but Guy Chamberlin's Frankford Yellow Jackets were better. The key game of the season featured the 12–0–3 Chicago Bears against the 12–1–1 Yellow Jackets on December 4, 1926. After three scoreless quarters, the Bears' halfback, Bill Senn, broke away for a 62-yard touchdown run. Chamberlin blocked the extra point attempt. As time was running out, Chamberlin's Yellow Jackets moved down field into scoring position. Houston Stockton hit his tiny 5-foot-5 back, Henry "Two Bits" Homan, who caught the ball and crossed into the end zone for a score. Canton's Tex Hammer kicked the extra point for the win. The Bears took second place with a 12–1–3 record.

Ahead of the pack in 1927 were the Giants at 11–1–1. The Bears battled to a 9–3–2 record—third best in the NFL that year. They lost to the Yankees, Cardinals, and Giants. In 1928, the Bears finished 7–5–1 with four teams finishing ahead of them. The Providence Steam Roller was the top team in the NFL.

Bears and Stock Market Crash in 1929

When there is trouble in the front office, it usually shows up on the field as well. Halas and Dutch Sternaman were having their differences at the end of the decade. In 1929, the Bears lost eight of their last nine games to end the season at 4–9–2. It was Halas's first losing season. At the same time, Halas's own playing career wound down and ended on December 15, 1929 as The Great Depression was taking hold of the country. Having played in the days of leather helmets, Halas had broken his jaw and his leg, twisted knees and ankles, bruised ribs and lived with a painful hip injury—he knew what the sport demanded. In the early days of professional football, several player-coaches took the field, but few would have Halas's stamina. His decade playing for the Bears naturally earned him growing respect among players and coaches as his association with the Bears continued.

Papa's Bears in the 1930s

In 1930, Halas and co-owner Dutch Sternaman hired Ralph Jones, who was athletic director at Lake Forest Academy, to coach the Bears. Halas believed it was a good step to take to resolve the differences that had crept up in the owners' relationship. They both knew Jones from his days at the University of Illinois. Jones made innovative adjustments to the Bears' offense that gave the team a more mobile attack. The Bears also added University of Minnesota standout, Bronko Nagurski, who gave the team one of the greatest power-runners of all time as well as a bone-crushing tackler. With Red Grange and several other excellent players on the roster as well, the Bears were a formidable power.

However, the Bears were almost derailed in 1931. Dutch Sternaman needed money and decided to sell his stake in the team. Tough negotiations between the two partners were followed by some desperate financial moves by Halas to raise the money at a time when many of the banks had gone out of business. A few good friends and some last-minute maneuvers saved Halas's stake in the Bears.

Overall, the Bears would continue their winning ways. In the first 5 years of the 1930s, the Bears would win, place, or show in each of those seasons. The number of teams were much more tightly controlled in the 1930s and the competition got tougher. The Bears would continue in the first three places again, but within their smaller conference. They were in the hunt for the championship in 1937, but would lose to the Boston Redskins.

1930 and 1931 Seasons

In Ralph Jones's first season in 1930, the Bears recovered nicely from 1929. For the season, the Bears scored 169 points and allowed 71 from their opponents. They finished 9–4–1 for the season for third place behind the first place Green

Bay Packers and the second place New York Giants. Two of the Bears' losses were to Green Bay.

Added to the 1931 Bears' roster was halfback Keith Molesworth. The Bears finished 8–5–0 in 1931 for another third place finish. The Packers were winding up a three year championship run under Curly Lambeau. The Portsmouth Spartans took second place. The Bears scored 145 points and allowed 92 from their opponents.

1932 Championship Season

Back George Corbett and Hall of Fame end Bill Hewitt were added to the Bears' roster in 1932. The season did not start out well for the Chicago Bears as they tied their first three games and then lost to the Green Bay Packers in their fourth. The Bears turned things around after that and won 6 while tying 3 to give them a 6–1–6 record for their regularly scheduled games. The Portsmouth Spartans ended the season at 6–1–4, which put them in first with the Bears. Tied games were not considered in the standings. It was determined that a championship game would be played in Chicago. Horrific weather sent the teams indoors to the Chicago Stadium, where the game was played on an abbreviated field. The Bears triumphed, 9–0, in a game that featured a Nagurski to Grange touchdown pass and a safety.

1933 Season and Championship

Jones left the Bears to become athletic director at Lake Forest College. Halas returned to coach the Bears in 1933. Papa Bear's coaching pattern was established. He would coach for a long period of time, take a few years off, and come back and coach again. It was a highly successful strategy that Halas managed masterfully as a coach-owner.

There were many changes in 1933. The Bears trained at the University of Notre Dame that year. End Bill Karr, back and kicker Jack Manders, Hall of Fame lineman George Musso, and back Gene Ronzani were added to the 1933 roster. Two league divisions were created: The Eastern Division included the New York Giants, Brooklyn Dodgers, Boston Redskins, Philadelphia Eagles and the Pittsburgh Pirates. The Western Division included the Chicago Bears, Portsmouth Spartans, Green Bay Packers, Cincinnati Reds, and Chicago Cardinals. The divisions would allow the leaders from each to battle for the title in a championship game.

The Bears won the West Division with a 10–2–1 record. For the season, the Bears scored 133 points and allowed 82 from their opponents. With Halas at the helm, the Bears played the Giants in the first scheduled championship game. It turned out to be the most spectacular game of the season featuring a trick play by the Giants early on and one by the Bears late in the game. It would also feature six lead changes.

On a damp cool foggy December 17, 26,000 fans showed up to see the championship battle. In the early goings, the Giants center Mel Hein reported as an eligible receiver. Harry Newman took the ball under center from Hein and handed it right back to him with a slight of hand. While the defense watched Newman fall back as if he was going to pass, Hein hid the ball under his jersey and quietly started to make his way up field. Not a particularly good actor, Hein got anxious and began to run. The Bears tackled him on the 15-yard line and although the play worked beautifully, the Bears held and the Giants did not score on that series.

After two Jack Manders's field goals, the Bears were ahead 6–0. Morris Badgro hit Harry Newman on a 29-yard touchdown strike and the Giants took the lead, 7–6. Again, Manders kicked a field goal for the Bears. The Giants scored another touchdown on a short run by Max Krause. Nagurski tossed an 18-yard pass to end Bill Karr and with a successful point after, the Bears led, 16–14. Ken Strong hit Newman on an 8-yard pass to give the lead back to the Giants, 21–16. Time was running out. It was time for the Bears' trick play. Bronko Nagurski faked a run and threw a 14-yard jump pass to Bill Hewitt who was attracting Giants. Hewitt lateraled to Bill Karr who then made his way to the end zone.[26] The Bears won 23–21 to take top honors in 1933.

1934 Season and Sneakers Game

Before the season started, the Bears played in the first Chicago College All-Star Game. Before 79,432 fans at Soldier Field, the game ended in a 0–0 tie. It was not a sign of things to come for Halas's team.

The Bears looked unbeatable in 1934 when they went 13–0 for the season. Halas had added a new halfback, Beattie Feathers, who rushed for 1,004 yards that season. The Bears won 18-straight games and were dominating the league. The championship game was one for the history books, or perhaps Ripley's Believe It Or Not. The Bears played the Giants in the Polo Grounds. The night before the game, a storm dumped freezing rain and sleet onto the field. Abe Cohen, who served part-time in the Giants' locker room and part time in Manhattan College's locker room, was asked to head over to the school and borrow their basketball sneakers to help the Giants improve their footing. On icy field conditions, the Bears took a 13–3 lead before Cohen hopped out of a cab with a supply of basketball shoes. The Giants changed from cleats to sneakers and were able to outmaneuver the Bears. The sneakered team scored 27 unanswered points for a 30–13 win.

The game is called the "Sneakers Game." Rather than bemoan the unfair advantage in equipment, Halas would remember the game for the freaky weather change and the sheet of ice on the field.[27]

1935 and 1936 Seasons

In 1935, the Bears tumbled from the top position they held much of 1934. Both Nagurski and Feathers were injured. Few Bears' rookies made much of an impression, but the Bears picked up center/linebacker Frank Sullivan and tackle/end Milt Trost. For the season, the Bears scored 192 points and allowed 106 from their opponents. They tussled with the top teams and finished 6–4–2, which gave them third place in the Western Division. They lost to the 1935 Champion Lions once and tied them as well. They split with the runner-up Giants and took it on the chin from the Packers twice.

In 1936, the first college draft was held. The Bears picked up two Hall of Famers, guard/linebacker Danny Fortmann and tackle Joe Stydahar. Halfback Ray Nolting also joined the squad before the season began.

The Bears had a solid season in 1936, ending with a 9–3–0 record for a second place finish in the Western Division. They scored 224 points and allowed 94 from their opponents. In the first game of the season, they shut out Green Bay, 30–0. They followed with five more wins before losing to Green Bay 21–10. After three more wins, they faced two teams they had barely squeaked by in the first half of the season: the Lions and the Cardinals. The Bears lost both games and those two defeats closed out their year and killed off any hope of a post season. The Packers won the NFL Championship game by defeating the Boston Redskins 21–6.

1937 Championship Challenge

The Bears picked up ultra-tough end/tackle Dick Plasman in the 1937 draft. The Bears roared back in 1937 with the best record in football at 9–1–1. For the season, the Bears scored 201 points and allowed 100 from their opponents. They won the Western Division. They split with the Packers, winning at home, 14–2, and losing away, 24–14. And they tied the Giants, 3–3. They beat every other opponent they faced.

For the Bears' Bronko Nagurski, 1937 would be his last year in the NFL, at least until he was coaxed into coming back during the war. Bronk was 29 years old and he had 73 rushes for 343 yards for a very fine 4.7 yards per attempt. It would also be Beattie Feathers last year with the Bears. Feathers, who had rushed for over 1,000 yards in 1934, was 29 years old in 1937 and rushed for 211 yards. Bears' quarterback Bernie Masterson completed 26 passes on 72 attempts for 615 yards. Bears' halfback Ray Nolting was the team's leading rusher with 424 yards.

In the league championship game the Bears played the Eastern Division Champions, Washington Redskins. The Redskins had moved from Boston after poor attendance created huge financial losses. Prior to the start of their inaugural season in Washington, the Redskins picked up an outstanding quarterback in Hall of Famer, Sammy Baugh, who led the league with 81

Snow Bears
Chicago History Museum

completions for 1,127 yards. Another Redskins' Hall of Famer, halfback Cliff Battles, led the league in rushing with 874 yards.

On a cold and bitter December 12, 1937, in Chicago's Wrigley field, the Bears and Redskins played for the NFL Championship. The field was frozen with jagged clumps of dirt that cut and bruised players. Yet, the athletes overcame the elements to provide spectators with a tremendous game. The Bears featured a running game that ground out yards with tough blocking and powerful runners. Chicago's defense was stingy and strong. In eight regular season games that season, they allowed their opponents 7 points or less.

Washington offered a balanced attack on the strength of spectacular Baugh along with a good receiving and rushing corps. The Redskins' defense was especially tough on running teams.

After the first few series, the Redskins and Bears swapped touchdowns. Baugh managed to sustain a drive and Cliff Battles took a handoff on a reverse and scored from 7 yards out.[28] Manders scored on a run up the middle for the Bears. As the first quarter was winding down, Baugh was intercepted by Bears' end George Wilson. A few plays later, Masterson hit Manders on a 37-yard touchdown pass. The teams moved remarkably well considering the field conditions, but in the second quarter the conditions likely contributed to Manders missing two field goal attempts.

Baugh had been shaken up in the second quarter, but came back in the third and tossed a 55-yard touchdown strike to end Wayne Millner. The Bears came back on a long touchdown drive that characteristically ground out yardage with Nagurski, Manders, and Nolting. Masterson's short pass to Manske gave the lead back to the Bears, 21–14. Rookie quarterback Baugh put on an exhibition from that point forward in the quarter. He threw two more touchdowns, including a long bomb of 78 yards to another Hall of Famer, Wayne Millner. Baugh's last strike of the day was to Ed Justice from 35 yards out.

Early in the fourth quarter the Bears drove downfield to a first down on the Redskins' 12-yard line. After moving the ball to the 7-yard line on two runs, Masterson was sacked back at the 12-yard line. A fourth down pass fell incomplete and the Redskins took over. The balance of the fourth quarter was dramatic, but sloppy. Playing for field position, Baugh attempted a quick kick on the Redskins' 28-yard line on a third down. His punt was blocked and recovered by teammate Bill Young. On fourth and 19, Baugh punted again, but this time the punt was mishandled by the Bears' Ray Buivid and recovered by the Redskins at their own 41. A few plays later, Cliff Battles fumbled the ball back to the Bears, but Masterson gave it right back when he threw an interception on the next series. The Redskins won the game, 28–21.

1938 and 1939 Seasons

The Bears picked up fullback/halfback Gary Famiglietti and halfback Bob Swisher. For the season, the Bears scored 194 points and allowed 148 from their opponents. They won their first three games, defeating the Cardinals, 16–13; the Packers, 2–0; and the Eagles, 28–6. Traveling to Cleveland to play the Rams in their fourth game, the Bears lost 14–7. The following week when Cleveland had their bye week, the Bears wrested a 34–28 win from the Cardinals. They faced a refreshed Rams team at home, but lost 23–21. They would go on to beat the Washington Redskins and Brooklyn Dodgers, but lost twice to the Lions and once to the Packers. The Bears would end the 1938 season with a 6–5–0 mark. The Packers won the Western Division, but lost to the Eastern Division Giants in the NFL Championship game.

In 1939, the Bears improved to 8–3–0. They increased their point total to 298 and the team allowed their competition to score 157. The Bears picked up quarterback Sid Luckman and fullback Bill Osmanski. Luckman would lead Halas's new powered offense of the 1940s and Osmanski would be one of the best fullbacks in the NFL. The Bears also added guard Ray Bray, guard/tackle Aldo Forte, and end John Siegel.

The Bears' three losses that season were one too many for a playoff spot. The Bears split with the Packers and Lions. The 1938 Champion New York Giants beat the Bears, 16–13. Halas's men finished strong with four straight wins. The Packers led the Western Division and won the NFL Championship by beating the Giants, 27–0.

Stunning the Nation with the Modified T Formation

In sports, teams have peaks and valleys. As the 40s approached, Halas began planning a new offense and "retooling" his team by acquiring new players. Knowing the tough nature of the game first hand, Halas certainly signed on more than his share of hard men. But at the same time, he had a penchant for innovation and he knew that he needed both physical toughness and intelligence in his players to carry out the new complexities. When it came to developing the plays and strategies needed to move forward, what Halas could not develop himself, he sought from the best minds in the game.

Although the T Formation had been one of the oldest formations in football, Halas and his coaches had been experimenting with modifications in the 1930s. Halas was a friend of Clark Shaughnessy who had been coaching at the University of Chicago. Halas hired Shaughnessy as a consultant. Shaughnessy helped design and implement a version of the T Formation that would make use of man in motion and other elements that made it much more difficult to defend.

The T Formation uses a quarterback directly behind the center, a fullback behind the quarterback and two halfbacks on either side of the fullback all forming a "T" behind the line of scrimmage. With four men in the backfield, the formation allowed for a seemingly infinite number of variations on handoffs, fakes, pass patterns from the backfield, etc. The quarterback in other formations was often the play caller and director, but with the T Formation, the quarterback would also hold the central position as ball handler and passer. In other formations, the halfback was often the passer. The T Formation would challenge defenders more than other formations to hold their position to make sure they understood where the play was headed because any one of four backs might be getting the ball.

The essential weakness in the T Formation had been the fact that defenses could focus on the center of the field; the T Formation was not as effective outside the opponent's ends.[29] Heading into the 1940 season, Shaughnessy was hired to coach the Stanford team and was preparing for the modified T Formation there. Shaughnessy was helping Halas prepare the Bears before he left for the west. Ralph Jones who was at nearby Lake Forest College would also be involved. Because new variations like the man-in-motion made the formation a much more complex offensive scheme, it was not something that Shaughnessy, Halas, and others had put together overnight. Halas snagged heady Columbia University quarterback, Sid Luckman in 1939 to run the Bears' version of it.

1940 Season

Halas was improving his strategy and his roster. In addition to Sid Luckman and Bill Osmanski who were added in 1939, Hall of Famers center and linebacker Clyde "Bulldog" Turner and George McAfee were acquired in 1940 prior to the season. Turner played center on offense, but also played guard and tackle as needed. As a linebacker on defense, Turner showed great speed. McAfee was a halfback, kick returner, and a defensive back. McAfee was a break-away threat who scared the opposition every time he touched the ball. Halas called him "one of the best players to ever wear a Bear uniform."[30] With a powerful lineup and new offense, the Bears were commanding, but not invincible. During the 1940 season they were 8–3, good enough to win the Western Division and battle the Washington Redskins for the championship.

1940 NFL Championship Game

The Bears clobbered the Redskins in the 1940 NFL Championship game. Three Bears' scores in the first quarter, including a Bill Osmanski 68-yard touchdown run, set the tone for the game. In the second quarter, Sid Luckman hit Ken Kavanaugh on a 30-yard scoring play to give the Bears a 28–0 lead heading into the half. Ray Nolting scored on a 23-yard run in the third quarter, but the Bears wowed the Washington crowd when they scored three more times that quarter on interceptions. Three rushing touchdowns in the fourth quarter gave the Bears a final 73–0 win—the highest score in NFL history.

The rest of the NFL flocked to the new T Formation thereafter. The trio of Shaughnessy, Jones, and Halas published *The Modern T Formation with Man-*

in-Motion, essentially a no-frills coach's manual with 70 diagramed plays and brief explanatory information.[31]

1941 Season

In 1941, the Bears scored 396 points and allowed just 147 from their opponents. They ended the regular season 10–1 on the strength of a powerful, balanced offense and a very good defense. They didn't just beat their opponents; they dominated them—with one exception. The Green Bay Packers had also finished out their season at 10–1, tied with the Bears for the Western Division crown. During the season, the Bears and Packers had split with each other. But this season, the competitors won while away and lost at home.

As the 1941 season was closing, the Japanese bombed Pearl Harbor on December 7, and the United States became a combatant in World War II. Just 7 days later, on December 14, the Bears played the Packers in a playoff game to determine the Western Division crown. After the Packers scored first on a short run by Clark Hinkle, the Bears came back with 30 unanswered points. Hugh Gallarneau started the rally with an 81-yard punt return for a score. After Bob Snyder kicked a field goal, the Bears' 6-foot-2, 238 pound first-round draft choice, Norm Standlee, crashed in for two scores to finish off successful drives. Bob Swisher ran one in from the 9-yard line to give the Bears a 30–7 lead before the Packers answered with a 10-yard touchdown pass from Cecil Isbell to Hal Van Every. Snyder kicked another field goal to give the Bears a final 33–14 victory. Although he did not score, George McAfee logged in a terrific 119-yard rushing performance.

1941 NFL Championship Game

The Bears played the Giants in the championship game at Wrigley Field. It was a surprisingly balmy 47° when the teams met on December 21. As the reality of a long war and its resulting impact on everyone seemed to settle in, the attendance was only 13,341 for the Championship Game.[32]

Bob Snyder led off the scoring for the Bears on a 14-yard field goal. Hall of Famer Tuffy Leemans of the Giants hit George Franck on a 31-yard touchdown play. In the second quarter, Bob Snyder kicked two field goals, one from 39 yards and a second from 37 yards, to give the Bears a 9–7 lead heading into the half. In the third quarter, Ward Cuff kicked a 16-yard field goal for the Giants. The Bears' big back, Norm Standlee, muscled his way into the end zone for two scores, one from 2 yards out and the second from 7 yards out. The Bears' defense closed down the Giants' passing game with interceptions by Danny Fortmann and Bulldog Turner. Hall of Famer George McAfee scored from 5 yards out. Ken Kavanaugh picked up a fumbled lateral and rumbled 42 yards for another Bears' score. The final was 37–9, in favor of the Bears.

1942 Season

Halas wanted to contribute more actively to the war effort than his assignment had allowed him in World War I. After he coached his near-perfect Bears to their first five wins in 1942, he left for duty at the Naval station in Norman, Oklahoma, and then on to the South Pacific. In the South Pacific, Commander Halas, USNR, used his considerable organizational, persuasive, and leadership talents to serve as recreational and welfare officer of Admiral Thomas Kincaid's Seventh Fleet. Kincaid supported McArthur's command and the commander was kept pretty busy.

The Bears were undefeated in the regular 1942 season. They beat the Packers by scores of 44–28 and 38–7, although the Packers had been the one team to challenge the Bears in 1941. Only the Cardinals and Rams came within 14 points of the Bears that entire season. Halas was gone, but most of the Bears starters from 1941 were still on the roster.

1942 NFL Championship Game

At season's end in 1942, the 11–0 Bears took on the Washington Redskins for the championship. The Bears scored first in the second quarter when defensive tackle Lee Artoe recovered a fumble by Redskins' halfback Dick Todd at the Bears 48-yard line and ran it into the end zone. Todd lost the ball when tackled after catching a Sammy Baugh pass. The Bears missed the extra point.

Baugh threw a 39-yard touchdown strike to Wilbur Moore. Fullback "Anvil Andy" Farkas, who is believed to be the first player to wear eye black to reduce glare, rushed for the Redskins' second score from 1 yard out after carrying the ball nine times on an 11-play bone-crushing drive.[33] The Redskins prevailed, 14–6.

1943 Season

The 1943 Bears would play without Halas as the war continued. The league suffered financially and players were in short supply. Assistants Hunk Anderson and Luke Johnsos coached the Bears to another great season. They were helped immeasurably when Bronko Nagurski was coaxed out of retirement after leaving football in 1937. Nagurski became a wrestler. Nagurski at 6-foot-2, 235 pounds, had the size to play fullback today and the heart to play it in any era. In his first professional football stretch, he played fullback and defensive line. When he came back to the Bears, he played tackle. When the Bears were trailing the Cardinals in a must-win game at the end of the season, Bronko returned to his fullback position, scored a key touchdown, and turned the tide in favor of the Bears. He returned again as fullback in the championship game in which the Bears beat the Washington Redskins 41–21. The Bears had won three of the last four championships.

1944-1945 Seasons

The Bears had done well in the early war years, but NFL teams were struggling to survive and even the best run teams were starting to unravel. Sid Luckman had joined the Merchant Marine in 1943. Although he was not able to practice, he was able to play on Sundays. In 1944, the Bears were 6–3–1 and they scored 258 points and allowed 172 points from their opponents. Green Bay beat the Giants for the 1944 championship. In 1945, the Bears ended the season 3–7–0. They scored 192 points and allowed 235 from their opponents. The Cleveland (soon-to-be Los Angeles) Rams won the championship. The Bears had dropped down in the standings in 1944 and 1945, but came back strong at war's end as their premier players and Coach Halas returned from war.

1946 Season

In 1946, the Bears racked up an 8–2–1 record. Luckman had returned to the Bears full-time along with others coming back from military service. For the season, the Bears scored 289 points and allowed 193 points from their opponents. They beat the Packers and Lions twice and won single meetings with the Eagles and the Redskins. They split with the Cardinals and tied the Rams in their first meeting and beat them their second. The only team that beat the Bears without receiving retribution from the Monsters of the Midway was the New York Giants who won 14–0 on October 27. It would be these Giants that the Bears would face in the post season.

1946 Championship Game

The Bears battled the New York Giants in the Polo Grounds on December 15, 1946 for the NFL Championship. After a Giants' fumble was recovered by Ed Sprinkle at the Giants' 31-yard line, the Bears' backs pounded the line on three straight runs that set up the defense for the pass. Luckman's tossed a 21-yard scoring pass to Ken Kavanaugh. A few series later, Dante Magnani picked off a pass thrown by the Giants' Frankie Filchock and ran it in 40 yards out for another Bears' score. The Bears led 14–0 when Filchock hit Frank Liebel on a 38-yard touchdown pass. After the extra point, the Bears' lead was cut to 14–7 as the first quarter came to a close. The second quarter was plagued by a series of untimely penalties and mistakes that killed off scoring opportunities for both teams.

In the third quarter, the Giants recovered a fumble on the Bears' 20-yard line. After moving the ball to the five yard line, Filchock struck again on a touchdown pass to fullback Steve Filipowicz. After the extra point, the score was tied at 14–14. When the Bears drove down field to the Giants 19-yard line, Luckman faked a handoff to the very dangerous George McAfee whom the Giants were keying on, and then the crafty quarterback bootlegged in the opposite direction for a score.[34] A Frank Maznicki field goal late in the game gave the Bears a 24–14 lead, which they held to the end.

The Bears could look back at one of the most remarkable runs in sports history: four championships in 7 years. The Staleys-Bears had won seven championships in 27 seasons.

Bears in 1947-1949

An 8–4 finish in 1947 placed the Bears second in the West to the Cardinals, a team that had beaten the Bears twice that season. The Bears scored 363 points and allowed 241 from their opponents. They had the highest rated offense in the league.

The Bears signed legendary Notre Dame lineman George Connor in 1948. Connor originally went to Holy Cross, served during the war, and then played for Notre Dame. The Fighting Irish won two consecutive national championships with Connor and another future Bear, Johnny Lujack. When the Bears had to stop a powerful Philadelphia Eagles running attack in 1949, Connor, who was an agile and fast 6-foot-3 and 240 pound tackle, was moved to linebacker by Halas and staff. His success there helped establish a larger prototype for that position.

The Bears' 10–2–1 record for 1948 was good enough for a second place finish in the West. The Cardinals 11–1–1 was the best in the West with Halas's old teammate Jimmy Conzelman as the head coach. The margin of victory was slim for the Cardinals who beat the Bears, 24–21, in the final game.

Like the 1948 Bears, the 1949 Bears finished second in the West. The Bears' 9–3–0 record trailed the Rams 8–2–2. The Bears finished out the decade with three second place finishes in their division in a row.

Postwar Difficulties

Although the war had come to an end, difficult times remained for the NFL. Arch Ward, a powerful Chicago Tribune Sports Editor, formed a new league, the All-American Football Conference (AAFC) that operated during the 1946-1949 NFL seasons. Many NFL players were not under contract during the war and it was a players' market as the conflict was drawing to a close. Former NFL players were courted by the new league and there was AAFC competition for players coming out of college. Financially, NFL teams were hurt by competition with AAFC teams—this was more acute in cities that had teams from both leagues.

AAFC teams had their problems as well. The Cleveland Browns dominated its competition in the new league and several of the lesser teams had difficulty holding on to fan support. Late in 1949, NFL Commissioner Bert Bell announced a merger agreement. Under the agreement, the AAFC Cleveland Browns, San Francisco 49ers, and Baltimore Colts would join the NFL in 1950. Other AAFC teams would disband. In the new NFL organization, the West and East Divisions were replaced by the American and National Conferences. In 1950, the American Conference was made up of the Browns, Cardinals,

Eagles, Giants, Redskins, and Steelers. The National Conference was made up of the Bears, Colts, 49ers, Lions, Packers, Rams, and Yanks.[35]

Bears in the 1950s

Throughout the 1950s, the Bears were true to their reputation as one of the toughest football teams in the NFL, but they would not win a league championship that decade.

In 1950, Johnny Lujack took over the quarterback duties from Sid Luckman. The Bears scored 279 points and allowed 207 from their opponents. Their 9–3 record tied them for the top position with the Rams in the newly formed National Conference. The Bears were one of the top contenders who came up just a little short that season. The Bears had beaten the Rams, 24–10, in the first game of the season. They beat them again, 24–14, on November 26, 1950. But in the conference playoff, the Rams turned the tables and won, 24–14. Joe Stydahar was the Rams' coach. Bob Waterfield threw three touchdown passes to fellow Hall of Famer, end Tom Fears. Waterfield also kicked a field goal giving him a key role in all 24 Rams' points. For the Bears, halfback George Gulyanics rushed for 94 yards, but the Bears' scores came from short touchdown runs by Al Campana and Fred Morrison who both had very modest rushing numbers on the day. The Rams faced the Browns for the league championship and lost, 30–28.

For the 1951 season, the Bears scored 286 points and allowed their opposition to score 282. They finished with a 7–5–0 record for fourth place in the National Conference.

In 1952 and 1953, Halas posted rare losing seasons. The Bears finished 5–7 in 1952 while they scored 245 and allowed 326 from opponents. The Bears finished 3–8 in 1953 and scored 218 points while allowing their opposition to score 262. For 1953, the American Conference was renamed the Eastern Conference and the National Conference was renamed the Western Conference.

The Bears improved to 8–4 in 1954 and took second place in the Western Conference. For the season, the Bears scored 301 points and allowed 279 from their opponents. The same 8–4 record in 1955 gave the Bears second place again. For the season, the Bears scored 294 points and allowed 251 from their opponents. The Bears' offense had become one of the best in the league.

1956 Season

In 1956, Halas turned head-coaching duties over to Paddy Driscoll. Driscoll coached the 1956 Bears to a 9–2–1 record for the top spot in the Western Conference. For the season, the Bears scored 363 points and allowed 246 from their opponents—their offense was the best in the NFL. On December 30, 1956, the Bears faced the New York Giants in the NFL championship on an ice covered field in Yankee Stadium.

NFL Championship Game

The Giants were a special team in 1956. They had an excellent offense and one of the top defenses in the league. Jim Lee Howell was the head coach with Tom Landry as defensive coordinator and Vince Lombardi as offensive coordinator.

For the championship game, the field conditions were bad, but players on both teams wore sneakers. Some suggest that the Giants had the latest shoes available from teammate Andy Robustelli's sporting goods store and that made a big difference.

From the opening kickoff, the Bears looked flat. On the other side of the ball, it was a big play day for the Giants. Rookie back Gene Filipski took the kickoff at the Giants 7-yard line and returned it to the Bears' 38. A 17-yard pass completion to Gifford helped set up a Mel Triplett 17-yard touchdown run. Triplett's score was followed by two field goals by Giants' kicker Ben Agajanian. The Giants' defense frustrated the Bears' offense. Quarterback Charley Conerly took advantage of good field position in the second quarter and pushed the Giants toward the end zone in a short series. A 3-yard touchdown run by Alex Webster added to the Giants' lead. Rick Casares scored the Bears' only touchdown on a 9-yard run following a Giants' turnover. Following the Bears' extra point, the Giants led 20–7. It would not get any better for the Bears. Another short touchdown run by Webster, a fumble recovery and run for a score by Henry Moore, and Conerly touchdown strikes to Gifford and Rote gave the Giants a 47–7 win.

Conerly, the Giants' tough seasoned veteran, threw 7 completions on 10 attempts for 195 yards. Frank Gifford caught four passes for 131 yards and one touchdown. Triplett rushed for 71 yards and Alex Webster was good for 100 combined rushing and receiving yards.

The game was a terrible disappointment for Halas and his staff, but it did have some redeeming value. Giants' player and Monday Night Football sportscaster, Frank Gifford, saw the game as a turning point for the Giants in the New York market:

I'll always believe that that game was the key to the development of the NFL today...once we played the game, we became heroes in New York. The thing just grew from there.[36]

Rebuilding in the Late 1950s

The Bears slipped to under .500 in 1957, finishing with a 5–7 record and scoring 203 points while allowing 211 from their opponents. Halas returned to coaching in 1958 for his fourth coaching "series." In 1958, the Bears finished

8–4 for second place in the Western Conference behind the Colts who would go on to win the NFL Championship. The Bears scored 298 points and allowed 230 from their opponents. In 1959, the Bears finished 8–4 and they scored 252 points and allowed 196 points from their opponents.

In the late 50s, the Bears were rebuilding. Johnny Morris and Abe Gibron came along in 1958. Linebacker Larry Morris, who had played for the Rams, was added in 1959. Safety Richie Petitbon was picked up in the 1959 draft and would be a stalwart addition to the defense at safety through the 1968 season.

Bears in the 1960s

Draft choices and acquisitions added Mike Ditka, Mike Pyle, Roosevelt Taylor, Bill Wade, and Dave Whitsell—all picked up in the early 1960s. Taylor, who had played for Eddie Robinson at Grambling, would not miss a single game in his eight-year career with the Bears.[37] In 1960, Halas signed Bob Wetoska who was released by the Redskins who had drafted him. Not flashy, but very reliable, Wetoska would perform yeoman's duty for the Bears, mostly at offensive tackle for the entire decade.

The Bears were making strides in the early 1960s and getting better each year. In 1960, they were 5–6–1. In 1961, they improved to 8–6–0. In 1962, they stepped up to 9–5–0. But the decade of the 1960s in professional football would be dominated by Lombardi and his Packers. To win in the 1960s, the Bears' number one obstacle was Green Bay.

Halas had not lost an ounce of his competitive fiber in 40 years. He passed it on to his players too, especially when they played the Packers. The Packers geared up for the Bears as well. On October 1, 1961, after Bears' middle guard/linebacker Bill George had tackled Packers' quarterback Bart Starr and bloodied his mouth, George warned the great quarterback:

You'll get a lot of that today, Bart. On every play.[38]

Starr responded with appropriate comments to Bill George before the quarterback went back to the huddle and led his team to a 24–0 victory. Later in the season, the Packers scored 28 unanswered points after a Wade to Ditka pass had put the Bears in front to start the game. A Paul Hornung field goal started off the third quarter, but the Bears peeled away at the Packers' lead with two Wade-to-Ditka scoring passes and one Rick Casares touchdown rush. When the gun sounded, the Bears fell short, Packers 31– Bears 28.

In 1962, the Bears improved, but the Packers were very strong and overrunning most of the NFL. The Packers easily won both games against the Bears that season by wide margins: 49–0 in the first contest and 38–7 in the second. The

13–1 Packers scored 415 points that season and only allowed 158 from their opponents. The Bears scored 321 points and allowed 287 from their opponents.

1963 Season

Halas was ready for another championship run in 1963. He knew his Bears would have to beat the Packers to win a championship. Halas and his coaching staff created plays for the Packer matchups before the season began, practiced those plays in training camp, and then sat on them until meeting the Packers in the regular season. On August 24, the Bears played the Packers in a preseason game. The Bears lost 21–7. They held back. On September 15, the Bears played the Packers at City Stadium in one that counted. It was a defensive battle. In the first quarter, Bob Jencks kicked a 32-yard field goal to put the Bears ahead. Jerry Kramer tied it up for the Packers with his own 41-yard field goal. In the third quarter, Joe Marconi had a 1-yard touchdown run. Jencks kicked the extra point. The Bears won 10–3. It was the first of five straight regular season wins for the Bears.

On October 20, the Bears played the San Francisco 49ers at Kezar Stadium. The Bears lost 20–14. During the flight home, Bill Wade poured out his sorrows to Coach Halas. Papa Bear listened patiently and then asked, "Who do we play next week?" Later, Wade wrote that Halas had a "great ability to constantly push forward and look ahead through hardship and defeat, heartache and disappointment."

On November 17, the Bears played the Packers at Wrigley Field. Starr was out and Hornung had been lost for the season, but the Packers were flying high on an 8-game winning streak seeking their third championship in a row. The Bears' defense was rock-solid and Wade played his usual tough, conservative, and mistake-averse game. The Bears derailed the Packers, holding them to just 7 points. True to their ball control nature that year, the Bears scored 12 points on four Roger Leclerc field goals. Willie Galimore dashed for a 27-yard touchdown and Wade cruised in from 5 yards late in the game. Tom Moore, who replaced Hornung, would get the Packers on the board late in the fourth quarter with an 11-yard touchdown run to avoid the shutout. In the face of the tough Bears' defense, seven Packer turnovers resulted and the Bears won 26–7.

On November 24, the Bears played the Pittsburgh Steelers at Forbes Field. In the fourth quarter, Mike Ditka caught a pass from Wade, broke six tackles, and set up a field goal that tied the game. Roger Leclerc kicked an 18 yarder, and the Bears salvaged a 17–17 tie. Ditka had 7 receptions for 146 yards.

1963 NFL Championship

The Bears finished the regular season 11–1–2 to win the Western Conference. The Packers were closely behind at 11–2–1. On December 29, the Bears played the New York Giants at Wrigley Field for the NFL Championship on a sunny,

Bill Wade Passing with Bob Wetoska Protecting

but bitter cold day with temperatures hovering in the single digits for much of the game. Spectators numbered 45,801.

The Bears received the opening kickoff and Wade led the team to midfield. A Wade fumble gave the ball to the Giants. The Moses of Quarterbacks, Y. A. Tittle, started to methodically move his mighty Giants down field. New York's offense was the best in the league that year, but they were up against a defensive juggernaut in the Bears. Tittle drove his team downfield ever so carefully, using his running backs to ground out yards. After a screen pass brought the ball down to the 14-yard line, he hit Frank Gifford in the end zone for a score. Tittle injured his knee on the play when the Bears' Larry Morris rolled into his leg as he let fly the pass. Tittle masked the injury the best he could and continued to play. [39]

When Galimore fumbled on the Bears' 31 yard-line, the Giants had another scoring opportunity. Tittle threw a pass to end Del Shofner in the end zone, but the steady receiver dropped it. When Tittle tossed the ball to Phil King, Bears' linebacker Larry Morris stepped in front for an interception and ran it all the way down to the Giants 5-yard line. Two plays later, Wade snuck in from the two. After the extra point, the score was tied at 7–7.

In the second quarter, the Giants drove downfield to the Bears' 3-yard line, but the Bears' defense stiffened and the best the Giants could do was a Don Chandler field goal. Later in the quarter, Chandler missed another field goal attempt and Tittle was whacked again, injuring his knee more severely.

In the third quarter, Ed O'Bradovich intercepted a screen pass in Giants' territory and took it down to the Giants' 14-yard line. Wade hit Ditka on a pass that brought the ball down to the 2-yard line. Wade took it in for the score on the next play and the Bears led, 14–10. Both defenses played tough. Tittle was injured and immobile. On the last Giants' drive in the waning seconds of the game, Tittle took aim at the end zone from about 50 yards away and tossed a wounded duck that Richie Petitbon intercepted.

The game was more than a defensive struggle, it was contest of endurance. Tittle played through injury and pain to give the Giants a chance. The Bears' defense disrupted the Giants' offense and handed its own offense opportunities. Wade capitalized on those. Halas said after the game: "This has to be my biggest personal satisfaction."[40]

The 1963 Champions were not treated to Disneyland or showered with priceless gifts, but they were invited to Chicago City Hall by Mayor Daley. Halas's son-in-law and future Bears' Chairman, Ed McCaskey, remembered how the post game hoopla affected Hall of Fame defensive tackle, Stan Jones:

After the Bears had won the 1963 championship, Mayor Richard J. Daley invited the team to City Hall to show appreciation. He said that a gift to everyone would be forthcoming. Stan and his wife, Darlis, went home and waited for it. With the playoff money, they bought

> *a glass table. Every day he would ask Darlis, 'Did the gift come from the mayor?' The answer was 'no' for several weeks. One day Darlis said, "Stan, Mayor Daley's gift arrived." In his haste to open the package, it slipped out of his hands and broke the glass table. The gift was a City of Chicago paperweight.*

Invited to speak at a 20-year reunion of the 1963 Championship team, was Bears' left guard, Ted Karras. Ted was one of three brothers who were all outstanding college and professional football players. Ted's brother Alex also achieved great celebrity as a television star after a stellar 12-year NFL career. But Alex's Detroit Lions teams never won the championship during his tenure. Playing on his champion status and punctuating his sibling rivalry with his celebrity brother, Ted said before the audience: "I'm a junior high school football coach and a physical education teacher and the amazing thing is my wife considers me a success."

Another member of the 1963 championship team, Bob Wetoska, looked back at 1963 over 30 years later and thought about fiery Coach Halas who led the Bears to the big win: "Deep down, everybody loved and respected the man—even if sometimes he got a little excited."[41]

Halas was named AP Coach of the Year, the Sporting News Coach of the Year, and the UPI NFL Coach of the Year for 1963.

1964-1967 Seasons

In August of 1964, while the Bears were preparing for the College All-Star Game, teammates Willie Galimore and John Farrington were killed in an automobile accident. It was a tragic beginning to a poor season for the Bears. The Bears did not play like a championship team and finished the season at 5–9.

The Bears came back much stronger in 1965 and finished at 9–5, good for the third spot in the West. Halas was named AP Coach of the Year, the Sporting News Coach of the Year, and the UPI NFL Coach of the Year for 1965.

Although the rest of the 1960s would be a disappointment in the record books as the Bears could not develop a run at the top of the standings, Chicago Bear fans remembered the remainder of the 1960s for two players who began their careers in 1965. On offense, Gale Sayers would light up the league with a full out running style that featured impossible cuts that made him amazingly elusive. In 1965, Sayers would score an incredible 22 touchdowns in his first season, including six in one game against the San Francisco 49ers. Sayers would average 5 yards a carry.

On the defensive side of the ball, Halas and the Bears greatly strengthened their tradition of toughness and passion by drafting Dick Butkus. Butkus was the perfect progeny of all the toughest Bears who had gone before him including fellow Illini Halas himself. From his earliest days outside his house in Chicago's Roseland neighborhood, Butkus started honing his football skills.[42]

In 1966, the Bears regressed to a 5–7–2 finish. In 1967, the Bears improved to 7–6–1 giving them a second place finish in the new Central Division of the Western Conference.

Prior to the start of the 1968 season, Halas retired from coaching after 40 seasons. Jim Dooley took over as coach in 1968 and the Bears posted a 7–7 record, which was followed by a 1–13 season in 1969—the worst in Bears' history. Dooley's Bears followed with 6–8 seasons in 1970 and 1971. Dooley's tenure was marked by tremendous highs and lows with key injuries often mixed with remarkable performances. It was during Dooley's head coaching years that Gale Sayers injured one knee, rehabilitated, recovered, gained over 1,000 yards, and then injured his other knee to effectively end his career. Dick Butkus played at a high level throughout the period regardless of his team's lack of success and in spite of his own injuries. It was also during Dooley's head coaching career that Brian Piccolo was diagnosed with cancer one season and then died from the disease the next.

Finks Era

The 1970s were about big change for the Bears' organization. The Bears played their final season in Wrigley Field in 1970 before moving to Soldier Field. In 1975, the Bears moved their training camp to Lake Forest after spending 31 years at Saint Joseph's College in Rensselaer, Indiana. And tragically, the Bears lost the team president, George "Mugs" Halas, son of Papa Bear, in the final days of the decade on December 16, 1979.

Team founder George Halas would be as busy as ever during his sixth decade of professional football leadership. He was elected president of the National Football Conference as the NFL and AFL merged in 1970. In 1974, Jim Finks joined the Bears as general manager. Finks named Jack Pardee, the first non-Bear in such a position, as head coach.

Walter "Sweetness" Payton was the Bears' first-round draft choice in 1975. He was simply the best football player ever. He could run, block, catch, pass, punt, and kick. There was nothing in football he could not do. He missed one game in his entire pro career and trained with legendary discipline and intensity—coming into each training camp in superb condition.

Payton played for 13 seasons with the Chicago Bears, from 1975 to 1987. He rushed 3,838 times for 16,726 yards—scoring 110 touchdowns. He rushed over 1,200 yards in a season 10 times. He also caught 492 passes for 4,538 yards and 15 more touchdowns. Altogether, he scored 125 touchdowns and he accounted for a record 21,803 combined net yards. He gained 100 yards or more from scrimmage in 108 games.

The Bears returned to the playoffs in 1977 under Coach Pardee. Chicago lost in the opening round of the Playoffs to the Dallas Cowboys.

Two years after their last trip to the playoffs, they were back with Coach Neill Armstrong, former defensive coordinator of the Minnesota Vikings. Armstrong posted a 30–34 record with the Bears and was gone after four seasons, but his tenure created some high spots for the team and its fans. In a gutsy performance on the same day that Mugs Halas died, December 16, 1979, the Bears honored his memory by scorching the Saint Louis Cardinals 42–6 to wipe out a 33 point differential they needed to make the playoffs. On Thanksgiving Day November 27, 1980, the Bears fell behind the Lions 17–3 going into the fourth quarter. After closing the gap to 17–10, quarterback Vince Evans drove the Bears 96 yards down the field with less than four minutes to go to tie the game. The Bears won the overtime coin toss, forcing the Lions to give the ball right back to them. Dave Williams received the kick, ran toward the center of the field, and then cut to the side lines and towards the end zone. He covered 95 yards in 21 seconds for the winning score—the Bears won 23–17. Another notable victory in the Armstrong era was the Bears' 61–7 massacre of the Packers on December 7, 1980.

Papa Bear's Last Run at the Championship

The Bears would turn the corner in the 1980s and become a dominant power in the middle of the decade. One of the last big moves made by George Halas was hiring Mike Ditka as head coach in 1982. On February 2, 1983, his 88th birthday, Halas told his grandchildren: "May the good Lord grant all of you as long and as wonderful a life as I have had." His family reported that in June of that year, Halas looked frail for the first time in his life. He died on October 31, 1983 as the Bears prepared to play the Los Angeles Rams. His grandson, Michael McCaskey, became president of the Bears.

In 1984, the Bears won the Central Division. They defeated the Washington Redskins in the divisional playoff to advance to the NFC championship game. That game was a disappointing loss for the Bears, but the 49ers' 23–0 victory was instructive. The Bears' defense had disrupted the play of 49ers legendary quarterback, Joe Montana. The Niners went into the half with two field goals and the Bears had two picks on Montana. But the Bears' offense was missing starting quarterback Jim McMahon. The defense wore out and the game proved a motivator for the Bears' next season.

Going into the 1985 season, the Bears looked to improve with the additions of William "the refrigerator" Perry and Kevin Butler. Perry would prove to be both literally and figuratively a huge boost to the Bears. On defense, he would help to shut down opposing offenses by filling running gaps. On offense, he would occasionally loosen up opposing defensive goal line stands with crushing blocks, power runs, and even the occasional pass pattern. Butler would prove exceptional—both a steady and a clutch kicker who provided much-needed points on the board.

Considered to be one of the finest football teams of all time, the 15–1 Bears were virtually unstoppable in the playoffs, crushing the Giants 21–0, the Rams 24–0, and the New England Patriots 46–10.

George Halas was not there to see the championship run, but in many ways the 1985 team was largely his in personality and spirit.

Football is an up-and-down game. In the hypercompetitive environment that is the NFL, no team can sustain a top tier position for long. Every team needs to build and then rebuild. The peaks and valleys are part of the process, and for Halas like other NFL Pillars, the game was more than a metaphor for life—it was life. And regardless of how tough things got, the resilient George Halas, would look forward and say, "Who are we playing next week, kid?"

Halas's Contributions to the Game

George Halas coached for 40 seasons and accumulated 324 wins, 151 losses, and 31 ties. The Bears won six NFL Championships with Halas as coach. He was enshrined in Pro Football Hall of Fame's charter class of 17 members on September 7, 1963. Halas was named AP Coach of the Year, the Sporting News Coach of the Year, and the UPI NFL Coach of the Year for the 1963 and the 1965 seasons.

If anyone could be called the Father of the NFL, it would be George Halas. In this way, his nickname, Papa Bear says it all. He loved the fans and was dedicated to his friends, family, and faith. On Thursday, December 10, 1981, Halas appeared before the House Judiciary Committee in Washington, D.C., with Pete Rozelle and Paul Tagliabue. Halas explained how the NFL was like a wheel: The league was the rim and the teams were the spokes. If you have a weak spoke, you have a weak wheel. That's why the teams with the worst records get to draft first. That's why the league schedules the games instead of the strong teams just playing each other. That's why the teams share the television money equally.

Halas and a small group of men developed the framework for professional football in the most humble circumstances—a meeting in a car showroom in Canton, Ohio. It took decades to make it work. No one worked as hard or as long as Halas.

Halas never really retired from football. Any awards and honors that came his way would take place during his "career." When he received the Sword of Loyola at the Conrad Hilton, he said:

Sixty years ago I offered my heart and my helmet to the Lord. My heart is still beating and my helmet still fits. I pray the Divine Coach finds me worthy to be on His first team.

George Halas
Art by Gary Thomas, © Goal Line Art, Inc.

Halas drove hundreds of men to make them the best players and men they could be. At times he could be ruthless in his pursuit of excellence, but he was always relentless in his abiding love of his team. Books are full of stories on how tough he could be. As a player, Halas broke his jaw and his leg, he twisted ankles and knees, and bruised and broke ribs. He led his teams as a players' coach and although he was tough and disciplined, he always treated his players as men.

In the early annals of the Bears, Halas had attracted the toughest of players. Even the name Bears conjures up an impression of physical abandonment that is in large part his making along with people like George Trafton, Bronko Nagurski, Doug Atkins, Ed Sprinkle, Dick Butkus, Mike Ditka, Mike Singletary, Brian Urlacher, and many others.

Halas is a larger-than-life figure for many sports fans. Although his life was hard, it was fantastic on so many levels. His life's story is a living history of 20th Century America. Stamped upon his character were lessons from the Great Depression, World War I, and World War II. In so many ways, his life was successful because he had faith, worked hard, and never gave up. He saw problems as opportunities. He moved on from setbacks at lightning speed.

It is customary for sportswriters to devote a chapter in their autobiographies that lists their own personal list of top athletes, coaches, teams, etc. In Warren Brown's book named after his long running Chicago American column, *Win, Lose, or Draw*, he wrote:

In the professional field George Halas and the Chicago Bears year in and year out, will do for me. I am not too hard to please as long as I have the best, doing anything.[43]

George Halas Timeline

1895

- February 2, 1895, George Stanley Halas is born in Chicago.

1913

- Halas graduates from Crane Tech High School in Chicago where he set many track records, and played baseball and lightweight football.

1914-1917

- Halas attends the University of Illinois and plays football, basketball, and baseball.

1917

- Halas joins the Navy and serves at Great Lakes Naval Station as recreation officer. He serves as player-coach of Great Lakes Bluejacket football team.

1919

- January 1, 1919, Halas is named Most Valuable Player in the Rose Bowl after he scores on a 45-yard touchdown pass from Paddy Driscoll and he runs back an interception 77 yards in the Great Lakes' 17-0 victory over the Mare Island Marines.
- Halas plays for the New York Yankees and their Minor League affiliate.
- Halas plays for the Hammond Pros semipro football team.

1920

- Halas is hired by A.E. Staley to manage and coach the Decatur Staleys, a semipro football team.
- September 17, 1920, Halas attends the original pro football organizational meeting in Canton at the Jordon Hupmobile showroom of Ralph E. Hay, owner of the Canton Bulldogs. Halas, Hay, and others present establish the American Professional Football Association.

1921

- October 6, 1921, a letter agreement from A.E. Staley formally turns ownership of the Staley team to George Halas. Halas becomes owner of the Staleys.
- Chicago Staleys capture the APFA (NFL) championship with a 9–1–1 record—it is Halas's first championship as a coach and owner.

1922

- Halas's team becomes the Chicago Bears.
- Halas's proposal to change the league name from the American Professional Football Association to the National Football League is accepted by membership.

1930

- Halas steps down as Bears' coach and Ralph Jones replaces him for the 1930-1932 seasons.

1932

- Chicago Bears, coached by Jones, capture the NFL championship with a 7–1–6 record.

1933

- The NFL creates the East and West Divisions, and establishes a post season game between the top finishers in each to determine the league champion.
- December 17, 1933, Halas-coached

Chicago Bears defeat the New York Giants, 23-21, to win the NFL championship.

1934

- December 9, 1934, New York Giants defeat the Chicago Bears, 30–13, in the NFL Championship game that came to be called the "Sneakers Game." The Giants' come-from-behind victory is in part facilitated by their use of basketball sneakers for better traction.

1940

- December 8, 1940, the Chicago Bears defeat the Washington Redskins, 73–0, to win the NFL Championship. The Bears' modified T Formation proves to be unstoppable that day.

1941

- December 21, 1941, the Chicago Bears defeat the New York Giants, 37–9, to win the NFL Championship.

1942

- Halas returns to the Navy to serve for the duration of World War II. The Bears are coached by Hunk Anderson and Luke Johnsos during this period.
- December 13, 1942, Washington Redskins defeat the Chicago Bears, 14–6, to win the NFL championship.

1943

- December 26, 1943, the Chicago Bears defeat the Washington Redskins, 41–21, to win the NFL Championship. It is the Bears' third championship in four seasons.

1946

- Halas returns to coach the Bears.
- December 15, 1946, Bears defeat the New York Giants, 24–14, to win the NFL championship.

1956

- Halas steps down from coaching for the 1956 and 1957 seasons. Paddy Driscoll takes over as head coach.

1963

- Halas is enshrined into the Pro Football Hall of Fame as part of the charter class of 17 members.
- December 29, 1963, the Bears defeat the New York Giants, 14–10, to win the NFL championship. It is Halas's sixth NFL Championship as coach and his eighth as owner.
- Halas is named AP Coach of the Year, the Sporting News Coach of the Year, and the UPI NFL Coach of the Year for 1963.

1965

- Halas is named AP Coach of the Year, the Sporting News Coach of the Year, and the UPI NFL Coach of the Year for 1965.

1968

- Halas steps down from coaching for the last time. Jim Dooley takes over as Bears' head coach.

1983

- October 31, 1983, George Halas dies at the age of 88.

Highlights

George Halas coached for 40 seasons and holds an overall NFL head coaching record of 324–151–31. The Bears won six NFL Championships with Halas as coach and a total of eight as NFL owner. Halas was present at the beginning of the NFL and worked tirelessly for over 60 years to see professional football succeed. Halas was named AP Coach of the Year, the Sporting News Coach of the Year, and the UPI NFL Coach of the Year for both 1963 and 1965. He was enshrined in Pro Football Hall of Fame's charter class of 1963.

If anyone could be called the Father of the NFL, it would be George Halas. In this way, his nickname, Papa Bear says it all. Halas and a small group of men developed the framework for professional football in the most humble circumstances—a meeting in a car showroom in Canton, Ohio. It took decades to make it work. No one worked as hard or as long as George Halas.

Endnotes

[1] George Halas with Gwen Morgan and Arthur Veysey, *Halas by Halas* (New York, McGraw Hill, 1979) 17.

[2] Eastland Disaster Historical Society summary, viewed at http://www.eastlanddisaster.org/summary.htm on April 12, 2013.

[3] Fighting Illini—Official Home of the University of Illinois Athletics, Photo Caption: "Robert Zuppke Helped Lead Illinois to Four of Its Five National Championships," http://www.fightingillini.com (viewed on October 27, 2010).

[4] Patrick McCaskey with Mike Sandrolini, *Bear with Me: A Family History of George Halas and the Chicago Bears*, (Chicago: Triumph Books, 2009) 5.

[5] McCaskey with Sandrolini, *Bear with Me: A Family History of George Halas and the Chicago Bears*, 7.

[6] McCaskey with Sandrolini, *Bear with Me: A Family History of George Halas and the Chicago Bears*, 22.

[7] *Bear with Me: A Family History of George Halas and the Chicago Bears*, 27·

[8] Halas with Morgan and Veysey, *Halas by Halas*, 35.

[9] George Halas, "My Forty Years in Pro Football," *Saturday Evening Post*, Nov. 25, 1957.

[10] Bob Carroll, "Ed Sprinkle," *The Coffin Corner*, Vol. 12, No. 1 (1990), viewed at http://www.profootballresearchers.org/Coffin_Corner/12-01-390.pdf on Sept. 5, 2013.

[11] Chicago Bears Official Website, "Chicago Bears in the Hall" viewed at http://www.chicagobears.com/tradition/bears-in-the-hall/george-connor.html on September 9, 2013.

[12] Maury White, "Keith Molesworth, Washington, 1990," *Des Moines Register*, Biography for Iowa Sports Hall of Fame, July 2, 2005, viewed at http://www.desmoinesregister.com/article/19900701/SPORTS11/50702014/Keith-Molesworth-Washington-1990 on October 17, 2013.

[13] For a concise description of Anderson's contributions to football see Emil Klosinski, "A Hunk of History: Hunk Anderson," *The Coffin Corner*: Vol. 3, No. 2 (1981) viewed at http://www.profootballresearchers.org/Coffin_Corner/03-02-058.pdf on December 18, 2013. Kosinski is the author of *Notre Dame, Chicago Bears and Hunk Anderson*.

[14] "Staleys Bow to Cardinals," *Chicago Herald and Examiner*, November 29, 1920.

[15] Official web site of the Chicago Bears, Tradition Page at http://www.chicagobears.com/tradition/bears-in-the-hall/paddy-driscoll.html.

[16] Bob Carroll, "Akron Pros 1920," *The Coffin Corner*: Vol. 4, No. 12 (1982), viewed at http://profootballresearchers.org/CC_1980s.htm on April 3, 2013.

[17] The agreement was made verbally and then spelled out in a letter agreement dated October 6, 1921, created by A. E. Staley and signed by Staley and Halas.

[18] Howard Millard, "Staleys Get Breaks to Defeat Islanders," *Decatur Review*, Oct. 11, 1921.

[19] Penn Quakers web site biography of Berry viewed at http://www.pennathletics.com/ViewArticle.dbml?DB_OEM_ID=1700&ATCLID=811431 on September 2, 2013.

[20] George Sullivan, *Pro Football's All Time Greats* (New York, Putnam, 1968) 128-129.

[21] Wally Provost, "Chamberlin Missed Call on Pro Grid Growth," from Nebraska's Greatest Guy series, September 1964. *Omaha World Herald*.

[22] See George Halas's telling of this incident in *Halas by Halas*, Halas with Morgan and Veysey, 83-85.

[23] Halas with Morgan and Veysey, *Halas by Halas*, 87.

[24] ESPN Sports Century website at http://espn.go.com/sportscentury/features/00014213.html

[25] "Reds First Game," *The Coffin Corner*, Vol. 6, Nos. 9 & 10 (1984), viewed at http://profootballresearchers.org/CC_1980s.htm on September 11, 2013. This publication

reproduces a Harry MacNamara story from the *Chicago Herald Examiner*, "Bears and Cards in Valiant Grid Battle."

[26] Pro Football Hall of Fame description viewed at https://www.profootballhof.com/history/story.aspx?story_id=2087&print=y on April 15, 2013.

[27] Joseph S. Page, *Pro Football Championships Before the Super Bowl: A Year-By-Year History, 1926-1965* (Jefferson, NC: McFarland & Company, 2011) 30.

[28] Page, Pro Football Championships Before the Super Bowl, 41.

[29] Clark Shaughnessy, Ralph Jones, George Halas, *The Modern "T" Formation with Man-in-Motion* (Chicago: Shaughnessy, Jones and Halas Publishers, 1941) 96.

[30] George Halas, "My Forty Years in Pro Football," Saturday Evening Post, Nov. 25, 1957.

[31] Clark Shaughnessy, Ralph Jones, George Halas, *The Modern "T" Formation with Man-in-Motion* (Chicago, Shaughnessy, Jones and Halas Publishers, 1941).

[32] Page, Pro Football Championships Before the Super Bowl, 60.

[33] Page, Pro Football Championships Before the Super Bowl, 64.

[34] Page, Pro Football Championships Before the Super Bowl, 86.

[35] The Yanks' origins are complicated. For simplicity sake, some view it as a renamed continuation of the 1949 New York Bulldogs of the NFL. See Bob Carroll, "How to Get from Dayton to Indianapolis by Way of Brooklyn, Boston, New York, Dallas, Hershey and Baltimore," The Coffin Corner, Vol. 17, No. 5 (1995), viewed at http://www.profootballresearchers.org/Coffin_Corner/17-05-621.pdf on September 11, 2013.

[36] Bill Jauss, "Carved in Ice, Bears-Giants Sneaker Title Game," *Chicago Tribune*, December 28, 1996, viewed at http://articles.chicagotribune.com/1996-12-28/sports/9612280042_1_sneakers-bears-skated-shoes on October 18, 2013.

[37] Lew Freeman, *Game of My Life: Chicago Bears: Memorable Stories of Bears Football* (Champaign: Sports Publishing LLC, 2006) 74.

[38] Tex Maule, "The Right to be First," *Sports Illustrated*, November 20, 1961, viewed at http://sportsillustrated.cnn.com/vault/article/magazine/MAG1073220/1/index.htm   on September 9 , 2013.

[39] Page, *Pro Football Championships Before the Super Bowl*, 189.

[40] Page, *Pro Football Championships Before the Super Bowl*, 192.

[41] Gary Reinmuth, "Ex-bear Wetoska Still Does His Job Quietly, But He Owns The Company," *Chicago Tribune*, August 9, 1994, viewed at http://articles.chicagotribune.com/1994-08-09/sports/9408090307_1_bears-tackles-offensive on September 10, 2013.

[42] Dick Butkus and Pat Smith, *Butkus: Flesh and Blood*, (New York: Doubleday, 1997) 2.

[43] Warren Brown, *Win, Lose or Draw*, (New York: G.P. Putnam's Sons, 1947) 269.

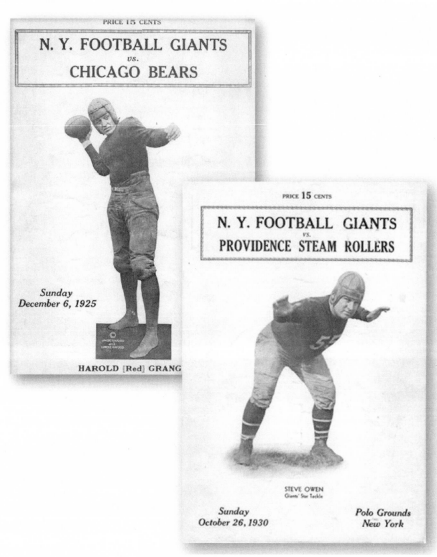

Football Programs

Guy Chamberlin

No one liked to play football more.

It is an early spring day in southeastern Nebraska in 1933. Guy Chamberlin looks out on his father's Gage County Nebraska farm. He is finished with football and along with his eldest brother, Warren, he will work the land that stretches out in front of him. Certainly his father has plenty of land to work in this Big Blue River Valley where he settled in the late 1800s.

Guy Chamberlin is 39 years old, lanky, but with an obvious athletic build—more like a basketball player than the football player he has been. Chamberlin has lived large for a farm boy from rural Nebraska. An excellent student athlete, he starred for both Nebraska Wesleyan and the University of Nebraska in football. He played in front of thousands of college football fans and by some accounts, single-handedly beat the Catholics of Notre Dame.[1] He served stateside in the U.S. Army during the Great War, and the moment he took his military uniform off, he put on a football uniform again.[2] He played and coached at the professional level and everywhere he went he would win games—demanding a great deal from his teammates and often outplaying everyone else on the field. He is called "Champ" for good reason.

Befriended by his childhood hero Jim Thorpe who introduced him to professional football in Canton, Chamberlin competed against the father of professional football, George Halas, one year; played with him the next two; and then competed against him again. He has met many of pro football's early greats and impressed most of them by his play.

Now that his playing days are over, Chamberlin is finished with coaching professional football. For Guy Chamberlin, sport is defined by active physical competition and football fits the bill. As Chamberlin would say many years later: "There never was a guy who liked to play football as well as I did."[3]

Coming from a no-nonsense Nebraska farm family, he is seeking a more stable career. Most of the professional football teams are struggling to survive. For many, if not most of its early participants, professional football does not offer a career. Certainly that is Chamberlin's opinion.

Bulldog intensity drives Guy Chamberlin. He has gone back to his roots to begin a new chapter in his life. But there will be years of hardship. Families in Gage County and others across the Great Plains will experience severe drought and dust to go along with the Great Depression throughout the remaining 1930s.

1915 University of Nebraska v. Notre Dame

It will be a difficult time, but Guy Chamberlin and his fellow Nebraskans will face their problems with courage.[4]

Early Life

Berlin Guy "Champ" Chamberlin was born on January 16, 1894 on a farm outside of Blue Springs, Nebraska, a village along the winding Big Blue River in Gage County. His mother was of German descent and she named him Berlin after the city in Germany.[5] He would never be called Berlin in Nebraska farm country—to almost everyone he would be known as Guy or sometimes the more formal B. Guy Chamberlin. Guy was the third child born to Elmer E. Chamberlin and Anna Tobyne Chamberlin.

Guy's father, Elmer, was born in February of 1861 just before the Civil War began. He was a serious man when it came to work, but he was also fond of telling stories and outgoing at the same time.[6] He came from historic Salem, New York, and moved out west with a friend in 1895. His brothers and sisters came west as well. Elmer's father, William, was a miller who had owned several farms out east. A practical man, Grandfather Chamberlin is said to have put his children to work clearing rocks from the soil and building rock walls at each new farm he bought. He also changed the spelling of the family name from Chamberlain to Chamberlin so it could fit better on his grain sacks.[7]

Anna Tobyne's parents, James N. Tobyne and Caroline Zeitz Strockey had moved west in a covered wagon from Belvidere, Illinois, where the family had owned a farm that was located in "very very very fine farmland."[8] They homesteaded near Blue Springs. James Tobyne constructed a stone building that served as a way station for travelers. His success in farming and other activities would allow him to give each of his children a farm of their own.

Elmer Chamberlin rented land for 10 years until he had enough to start his own farm. His wife Anna was remembered as quiet and thrifty. The Chamberlin and Tobyne families were successful and hardworking. Elmer and his wife Anna raised their children to be the same.

One Tobyne family farm would become part of the Chamberlin holdings. Over time, Elmer owned about 1,000 acres in Gage County and a parcel of land in Canada as well.[9] Elmer became a prominent farmer in Gage County.[10] Farming in Nebraska is by no means an easy occupation and it is often made more difficult by dry conditions.

The oldest son of Elmer and Ann was Warren who went into farming. Next in line was William who would quit farming as a young man and become a banker. William was followed by Guy and then twin girls Frances and Ramona. The youngest child was Truman, who was always known as Pat. Pat would become the Chamberlin farm's mechanic and would manage part of the farm after his father's death. Eventually, Pat owned a Packard dealership in nearby Wymore.

Guy and his siblings went to a little rural school called Valley Center where their Aunt Fannie, their father's maiden sister, taught. Fannie was

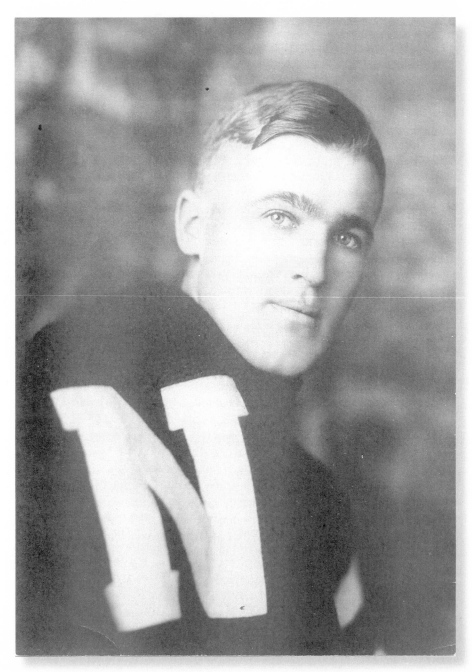

Guy Chamberlin at University of Nebraska

strict with her Chamberlin relatives. After graduating from Valley Center, Guy Chamberlin attended Blue Springs High School. There was no football team at Blue Springs because the school was not big enough to field one, but Chamberlin and some friends put together their own team along with kids from another small town, Wymore. Occasionally, their pick-up team played the Beatrice High School team in scrimmages.[11] Chamberlin graduated from high school in 1911.

College Career

Chamberlin attended Nebraska Wesleyan in Lincoln and played football. After his sophomore year, he transferred to the University of Nebraska. He played halfback at Wesleyan, which was coached by William G. Kline. In 1911, his first year at Wesleyan, Chamberlin and his team won seven games with no losses. Chamberlin decided upon the smaller school because he thought he would have a better chance of making the team.[12] He did not have to worry about that. Chamberlin made the Omaha World Herald's All-Nebraska team. He also played baseball and competed in track and field that year. In his second year at Wesleyan, the football team suffered two losses and posted a 5–2–1 record, but Chamberlin once again gained all-state honors. He was 6-foot-2 and thin, but a strong aggressive runner who could knock opposing tacklers off their feet.

Coach Kline helped Guy improve his running stride and speed. After working with Chamberlin on the basics, he clocked Guy at a blazing fast 10 seconds for the 100-yard dash. In track and field competition at Wesleyan, Chamberlin threw the discus, and he ran the 100-yard dash, the 440, and the half mile.[13] An all-around excellent athlete, as a sophomore, Chamberlin lettered in football, track, and baseball.[14] He also found time to teach Sunday school at the First Methodist Church. Anna Chamberlin moved to Lincoln and looked after her sons William and Guy when they were in school.

After transferring to the University of Nebraska in Lincoln, college rules prohibited Guy from playing on the varsity squad in the 1913 season. At Nebraska, Chamberlin played for Ewald "Jumbo" Stiehm (pronounced steam), a remarkable, intense coach whose winning percentage of .913 is the highest of any coach in school history. When Stiehm was coaching, the team was sometimes called the "Steamrollers." Otherwise they were the Bug-Eaters or the more popular Cornhuskers or Huskers.

Chamberlin was a member of the Beta Theta Pi fraternity. In those days, the fraternity met often, but members were not living together in a designated house. As a transfer student, the farm boy from Blue Springs, who lived with his mother, was not welcomed by several of the Nebraska football players. Early on, some of the varsity players mocked Chamberlin with remarks about how he was going to show them how to play the game. Chamberlin was known to his family as friendly and sociable, but he did not see any humor in this situation. He quietly fumed and waited for an opportunity to prove

Chamberlin Running Track at Nebraska Wesleyan University

himself. When he finally got a chance to show his football prowess in practice as a defensive end against the varsity, he started knocking out varsity Cornhuskers like shooting ducks. With two players already on the sidelines from Chamberlin play, he broke a quarterback's ankle with a vicious tackle on a punt return. Coach Stiehm had to intercede on the varsity's behalf.[15] Throughout Chamberlin's career, like many great players, he would exhibit a calm demeanor off the field and become something else entirely inside the white chalk lines. Like many players of his day, Chamberlin played offense and defense. At the University of Nebraska, he played end and halfback in his first year. He was often called upon to pass the ball, which the left-hander did well along with many other things. In 1914, Nebraska posted a 7–0–1 record winning the Missouri Valley Conference Championship with Chamberlin. Chamberlin scored nine touchdowns for the season. He ran back a kickoff for 90 yards against Michigan. On defense, he was an especially aggressive end who was excellent at breaking up plays.

In his senior year in 1915, on offense, he moved primarily to end, but he was versatile enough to return to the backfield and play any position there—making him someone whom opponents feared.[16] It was a brilliant season for Nebraska; they finished 8–0. Nebraska won the Missouri Valley Conference Championship for the second year in a row. Chamberlin scored 15 touchdowns. He was named to the All-Western and All-American teams.

In that 1915 season, Chamberlin and the Huskers started out strong by clobbering Drake, Kansas State, and Washburn on their way to a showdown with a strong Notre Dame team coached by Jesse Harper. On staff for Notre Dame was Assistant Coach Knute Rockne who would go on to a legendary head coaching career starting in 1918. Rockne had famously scouted the Huskers. Notre Dame's defense was instructed on apparent weaknesses in Chamberlin's running game that Rockne had discovered. Rockne also noted that Chamberlin licked his fingers before any passing play. The scouting report did not help—Chamberlin displayed no weaknesses at all. Long after the game, Rockne laughed when he recalled his predictions on Chamberlin's play. Chamberlin joked that he licked his fingers regardless of what he was going to do with the ball, but on that day, he fingered a wet sponge that he somehow affixed to his uniform to fight off the dryness.

The Nebraska-Notre Dame game was a tight match from beginning to end, but Nebraska prevailed 20–19. During the game, Nebraska fans across the state gathered at railroad stations to hear the latest game news read by telegraph operators coming over the wires while the contest was being played.[17] Chamberlin scored on two end-around plays and he passed for another touchdown. Notre Dame missed two extra points while Nebraska made two of three. The extra point differential turned out to be the difference. Chamberlin was the star of the game.

Lincoln Nebraska sports writer Cy Sherman called Chamberlin, "the most brilliant player ever developed in the annals of Missouri Valley football."[18]

After graduating in 1916, Chamberlin served as coach of athletics at Lexington High School. Despite the best efforts of President Wilson to stay out of the European conflict, the United States entered the Great War in 1917. Chamberlin's teaching career was cut short, but teaching was something he'd do very soon in the service and then much later in life at an unusual setting.

Military Service

Guy Chamberlin served in the U.S. Army as a Second Lieutenant from 1918-1919.[19] His first stop was Camp Zachary Taylor in Louisville, where he attended the Field Artillery Central Officers Training School. He moved on to Fort Sill School of Fire for instruction on the "latest weapons and fire direction procedures." He finished his service at Camp Kearney in California where he instructed in the 48th U.S. Field Artillery. When the end of the War came on November 11, 1918, he stayed and directed athletics at the Camp from February to September 1919.[20] It was during his military service that Chamberlin married Lucile E. Lees on January 3, 1919. Guy and Lucile had a daughter, Patricia Ann.

Chamberlin in Professional Football

Chamberlin was recruited by Jim Thorpe to play on the Canton Bulldogs in 1919. The Bulldogs were owned by Ralph E. Hay who owned a dealership in town that sold Jordan Hupmobiles and Pierce-Arrows. Hay would be remembered for his work with George Halas and others to establish the NFL itself.

Chamberlin played halfback as well as offensive and defensive end for the Bulldogs. Thorpe built his team around three leading offensive players in the backfield from the Carlisle Indian School: Joe Guyan, Pete Calac, and Thorpe himself. In Chamberlin, Thorpe had another game breaker. Although Chamberlin's talents were evident, he had to earn more playing time as the season continued. He did. According to the *Detroit Free Press*:

> *Chamberlain was in every play. A good ground gainer and a splendid defensive man, he time and again nailed the recipient of punts in his tracks, made many other tackles and repeatedly threw his lengthy frame in front of the ball to break up Herald's passes.*[21]

After the football season, Chamberlin played for the Canton Noakers baseball team. Chamberlin was an excellent pitcher and an excellent batter who hit over .500. He was a popular player whom the Noakers and fans were sorry to see leave before the 1920 season.

The 1919 Bulldog season took place before the famous meeting in Canton that established the first national professional football league called the

American Professional Football Association (APFA).[22] The APFA would be renamed the National Football League in 1922. The meeting took place at Ralph Hay's automobile dealership in Canton. The Bulldog owner played host to interested parties who established the league.

When Chamberlin joined the Canton Bulldogs in 1919, they were a semipro team, not so much due to talent, but based on their schedule and the competition at the time. Football historians acknowledge the central position of the Bulldogs and the city of Canton in early football. Most historians look at the year 1920 as the beginning of professional football—at least as a formerly organized activity, and that is certainly the starting point marked by the Pro Football Hall of Fame. The Bulldogs were one of the charter members.

Decatur Staleys-Chicago Staleys

A young engineer in charge of the Staley athletic teams, George Halas, scouted Chamberlin and asked him to join his industrial—soon to become professional—team. Chamberlin played with Halas and the Staleys from 1920-1921. The 1920 team was located in Decatur and was called the Decatur Staleys because it was owned by the Staley Starch Company. Players received jobs working for the Staley Company. In addition to football, Chamberlin also played on the Staleys' baseball team that featured the great Iron Man Joe McGinnity as player-manager.

Decatur Staleys' 1920 Season

There were 14 member teams of the APFA in 1920. It was entirely possible for the two top teams to finish the season without a single common opponent. The teams were also scheduling games outside the league to teams that ran the gamut in quality from poor to highly competitive.

All of Chamberlin's teammates on the Staleys in 1920 were considered rookies because it was the first year of play in the APFA. The three most senior men on the team were 28 years old. Guy Chamberlin, at the age of 26, was a year older than his boss, player-coach George Halas. Chamberlin played left end and Halas played right end. Loaded with talent, in addition to Halas and Chamberlin, the Staleys featured Hall of Famer George Trafton, Jimmy Conzelman, Halas's future Bears' partner Dutch Sternaman, and others. By most accounts, players in those days were very rugged men. Trafton was one of the biggest and roughest at 6-foot-2 and 230 pounds. He was known around the league for his aggressive style of play. According to Trafton's Pro Football Hall of Fame biography:

Trafton was strongly disliked in every NFL city, with the exception of Green Bay and Rock Island. In those places, he was hated.[23]

Guy Chamberlin at University of Nebraska Ready to Play

Conzelman was a versatile back who would go on to win two NFL Championships as a head coach. The new team brought great excitement to Decatur and the Staley Starch Company. In make-up, the team looked like a College All-Star team that could compete with any team in the country.

In the first two games of the season, the Staleys blew away two industrial teams, the Moline Universal Tractors, 20–0, and the Kewanee Walworths, 25–7. In the first match against a league rival, the Staleys traveled to Rock Island and beat the tough Independents, 7–0. Traveling to their future Chicago home, the Staleys shut out the Chicago Tigers, 10–0, at Cubs Park.[24] After beating Rockford 29–0, they played the Rock Island Independents again, but this time the game ended in a 0–0 tie. The media lauded the excellent wing play of the Staleys, that of Halas and Chamberlin. Also praised was Chamberlin's high knee action that makes him a terror to all opponents.[25]

The Minneapolis Marines gave the Staleys a tough game, but the Staleys prevailed, 3–0. The Staleys beat the Hammond Pros, 28–7, and once again shut out the Chicago Tigers, 6–0. Back to back battles against Paddy Driscoll's Chicago Cardinals pinned a 7–6 loss on the Staley's pristine record, but the Staleys regrouped for another win, 10–0.

Hall of Famer Paddy Driscoll, who was a player-coach for the Cardinals, joined the Staleys for one game at the end of the season against the Akron Pros in what was billed the league championship.[26] The game featured the two best teams in the league, but a true championship game would not be built into the schedule for over a decade. The Akron Pros and the Decatur Staleys fought to a 0–0 tie.

The Staleys scored 164 points and allowed just 21 points from their opponents in 1920. They had a brilliant 10–1–2 season, but the Akron Pros finished with an 8–0–3 record. In the early days of the league, the champion was typically announced at the team owners' annual meeting and decided upon strictly by winning percentage with ties having no bearing. But by having the team owners make the decision after the season, arguments could at least be made. There were no playoffs, but there were disputes about who truly deserved the top honor until the playoff system was introduced.

The Akron Pros had an awesome defense that year and scored 151 points while allowing just 7 from their opponents in the entire 11-game season. One notable contributor to the Akron championship effort was Fritz Pollard, an African-American running back and Hall of Famer. On April 30, 1921, when the team managers got together long after the season had ended, they voted Akron the league champion and gave them a loving cup that had been provided by the Brunswick-Balke Collender Company.[27]

The men running professional football teams were some of the most highly competitive sportsmen in the nation. Yet, everything about football was young in those days. There were many things that went on in the early days of professional football that would eventually get weeded out under the auspices of President Joe Carr. Originally, actions that might help one team, but hurt the league, were commonplace. Jockeying schedules, late cancellation of games, players jumping from team to team, and other such dealings were common. The owners wanted to eliminate such practices that might be against the spirit, if not the letter of the league rules, but they needed a strong unifying figure—a man who could enforce the rules authoritatively across the league. Carr was that man.[28]

Chicago Staleys' 1921 Championship Season

Although football had been around for several decades, in many ways the professional game was in its early stages of development. The Decatur Staleys had shown themselves to be one of the best teams, but their home field had seating for only about 1,500. Some teams were attracting more than 5,000 spectators. The Staleys also employed their players at the plant and shared the gate receipts with them. When the economy was hit by a recession, Mr. Staley turned team ownership over to Halas for 1921 with some seed money in exchange for the continuation of the Staley team name for one more year plus some advertising. The team was called the Chicago Staleys in 1921 and became the Chicago Bears in 1922.

In 1921, the Chicago Staleys captured the APFA championship with a 9–1–1 record. Guy Chamberlin played in every game. Chamberlin greatly contributed to the team's success, but no one player was exalted above all others on the Staleys. It was truly a team effort. For the season, the Staleys scored 128 points and allowed 53 from their opponents. The Staleys' one loss came at the hands of the Buffalo All-Stars who beat them 7–6 on November 24. Two weeks later on December 4, the Staleys avenged that loss by beating the All-Stars 10–7. In that game, Chamberlin intercepted a pass and ran it back 70 yards for the Staleys' one touchdown.[29] During the season, Chamberlin had two touchdown receptions.

Canton Bulldogs-Cleveland Bulldogs

Chamberlin's former team, the Canton Bulldogs, had made the transition from semi pro to professional football. The name Canton Bulldogs was used by a team from 1906-1908. A team founded in 1911 called the Canton Professionals picked up the Bulldog moniker in 1915.[30] Ohio was a hotbed for football even back then. The Bulldogs of 1916 and following were a prominent team with a penchant for winning.

Canton Bulldogs' 1922 Championship Season

Chamberlin was back with the Canton Bulldogs as player and coach in 1922. Chamberlin would recall being "paid $7,000 the 2 years I was at Canton."[31] He brought in a number of new players and perhaps none was as important to the team's fortunes as Chamberlin himself. He scored seven touchdowns in 1922 and his 42 points made him leading scorer for the team. The Bulldogs would score 184 points while only allowing the opposition to score 15 points.

On the field, the Bulldogs were a success, but they played at Lakeside Park, a minor league baseball park that was not big enough to bring in the kind of gate receipts needed to support professional football. Chamberlin was able to quickly assemble a dominating team with a tough front line, but the bottom line was in trouble.

Chamberlin managed a team that was true to its name; the Bulldogs had size and strength. Playing right tackle was Hall of Famer, Wilbur "Fats" Henry, who was a force at 235 pounds. The left tackle was Link Lyman, another huge lineman for the time at 233 pounds who would also achieve Hall of Fame status after a great career. Lyman hailed from Chamberlin's alma mater, the University of Nebraska. Chamberlin who was generous in giving his players credit, praised Henry and Lyman this way:

Lots of fans said that they [Henry and Lyman] were responsible for our success and they were about right.[32]

The Bulldogs were fearsome in 1922, but they didn't start out that way. After pounding the Louisville Brechts, 38–0, a team that would only play four games that year, the best the Bulldogs could do was to tie the Dayton Triangles, 0–0, in their second outing. They beat Jim Thorpe's Oorang Indians team, 14–0, but that was not much comfort to them. The Oorang Indians of LaRue, Ohio, had a competent group of players, but owner Walter Lingo had many interests. Lingo's Oorang Kennels was the largest mail order dog breeding business in the country specializing in Airedales.[33] Lingo had a love for his dogs as well as American Indian lore, and he concocted a show that he put on at games to promote his interests. It is said that the show was so elaborate that the players felt like the game itself was of secondary importance.[34]

After the Oorang game, the Bulldogs beat the Akron Pros soundly, 22–0. A critical win came next when the Bulldogs beat the Chicago Bears, 7–6. The difference in the game was a missed extra point.[35]

The Bulldogs sputtered and tied the Toledo Maroons 0–0 before facing a very tough Buffalo All-Americans team. Things looked grim against Buffalo who had a fourth quarter 3–0 lead, when Guy Chamberlin blocked a punt that big tackle "Fats" Henry recovered. With the line of scrimmage at the 11-yard line, Wilbur Henry kicked a field goal to save the Bulldogs unbeaten streak under Chamberlin. The game ended in a 3–3 tie.

Canton proved to be unstoppable the rest of the season by winning their next six games including two matches against the Chicago Cardinals, a team the runner up Bears could not handle that year. Canton's 10–0–2 record gave Chamberlin's team the league championship. Despite the championship in 1922, Canton Bulldogs Owner Ralph Hay could not afford to hold on to the

1922 Canton Bulldogs

Bulldogs and he sold the team to Canton businessmen before the 1923 season. He credited Chamberlin in a letter to his team and fans:

The assistance of my organization, the loyal support of the Canton fans and the wonderful harmony that Coach Chamberlin brought into the heart of every player who was with this team in 1922 was the fundamental reason for our success.[36]

Canton Bulldogs' 1923 Championship Season

By the score differential, one would think that Canton bullied the rest of the league in 1923. They scored 246 points and allowed just 19 from opponents. But after shutting out their first three opponents, the Bulldogs played four challenging games against the league's best that turned out to be squeakers, every one. They beat a tough Bears' team 6–0. Next came the Akron Pros, and the Bulldogs prevailed by 7–3. They beat the Chicago Cardinals by the same score, 7–3, and then tied the Buffalo All-Americans 3–3. They slaughtered their next three opponents: Oorang Indians, 41–0; Cleveland Indians, 46–10; and Toledo Maroons, 28–0. Their final two games went down in favor of Chamberlin's team: Bulldogs 14–Buffalo All-Americans 0; Bulldogs 10–Columbus Tigers 0.

With a record of 11–0–1, the Bulldogs wrapped up another championship and once again Chamberlin's old team, the Chicago Bears were runners up at 9–2–1. Chamberlin's old teammate and coach, George Halas, would describe Chamberlin as the best end in professional football and would go on to lament the fact that he did not hold onto him.

Cleveland Bulldogs' 1924 Championship Season

On July 8, 1923, a Cleveland jeweler and sports promoter named Samuel Deutsch formed the Cleveland Indians. Based on winning percentage alone with ties having no bearing, the Indians' 3–1–3 record was good enough for a fifth place finish out of 20 teams in the NFL. Deutsch wanted more. He bought the Canton Bulldogs after the 1923 season, which he left inactive, but he moved many Canton Players into his Cleveland team calling the amalgamation, the Cleveland Bulldogs.[37] Chamberlin moved on to Cleveland joining the new team. With Chamberlin at the helm, and an amalgamation of players from two teams, the Cleveland Bulldogs notched a 7–1–1 season in 1924, which earned them the league championship.

In the first game, Chamberlin's Bulldogs beat the Bears, 16–14. The two point difference would give the championship to the Bulldogs based on percentages. After their first win, the Bulldogs tied the Frankford Yellow Jackets, 3–3. They notched a 27–14 win against the Akron Pros who had not done well since their 1920 championship season. Chamberlin's team slaughtered the Rochester Jeffersons, 59–0, who were not a professional caliber team. The Bulldogs mauled the Dayton Triangles, 35–0, and beat the Akron Pros again, 20–7. They lost for the first time that season to the Frankford Yellow Jackets, 12–7. As the season wound down, they shutout the Columbus Tigers, 7–0, and then showed championship form in beating the Milwaukee Badgers, 53–10.

In a challenge match against the second place Chicago Bears on December 7, they lost 23–0. At the league meeting, the owners awarded the championship to Chamberlin's Bulldogs based on season dates that had been agreed upon the previous year. The final game against the Bears was ruled an exhibition.

The three championships in a row were certainly a great achievement for Chamberlin, but because two different teams were involved, the accomplishment is often overlooked in articles and postings that call attention to Lambeau's and Lombardi's three football championships in a row at Green Bay. Chamberlin left the Bulldogs after the 1924 season after assembling a record of success that would stand out in NFL history.

Frankford Yellow Jackets

Chamberlin moved on to play and coach the Frankford Yellow Jackets for the 1925 and 1926 seasons. The Yellow Jackets played from 1924-1931. Frankford itself is a neighborhood in northeast Philadelphia. Chamberlin settled into the area, rented a home, pitched for the American Legion in the baseball season, and worked as a truck driver in the off season. Pennsylvania's blue laws prohibited professional football on Sundays so the Yellow Jackets would often schedule two games on the same weekend, a Saturday home game and a Sunday away game.

1925 Frankford Yellow Jackets' Season

In 1925, the NFL was a bloated 20-team league. Scheduling was seriously out of sync. The Yellow Jackets played 19 games while the Duluth Kelleys played just three. Five teams did not win a game all season. The Yellow Jackets had an excellent first half of the season winning 9 of 10 games and then fell apart in the second half winning 3 and losing 6. It is likely that their heavy schedule contributed to the lapse in the second half of the season. Before their swoon, they beat the Pottsville Maroons, 20–0, on November 14. Two weeks later, Pottsville destroyed the Yellow Jackets, 49–0. They did not play the Chicago Cardinals who took the championship with a record of 11–2–1. Pottsville was runner up with a 10–2–0 record.

1926 Frankford Yellow Jackets' Season

Guy Chamberlin brought it all together for the Yellow Jackets in 1926. The Yellow Jackets had another exhausting schedule. They played 17 games. They scored 236 points and allowed 49 from their opponents. There was a kind of perfect symmetry to their season record. They tied the first and last game of the season and lost game 8 to the Providence Steam Roller 7–6. They won every other game on their schedule to end at 14–1–2 for the Championship.

On December 4, 1926, with the Yellow Jackets holding a 12–1–1 record, they played the key game of the season against the Chicago Bears who held a 12–0–3 record. For the first three quarters, the offenses struggled to get into scoring position. In the third quarter, the Bears finally got close enough for a Paddy Driscoll field goal attempt. It was blocked by Guy Chamberlin. In the fourth quarter, the Bears' halfback, Bill Senn, cut loose for a 62-yard touchdown run. Chamberlin blocked the extra point attempt. The Bears held a 6–0 lead as time was pulling away from Frankford. With one last run at the end zone, Chamberlin's Yellow Jackets moved down field on the strength of a long pass play. Then, Houston Stockton hit his tiny 5-foot-5 back, Henry "Two Bits" Homan, who caught the ball and crossed into the end zone for a score. Frankford's Tex Hamer kicked the extra point for the win.

On November 29, 1926, Raymond Hill of the Philadelphia Evening Bulletin described Chamberlin and his play:

> *… consistent performer all year…a brainy player and wide-awake on the field….He has been performing life saving feats for the Jackets all year, besides getting down fast under punts, grabbing passes and breaking up end runs…his play is one of the main reasons for Frankford being up in the fight.*[38]

Chamberlin left the Frankford Yellow Jackets after the championship season of 1926 and went to the Chicago Cardinals. His reasons are lost to history. Some suggest that the Cardinals were hardly in a position to offer more money to Chamberlin and therefore it was more likely to do with some other dispute between coach and management.[39] Chamberlin's accomplishments were great regardless of where he went, but the teams that he coached all had one thing in common, financial trouble.

1927 Chicago Cardinals' Season

Chamberlin was on top of his game in coaching when he moved from the Frankford Yellow Jackets to the Chicago Cardinals in 1927. Once again he served as player-coach, but he played little. The Cardinals would prove to be a difficult assignment. The Chicago Bears shut the Cardinals out in the season opener, 9–0. They managed to defeat Pottsville 19–7 and the Dayton Triangles 7–0 in their next games. Two losses followed—the Packers shut them out, 13–0, and the Yankees got past them, 7–6. Chamberlin's team showed improvement when they tied the Packers in their second meeting of the season, 6–6. But they lost to the Yankees in their second meeting, 20–6. Chamberlin's old team, the Frankford Yellow Jackets beat the Cardinals 12–8, and the Giants roughed them up 28–7. The Cardinals' President, Chris Obrien, fired Chamberlin before the Cardinals big game against the Bears on Thanksgiving. Chamberlin had coached his last game. Ben Jones filled in as coach for the final two games.[40] Under Jones, the Cardinals squeaked by the Bears 3–0, but they were slaughtered by the Cleveland Bulldogs, 32–7, the following week.

Chamberlin was not the last coach who would find the Cardinals a difficult assignment during that period. A series of coaches were hired and fired in the next several years.

Guy Champ Chamberlin was true to his nickname. He won almost everywhere he went and with each championship, there was one common runner up: the Chicago Bears.

> 1922 Champion: Chamberlin's Canton Bulldogs; runner up, Chicago Bears
> 1923 Champion: Chamberlin's Canton Bulldogs; runner up, Chicago Bears
> 1924 Champion: Chamberlin's Cleveland Bulldogs; runner up, Chicago Bears
> 1926 Champion: Chamberlin's Frankford Yellow Jackets; runner up, Chicago Bears

Football fans look back at Chamberlin's record and wonder how anyone could win four championships coaching three different teams in 5 years.

After Football

Guy followed in his father's footsteps after his football career and farmed, but in time he also branched out to owning other businesses. For the most part, neighbors might reminisce about the Cornhuskers and their neighbor who had been a football star, but there was very little hero worship going around upon his return to Gage County. Depression, drought, and dust must have dampened enthusiasm for what Guy Chamberlin had done. If anything, perhaps his neighbors would have heightened expectations of what Guy Chamberlin would accomplish outside of football. Chamberlin would be judged on what he was doing, not what he had done.

Chamberlin would say later in life that he had no idea that professional football was going to be successful—and that's likely why he did not continue to work in the NFL. He returned to his father's farm. Unlike modern players, there would have been no expectations that his college or professional football career was going to make his fortune. Like so many athletes of his day, he struggled to adjust to a life after his professional career. He and his brothers would live around the farm and at times each of them would be called to run it. As older farm couples are prone to do, Guy Chamberlin's parents, Elmer and Anna, moved into town, but Elmer kept his hands in the operation. Elmer lived to be 96 years old. Eventually, the Chamberlin farm would be sold in the 1950s.

In middle age, Chamberlin would have bouts with various health issues that would eventually separate him from farming and some other physically difficult jobs. He would own a Ford Dealership, work for a farm implements store, and later serve in a state prison reformatory. It would be working with troubled young men at the reformatory that Chamberlin would hit his stride again. Helping underdogs do their best was a natural fit for Chamberlin.

As one of the most important figures in both college and professional football, Chamberlin was called upon to speak before interested audiences. He also offered his insights on University of Nebraska football to fans during the season.

Guy Chamberlin passed away in Lincoln, Nebraska on April 4, 1967 at the age of 73.

Chamberlin's Contributions to the Game

Nebraska Wesleyan was undefeated in Chamberlin's first year and when Chamberlin played for the University of Nebraska, they won the conference championship both years. Wherever Chamberlin went, he earned his moniker "Champ."

To honor Chamberlin's memory, the University of Nebraska created the Guy Chamberlin Trophy inaugurated in 1967. The award is presented to the senior player who has "shown by the play and contributions to the betterment of the University of Nebraska football squad that he has the qualities and dedication of Guy Chamberlin to the Cornhusker tradition." Lincoln radio station KFOR donated the permanent trophy and each recipient receives a replica through funds contributed by the Chamberlin family and friends. The Chamberlin Memorial Fund is administered by the University of Nebraska Foundation. Sportswriters and broadcasters who cover all Nebraska games vote on the award.

Unlike any other of the top NFL coaches, Guy Chamberlin's play was inextricably woven into his total contribution to the game. Certainly George Halas and Curly Lambeau had long careers as player-coaches, but both went on for much longer periods of time coaching and not playing. But in Chamberlin's case, in most of his coaching career when he was winning championships, he was one of the top performers, if not his top player.

Chamberlin's professional career compared in some ways with Lombardi, in that his accomplishments were tremendous, but confined to a relatively short period of time. However, in many ways the similarity ends there. Lombardi was middle aged by the time he took on the head job at the Green Bay Packers and had coached in high school and college. Chamberlin was still learning the ropes when he took over the Canton Bulldogs and he was still a young man when he retired. Chamberlin was a professional football pioneer.

Chamberlin coached from 1922-1927. In those 6 years, he won four championships. Prior to his coaching career, he played for George Halas and the Decatur-Chicago Staleys in 1920-1921. The Staleys won the Championship in 1921; thus in an eight year period, Chamberlin was a part of five championship teams. When Chamberlin played for the Canton Bulldogs in 1919, before the

Second Lieutenant Chamberlin at Camp Kearney in California

start of national professional football, his team was considered the champion of the Ohio League. The Ohio League was in part the nucleus of what would become the APFA and then the NFL.

Chamberlin would find his place preserved in the College Football Hall of Fame in 1962 and the Pro Football Hall of Fame in 1965. When notified of his honor to the Pro Football Hall of Fame, Chamberlin characteristically commented:

> *Winning an award such as the Football Hall of Fame makes a fellow feel mighty humble. Every time you receive an award you realize the recognition was made possible by 10 other boys you had around you. They deserve the award as much as I do.[41]*

The Pro Football Hall of Fame is located in Canton, home of the Canton Bulldogs, Chamberlin's first pro football team. In Canton at Chamberlin's enshrinement, Canton teammate Doc Elliott called Chamberlin simply "the winningest guy of all time."[42]

Regardless of the honors bestowed on him, Chamberlin remained self-effacing. After the Canton enshrinement festivities, Chamberlin quipped about his Hall of Fame likeness:

> *Ever since I got into pro football, I thought I was a little touched in the head, I looked into my bust, and sure enough, I've got a hole in my head.[43]*

The men at the state prison reformatory showed their appreciation of the modest man and his kind attitude towards them by building a field, naming, and dedicating it to Guy Chamberlin.

Chamberlin was enshrined in the Nebraska Football Hall of Fame posthumously in 1971. Chamberlin is one of the top ten coaches in professional football history based on championship wins. What sets Chamberlin apart is that his playing contributed so much to those wins. George Halas, who had seen it all from the beginning of professional football into the modern era, wrote:

> *He had all the attributes of a great football player and as you can imagine in those early days players were far more rugged than they are today...professional football was very fortunate in having a man of his caliber as one of its pioneers.[44]*

Guy Chamberlin Timeline

1894

- January 16, 1894, Berlin Guy "Champ" Chamberlin is born on a farm outside of Blue Springs, Nebraska.

1911

- Guy Chamberlin graduates from Blue Springs High School, a school that is too small to field a football team.
- Chamberlin attends Nebraska Wesleyan in Lincoln leading the team to an undefeated season while playing halfback under Coach William G. Kline.
- Chamberlin makes the Omaha World Herald's All-Nebraska team for football, and he plays baseball and competes in track and field.

1912

- Chamberlin once again receives all-state honors for his football play at Wesleyan.

1913

- Chamberlin transfers to the University of Nebraska, but he is ineligible to play varsity his first year.

1914

- Chamberlin plays varsity football under Coach Ewald "Jumbo" Stiehm.
- Nebraska posts a 7–0–1 record to win the Missouri Valley Conference Championship with Chamberlin scoring nine touchdowns.

1915

- October 23, 1915, Chamberlin who has been moved to end, scores on two end-around runs and passes for another touchdown as Nebraska beats Notre Dame, 20–19.
- Nebraska finishes 8–0 for its second Missouri Valley Conference Championship in a row.
- Chamberlin scores 15 touchdowns and is named to the All-Western and All-American teams.

1916

- Chamberlin teaches and coaches at Lexington High School in Nebraska.

1917-1919

- Chamberlin serves in the U.S. Army as a Second Lieutenant.

1919

- Chamberlin plays for Jim Thorpe on the Canton Bulldogs.

1920

- Chamberlin plays for George Halas and the Decatur Staleys.

1921

- The Chicago Staleys capture the APFA (NFL) championship with a 9–1–1 record.

1922

- Chamberlin returns to the Canton Bulldogs to serve as a player-coach— he scores seven touchdowns and 42 points to make him the leading scorer on Canton's 1922 championship team.

1923

- Chamberlin's Bulldogs wrap up a second NFL Championship with an 11–0–1 record.

1924

- Chamberlin is player-coach of a new team that is born out of an amalgamation of teams from Canton and Cleveland owned by the same man. Chamberlin's Cleveland Bulldogs notch a 7–1–1 season, which earns them the NFL Championship—Chamberlin's third in a row.

1925

- Chamberlin becomes player-coach of the Frankford Yellow Jackets.

1926

- Chamberlin's Yellow Jackets win the NFL Championship with a 14–1–2 record. It is Chamberlin's fourth championship in 5 years on three different teams.

1927

- Chamberlin becomes player-coach of the Chicago Cardinals, a team that is struggling financially. He is released towards the end of the season and he retires from football.

1962

- Chamberlin is enshrined into the College Football Hall of Fame.

1965

- Chamberlin is enshrined into the Pro Football Hall of Fame.

1967

- April 4, 1967, Guy Chamberlin dies in Lincoln, Nebraska, at the age of 73.
- To honor Chamberlin's memory, the University of Nebraska creates the Guy Chamberlin Trophy.

1971

- Chamberlin is enshrined in the Nebraska Football Hall of Fame posthumously.

Highlights

Guy Chamberlin coached from 1922-1927. He won four championships. Prior to his coaching career, he played for George Halas and the Decatur-Chicago Staleys in 1920-1921. The Staleys won the Championship in 1921; thus in an eight year period, Chamberlin was a part of five championship teams. Chamberlin holds an overall NFL head coaching record of 58-16-7, which likely includes a few losses that occurred after he left his last team.

Guy Chamberlin's play was inextricably woven into his total contribution to the game over his career. When he was winning championships, he was winning them on the field as a hands-on coach. Chamberlin was a game-changer.

Endnotes

[1] Notre Dame teams were not yet formally called the "Fighting Irish" at that time although they did have nicknames. Some would have referred to them as the "Catholics" although the school has a long history of including students of other faiths. According to a post at the Notre Dame official site for athletics at http://www.und.com/trads/nd-m-fb-name.html, University President Rev. Matthew Walsh, C.S.C., officially adopted "Fighting Irish" as the Notre Dame nickname in 1927.

[2] World War I was called the Great War until the start of World War II.

[3] Wally Provost, "War Interrupts Gridiron Exploits," *Omaha World Herald*, September 2, 1964, p. 27.

[4] In Lincoln, Nebraska the years 1934-1939 averaged 20.8 inches of rainfall per year when the average is 27.6 according to Michael Hays, Cody Knutson, Q. Steven Hu, "Multiple Year Droughts in Nebraska (Lincoln, NE, The Board of Regents of the University of Nebraska) 2005. Viewed at http://www.ianrpubs.unl.edu/live/g1551/build/g1551.pdf on March 28, 2013.

[5] Wally Provost, "From Farm in Gage County Came a N.U. and Pro Giant," from Nebraska's Greatest Guy series, August 29, 1964, *Omaha World Herald*.

[6] Dorothy Chamberlin Savener Interview conducted by E. A. Kral, May 23, 1996, Wymore, NE. Subject: Berlin Guy Chamberlin (Interviewee is niece of subject), transcript obtained from Gage County Historical Society.

[7] In a 1996 interview, Dorothy Chamberlin Savener, stated that Elmer had said his father, William Chamberlin, changed the name for this reason. Other sources state that Elmer changed it, but it seems more likely that Dorothy Savener Chamberlin had it right that William Chamberlin, would have done it; he was a miller.

[8] Dorothy Chamberlin Savener Interview conducted by E. A. Kral.

[9] Hugh Jackson Dobbs, *History of Gage County Nebraska* (Lincoln, NE, Western Publishing and Engraving) 736.

[10] Gage County was developed in part through the Homestead Act and ambitious young people moved into the area to stake their claims. The Homestead National Monument resides in the vicinity.

[11] Wally Provost, "Plow Shoes, Overalls Farm Boy's First Uniform," from Nebraska's Greatest Guy series, September 1964. *Omaha World Herald*. Some sources indicate that Guy Chamberlin was a high school football star, but Chamberlin himself indicated that he only played "choose up" at the time.

[12] George Sullivan, *Pro Football's All Time Greats* (New York, Putnam, 1968)127.

[13] Blue Springs Weekly Sentinel of May 15, 1913, reprinted in special anniversary booklet.

[14] Wally Provost, "State College Set Must Have Cheered Chamberlin's Transfer to Husker," from Nebraska's Greatest Guy series, *Omaha World Herald*, August 26, 1964.

[15] Wally Provost, "Frosh Chamberlin Made Believers of N.U. Varsity," from Nebraska's Greatest Guy series, *Omaha World Herald*, August 27, 1964.

[16] "Top Season Follows Defeat of Irish—20–19 Win 1 of Chamie's Top Frays," *Omaha World Herald*, April 4, 1962.

[17] Frederick Ware, *Fifty Years of Football: A Condensed History of the Game at the University of Nebraska* (Omaha, Omaha World-Herald, 1940) 25.

[18] Mike Babcock, *Go Big Red* (NY, Macmillan, 1998) 31.

[19] http://www.zoominfo.com/people/Chamberlin_Guy_1262207.aspx

[20] John Rueben Johnson, *Representative Nebraskans* (Lincoln, NE, Johnsen Publishing Company, 1954) 43.

21   "Canton's Team Beats Heralds," *Detroit Free Press*, October 27, 1919. (Note misspelling of "Chamberlin," a common occurrence throughout Guy Chamberlin's career and beyond.)

22   More professional football history, including the Canton meeting, can be found in the chapter on George Halas.

23   Pro Football hall of Fame Biography at http://www.profootballhof.com/hof/member. aspx?PLAYER_ID=215 viewed on April 7, 2013.

24   Cubs Park was renamed Wrigley Field in 1926.

25   Wally Provost, "Chamberlin Missed Call on Pro Grid Growth," *Omaha World Herald*, September 5, 1964. (Provost quotes Chicago Daily News "terror to all" moniker for Chamberlin.)

26   Official web site of the Chicago Bears, Tradition Page at http://www.chicagobears.com/tradition/bears-in-the-hall/paddy-driscoll.html

27   Bob Carroll, Akron Pros 1920, *The Coffin Corner*: Vol. 4, No. 12 (1982), viewed at http://www.profootballresearchers.org/Coffin_Corner/04-12-119.pdf on April 3, 2013.

28   For more information on Joe Carr, see Chris Willis's book, *The Man Who Built the National Football League: Joe Carr*, Scarecrow Press, Lanham, Maryland, 2010.

29   George Sullivan, *Pro Football's All Time Greats* (New York, Putnam, 1968)128-129.

30   "Canton Bulldogs,' *Ohio History Central*, March 21, 2013, http://www.ohiohistorycentral. org/entry.php?rec=2109&nm=Canton-Bulldogs

31   Chris Willis, *The Man Who Built the National Football League: Joe F. Carr* (Lanham, Maryland, Scarecrow Press, 2010) 155.

32   Charlie Powell, "Chamberlin Enjoyed Fabled Career, Thought Pro Ball Wouldn't Progress," *Canton Repository*, April 12, 1965.

33   Robert W. Peterson, *Pigskin: The Early Years of Pro Football* (Oxford, UK, Oxford

34   For more information on the Oorang Indians see the Pro Football Hall of Fame article at: http://www.profootballhof.com/history/decades/1920s/oorang.aspx

35   Roy Sye, "Almost Champions, 1920-1932 Revisited," *The Coffin Corner*, Vol. 25, No. 1, viewed at http://www.profootballresearchers.org/Coffin_Corner/25-02-976.pdf on August 20, 2013.

36   Chris Willis, "Ralph Hay, A Forgotten Pioneer," *The Coffin Corner*, Vol. 25 (2004).

37   "Cleveland Indians, National Football League, 1923," *Ohio History Central*, March 21, 2013, http://www.ohiohistorycentral.org/entry.php?rec=2285

38   Raymond A. Hill, "Phila. Teams May Play for Pro Title," *Evening Bulletin*, November 29, 1926, viewed at http://home.comcast.net/~ghostsofthegridiron/Quakers_Yellowjackets_1926.htm on April 10, 2013.

39   Frank Fitzpatrick, "Why Did Winning Coach Leave Philly; He Led the Yellow Jackets to 14 Wins and an NFL Title in 1926. Then He Was Gone," *Philadelphia Enquirer*, February 15, 2007, viewed at http://articles.philly.com/2007-02-15/sports/25238450_1_yellow-jackets-nfl-title-frankford viewed on April 10, 2013.

40   Joe Ziemba, *When Football Was Football* (Chicago, Triumph Books, 1999) 400.

41   Gregg McBride, "Hall of Fame Picks Ex-Nebraska Star: Chamberlin, Blue Springs Product, Join Weir, Sauer in Grid Shrine," Omaha World Herald, April 4, 1962, Sports Section, p. 27.

42   Charlie Powell, "Colorful Show Climaxes Greatest Grid Weekend: HOF Adds 7 Notables to Shrine," *The Canton Repository*, Sept. 13, 1965.

43   Charlie Powell, "Colorful Show Climaxes Greatest Grid Weekend: HOF Adds 7 Notables to Shrine," *The Canton Repository*, Sept. 13, 1965.

44   Halas letter to Chamberlin's daughter, Mrs. Patricia Sherwood, on May 6, 1967, provided by Robert Sherwood, grandson of Guy Chamberlin.

Curly Lambeau

Ready to conquer the world

It is 1929, the year of the stock market crash and the beginning of the Great Depression. Earl Louis Lambeau, the Green Bay player-coach, has other things on his mind right now. He stands out on a no frills practice field in Green Bay and barks out instructions to his team. The cold autumn wind whips through the dark wavy hair that has given him the moniker, Curly. He is 5-foot-10, handsome, and built like a prizefighter. He can still play football, but he will only cross the sideline in uniform in one game this season.

Lambeau is restless, competitive, and perhaps more than anything, he is confident in everything he does. Football is a fitting game for him. It is a man's game—something made for his temperament. It is a game that intrigues and challenges him—a channel for his endless energy.

Lambeau's temper flares as he looks at a player who is not following his instructions. He approaches the man and shouts out directions that he gave a few minutes ago—this time with exaggerated gestures. He is not the most patient "teacher." He was not the most patient student either. In fact, he dropped out of two different colleges a decade ago and made no plans to go back.

Laumbeau has intelligently built a team of excellent athletes over the past eight seasons in the National Football League.[1] He is a much more mature coach now at 31 years old than when he started. There is no college draft yet in the NFL, so Lambeau talks to whomever he wants coming from the college ranks. It has not been easy, but Lambeau is persuasive. He ably recruits players for Green Bay, a relatively small Midwestern city that is known for iron smelting, papermaking, lumber milling, manufacturing, and to some extent, meatpacking. It is a place that does the difficult.

Some players prefer the college-like atmosphere of Green Bay and its small town feel. Green Bay has been a good place for jobs, but its population is less than 40,000. It is a tough place to live in December, January, and February when the average low temperature is under 20° and it often trails off below zero. Over 50 inches of snow routinely bury the town each year.

The hard-scrabbled citizens that include many immigrants, and sons and daughters of immigrants, do not complain about the weather in Green Bay. They are hardworking people who support Lambeau and his team. In fact, the people in the community have come to own the team through stock purchases and they sustain it by attending games in great number.

The newspapers praise Lambeau. The community is fond of him. The team itself is a different story. Coaches are not necessarily loved by their players. Lambeau motivates his men by almost any means. He threatens. He intimidates. He is quick to release any man who cannot help the team any longer. He insists on physical conditioning. He has no patience for players who are out of shape or who do not listen. But, he can manage difficult players as well as anyone in football when they are critical to the team's success. Some players do not like him. Others do not respect him. But most are confident that he will get more out of these Packers than anyone else on the planet.

Lambeau is a coach who takes his wins and losses personally. He can be miserable for days before a big game and even more miserable if they lose. He can be exuberant after a win, when he often tells his players in post game: "The lid's off tonight boys, just don't get arrested."

Coaching, like life, can be tenuous. If Lambeau's coaching career came to an end on this cold day in 1929, the Packers might fade away as so many other early small-market teams have done. Green Bay may have remained a relatively quiet Wisconsin town—a good town where industry flourished and workers went about their business, but a town of no special note nationally. But Lambeau sticks it out and his Packers are on the threshold of winning three championships in a row. Under Lambeau, the Packers will win six championships overall. In a few months and continuing for years, the national media will report on a fascinating "David and Goliath" story—little Green Bay beating the big city teams. Green Bay will become famous all over the world and Curly Lambeau will become its first superstar.

But today's practice is not about notoriety or glory, fame or fortune; it's about a local man coaching a group of men on a cold day and giving them a sense of potential and purpose with a dash of promise.

Early Life

Curly Lambeau was born Earl Louis Lambeau on April 9, 1898, to Marceline Marcel Lambeau and Mary Sara Latour Lambeau in Green Bay, Wisconsin. Curly's grandparents emigrated from Belgium. His paternal grandfather was a bricklayer. His father, Marcel, owned his own construction business. Earl Louis was the oldest of the four Lambeau children; Curly had two brothers, Raymond and Oliver, and a sister, Beatrice.

From his earliest days, Curly displayed great athletic ability and a great interest in sports. At Green Bay East High School, Curly captained both the football and track teams. In his senior year, he led the football team to an undefeated season that included a rare win over chief rival Green Bay West High School. That season, Lambeau would run, throw, kick, and punt his team to victory. He graduated as a member of the Class of 1917.

Lambeau was fond of throwing the football even though its rounded shape was more conducive to rugby than modern football. Throwing was a small part of the game at the time.[2] Lambeau was also adept at the dropkick, which would later become a lost art when the ball shape changed making the modern placekick more suitable. In track, Lambeau threw the shot put, the hammer, and the discus, and he performed the broad jump.[3] Lambeau was one of the best athletes in Green Bay and he knew it. His message in the East High yearbook:

When I get through with athletics I'm going out and conquer the rest of the world.

After high school, Lambeau worked for his father's construction business, but he was encouraged to attend college. Lambeau briefly attended the University of Wisconsin in 1917. He left when he found out there would be no football for freshmen.

Lambeau and ND Legends

In 1918, Lambeau attended Notre Dame where he rubbed shoulders with future college football legends. At Notre Dame, Lambeau shared the backfield, albeit for a single season, with George "Gipper" Gipp, the storied back who would lead the team in both rushing and passing from 1918-1920. Lambeau played under new head coach, Knute Rockne. Like Lambeau, Rockne was a fan of the pass and in South Bend, Lambeau learned the Notre Dame box, a formation based on the commonly used single wing. This would be the formation Lambeau used extensively at Green Bay with modifications until the late 1940s.

During Lambeau's stay in South Bend, World War I was raging, but it was a flu epidemic that shortened the football season. Notre Dame posted a 3–1–2 record. In one tough game against the Great Lakes Naval Station, Lambeau faced future rival and Chicago Bears founder, George Halas, who played end. The teams tied.

As a freshman, Lambeau had a supporting role in the Notre Dame backfield. He was no threat to superstar Gipp who among other astonishing feats, held the ND rushing career mark of 2,341 yards for more than 50 years. Tragically, after his senior season, Gipp developed a strep infection and died. On his deathbed, Gipp's last conversation to Rockne was quoted as:

The Four Horsemen of Football

I've got to go, Rock. It's all right. I'm not afraid. Some time, Rock, when the team is up against it, when things are wrong and the breaks are beating the boys, ask them to go in there with all they've got and win just one for the Gipper. I don't know where I'll be then, Rock. But I'll know about it, and I'll be happy.

Rockne would famously use the deathbed story to motivate his underdog Notre Dame team against Army in 1928. The quote would also make its way into movies and politics.

The Fighting Irish player roster described Lambeau as flamboyant, an excellent blocker, and a good short-yardage runner.[4] After the football season, Lambeau had a bout of tonsillitis. Recuperating at home, he decided not to return to South Bend, and subsequently quit school for good.[5] Although Lambeau had a brief career at Notre Dame, he would be called an "ex Notre Dame Football star." He was proud of the connection. Lambeau did not forget Rockne. The two corresponded and Lambeau occasionally recommended a high school player to the Notre Dame coach and he encouraged the student to head to South Bend.

Lambeau's practice of recommending Green Bay players to his old coach created yet another Notre Dame legend. One player who would go to Notre Dame on Lambeau's recommendations was Jim Crowley. Crowley would become one of the fabled Four Horsemen of Notre Dame—christened and made famous by Grantland Rice, a poetic sportswriter for the *New York Herald-Tribune* in an era when such craft was appreciated. After Notre Dame's 13–7 victory over Army on October 18, 1924, Rice penned one of sports journalism's favorite passages:

Outlined against a blue, gray October sky the Four Horsemen rode again. In dramatic lore they are known as famine, pestilence, destruction and death. These are only aliases. Their real names are: Stuhldreher, Miller, Crowley and Layden. They formed the crest of the South Bend cyclone before which another fighting Army team was swept over the precipice at the Polo Grounds this afternoon as 55,000 spectators peered down upon the bewildering panorama spread out upon the green plain below.[6]

Notre Dame student-publicity aid, George Strickler, who would become the sports editor of the *Chicago Tribune*, had a photo shot of the four ND players on horseback, which was picked up by newspapers across the country. The photo memorialized the passage, the players, and the team.

Crowley "recovered" from the notoriety and later coached at Fordham University. At Fordham, Lambeau's work would come full circle. One of Crowley's players by the name of Vince Lombardi would go on to coach the Packers in one remarkable decade.

Birth of a Franchise

The birth of the Packers' franchise and other professional team franchises involves a long evolution of city and town teams that had played amateur and semiprofessional football for decades. Untangling the roots of the professional team family tree is tedious work. Once exposed and disentangled, these roots lead to a series of fits and starts rather than a clear line of ancestry. Teams begin, end, and resume again sometimes with some of the same players, sometimes with the same name, sometimes with the same coach or manager. Unlike a human bloodline, that once it ends, ends forever, a team's ancestry is often traced through tenuous connections. Team history is especially murky before formal leagues existed to collect it. Historians often disagree on the basics, such as how a professional football player and team are defined. Most people would not think of a local team that plays another local team for a round of drinks and a wager as professional. However, some writers call such a team professional if they bring in a few ringers from out of town.

In pro football, it is far simpler to go back to the time when the NFL (originally called the American Professional Football Association (APFA)) was itself established and work forward. No one disputes the validity of the National Football League as a league of professional teams and players. This approach allows clarity. The National Football League was also the first league to have national aspirations.

The Packers started in professional football on what might be called the "Abrams to Lambeau to Peck to Calhoun" play. An old pal of Curly Lambeau, Nate Abrams, whose family had a cattle business, played on a team in Green Bay called the Green Bay Whales. Lambeau joined. Teams like the Whales popped up year after year, but often they were organized from scratch each season. Abrams introduced Lambeau to an acquaintance of his, Frank Peck, who ran a meat packing company called the Indian Packing Company. Peck signed Lambeau on staff as a high priced shipping clerk.[7] Lambeau also got to know newspaper reporter, George Calhoun, who had managed the Whales and was actively involved in Green Bay sports.

Lambeau was the local talent who just might make a professional team work. Together, Lambeau and Calhoun planned a new team. Some would say they continued the remnants of an existing one that was now sponsored by Frank Peck's Indian Meat Packing company. Sponsorship that year was not much more than what is required of a business that sponsors a local softball team today.[8] On August 14, 1919, the team officially began and it was Lambeau doing much of the managing.[9]

Abrams could certainly be considered the chief catalyst, a Lambeau friend, and supporter from the earliest days—introducing Lambeau to some key players and helping Lambeau through some rough financial times. Peck bankrolled the team in its first season, paid for the uniforms, and helped establish its early identity by association with his packing company. Calhoun was the chief alchemist—it was his tireless work in the press that turned the team from a minor amusement to a national institution. If Calhoun had not successfully beaten the bushes for fans and supporters, the Packers might never have gotten off the ground. Lambeau of course, was the field general and chief of staff—the father of the Packers. He led the football revolution with his own blood and sweat. Many others helped the Packers survive and thrive over the years, but it was these four who did the most in that first year.

In the local *Press-Gazette*, George Calhoun referred to the new team as the "Packers," shorthand for the "Indian Packing Company Team." But in the early days, they were often called the "Bays" and a few other names. Team nicknames attached themselves over time. Even in the more established sport of professional baseball, team nicknames were often slow developing and some changed over the years depending upon what was going on with the team. Often, the newspaper writers used several names and eventually the fans and the team settled on one over the others.

The Packers played a limited number of teams within a confined area who were not highly skilled. Some called such teams, "town teams"—they had been around for decades. In a place with more than one team, a town team would often be a kind of all-star team that grouped the best players together for certain contests with other towns. In their first year of operation, the Packers played in Hagemeister Park, which had no bleachers at the time. Fans stood behind ropes that secured the sidelines. Primitive perhaps, but the spectator experience was up close and personal. It also provided good exercise! Fans ran up and down the sidelines to see each play progress. During halftime when the teams sat on blankets at each end zone, fans would come over and circle the players and listen to the discussion. Calhoun "passed the hat" around and shared the proceeds with the players at the end of the season.[10] In 1921, stands were built at Hagemeister Park and tickets were sold for admittance.

As the Packers grew in popularity, Green Bay's venues grew in size. Much of the construction work done on Green Bay "stadiums" over time was done by Lambeau's father. Initially, this work was modest. Later projects became more ambitious.

Packers Go Pro

Ohio is considered the cradle of professional football and there had been loose associations there in the early years of semipro football. If the Packers were going to thrive as a professional football team, they needed to ally themselves with the American Professional Football Association (APFA), an organization born in Canton, Ohio, in 1920. APFA was named the National Football League in 1922 and it would become the first successful national league.

Newspaper man George Calhoun was aware of the American Professional Football Association and understood what it might offer to Green Bay. But challenges loomed. Another packing company, the Acme Packing Company merged with the Indian Packing Company before the start of the 1921 season. The consolidated company retained the name, Acme Packing Company.[11] John Clair from Acme was persuaded to apply for an NFL franchise. At the league's meeting, Clair's representative obtained the franchise for the tidy sum of $100.[12]

Lambeau's Players

In the first few seasons, Lambeau fielded few stars who would last long in the NFL, but chief among that group was Peaches Nadolney, Cub Buck, Charlie Mathys, Whitey Woodin, Moose Gardner, and Curly himself. Lambeau struggled to make good with his team, but it would take time. Three exceptional players that Lambeau added in 1929 were essential to his first championship run: Johnny "Blood" McNally, Cal Hubbard, and "Iron Mike" Michalske. The early era Green Bay title teams also featured veterans Red Dunn, Verne Lewellen, Bo Molenda, Jug Earp, Jim Bowdoin, Lavvie Dilweg, Tom Nash, Hank Bruder, and others. Outstanding players who made an impact later include Clarke Hinkle, Don Hutson, Arnie Herber, and others.

Lambeau favored the pass more than most coaches, but in his formations, the tailback or halfback would do most of the passing. Lambeau himself was an excellent passer and over the years he had a knack for acquiring the best pass receiving talent in the NFL.

Arnie Herber

A local boy who worked as a handyman in the Packers' clubhouse after college, Arnie Herber had a Packers' destiny. Lambeau gave the young man a tryout and an 11-year Packers' career followed. There was something magical about Herber—something akin to Roy Hobbs's from *The Natural*. Herber did not need Hobbs Wonderboy baseball bat in the NFL; he had a supernatural arm and an unconventional throwing motion that produced results. Herber had small hands and he would palm the ball tossing 60-yard passes with accuracy. When Don Hutson joined the team, what many call the NFL's first great passing-receiving tandem, Herber to Hutson, was born.

Bo Molenda

Bo Molenda was one of the finest fullbacks in the NFL and he helped round out the Green Bay backfield. He was an exceptional all-around athlete.

Cal Hubbard

Huge for his time, Cal Hubbard was a 6-foot-4, 250 pound lineman with excellent speed who played tackle. The Hall of Famer helped bolster the Packers' offensive line and was a force on defense where he was known to roam at times like a linebacker. Hubbard is considered to be among the best tackles in the first 50 years of professional football.

Clarke Hinkle

Clarke Hinkle lit things up for the Packers on both offense and defense. When the Hall of Famer hit someone from his linebacker position, it was explosive. He was also a leading rusher in a number of categories. He played 10 memorable seasons for the Packers.

Cub Buck

Cub Buck was Lambeau's first "professional strength" lineman. Although he was just 6-foot, Buck hit the scales somewhere between 260-280 pounds and was not going to be pushed around by anyone in the league. He played tackle on both offense and defense, and he punted and kicked as well. In the early days of professional football, no extra point or field goal was a sure thing. Often, several players on a team would take their turn at kicking.

Don Hutson

Hall of Famer Don Hutson redefined the measure of excellence for the end position. Hutson, the "Alabama Antelope," is often called the first modern receiver in football. At 6-foot-1 and 180 pounds, he ran the 100 yards dash in 9.7. He had large soft hands and he could pull down balls that others missed and he was a good leaper.

Hank Bruder

Bruder was a durable passionate player who fit well with Lambeau's program that called for well conditioned players with strong work ethics. Bruder played running/blocking back and defensive back for nine seasons in Green Bay. He could run, catch—and pass when called upon. On defense he was a sure tackler.

"Iron Mike" Michalske

The quick-moving Hall of Famer, Iron Mike Michalske, was a leading guard in the NFL whom teammate McNally described as "a fierce competitor" who would "start moving before his opponents."[13] Michalske at 6-foot and 210 pounds was built like a fullback and on defense he used his strength to stop the run and his speed to rush the passer.

Jim Bowdoin

Jim Bowdoin was a 6-foot-1, 227 pound guard from the University of Alabama. He played during Lambeau's 1929-1931 championship streak and bowled down defenders for the Packers' rushing game.

Johnny "Blood" McNally

Hall of Famer Johnny Blood McNally walked on hotel ledges, climbed flagpoles, ran along the top of railroad cars, and hung out with social outcasts. In addition to being a very good football player, the quirky, highly intelligent McNally was a poet, public speaker, seaman, bartender, hotel clerk, cryptographer, and economics professor.[14] He was one of the most colorful players in NFL history, if not the most colorful, and Lambeau managed to keep his off-field antics in check long enough for "Blood" to achieve great results in Green Bay. McNally was a speedy halfback who was a superb receiver. He was often the difference between losing and winning—a game breaker.

Jug Earp

Jug Earp was a formidable center who at 6-foot-1 and 235 pounds was a juggernaut in the middle of the line. He also played tackle and his play rivaled that of the great Hubbard.

Lavvie Dilweg

Dilweg was a tall end and defensive back who would be one of the key players of the early championship seasons. He was recognized as one of the best ends in football.

Red Dunn

Dunn was a quarterback/tailback/blocking back and a dependable passer who played unselfishly for the Packers during their first championship run. Formations in early NFL football called on players in the backfield to be versatile. A "running back" might do a lot more than run and a quarterback might call the signals and block—often not handling the ball much.

Tom Nash

Like Dilweg, Tom Nash was a tall end, in fact, identical in size at 6-foot-3 to Dilweg. Nash performed well on the opposite side of the line from Dilweg.

Verne Lewellen

Verne Lewellen played in the backfield and he could catch, run, pass, and block. "Lew" as he was called by the press, was one of the early Packers' star players at halfback and an excellent punter, capable of soaring punts of 60-70 yards. He was also one of Green Bay's best defensive players.[15]

1921-1928 Packers' Seasons

Lambeau formed his early teams in large part with local players from Wisconsin. Although Wisconsin certainly provided a fertile ground for football recruits, he would need to expand his base to be competitive. Many of his first year players would only play a season or two in the pros. Some were not top prospects and others would simply find better jobs—being a professional football player did not offer much security. Many of Lambeau's early recruits had not gone to college. Although there were 21 teams in the league and no divisions, the vast majority of teams played eight games or less in the 1921 season. Teams scheduled their own games and there were few league requirements. The Packers finished 3–2–1 in their first professional season. Their most interesting games were their first and their last of the season.

The Packers opened the season against the Minneapolis Marines at home in Hagemeister Park. After falling behind 6–0, the Packers took possession in the middle of the fourth quarter on an interception. A Lambeau pass to back Buff Wagner from Carroll College brought Green Bay into the red zone. From there, the Packers pounded the ball into the end zone with a series of short runs. Lambeau dropkicked the extra point for the 7–6 lead, which held up until the final gun.

The last game of the season began the famous Bears-Packers rivalry. In 1921, the Chicago team was in the hands of George Halas, but it was called the Chicago Staleys based on the sponsorship of the Staley Starch Company of Decatur, which had originally owned the team. The game was played at Cubs' Park in Chicago and George Halas himself caught a pass for the final touchdown. Lambeau's Packers lost to Chicago 20–0. In contrast to Green Bay, the Bears were made up of players who had attended college and many of them were college stars such as Hall of Famers Guy Chamberlin from Nebraska and George Trafton from Notre Dame.

Packers-Bears Rivalry

The Chicago Bears and the Arizona Cardinals are the two original professional football teams that survive from the first national team organization that was established in Canton, Ohio. The Packers followed a heartbeat later. At the time of the league formation, the Cardinals were called the Racine Cardinals because most of its players came from Chicago's south side around Racine Avenue. This has confused people from the beginning—even an official league document has "Wisconsin" typed out after "Racine." Eventually, the Cardinals moved to St. Louis and then on to Arizona. Certainly, the rivalry between the Bears and the Cardinals was passionate, especially when they were competing for the loyalty of Chicago fans. Never-the-less, the Packers-Bears rivalry exceeds all others in the NFL for intensity. Calhoun's articles in the *Press Gazette* and the work of the reporters for the *Chicago Tribune* did much to get the fans' blood pumping. The beat continues today over 90 years later. Calhoun was a master at building up opponents and games over the course of his long career. The Packers and Bears coaches and players continue to maintain the rivalry that is considered without exaggeration one of the greatest in all sports.

Lambeau-Halas: A Personal Rivalry

There was also a strong personal rivalry between Lambeau and Halas. In many ways, the rivalry may have been more about their likenesses than their differences. Although Lambeau only owned the Packers for one season, he was the face of the Packers and managed the team for decades as if he was the owner. Lambeau and Halas faced each other on the field as players during the first decade and as coaches for many years. Although football consumed both men, they both had successful business careers outside the game. They were competitive in all they did. Both men had very strong ties to their communities. Lambeau was synonymous with Green Bay. He put Green Bay "on the map." Halas loved Chicago unconditionally. In later years, Halas patiently remained in Chicago while teams all over the country were moving their operations and stadiums to the suburbs. Lambeau and Halas attended rival universities and were excellent college athletes who played under legendary coaches. Halas had attended the University of Illinois where he played football under Coach Bob Zuppke. Lambeau had played at Notre Dame under Coach Knute Rockne. Both Lambeau and Halas came from immigrant families with hardworking parents.

From Town Team to the Pros

Although, Green Bay had dominated teams in their "town" team circuit, Lambeau had no such illusion that the professional team circuit was going to be easy. He knew that unless he improved his roster, he would not be competitive. In the early days of professional football, the rosters might continue to evolve during the season. Weaknesses might be spotted in preseason or early season and deficiencies addressed at most any time.

One of the first acquisitions Lambeau made to his 1921 club, which would help him play with the "big boys," was a big man by the name of Cub Buck. Buck had played for Jim Thorpe at Canton before Lambeau picked him up. He played tackle on both offense and defense, and he punted and kicked as well. A bonus to Lambeau was the fact that Buck also coached linemen. Buck would also hold coaching jobs at Lawrence College even while playing professional ball. With Buck's size and professional experience on his line, Lambeau knew that he had someone who was not going to be pushed around by anyone in the league. Lambeau understood that over time he would need to build his team with players like Buck, if he was going to succeed in professional football.

Modest Operation

In the beginning, the Packers' operation was very modest. Players would get dressed at home and put their cleats on at the field. Each year, more bleachers would be added and very early on, canvas sheets would shield the perimeter of the field making it necessary for everyone who wanted to see the game to buy a ticket. When a water boy would run onto the field with a bucket of water, the players used a dipper to drink. The Packers were a community-supported team in most every way. Unpaid volunteers were present to help out any way they could. One of the more celebrated features of the team was its Lumberjack Band that was put together by George DeLair's restaurant to play at the home games.[16] The Lumberjack band would also attend away games in Chicago and whoop it up in the Windy City, displaying the exuberant side of Green Bay fandom that has always been there in good times and bad, boom and bust years, war and peace, warm September contests and frigid games in December.

After the 1921 season, the Packers were kicked out of the league because they had violated league rules, by using college players in a game. Green Bay was not alone, but other violations with college players heightened the issue for the press and college administrators. Three players from Notre Dame would be implicated in this matter, causing a potential rift in the relationship between Lambeau and Coach Rockne. No coach would be pleased to have his players involved in such a scandal. The rift didn't happen. Rockne continued to communicate with Lambeau and accept his leads on Wisconsin talent from his former player.

Lambeau borrowed money to repurchase the NFL rights. It required a $50 league entry fee for the team and a $1,000 security deposit or forfeit fee to insure that teams would not tamper with college players. This fee was "required" of all teams in the league. After the requisite franchise forms were filled out, what followed was a hiatus of several months in which the Green Bay franchise technically did not exist. Lambeau was left to wait for approval, but at the time, the NFL seemed intent to respond to criticisms of the professional game. Some college administrators thought that professional football was deficient in ethics and should not be tolerated. Football fans were slow to respond to the professional game as well and the league leaders were determined to improve its reputation. Although Lambeau's purchase of the team essentially put it back in the hands of those who had violated league rules, the delay suggested in a small way that the league managers had some consideration for the college game. In time for the 1922 season, the league approved Lambeau's request.

Although the Packers lost their first three games in the 1922 season, they ended with a 4–3–3 record for a modest improvement over 1921. Again, most of Lambeau's players were local who did not last long in the league. Peaches Nadolney, Lambeau's old roommate from Notre Dame, played guard/tackle for the Packers in 1922 and then moved on to Milwaukee. Whitey Woodin from Marquette signed on with the Packers that year and stayed for a decade. Woodin was a defensive end and offensive guard.[17] Charlie Mathys was another 1922 addition. He contributed as a blocking back and passer for 5 years. Lambeau signed Moose Gardner, a sturdy guard from Ashland, Wisconsin, a port city on Lake Superior. Jug Earp, another stout lineman, joined the team at midseason and would play both center and tackle for 11 seasons with intermittent service with other teams.

Lambeau's limited college playing experience and the fact that he had not coached much at any level meant that he was learning on the job with the Packers. Some of the early players were highly critical of this fact, but the early days of professional football were educational for everyone involved.

Green Bay put together an impressive 7–2–1 record for 1923. The Packers also moved to Bellevue Park for the next two seasons as Hagemeister Park was destroyed to make way for a new high school building. Bellevue was a baseball field that was reconfigured when the Packers played there.

Fans were excited to see the Green Bay Packers-Chicago Bears game on October 14, 1923. In just their second meeting, the rivalry had already been established. An over-capacity crowd of at least 4,500 cheered on the Packers at home. Unfortunately for Packers' fans, it would be a low-scoring disappointment that Chicago would win on a field goal, 3–0.

Hungry Five

There were more important concerns for the Green Bay franchise than its wins and losses in 1923. The team faced bankruptcy before some prominent Green Bay business leaders and friends stepped in to help Lambeau. Two game-day rain storms placed the Packers in serious financial jeopardy. Guarantees were made to visiting teams to insure they could at least cover basic expenses when traveling. Lambeau was short on funds to pay these. *Press-Gazette* executive A.B. Turnbull loaned Lambeau money to cover guarantees to visiting teams.[18] Curly Lambeau, A.B. Turnbull, Leland H. Joannes (a wholesale grocer), Dr. W. Webber Kelly, and attorney Gerald Clifford formed the "Hungry Five."[19] These men would help establish a corporation in 1923 that would sell shares in the team to keep it afloat. Shareholders would own the Packers, which became a nonprofit. Shareholders would not only buy shares that essentially offered no dividends, but they would also agree to buy season tickets. A fifteen-member board of directors and a five-member executive committee were set up to oversee the operation. Earnings would go to the Sullivan American Legion Post in Green Bay.[20] Selling shares did not catch on immediately throughout Green Bay, but this arrangement helped make the Packers sustainable and allowed Lambeau to look for better talent outside the region. It would still be difficult to manage the team and its expenses in the beginning. In times of need, the Packers would go back to the community for support through sales of shares. The groundwork for this safety valve approach was established in 1923.[21]

In 1924, the Packers played their home games at Bellevue Park—their last season at the baseball field. Lambeau signed on Verne Lewellen, a back who would contribute to the Packers for nine seasons. Tillie Voss, an end from Detroit, signed on and played for one season. The Packers finished the season at 7–4. Lambeau was working on his passing game.[22] The Packers beat the Milwaukee Badgers in two meetings and likewise the Kansas City Blues. The Milwaukee Journal reported that the Packers displayed a "slashing attack" when beating Kansas City, 16–0, on October 12, 1924. Tillie Voss caught a Lambeau pass and "scampered" 20 yards for a touchdown in the first period. Lewellen rushed for another Packer score in the third and fullback Dutch Hendrian kicked a 30-yard field goal for a 16–0 final. The Packers' "air drive" worked nicely according to the paper, but "intercepted forward passes halted their advances."[23]

The Packers played the archrival Bears in Chicago and Joey Sternaman, younger brother to Halas partner, Dutch Sternaman, scored the only points on a 20-yard drop kick field goal. Although Lambeau wanted to open the game up more to his passing attack, many early games would be low-scoring affairs. It was a game played for field position and taking advantage of turnovers. It was a Mathys's fumble on the Green Bay 28 that set up the Bears' score. Likewise, a Bears' miscue deep in their territory gave the Packers a scoring opportunity, but Cub Buck missed the field goal. Lambeau threw an interception late in the game and the game ended with the ball on the Packers' 5-yard line with the Bears winning 3–0.[24] Trivia buffs remember the game because Chicago's Frank Hanny and Green Bay's Tillie Voss became the first NFL players ejected for fighting.[25]

The Packers ended the season with a frustrating 7–0 loss to the Racine Legion on November 30. Former Notre Dame Quarterback Johnny Mohardt tossed a 25-yard pass to Milt "Mitt" Romney for the score.[26] The Packers completed 5 of 17 passes with a whopping five interceptions. A third quarter Packer passing touchdown was called back on an offside penalty.[27]

In 1925, the Chicago Cardinals won the NFL Championship. The Packers went 8–5 taking the 9th position in a bloated league of 20 teams. It was the Packers' first season in which they played their home games at City Park, also called City Stadium. The Park originally had seating capacity of 5,000 and would grow over the 32 years it would be the Packers' home field into a 25,000 seat-capacity facility. The Packers were undefeated in their new park for the 1925 season.

In 1926, the Packers moved up to fifth place out of 22 teams in the league. They compiled a 7–3–3 record. Cub Buck, who had helped Lambeau gain his footing in professional football, moved on to coach at the University of Miami.

In 1927, Green Bay compiled a 7–2–1 record which gave them second place out of 12 teams. NFL President Joe Carr, concerned about the watered down talent pool of the league and poor financial state of several teams, eliminated weaker teams thus reducing the number of franchises from 22 to 12. The Packers picked up Lavvie Dilweg, a newly minted lawyer from Marquette University who had played in Milwaukee for 1 year. Dilweg was an end who would play through the 1934 season. Hard to imagine today, but Dilweg would practice football in the mornings and law in the afternoons.[28] Perhaps even harder to imagine, Dilweg would not be the only attorney on the Packers. Verne Lewellen, who played from 1924-1932, was also an attorney.

In 1928, the Packers compiled a 6–4–3 record for fourth place in the 10 team league. They scored 120 points and allowed their opposition to tally 92 against them. The Packers tied the Bears in their first meeting and beat them in their second and third. They beat the teams that everyone else was beating up that year: the Chicago Cardinals and Dayton Triangles. They split with the Pottsville Maroons and the New York Giants. They lost twice to the Frankford Yellow Jackets. Yet, they were on the verge of greatness.

1929-1931 Seasons: String of Championships

In the early days of the NFL, Lambeau was an excellent motivator and first-rate at team preparation, but perhaps his greatest skill was his ability to find and sign talent. In 1929, the Packers won their first NFL Championship with a collection of superb players.

1929 Season

The 1929 Packers would go undefeated with only one tie to blemish their record. They scored 198 points and grudgingly allowed only 22 points from their opposition.

The Packers faced the Dayton Triangles in their first 1929 match. Although one of the original NFL teams, the Triangles had not been able to afford top talent and after 1922 played mostly as a traveling team that featured local players. When traveling, teams would routinely get a guarantee minimum to show up for an away game. Teams that did not draw well at home, could make money when traveling. Taking it on the chin, 9–0, from the Packers, the Triangles provided a respectable warm up game for Green Bay. At the end of a long drive, the Packers scored when Red Dunn hit Lewellen on a 20-yard pass in the end zone. Dunn kicked the point after. A safety was scored when Triangles' back Steve Buchanan was tackled in the end zone attempting to punt. Next, the Packers shut out the Bears, 23–0, in game two and knocked off another Chicago Team, the Cardinals, 9–2, in game three. Green Bay easily defeated the Frankford Yellow Jackets, 14–2, and the Minneapolis Red Jackets, 24–0, before they squeaked past the Cardinals, 7–6, in their second meeting of the season. Then they defeated the Red Jackets, 16–6, the Bears, 14–0, and the Cardinals, 12–0, yet one more time.

When they played the Giants on November 24, the game was broadcast on Milwaukee's WTMJ radio—a first for Green Bay. It may seem odd to radio listeners today, but no one from the station was actually in New York to do the broadcast. Announcer Russ Winnie broadcast the game by interpreting the teletype report of events.[29] Winnie worked at WTMJ into the late 1950s and the station itself continues to cover the Packers to this day. The Packers easily defeated the Giants, 20–6, in person and on the teletype as well. After a 0–0 tie with the Yellow Jackets, the Packers slammed their last two opponents: the Providence Steam Rollers, 25–0, and the Chicago Bears, 25–0.

The 1929 Packers were a special team, even for a championship team. The Packers played the last eight games on the road and they handily beat their chief rivals, the Chicago Bears, three times in one season. The Cardinals were not a problem and the Packers beat them three times as well. The mighty Giants went down easily enough. In fact, Green Bay shut out their opponents that season in eight games and no opponent scored more than 6 points against them. Their 12-0-1 record won them the NFL Championship.

1930 Season

The Packers won their second championship in 1930 with a 10–3–1 record. They scored 234 points and allowed 111 points from their opposition. The Packers shut out the Cardinals in their first contest of the year, 14–0, and then blanked the Bears, 7–0, a week later. They beat the mighty Giants, 14–7, in Green Bay City Stadium before 11,000 fans.

The Giants' offense featured Benny Friedman, who was considered by many to be one of the finest passers in the game. Early in the second quarter, Packers' rookie Wuert Englemann, jumped high to intercept a pass, evaded a few tacklers and then, according to *Milwaukee Sentinel* writer Stoney McGlynn, "was on his way with snakelike wiggles, cross steps and everything else in his repertoire" before he was brought down on the Packer 45-yard line.[30] Running plays by McNally and Lewellen brought the Packers down the field for two first downs. Then Lewellen connected with Tom Nash who ran over Friedman into the end zone. Dunn kicked the extra point.

Friedman was lauded for his stealthy rushing and accurate passing, but the Giants' offense self destructed with dropped passes and fumbles. The Packers were not perfect either. A blocked Packer punt gave the Giants the ball on the Packer 25-yard line. The Packers' defense played tight after a single Giants' first down, but on 4th down, Friedman found Len Sedbrook for a completion in the red zone where he powered his way into the end zone for a touchdown. Friedman kicked the extra point.

The game was decided by the Packers' game-breaker, Johnny Blood McNally. In the fourth quarter, Red Dunn tossed a pass to McNally 15 yards downfield. McNally exploded for another 55 yards with a key block from

Lewellen who was running with him step for step. Blood successfully stiff-armed Friedman, who was the last man between him and the end zone. The Packers won, 14–7.

The Packers' next opponent, the Frankford Yellow Jackets, succumbed to Green Bay by a score of 27–12. The Minneapolis Red Jackets were beat 13–0 at home and a week later in Green Bay, 19–0. After the Jackets games, the Packers whipped the Portsmouth Spartans, 47–13.

Once again, the Packers played Chicago teams two weeks in a row as they did at the beginning of the season, but this time it would be on the road. The Packers squeaked past the Bears, 13–12, before 21,000 fans in Chicago. The following week, the Packers lost to the Cardinals, 13–6. A loss to the Giants, 13–6, was followed by the Packers second win against the Yellow Jackets—this one by a score of 25–7. The Staten Island Stapletons were next on the schedule and the Packers beat them, 37–7.

Next up for the Packers was the Chicago Bears, whom the Packers had beaten twice already. Football coaches express angst when they have to play an opponent three times in a season. In today's NFL, a third meeting of two teams happens only in the post season. In 1930, sometimes teams played a rival three times in the regular season. When the Packers lost 21–0 to the Bears in the 13th game of the season, Green Bay did not look like league champions. Nevertheless, the following week when they tied the Portsmouth Spartans, 6–6, they won the championship. Before the playoff system was in place, it didn't matter whether a team was hot at the beginning, the end, or the middle of the season; the team needed to be hot enough at some point to win more games than anyone else.

In a move that would have impact for many years, Lambeau added a 20-year-old local boy to the team, Arnold "Flash" Herber, who would become one of the great long passers in the game. Herber, who could toss the ball 80 yards downfield, would contribute most from 1933 to 1940.[31]

1931 Season

In 1931, the Packers won their third championship in a row with an excellent 12–2 record. They scored 291 and allowed 87 from their opponents. They began the season with a monster streak of nine wins in a row, besting the Cleveland Indians, Brooklyn Dodgers, Chicago Bears, New York Giants, Chicago Cardinals, Frankford Yellow Jackets, Providence Steam Roller, Chicago Bears (again) and the Staten Island Stapletons. In the 10th game of the season, they finally tasted their first defeat at the hands of the Chicago Cardinals, 21–13. After beating the Steam Roller and Dodgers again, they lost a squeaker to the Bears, 7–6, in their final game of 1931.

For the season, McNally scored 13 touchdowns and he was named to the First Team All Pro along with Green Bay linemen, Cal Hubbard, Mike Michalske, and Lavvie Dilweg. Lambeau proved his mettle by winning three world championships in a row: 1929-1930-1931. Chamberlin had done it in the 1922-1923-1924 seasons and Lombardi would match the feat in the 1965-1966-1967 seasons.

1932-1935 Seasons

In 1932, Lambeau signed Clarke Hinkle, a fullback from Bucknell who would be known as one of the hardest hitting backs to play the game and the leading rusher in a number of categories during his career. He would play 10 seasons in the pros, all for the Packers.

Hinkle was valuable to the Packers in so many ways and he played a large role in the ongoing rivalry between the Packers and the Bears. Although Hinkle was smaller than the Bears fullback/linebacker sensation Bronko Nagurski, he was every bit as aggressive and gutsy. In a famous Nagurski versus Hinkle episode in 1934, Hinkle was carrying the ball and being run out of bounds by the oncoming Nagurski. Just as Nagurski was about to smash Hinkle across the sideline, Hinkle turned to hit Nagurski with everything he had. Nagurski was laid out on the field with a broken nose and cracked rib. Despite a continuous clash of these titans, they would develop a lasting friendship over the years. It would be Nagurski who would present Hinkle for his Hall of Fame induction. The Packers 10–3–1 record for 1932 would leave them just shy of yet another title.

In 1933, the league established two divisions, the East Division and the West Division. The league championship would be decided by a game that pit the top team from each division. The Packers dropped down to a third place finish in the West Division with a record of 5–7–1. The Packers outscored their opponents by 63 points for the season. The Bears beat the Packers three times and the Giants beat the Packers twice to essentially put the season on ice for Green Bay. The Bears beat the Giants for the championship that year.

The 1934 Packers were out of the running. They finished with a 7–6 record for third place in their division. The Packers outscored their opponents by 44 points for the season. Johnny Blood McNally was sold to Pittsburgh where he played during the 1934 season. Lambeau would meet up with Blood again, and re-sign him for the 1935 and 1936 seasons.

Lambeau, like all great coaches who succeeded over a long period of time, hated mediocrity. He made changes in preparation for the 1935 season. He changed the Packers' colors from blue and gold to green and gold for 2 years. He also set up a one week camp at the Pinewood Lodge on Lake Thompson in the woods of Rhinelander rather than Green Bay. There would be football, fishing, horseshoes, swimming, and other healthy outdoors activities. Lambeau also made a key acquisition that would serve the Packers well for a decade.

Don Hutson

Joining the Packers in 1935 was Don Hutson, a receiver who would go on to break many NFL records in his 11-year Packers' career. He ran excellent routes—some that he had devised himself. He had subtle moves that fooled defensive players. After playing against Hutson, run-oriented coaches would experience firsthand what the passing game might provide given the right personnel. Hutson was in a league by himself—he led the NFL nine times in touchdown receptions. In 1942, his 17 touchdown receptions eclipsed the old record by 8 scores. Hutson was also the first receiver to break 1,000 yards when he gained 1,211 that same year.

Lambeau scouted Hutson at the Rose Bowl played on January 1, 1935. Hutson's Alabama team defeated Stanford 29–13. Hutson scored two touchdowns that game and afterwards many teams were in hot pursuit of the young receiver. Shipwreck Kelly, owner of the Brooklyn Dodgers, had the inside track after assuring Hutson he would match any offer. However, Lambeau convinced the Hall of Famer Hutson to sign a contract with the Packers when Kelly was nowhere to be found. Immediately after signing the Packer contract, Kelly showed up at Hutson's doorstep. Kelly convinced Hutson to sign a Dodgers' contract and allow NFL President, Joe Carr, to settle the issue. Carr ruled in favor of Green Bay, which was a good move for football given Lambeau's desire to develop a strong passing game that would use Hutson's talent.[32]

According to Hutson, Lambeau paid him $300 a game, but the coach was concerned about the rest of the players learning the salary so he paid Hutson in two checks and asked him to cash each one at different banks in Green Bay.[33] Hutson and Lambeau got along well throughout their entire lives.

Lambeau's preseason preparations and his more disciplined, back to basics approach would pay dividends. The Packers improved to second place in 1935 with an 8–4 record. The Packers outscored their opponents by 85 points for the season.

In the early days of professional football, players often played a full 60 minutes a game and the same position on offense and defense. Thus an end would play offensive end and then turn around as defensive end as well. Lambeau is credited with modifying this strategy and thereby extending Hutson's career and effectiveness. Lambeau used Hutson as a defensive back later in his career and used a more durable blocking back to play the physically demanding defensive end position.

In 1935, the Packers would also offer their second stock sale. The Team was in desperate financial straits and the stock sale raised $15,000 to pay off debts.[34]

1936 Season

In 1936, the NFL held its first college draft. Like today, teams with the worst records picked first. The Packers were back on top in 1936 and won their fourth championship that year. They posted a 10–1–1 record; their only loss was to the Chicago Bears. In the second week of the season, the Bears gave the Packers a 30–3 drubbing that the Packers would avenge in a week seven 21–10 win. The Herber-to-Hutson combination led the way to Green Bay's total of 1,629 yards in the air.[35] Herber's 1,239 yards passing made him the first NFL player to pass for over 1,000 yards in a single season. Clarke Hinkle rushed for 476 yards on 100 carries. Hutson had 34 receptions for 536 yards. The Packers had a balanced attack. They moved the ball in the air for 1,629 yards and on the ground for 1,664 yards. The Packers outscored their opponents by 130 points for the season and were the top team in their division.

In the championship game, the Packers faced the Boston Redskins at a neutral site: the Polo Grounds in New York. The Redskins' games were poorly attended in Boston and the following year, the team would move to Washington, D.C. But in New York, 29,545 fans turned out.

The Redskins' exceptional running back, Cliff Battles was injured in the first few minutes of the game. If there had been television at the time, the highlight might have been a 48-yard Herber-to-Hutson pass in the early going.[36] Pug Renter, replacing Battles, helped lead the Redskins on a 78-yard touchdown drive, but the point after was missed. The 7–6 score was the closest Washington would get for the remainder of the game. Herber connected with Johnny "Blood" McNally on a 58-yard pass that brought the Packers down to the 8-yard line. Herber was back to pass when he was hit while releasing the ball. Charlie Malone of the Redskins scooped the ball up and ran it back 90 yards, but the play was called back on review.[37] Seconds later, Herber hit Milt Gantenbein in the end zone for the Packers' second touchdown. After a blocked punt gave the Packers the ball at the Redskins' 3-yard line, Bob Monnett ran the ball in for a touchdown, which was followed by a successful extra point, which ended the scoring for the game. The Packers defeated the Boston Redskins, 21–6, to win another championship under Lambeau. The Redskins picked up stakes and moved to Washington, D.C. in 1937.

1937-1938 Seasons

In 1937, the Packers finished second in the West Division with a 7–4 record. The Packers outscored their opponents by 98 points for the season. They lost their first two games and their last two, but won seven in a row in between. Although they were a top ranked offense, in every loss they lacked scoring power—averaging just about 4 points.

Lambeau would make good use of the 1938 draft and pick up another excellent passer, Cecil Isbell, from Purdue. Isbell was accurate from any distance and a first-rate rusher. In the 1938 season, Isbell led the Packers' rushing game with 445 yards. Isbell, Herber, and Monnett made substantial contributions in the passing game to help the Packers win the west in 1938. The Packers had a balanced attack that season gaining 1,571 yards on the ground and 1,466 in the air.

For the season, the Packers were 8–3 and they outscored their opponents by 105 points. They lost to the Bears and Lions in the first half of the season, but came back and beat them both in the second half. The Giants beat them in the last game of the season, 15–3, but the Packers were atop their division at season end.

1938 Championship Game

The Packers played the New York Giants on December 11, 1938, in the Polo Grounds for the league championship. It was an inhospitable game for the Packers. Their Hall of Fame end Don Hutson was banged up heading into the game and despite a gallant attempt, he spent most of the game on the bench nursing his injuries. The Packers had two punts blocked early in the game that gave the Giants scoring opportunities. One that led to a field goal and the second that led to a drive that ended with a Tuffy Leemans's touchdown run from 6 yards out. After the extra point was missed, the Giants led, 9–0. An interception gave the Packers the ball at midfield to start their first scoring drive. A few plays into the drive, Herber hit Carl Mulleneaux on a 40-yard touchdown pass. After the extra point, the Giants led, 9–7.

The Packers helped the Giants to good field position on another series when they turned the ball over at midfield. A few plays into the Giants' drive, Ed Danowski found Hap Barnard on a 21-yard touchdown pass. The Giants led, 16–7, after the extra point. When the Packers were back on offense, end Wayland Becker caught a short pass from Isbell that he turned into a long 66-yard gain. The Packers' fullback, Clarke Hinkle, crashed the line on five successive rushes, fighting his way into the end zone. The Giants led 16–14 after the Packers' extra point. Early in the second half, 238 pound "Tiny" Engebretsen kicked a 15-yard field goal to put the Packers ahead, 17–16. The Giants responded with a 61-yard touchdown drive that featured some tough running and receiving by back Hank Soar. The Giants led, 23–17, and that's how the game ended. The Packers had ample opportunities to come back and win, but they were frustrated by turnovers, tough penalties, and the Giants' defense.

1939 Season

In 1939, the Packers won their division again. Lambeau's passing game came up big in 1939 with Arnie Herber throwing for 1,107 yards and Cecil Isbell throwing for 749. The Packers' passing yards totaled 1,871. Don Hutson had 34 receptions for 846 yards.

The Packers finished their season, 9–2, outscoring opponents by 80 points over the season. Their two losses were both 3 point decisions—one to the Rams and the other to the Bears—teams the Packers also beat that season. The Packers faced the Giants in the 1939 league championship.

1939 Championship Game

The venue for the 1939 Championship Game was the hospitable State Fair Park in Milwaukee. It was a cold windy day in Milwaukee that made passing and kicking difficult, but the field conditions were adequate and dry. It was a day for running the football and short passes. The Packers scored first when Herber tossed a 7-yard pass to Milt Gantenbein for a touchdown. On two

Giants' drives, when the offense stalled, two field goal attempts were blown off course. Early in the third quarter, Engebretsen kicked a 29-yard field goal to put the Packers ahead, 10–0. On the Giants' possession, Danowski was intercepted by Gantenbein giving the Packers excellent field position on the Giants' 33-yard line. Isbell threw a floater that miraculously made its way into halfback Joe Laws's hands for another Packers' touchdown.

Most of the time, the Giants failed to move the ball, but when they did, they turned it over. Ernie Smith kicked a 42-yard field goal, somehow between the 35 mile per hour wind gusts that day. Bud Svenson intercepted a rare pass by back Len Barnum that gave the Packers the ball at the Giants' 15-yard line. Barnum was getting a workout—he had intercepted a pass and missed a field goal attempt earlier in the game. Two plays later following a beautifully executed double reverse that took the ball down to the 1-yard line, the Packers' sparkplug of a fullback, short and stocky Ed Jankowski took the ball in for the final score of the game. Lambeau and his Packers had won the championship, 27–0.

The December 18, 1939 *Life Magazine* featured an article entitled: "Little Wisconsin Town Produces World's Most Famous Team." The article features photos of Lambeau and several Packers' players and presents the David and Goliath image of the team: "once more Lambeau's Green Bay Packers, representing a little town of 37,000, had played and beaten most of the expensive teams of New York, Chicago, Pittsburgh, and Washington." The article romanticizes that Lambeau's success in bringing such great talent to Green Bay was because rather than just fire "pro stars when they are too old to play, he finds them regular jobs, enables them to have a home, settle down in Green Bay."

As 1939 champions, the Packers played against the College All-Stars in the annual charity game in Soldier Field in August, 1940. The game was important and Lambeau urged his players to stay in shape over the offseason so they could win it. The Packers beat the All-Stars, 45–28, before a record crowd of 84,567 in the 7th Annual Chicago Tribune All-Star Charity Football Game. Many still considered the college game and its athletes who had won 4 out of 7 all-star matches, far superior to professional football. Lambeau and others wanted to change that.

1940 Season

A record of 6–4–1 in 1940 got the Packers second place in the West Division. It would be the last Packer season for Arnie Herber. The Chicago Bears, who beat the Packers twice that season, took the division and then beat Washington for the championship. Lambeau, who had run the team since 1922, received a new contract in 1940. He would be paid $10,000 a year plus a percentage of net proceeds from events such as the Chicago Tribune All-Star, playoff, and exhibition games.

1941 Season

In 1941, the Packers and Bears would finish atop the West Division with identical 10–1 records.

As the 1941 season was closing, the Japanese bombed Pearl Harbor on December 7, and the United States became a combatant in World War II. Just 7 days later, on December 14, the Packers played the Bears in a playoff game to determine the west crown. After the Packers scored first on a short run by Clarke Hinkle, the Bears came back with 30 unanswered points. The Bears led 30–7 before the Packers answered with a 10-yard touchdown pass from Cecil Isbell to Hal Van Every. Bob Snyder kicked a field goal in the fourth quarter to give the Bears a final 33–14 victory.

The Bears moved on to the championship match in which they trampled the Giants 37–9 before a Spartan crowd of 13,341.

1942-1943 Seasons: Early War Years

Before the 1942 season began, the NFL was strongly affected by the war. The league had lost a third of its players to the armed services. The Cleveland Rams suspended their operations. The Pittsburgh Steelers and Philadelphia Eagles merged to save money. The hybrid team was called the "Steagles." As the war continued, teams would lose more men to the service. The quality of the game suffered.

Second place finishers in the west in 1942 at 8–2–1, the Packers were bested again by archrival Chicago Bears who would go on to lose to the Washington Redskins, 14–6, in the championship game. Green Bay's Cecil Isbell had a phenomenal season; his 2,021 yards passing marked the first time an NFL player exceeded 2,000. He also notched the Packers' first 300-yard passing game. In a surprise move, Isbell retired from the Packers after the 1942 season to become an assistant coach at Purdue. His early departure from the Packers would become a curiosity for many years. Isbell would later say that he had seen his coach tell several good players to pack it up and he wanted to go out on his own terms.

It would be a second place finish for Lambeau and his 7–2–1 Packers in 1943. Don Hutson would excel with 47 receptions for 776 yards and 11 touchdowns. He also threw a touchdown pass, kicked three field goals, and made 36 out of 36 extra point attempts. Again, the Chicago Bears would take top position in the West Division, and then go on to defeat the Redskins, 41–21, in the championship match.

1944 Season

The year 1944 was another championship season for the Packers. Irv Comp who was drafted the previous year would step in as the primary passer in 1944.

The Packers won their division with an 8–2 record and then beat the Giants in the championship game 14–7. In the championship game, the Giants keyed on the Packers' incomparable receiver Don Hutson who had 58 receptions for 866 yards and nine touchdowns that season. Lambeau fooled the Giants by calling fullback Ted Fritsch's number all day. Fritsch scored both Green Bay touchdowns: one rushing and a second one on a reception from a Comp pass. Fritsch had gained 322 yards that season on 94 rushes.

1945-1949 Seasons: Postwar Years

On August 14, 1945, the War came to an end. Lambeau faced the daunting task of rebuilding his team in a new postwar environment. The middle of the pack with a 6–4 record was the best the Packers could do in 1945. Players started to return from the war, but the season would mark Don Hutson's final year. Hutson was simply irreplaceable. Buckets Goldenberg and Joe Laws would also hang up their cleats after the season. The Cleveland Rams beat the Washington Redskins, 15–14, for the championship.

As if the postwar rebuilding efforts were not challenging enough, Arch Ward, a powerful Chicago Tribune Sports Editor, formed a new professional football league, the All-American Football Conference (AAFC), in 1945. The League would be ready to begin playing in September 1946. The AAFC would provide another great challenge to NFL team management on the heels of the World War. Initially, the AAFC had substantial financial backing that would often result in the new league capturing talent before many NFL teams had truly retooled from the war years. Many former players along with college prospects were attracted to the new league. NFL teams that had continued to operate during the war, often with desperate financial conditions, were not prepared to compete in the new marketplace for top players.

Lambeau was not able to rebuild the Packers to their prewar condition during the period, but this is not surprising. One of Lambeau's strengths was his ability to discover talent and attract players to the Packers. After all, it was Lambeau's pre-NFL draft teams that won three championships in a row. Plus, the 1936 championship was accomplished mostly with pre-draft players as well. When Lambeau was working in an unfettered recruiting environment, he was at his best. When the NFL draft was instituted, it created a much more controlled recruiting environment. When the AAFC went after players, the challenges mounted. In the postwar period many of Green Bay's highest draft picks were signed by AAFC teams. Canadian teams were also vying for players. Other NFL teams were challenged in this way as well.

The postwar Packers were not a top tier team and Lambeau was finding it difficult to fix their weaknesses. Johnny Strzykalski, the Packers' first-round draft choice in 1946 ended up playing for the San Francisco 49ers of the All-American Football Conference. The Packers would drop to a 6–5 third place finish in the west in 1946.

In the 1947 draft, Green Bay selected UCLA quarterback Ernie Case in the first round. Case played at UCLA before and after the war. He was a bomber pilot who had been shot down in combat in Italy and captured as a POW. Case escaped his capturers. A recipient of the Purple Heart, Case would go on to play for the Baltimore Colts of the All-American Football Conference not the Packers. The Packers' 6–5–1 record would give them another third place finish in the West Division in 1947.

Earl Francis "Jug" Girard was the Packers' first draft choice in 1948 and the Packers were able to sign him—the first top draft choice of the Packers signed in 3 years. Girard was a versatile player who could pass, receive, and punt. But Lambeau was running out of time. The Packers' 3–9 record would fetch a fourth place finish in the west in 1948.

Stan Heath was the Packers' first draft choice in 1949 and although the Packers were able to sign Heath, he only stayed with the team for 1 year and then went on to a career in Canadian Football. As a senior at the University of Nevada in 1948, Heath led the nation in passing, total offense, and touchdown passes.

The 1949 campaign was Lambeau's final season in Green Bay. The team's 2–10 record was Lambeau's worst in his time as coach.

Changes in Green Bay

Lambeau himself had raised the bar very high in Green Bay and once that bar was raised, it seemed that he, and every coach that came after him, had a gold standard to meet. In Green Bay, winning was often a matter of survival for the team. In the postwar period, everyone involved in professional football was working under especially difficult circumstances. Money was short and new talent was being courted by not only other teams in the NFL, but a new league.

Postwar changes brought a more decentralizing organization to the Packers. Lambeau had been at his best when he was a freewheeling team leader, talent scout, and task master. He resigned before the 1950 season began.

1950-1951 Chicago Cardinals' Seasons

In 1950, Lambeau took a job coaching the Chicago Cardinals. Once again he would be back on the pages of *Life Magazine*, but he was no longer featured in a "David and Goliath" story. The Cardinals and Packers scheduled a preseason game for August 16. Various gifts were collected and presented to Lambeau before the game started in Green Bay. The Packers went on to squeak by the Cardinals and a Life photo captured a distraught Coach Lambeau taking the loss to his old team to heart.

Lambeau would coach the Chicago Cardinals to a 5–7 record in 1950 and a 3–9 record in 1951. He would be replaced with a few games remaining in 1951.

1952 Washington Redskins' Season

Lambeau moved on to Washington in 1952 where he took the Redskins to a 4–8 record in 1952 and a 6–5–1 record in 1953. The 1953 season was a respectable effort in which two of the Redskins losses were at the hands of the Cleveland Browns who were beating everyone at the time. In Lambeau's last game, the Redskins were riding a 13–7 lead over the Steelers when Pittsburgh Hall of Famer Jack Butler intercepted an Eddie LeBaron pass and ran it back for a touchdown and the 14–13 win. It would be Butler's fourth interception of the day. In the 1954 preseason, Lambeau was discharged.

Lambeau's Contributions to the Game

Curly Lambeau made remarkable contributions to professional football. First, he was as close to the start of the NFL as you can get without being at the first meeting in Canton. Like other early team founders, his work helped define professional football. He loved the game and dedicated himself to it. Like George Halas, he was also a player and coach who directed a franchise. Lambeau was one of those few NFL founders who actually played the professional game. No one could honestly say to Lambeau that he did not understand what it meant to play the game. As a coach in the earliest of days, his handling of players was remarkable from day one. He was not loved by everyone, but he got results. His teams improved over time, and he only had two losing seasons. Like many early pioneers, Lambeau was not the perfect strategist and game planner to start. He simply did not have the coaching experience that some of the other greats had coming into the league. But he climbed a coaching summit few others have reached. Lambeau won six NFL championships including three in a row, 1929-1931. In 33 years of coaching, he would rack up a 266 wins, 132 losses (and 22 ties) for a .631 winning percentage.

Most will remember Lambeau for developing the only successful NFL franchise in a small market. Green Bay provided challenges that no other franchise overcame to continue into the modern era. In many years, the Green Bay attendance was half of what some big city franchises were reporting. Over time, Lambeau and his supporters developed Green Bay into a first class venue for games that consistently commanded attendance figures that could support the team.

Lambeau promoted the passing game, which had a huge impact on the development of professional football. Along with others who promoted a faster more exciting game, Lambeau helped professional football turn a corner to command a huge fan base. As Lambeau's coaching career was coming to an end, the NFL was poised to grow to new heights of popularity in the age of television. He was one of those that helped set the table for the banquet.

Lambeau was one of the best at finding and developing great talent. And he never rested on his team's accomplishments—he was always working to improve his roster. Lambeau became an international celebrity and advocate for professional football throughout the world. He was enshrined in the charter class of 17 members in the Pro Football Hall of Fame in 1963.

He holds the NFL's fourth highest win total in the 20th century. In his honor, the Green Bay Packers fittingly christened their stadium Lambeau Field on September 11, 1965 following the great coach's death the previous June.

Curly Lambeau Timeline

1898

- April 9, 1898, Earl Louis Lambeau is born in Green Bay, Wisconsin.

1914-1917

- Lambeau attends Green Bay East High School and plays football along with track and field.

1916

- Lambeau leads Green Bay East High School to an undefeated season.

1917

- Lambeau graduates from Green Bay East High School.
- Lambeau briefly attends the University of Wisconsin.

1918

- Lambeau attends Notre Dame for one year and plays football. He shares the backfield with George Gipp playing under Coach Knute Rockne.

1919

- August 14, 1919, Lambeau and newspaper man, George Calhoun, startup the Green Bay Packers.

1921

- Green Bay sponsor, the Acne Packing Company, applies for and receives an APFA/NFL franchise.
- Following the 1921 season, the Green Bay Packers are expelled from the league due to a rule violation that prohibits team use of college players.

1922

- Player-coach Curly Lambeau himself applies for an APFA/NFL franchise and receives it. His franchise replaces the former Green Bay franchise before the 1922 season begins so the team misses no games.

1923

- Troubles persist for the Packers as Lambeau's team faces bankruptcy. The "Hungry Five," a group of local Green Bay businessmen including Lambeau, establish a non-profit corporation that can sell shares to Packer fans to support the team. Lambeau no longer owns the team.

1929

- Green Bay Packers win their first NFL Championship with a 12–0–1 record.

1930

- Green Bay Packers compile a 10–3–1 record and win their second NFL Championship in a row.

1931

- Green Bay Packers compile a 12–2 record and win their third NFL Championship in a row. Lambeau has matched Guy Chamberlin's record for consecutive championships, but has done it with the same team.

1936

- Green Bay Packers compile a 10–1–1 record and are the top team in the West Division.
- December 13, 1936, the Green Bay Packers defeat the Boston Redskins, 21–6, to win the NFL Championship—Lambeau's fourth.

1938

- December 11, 1938, the New York Giants defeat the Green Bay Packers, 23–17, to win the NFL Championship.

1939

- Green Bay Packers' 9–3 record earns them the top spot in the West Division.
- December 10, 1939, the Packers defeat the New York Giants, 27–0, to win the NFL Championship—Lambeau's fifth.

1944

- Green Bay Packers' 8–2 record earns them the top spot in the West Division.
- December 17, 1944, the Green Bay Packers defeat the New York Giants, 14–7, to win the NFL Championship. It is Lambeau's sixth and final championship.

1946-1949

- Green Bay Packers face significant financial constraints and team-building problems in the postwar years. A new professional football league competes for top draft picks and money shortages are not abated.

1950

- Lambeau resigns his job with the Green Bay Packers and becomes the head coach of the Chicago Cardinals.

1951

- Lambeau is released from the Chicago Cardinals towards the close of the season after compiling a 7–15 record with the franchise over two seasons.

1952

- Lambeau becomes the head coach of the Washington Redskins.

1954

- Lambeau is discharged from the Washington Redskins in the preseason after compiling a 10–13–1 record over two seasons.

1963

- Lambeau is enshrined into the Pro Football Hall of Fame as part of the charter class of 17 members.

1965

- June 4, 1965 Lambeau dies at the age of 67.
- September 11, 1965, New City Stadium in Green Bay is renamed Lambeau Field in honor of Curly Lambeau.

Highlights

Curly Lambeau won six NFL championships including three in a row, 1929-1931. In 33 years of coaching, he holds an overall NFL head coaching record of 226 –132 –22. He developed the only successful surviving NFL franchise in a small market. He was one of the few highly successful player-coaches in the NFL and he was one of the earliest promoters of the passing game. His Packers were perhaps the greatest David and Goliath story in sports history.

Curly Lambeau became an international celebrity and advocate for professional football throughout the world. He was enshrined in the charter class of 17 members in the Pro Football Hall of Fame in 1963. He holds the NFL's fourth highest win total in the 20th century. In his honor, the Green Bay Packers fittingly christened their stadium Lambeau Field on September 11, 1965 following the coach's death the previous June.

Endnotes

[1] The National Football League began in 1920 although the name National Football League was not adopted until 1922. Lambeau's team joined the professional league that we think of as the NFL in 1921.

[2] Stuart Stotts, Curly *Lambeau: Building the Green Bay Packers* (Madison, WI, Wisconsin Historical Society Press, 2007) 9.

[3] David Zimmerman, *Curly Lambeau: The Man Behind the Mystique* (Hales Corner, WI, Eagle Books, 2003) 33.

[4] David Zimmerman, *Curly Lambeau: The Man Behind the Mystique*, 37.

[5] Stuart Stotts, *Curly Lambeau: Building the Green Bay Packers*, 11-16.

[6] Originally appeared in Rice's story in the *New York Herald Tribune* on October 18, 1924. For more information see the Official Site of Notre Dame Athletics, viewed on 1/13/13 at http://www.und.com/trads/horse.html.

[7] Stuart Stotts, *Curly Lambeau: Building the Green Bay Packers*, 18.

[8] Indian Meat Packing supplied uniforms that first year. Football team sponsorship could become much more expensive in years following.

[9] Stuart Stotts, *Curly Lambeau: Building the Green Bay Packers*, 19.

[10] David Zimmerman, *Curly Lambeau: The Man Behind the Mystique*, 45.

[11] "Acme Packers Absorb Another Firm," New York Times, (1/11/1921) viewed 1/9/13 at http://query.nytimes.com/mem/archive-free/pdf?res=9906E0DD153CE533A25752C1A 9679C946095D6CF.

[12] Some say Clair's brother made the trip to Canton on John Clair's behalf. Some also say that the fee was $50 not $100. The minutes for the first meeting use the $100 amount.

[13] "Former Packer Star Dead at 80," *Milwaukee Journal*, October 27, 1983, 11, viewed at http://www.jsonline.com/historicarchive.

[14] Denis Gulickson, *Vagabond Halfback: The Life and Times of Johnny Blood McNally* (Madison, WI, Trails Books a Division of Big Earth Publishing, 2006) xii.

[15] Bob Carroll, "Verne Lewellen," *Coffin Corner*, Volume 12, No. 1, (1990) viewed at http://profootballresearchers.org/CC_1990s.htm on December 3, 2013.

[16] David Zimmerman, *Curly Lambeau: The Man Behind the Mystique*, 56.

[17] Hoard Historical Museum, http://www.hoardmuseum.org/23.asp?page=23.asp&ID=62 viewed on 1/13/13.

[18] Jonathan Rand, *The Year that Changed the Game: The Memorable Months that Shaped Pro Football* (Washington, DC, Potomac Books Inc., 2008) 26.

[19] Reasons for the "Hungry Five" name may be one of those odd mysteries lost in sports history. They were certainly hungry for a winner in Green Bay, but the name could just as easily have been established by a waitress who was impressed by the appetites of these local men who met in a restaurant to discuss the local team's business.

[20] David Zimmerman, *Curly Lambeau: The Man Behind the Mystique*, 65.

[21] As of January 2013 the Packers have held five stock sales. In a 2012 sale, more than 268,000 shares were sold at $250 apiece during a 12-week sale that contributed $67 million in revenue toward the $143 million project to improve and expand Lambeau field. There are more than 360,000 Green Bay shareholders.

[22] Early football formations often had several individuals who would occasionally pass the ball. More often than not, a halfback might pass more than a quarterback who was often used to call signals and block. Positions do not correspond exactly with those of the modern game. Player statistics are not necessarily available or useful.

[23] "Packer Eleven Trims Kaysees," *Milwaukee Journal*, October 13, 1924, 17.

24 "Field Goal Beats Green Bay: Joe Sternaman Hero as Game Ends 3-0," *Milwaukee Journal*, November 24, 1924.

25 Mark Concannon, "History is Special Between Old Rivals," FOXSportsWisconsin.com, viewed at http://www.foxsportswisconsin.com/01/21/11/History-is-special-between-old-rivals/landing.html?blockID=395657 on April 11, 2013.

26 Milt "Mitt" Romney was a cousin of Governor George Romney whom the Governor liked so much he would name his son Willard Mitt Romney in his honor. Milt would go on to play in the NFL from 1923-1929. He played for the Bears from 1925-1929.

27 "Mohard's Passing Attack Baffles Bays," *Milwaukee Journal*, December 1, 1924, 16.

28 Terry Bledsoe, "Halas Helped Make Delwig a Packer," *Milwaukee Journal Sports*, October 7, 1965, 21 Viewed at http://www.jsonline.com/historicarchive.

29 Randall Davidson, *9XM Talking, WHS Radio and the Wisconsin Idea* (Madison: University of Wisconsin Press, 2006) 222. See also Packers history web site: http://www.packershistory.net/1929PACKERS.html.

30 "Packers Beat Giants, 14-7, on 70 Yard Pass Play," *Milwaukee Sentinel*, October 6, 1930, 11, viewed at http://www.jsonline.com/historicarchive.

31 David Zimmerman, *Curly Lambeau: The Man Behind the Mystique*, 89.

32 Richard Whittingham, *What a Game They Played: An Inside Look at the Golden Era of Pro Football* (Lincoln, NE, Bison Books, 2002) 121-122.

33 Richard Whittingham, *What a Game They Played: An Inside Look at the Golden Era of Pro Football*, 122.

34 Jonathan Rand, *The Year that Changed the Game: The Memorable Months that Shaped Pro Football* (Washington, DC, Potomac Books Inc., 2008) 26.

35 The Green Bay backfield included several other players who passed during the season accounting for the difference between Herber's 1,239 and the 1,629 team total.

36 Richard O. Davies, *Rivals:The Ten Greatest American Sports Rivalries of the 20th Century* (Malden, MA, Wiley-Blackwell, 2010) 88.

37 Page, *Pro Football Championships Before the Super Bowl*, 37.

Paul Brown

Players will be lean and hungry

The "professor" standing in front of the classroom at Hiram College is a serious dark-haired man who is 5–foot–8 and 150 pounds. There is no doubt in his voice as he directs his students to find their seats. There is no hesitation as he gives directions—he exudes confidence. The class is made up of mostly big men who seem out of place in the classroom setting. Perhaps it's the way they spill out of their chairs. But this isn't a college class; this is the first day of training camp for the Cleveland Browns' football team. These students are professional football players. Their instructor is Coach Paul Brown.

Paul Brown instructs his athletes on success and his system of play. Brown is one of the most successful coaches in professional football history. His hour-long talk is an important part of his winning program. He says:

This is what I believe. I am not here to psyche you out.

Brown discusses proven principles that he has honed at every level of play. In fact, his talk covers much of the same ground that he covered many years ago with his high school players:

PLAYERS SHOULD EXPECT TO WORK HARD EVERY DAY REGARDLESS OF WEATHER CONDITIONS.

ENTHUSIASM IS EXPECTED; CYNICISM IS DISCOURAGED.

PLAYERS MUST BE TOUGH, HARDNOSED, HARD-HITTING, BUT NOT OBNOXIOUS.

SACRIFICES WILL MAKE THIS TEAM SPECIAL.

EVERYONE STARTS FRESH EACH YEAR.

Brown's expectations are sky high. He likes tough football players, but he also says, "I do not like 'thugs.'" He likes players who are achievers, but he does not like selfish athletes. Players must be clear-headed. Brown will expect them to understand every play in detail and to diagram them as well. Players are tested on their playbooks. And although camp is not designed to punish, Browns' camps are highly competitive and both intellectually and physically difficult.

Brown tells his players what is expected of them both on and off the field. Each day in practice, he introduces the day's tasks and goals. Brown consistently tells his players "why" they need to do something.[1] Brown wants a serious single-minded team. He knows he cannot make everyone believe in his "system," but he will never waiver.

Paul Brown: A Why Kind of Person

Brown is viewed by many as more of a business executive than a coach. He was the man who developed the first highly organized football program. But underneath it all was Brown's belief in the importance of managing human beings and guiding them to be their best. He told his players things that other coaches may have assumed that they would know. He tested his athletes for intelligence because he wanted to make sure they were capable of following his program and growing with it.

Brown himself understood the importance of knowing "why" things are done and he also liked to test out every aspect of his plans, plays, and program. If something did not work, why do it? He demanded precision in what his team did, often down to the smallest detail, but he was also open to innovation throughout his career. Why not split the end from the tackle and give him more room to maneuver and spread the field? Why not move a halfback out beyond the tight end off to the side or the "flanker" position? And why not take the fullback and the remaining halfback and have them aligned horizontally and spread them out a few feet to provide quicker play development and more options? Brown's pro-set development was based on such adjustments that he and others made to the T Formation and earlier schemes that were used in professional football for decades.[2]

Brown was innovative, sure, but what made it all work so well, was that he was able to lead his players in confidence, help them develop their skills to the maximum, and then make sure that everything was in place so they could execute. Discipline was fundamental. Execution was key. Results dictated strategy.

Early Years

Paul Brown was born on September 7, 1908, in Norwalk, a town in northern Ohio that is centered between Cleveland and Toledo. It is located in Huron County in an area called the Firelands of Ohio, so called because during the Revolutionary War, towns in the area were scorched by British troops attempting to destroy industries that were supporting the Continental Army. Norwalk with a population of 7,858 was an idyllic small-town setting for a young boy in 1910.[3]

When Paul Brown was nine, he and his family moved to Massillon, Ohio. Massillon is close to Canton in the east central portion of the state. When Brown was 12 years old, Massillon's population was 17,428.[4] In Massillon, Paul Brown's father, Lester Brown, worked as a dispatcher for the Wheeling and Lake Erie Railroad. A railroad man with a watch, he was serious and disciplined. Something his son inherited and crafted to an art form. Lester Brown and Paul's mother, Ida Sherwood Brown, were born of English ancestry.

Brown played football, basketball, and track at Washington High School in Massillon where a talented man named Dave Stewart coached all three sports. Brown was small, but rose to first string quarterback in his junior year. He replaced another talented quarterback, Harry Stuhldreher, who went from Washington High School to Notre Dame where he became one of the vaunted Four Horsemen backfield.

Brown was confident. At times, he instructed his own teammates as if he was the coach, but Stewart tolerated it.[5]

After high school, Brown enrolled at Ohio State University, which was the center of the universe for all Ohio boys wanting to play college football. But at Ohio State, Brown was denied the opportunity to try out for the football team based on his 5–foot–8 size and slim build.

Brown found another Ohio school more his size, Miami University in Oxford, and he transferred the following year. Miami University would go on to achieve fame as the "Cradle of Coaches," so called because it produced so many noted football coaches. At Miami, Brown played varsity football his last 2 years of college when he became eligible to play after his transfer. Coach Chester Pittser's offensive formation was modeled after the one used by Bob Zuppke, the legendary coach at the University of Illinois. As quarterback, Brown would line up behind center and then shift to a tailback position where he might be asked to run, block, throw or punt. Brown also served as a punt returner and he held for the placekicker. As Brown himself put it, "I was in it thick."[6]

High School Coaching

In 1930, after Brown graduated from Miami University, he took a job teaching at Severn Prep in Maryland whose students would often go on to the Naval Academy in Annapolis. At Severn, he taught English and History, while coaching football, lacrosse, and track.[7] Severn's football team record in the 2 years Brown served was 16–1–1. When Brown was offered a teaching and coaching position at his alma mater, Washington High School in Massillon, he happily accepted. Dr. H.W. Bell, the president of the Massillon School Board, who would serve the Browns as their family physician, selected Brown on the recommendation of Dave Stewart.

Poor equipment, old uniforms, rickety stands, and a horrible playing surface greeted Brown on his return to Massillon. The new coach also inherited an undersized team that got beat up the last half of his first season.[8] Although

Paul Brown at Miami University

it was the midst of the Great Depression, nothing would deter Brown from quickly building a first-class program.

There was something in Paul Brown's character that was expansive. Brown accepted responsibility for the entire athletic department at Washington High School and then became director of athletics for the entire city. Brown brought team and community together. Community pride was enhanced as a result of the football program and strengthened more by the connections that Brown was making throughout the entire school system. Massillon School Superintendant L. J. Smith supported Brown's athletic efforts. Brown, on his part, was willing to support all efforts to improve the Massillon schools' academic performances. During Brown's tenure at Washington High School, a Booster Club was formed to help garner even more support for the programs. In 1938, a new 16,600 seat stadium was built with Works Progress Administration (WPA) funds that served Washington High School and others in the community. Eventually this stadium would be called Paul Brown Tiger Stadium. The gate receipts from this huge facility improved the financial situation for the Washington High School football team. Better uniforms and equipment were purchased. The previous year's equipment was passed down to each of the junior high schools in Massillon each year.[9]   Stadium receipts also supported extracurricular activities. Brown saw that the junior high school coaches were high-caliber individuals and that their programs delivered conditioned athletes that fed into the Washington High School program.

Brown groomed athletes to be their best. Rules extended to activities outside the football field. Players were expected to take part in offseason activities. Each practice session was choreographed for maximum effect. Assistant coaches were not just helpers, they played an integral role. Scouting was valued. Athletes needed more than skills and abilities in sport, they needed knowledge. Brown provided playbooks for each of his athletes.

Brown was innovative, but he took ideas from the best practitioners of the game and adapted their methods and strategies as he saw fit. He was credited with his own inventions—the first football facemask, the first known pass-blocking schemes, and many new plays. But more than anything else, it was Brown's penchant for organization that was without rival at every level of play he coached.

Brown used the large Paul Brown Tiger Stadium to his advantage by inviting football powerhouses to come to Massillon and share in a larger gate receipt. In 9 years at Massillon, Brown amassed a record of 80–8–2, which was good for six consecutive state championships and four national scholastic championships.[10] Brown's winning percentage was .909. He was a legend in Ohio, the state of football legends, before he ever coached a single college game.

Ohio State University

When the head coaching position opened up at Ohio State, Paul Brown received the ardent support of the Ohio High School Football Coaches Association. Once the coaches made their candidate known, newspapers supported Brown and then notable Ohio State alumni started writing the Athletic Director, Lynn St. John.[11] Some joked later that perhaps his fellow coaches supported his candidacy as a means to remove him from Ohio high school competition to give someone else a chance to win.

On January 14, 1941, Paul Brown was named head football coach at Ohio State by St. John. Like a politician elected to office, Brown immediately began a speaking tour throughout the state to rally support for the team and his program.

Seasons at OSU

Ohio State had been smashed by Michigan 40–0 in the 1940 contest when Francis Schmidt had coached the Buckeyes. Ohio State had no answer for Michigan's All-American halfback, Thomas Harmon, who passed for three scores and rushed for two more. Harmon also kicked four extra points! His career touchdown tally of 33 surpassed the old mark of 31 set by Red Grange.[12] Harmon won the Heisman Trophy and lived a long remarkable life after surviving two plane crashes during his highly-decorated military service in World War II.

In 1941, Brown's first season with the Buckeyes, he delivered a 6–1–1 record, good for second place in the Western Conference, which Ohio State shared with archrival Michigan.[13] In the season's big game, Ohio State and Michigan fought to a draw. The game was dead even in every way. The teams were tied 7–7 at half and 14–14 in the third quarter. Remarkably, both teams scored in the fourth quarter and each one missed the extra point attempt.[14] The Minnesota Gophers took first place that year. Ohio State University's only loss that season was to Northwestern University, a team that featured a talented tailback named Otto Graham who was cool under pressure and was excellent at both the run and pass. Graham impressed Brown so much that the coach would seek his services after the war.

In 1942, following the December 7, 1941, attack on Pearl Harbor, college sports programs continued the best they could as the country began to fully develop the military might that would defeat its enemies. The 1942 college football season went forward, albeit altered in many ways. Ohio State began and ended its season playing service teams—those made up of men serving in the military that included both excellent college and professional players. The Buckeyes' first game was a decisive 59–0 victory over Fort Knox. Wins against Indiana, Northwestern, and Southern Cal followed. Their next stop was Madison where they faced the University of Wisconsin. The players drank contaminated water on the train from Columbus to Madison and many of the Buckeyes were sick or weakened for the game. Wisconsin won 17–7.

The Wisconsin game proved that there was no limit to details that might impact a game. After coming back the next week to defeat Illinois, Brown's Buckeyes faced mighty Michigan for what amounted to the conference championship. Ohio State won the game 21–7 on three passing touchdowns.

The season finale was a 41–12 victory over Iowa Pre-flight, a service school that lost just one other game that season and it was to Notre Dame. In Brown's second year of coaching, Ohio State was the National Champion based on its number one ranking in the final AP Poll.[15]

As more Americans went into the service, the 1943 season featured teams with players associated with military programs. Due to military impact on colleges, some schools were loaded with talent while others had little. Some schools joined the Navy's V-12 program whose students were permitted to play college ball. Schools like Ohio State that were in the ROTC program, lost eligibility for those member students over 18 years of age. ROTC schools fielded especially young players while those in the V-12 Programs had the decisive edge. The Buckeyes went 3–6 for the season although the ultra-competitive Brown never gave up. According to Brown in his biography, *PB: The Paul Brown Story*, he was frustrated by the situation faced by his underage, undersized, and overwhelmed players that year. The "Baby Bucks" suffered many injuries playing against larger more mature players that year. Brown would also come to say:

I was not proud of the way we conducted that season, the only time during my entire coaching career that I ever felt that way.[16]

Great Lakes Naval Station

Although Brown was 35 years old in 1944, he was still eligible for the draft. He joined the Navy and received a commission as a Lieutenant assigned to the Great Lakes Naval Station with the understanding that he would be at least initially employed in their football program. Tony Hinkle, the current head football coach at Great Lakes, was being deployed to the Pacific in the coming months. Deployment was a possibility for coaches and a likelihood for players.

Military and government leaders saw the service teams as a great way to increase morale and condition young men. An athlete might play for his university one year and find himself on a team like the Great Lakes Naval Station Bluejackets playing against his alma mater the next. The following year, he might find himself on a ship in the Pacific. When a notable athlete came to Great Lakes, the coach might be allowed to have that athlete transferred to the football team or one of the other teams for the season. After the season, the athlete was placed right back into normal duties. The rules had changed for 1944, and professional players were not added to the service teams that year.

With key losses to Notre Dame and Ohio State, the 1944 Great Lakes team managed a 9–3 record. Certainly an enviable record for most coaches, but not Paul Brown. In 1945, many of the players coming to Great Lakes were sent to a California base. Brown secured the services of several key players who had been overlooked. Marion Motley, a powerful fullback and linebacker, gave Brown a player that at times was untouchable. Paul "Bucky" O'Connor, George Terlep, and Marty Wendell were standouts on the Notre Dame team that had defeated Brown's Bluejackets the year before, but were now on Brown's team in 1945. A young man by the name of Bud Grant, who would later achieve coaching fame with the Minnesota Vikings, gave Brown a swift receiver with great hands.

The 1945 Bluejackets managed a 6–2–1 record in Brown's final year of service. The highlight of the year was a win against a very talented Notre Dame Fighting Irish team that would win the National Championship the following year. Brown was so obsessed with beating the Fighting Irish that he used some practice time during preceding weeks when he was facing other opponents to work out schemes for the Irish.[17] Despite this "cardinal sin" of football coaching, Brown's team did not seem to suffer from "looking ahead" and beat the Irish, 39–7. Motley and another key player, Grover Klemmer, stayed on after their actual eligible discharge dates to participate. According to Brown, the Irish could not handle Motley.[18]

What set the Great Lakes team's win in motion against the Irish was a run by a small halfback from Milwaukee, Francis Xavier Aschenbrenner, who was born in Germany. "Asch" took the opening kickoff for 53 yards to give the Bluejackets excellent field position leading to the first score. Remarkably, after his military service, Aschenbrenner played for Northwestern University and was the most valuable player in the 1949 Rose Bowl. In the only bowl game victory by Northwestern in the 20th Century, Aschenbrenner helped defeat the University of California at Berkley, 20–14. His 73-yard touchdown run was the longest run in the Rose Bowl for 44 years.

Brown's Professional Career

Paul Brown made his mark in professional football like few have done. He established the Cleveland Browns, a new team in a new league. He quickly moved the Browns into the top tier of the National Football League. He was fired from the Browns that he all but owned and then started all over again with the Cincinnati Bengals that he built from the ground up.

Mickey McBride

At the turn of the 20th Century, Mickey McBride was a tough newsboy on the south side of Chicago. He worked his way to one of the most critical jobs in the newspaper business, circulation manager. McBride was good at his work. He moved to Cleveland and got a position doing the same thing. In time, he also made money in real estate, taxi cabs, and a wire service. McBride became a wealthy business owner.

McBride's sons attended Notre Dame and he became interested in football while they were attending school. He decided that he wanted the challenge of owning a professional football club. First, he tried to persuade the Cleveland Rams owner, Daniel Reeves, to sell his NFL franchise. Reeves would not sell. When Arch Ward, a powerful *Chicago Tribune* Sports Editor, began to form a new league, the All-American Football Conference (AAFC), McBride signed on to establish a team in Cleveland. McBride knew little about how to start and manage a team. He needed a strong coach to manage the team's operations. He sought out Frank Leahy, the Notre Dame coach, who at the time was serving in the military. But when it looked like Leahy was ready to become McBride's first coach, Father Cavanaugh, President of Notre Dame University, persuaded McBride that Notre Dame needed Leahy. McBride was then directed to Paul Brown. Arch Ward was pressed into service to broker a deal with the coach.

Brown Signs with Cleveland

In order to woo Brown, McBride agreed to provide $25,000 a year, a 5% stake in the franchise, and a stipend for Brown while he was still in military service. Back in Columbus, Ohio State's Lynn St. John had balked at an all-out effort to draw Brown back. According to Brown, St. John would take Brown back per his assurances made before Brown began his military service.[19] However, Carroll Widdoes, who had taken over for Brown, had just finished an undefeated season. Mixed signals from St. John that Brown was either getting, or feeling like he was getting, turned him away from what he would call "the only job I had ever wanted." Brown signed on to coach Cleveland's new professional football team.

After a couple fan contests for a name for the new team, McBride would settle on the "Browns" name in the coach's honor. After the team was named, McBride left Brown alone to manage it. In typical Paul Brown fashion, the coach threw himself into the process of building a staff, creating an organization, and getting the best players. The All-American Football Conference had no player draft prior to its first season. Brown identified players he knew from his work at Great Lakes Naval Station, Ohio State, and Washington High School. He handpicked and fashioned a team that would be immediately successful.

After the NFL Cleveland Rams moved their organization out west to play in Los Angeles, locals called them the "Scrams."[20] Some of the Rams' players had no interest in moving to California and Brown signed them on. The players' contracts were challenged in court, but the court agreed with the players that they had signed on to a Cleveland team not one in Los Angeles.

Brown's Coaches

Brown assembled his first year coaches: Blanton Collier, Fritz Heisler, Bob Voights, Ted Conkright, and John Brickels with Creighton Miller advising on acquisitions. Collier, Heisler, and Brickels would be Brown's most important assistants.

Blanton Collier

Brown met Blanton Collier at Great Lakes. Collier would be one of Brown's assistants and eventually became Cleveland head coach after Brown left. Working initially with defensive backs, Collier is remembered as a brilliant perfectionist with patience who promoted the technical details.[21]

Fritz Heisler

Fritz Heisler played for Brown in high school and coached after his playing days at Miami of Ohio. He worked for Brown at Massillon and OSU. In Cleveland, he originally coached the guards on both offense and defense. Eventually, he became the offensive line coach.[22]

John Brickels

At Brown's behest, former rival Ohio High School coach, John Brickels, ran the Browns' operation and helped recruit players before Brown obtained his discharge from the Navy. This was a critical job in the earliest days of the team. When Brown returned home, Brickels became the backfield coach in the Browns' first two seasons.

Unique Timing of the New League

The AAFC needed media exposure. Brown brought it. The AAFC needed excellent teams. Brown developed one. The AAFC needed owners with deep pockets. Mickey McBride and several others had them. It wasn't enough. A handful of frail franchises would weaken the league.

The Browns played their home games at Cleveland Municipal Stadium for half a century. The park opened in 1931 and had a capacity that varied slightly, but was roughly 80,000 over the years. Outside the stadium was Lake Erie and the winds off the lake could make conditions difficult.

Many players were not under contract during the war and it was a players' market as the conflict was drawing to a close. Had the AAFC existed before the war, perhaps the NFL would have managed contracts differently. Moreover, some of the NFL owners like George Halas thought that the AAFC would not last long so even if they lost college players to the new league, those players would be available to the NFL soon.[23]

It was a unique time for professional football. Brown could select former NFL players who were currently unsigned and great college players who had not been recruited during the war. In order to get players securely signed while they were still in military service, Brown offered retainers that paid players a monthly stipend until they were discharged. The same strategy had been used by McBride to lure Brown himself.

The war years had been challenging times for the NFL—some teams were combined to share expenses—most struggled to stay in business. NFL teams would have been hard-pressed to offer retainers to men still in the service. While Brown was getting started with a significant source of funds, for many teams it would take TV revenues before real security existed.

Mickey McBride was resourceful in other ways. McBride also owned a large taxi cab company and when Brown had a player whom he liked, but had no room for him on his team, McBride could give him a job as a taxi cab driver. Then, if Brown needed to fill a slot quickly he went to his "taxi squad" for help.

Brown's Players in Cleveland

Going back in time, what would it be like to play for Paul Brown? Brown says conditioned athletes are better than the huge blubbering type players that are popular with some teams. Players should be lean and hungry, but they should also be good men. He tells players their futures depend upon these things.[24] "If you are a bum, a boozer or a chaser, I have no interest in you making our team," warns the coach.[25] Paul Brown seeks players and coaches who know what to do and do what they know. Players will be driven, but never with emotion that will quickly swell and wane.

Because of his controlled approach and strict disciplined ways in most everything, Brown is sometimes viewed as a kind of football automaton. But Brown wants players who love the game as he does; players who are loyal to Brown and his program; and players who can commit to being part of a team that can dominate the competition. He wants his guys to play for the "sheer desire of licking someone."[26] More than x's and o's, or dollars and cents, Brown wants to win. And because his pinpoint focus is on success on the football field, he is strong-willed and at times unmoving.

For players who are not completely devoted to the team and his system, he prods them: "We'll keep you until we can replace you." "Maybe you should be in another profession." "What do you plan to do next year?"[27] According to kicker Lou Groza, who played for 16 years with Brown in Cleveland: "The big thing is you didn't want to get him on your back because he could be very caustic." That was certainly one side of Brown, but Groza also praised Brown. "He was a great coach and I think he set the stage for others to emulate him."[28]

Brown loves football, but he also does not mask the uncertainty that exists for professional football players. Although Brown establishes football playing as a year-round vocation, he believes players will need to hang up their cleats at some time and find a new line of business.

In recruiting, Brown seeks the intelligent, hungry, quick, and hard working. He does not care about race and when he fields his "best 11 men" on the field, they are the best 11 men he can get. He works his players hard and expects full devotion to the game. He eliminates those who do not fit his system. They "waste the team's time." Brown had the ability to recognize talent and right from the start, he signed on great players.

Abe Gibron

Superb guard Abe Gibron played at 5-foot-11 and a mountainous 250 pounds, but he was quick off the ball and fast. He opened holes for the Browns' backs and was an excellent pass protector. Brown especially liked his ability to keep pace with the running backs when he pulled out to lead sweeps.[29]

Bill Willis

Bill Willis was an African American player who would help Brown turn his new team into a powerhouse. Willis had played tackle for Brown at Ohio State University and Brown acquired his services just as Willis was heading up to Canada to play football. Hall of Famer Willis was super quick and played center guard on defense, a position that lined up in front of the offensive center and could drop back for pass protection as well.

Bobby Mitchell

Hall of Famer Bobby Mitchell played halfback for Paul Brown for four seasons somewhat in the shadow of fullback Jim Brown. Mitchell was also an excellent receiver.

Dante Lavelli

Dante Lavelli played wide receiver for Brown at Ohio State University. Lavelli had only played a few games for Ohio State before his military duty so few people in professional football knew of him. His nickname was "Glue Fingers" given him by radio play-by-play announcer Bob Neal, and he would be remembered as a tough, clutch player.[30] The Hall of Famer was the son of Italian immigrants. Lavelli would play for 11 years.

Dub Jones

Starting in 1948, Dub Jones played eight seasons for the Browns. He played halfback and developed into a flanker. The 6-foot-4 Jones was a threat at running and receiving—one of Brown's key offensive weapons.

Frank Gatski

Hall of Famer Frank "Gunner" Gatski played center for the Browns for 11 years. The tough lineman helped protect the Browns' superstar quarterback, Otto Graham.

Gene Hickerson

Hall of Famer Gene Hickerson was an exceptionally fast and mobile offensive guard who was at his best when pulling out on sweeps and pitchouts around end.

Horace Gillom

Horace Gillom played 10 seasons with the Browns. Gillom was an African American who played for Brown in Massillon. He played both offensive and defensive end, but he gave the Browns a great edge over most teams with his towering punts that would travel over half the length of the field at great heights.

Jim Brown

Hall of Famer Jim Brown was immediately an impact player for Brown. After his career ended, some considered him the finest fullback in professional football.

Len Ford

The Browns acquired Hall of Famer Len Ford before the 1950 season. Ford was especially valuable as a pass rusher. He would play eight seasons for Paul Brown.

Lou "the Toe" Groza

Kicker Lou Groza was a very accurate kicker who would often kick field goals much longer than normally attempted at the time. Groza was another key player who made the Browns a dominant team. He and several other teammates would be inducted into the Pro Football Hall of Fame.

Mac Speedie

Mac Speedie played against Brown's Bluejackets team from Great Lakes Naval Station. Speedie was a 6-foot-3 end who was one of the best receivers in football. He helped the Browns develop an exceptional pass attack. Speedie had suffered from Perthese disease as a young boy, a condition characterized by a temporary loss of blood supply to the hip joint. The disease left Speedie with an odd gait that made it more difficult for defenders to cover his pass patterns.

Marion Motley

Marion Motley was someone most other coaches overlooked. Motley was an African American who Brown knew well. He played for one of Brown's Washington High School rivals, Canton McKinley High School, and he played for Brown's Bluejackets at the Great Lakes Naval Station. As a fullback, Motley was powerful in the same way Bronko Nagurski was a generation

Paul Brown in the Classroom

before. Motley was a peerless blocker who protected Otto Graham and an excellent ball carrier who is credited with much of the success for Brown's draw play.[31] The Hall of Famer could also play linebacker.

Mike McCormack

Hall of Famer Mike McCormack was a right tackle who along with a cadre of other great lineman helped open holes for Jim Brown and protect Otto Graham.

Otto Graham

Brown wasted no time signing Otto Graham who was at Glenview Air Station—a short distance from Great Lakes Naval Station. Graham had impressed Brown with his vision of the field and his athleticism when he led Northwestern to victory against the Ohio State Buckeyes in Brown's first season in Columbus. Graham was also Brown's kind of player: disciplined, calm under pressure, and committed to the game. He adjusted to playing quarterback in Brown's T Formation quickly.

Tommy James

Tommy James joined the Browns in 1948 and played halfback and defensive back. James was a superb pass defender and crucial member of the Browns' defense.

Tony Adamle

Tony Adamle joined the Browns in 1947. Adamle played linebacker and fullback. Intelligent and self assured, Adamle was a team leader. He and the Browns' line-backing corps helped make the defense formidable. At fullback, he was especially valuable when he was able to play in relief of Marion Motley when the great star was injured.

Warren Lahr

Warren Lahr joined the Browns in 1949 and played for 11 years. As a defensive back, he was an excellent pass defender and frequently came up with interceptions at critical times.

Browns in the AAFC

It would be with players like Graham, Willis, Lavelli, Motley, Groza, and Speedie that Brown would establish his dominant Cleveland team. Brown would pattern his team like the New York Yankees baseball team and insist that his players dress and act with decorum in public. No smoking or swearing in public. Brown wanted his team to be a dynasty right from the start.

Teams of the AAFC

The AAFC was organized in two divisions: the East and West. The East Division included the New York Yankees, Buffalo Bisons, Brooklyn Dodgers, and Miami Seahawks.[32] The West Division included the Cleveland Browns, the San Francisco 49ers, the Los Angeles Dons, and the Chicago Rockets. The league championship would be decided by the top team from each division battling it out in a final game.

Browns' Inaugural Season: 1946

The year 1946 marked the inaugural season for both the Cleveland Browns and the eight-team All-America Football Conference. The league featured a few strong teams, several lesser teams, and a lot of lopsided games. On display were many of the finest players in professional football.[33] The AAFC sought out, attracted, and retained black athletes—a practice that enhanced the AAFC teams and helped draw thousands of black fans to its venues.

The Cleveland Browns were the elite of the league. The Browns opened the season by defeating the Miami Seahawks, 44–0, in Cleveland. They had little problem defeating their next five opponents: the Chicago Rockets, Buffalo Bisons, New York Yankees, and Brooklyn Dodgers. When they played the Yankees again, they beat them, 7–0. After besting the Los Angeles Dons, 31–14, the Browns fell to the San Francisco 49ers, 34–20, and lost a close one to the Los Angeles Dons, 17–16. The Browns finished strong by beating the Rockets, Bisons, Seahawks, and Dodgers in the last four weeks of the season. The Browns were champs of the Western Division compiling a 12–2 record, which entitled them to play the New York Yankees in the league title game.

1946 AAFC Championship Game

The championship game was played at Cleveland's Municipal Stadium in front of 41,181 fans. The Yankees scored first on a 21-yard field goal by Harvey Johnson. Brown's strategy called for Graham throwing short bullet passes rather than the long passes the Yankees may have planned on defending. A second quarter Cleveland drive that featured a series of Graham passes was finished off by a 2-yard touchdown run by Motley. In the third quarter, the Yankees were able to sustain a long 80-yard drive with running back Spec Sanders taking it in from the 2-yard line. A blocked extra point kept the score, 9–6, Yankees. In the fourth quarter, Graham led the Browns downfield all the way from their own 25-yard line with a series of passes. On a critical third down, Edgar Jones made a shoestring catch in the middle of the field to keep the drive going. The winning score came when Lavelli beat his man into the end zone and snagged a Graham pass. After Groza's point after, the Browns led, 14–9, and held on from there for the win. Groza, led the AAFC in points scored, with 84—including 13 field goals in 29 attempts and 45 extra points on 47 attempts. Groza also had exceptionally long field goals of 50, 51 and 49 yards.[34] The professional football kicking game was improving during this period and Groza led the way.

Brown Adds More Talent

Added to the 1947 roster were punter Horace Gillom and linebacker/fullback Tony Adamle. Gillom would help the Browns keep the opponent's offense from good field position, while Groza's field goal abilities gave the Browns the opportunity to score from long distances. Adamle had a reputation for toughness and leadership both on the field and in the locker room. He was one of the few players who could talk back to Brown and not end up in the dog house.[35] Adamle would serve the Browns well and eventually leave the team after the 1951 season in part to pursue a medical degree. He would return for a year in 1954. His son, Mike Adamle, was an All-American fullback at Northwestern University and he played for 6 years in the NFL.[36]

1947 Season

Cleveland's second season was better than the first. Attendance would average 55,848, the highest of *any* professional football team that year. The Browns finished with a 12–1–1 record, winning the western division again and facing the Yankees again for the league championship.

It was Friday night football when Cleveland opened in front of 63,263 fans at home at Municipal Stadium on September 5, 1947. The Browns faced the Buffalo Bills who had changed their name from the Buffalo Bisons. The Browns smashed the Buffalo Bills, 30–14. The Dodgers were whipped next, 55–7. The Browns shut out Baltimore, 28–0, and then beat the Chicago Rockets, 41–21.

The next opponent for the Browns was the talented Yankees team that featured the tiny, but sensational runner Claude "Buddy" Young. At 5-foot-6, Young had equaled Red Grange's 10 touchdown season record at Illinois. It was not easy, but the Browns held Young in check and prevailed, 26–17, in front of 80,000 plus fans in Cleveland.

The Browns suffered their first and only loss of the season to the Los Angeles Dons by a score of 13–10. They would follow with wins against the Rockets, 49ers, Bills, Dodgers, and 49ers. In another big contest against the Yankees, the best the Browns could do was a tie, but they came from 28 points behind to do it. The Browns finished the regular season with a 27–17 win over the Dons and a 42–0 drubbing of the Colts.

1947 AAFC Championship Game

On an icy field, the Browns faced the Yankees in Yankee Stadium, the "House that Ruth Built," for the league championship on December 14, 1947, in front of 61,879 fans. A 51-yard run by Motley that brought the ball into the red zone highlighted a Browns' scoring drive in the first quarter. A Graham toss to

Speedie brought the ball to the 1-yard line where Graham took it in on a sneak. The Yankees kicked a field goal for their first score. A Yankees' Spec Sanders pass was intercepted by the Browns' Tommy Colella at his shoe tops—giving Cleveland possession at the New York 41. Motley powered his way toward the end zone for 16 yards. A 4-yard rush by Edgar Jones gave the Browns their next score and the 14–3 victory gave Cleveland its second championship in a row.

Graham received the league's MVP award while passing for 2,753 yards and 25 touchdowns. Speedie led the league in receiving. *Pro Football Illustrated* lauded Brown as Coach of the Year.

1948 Season

The Browns went undefeated in their third year with a regular season mark of 14–0. San Francisco finished 12–2 and the rest of the teams lagged far behind at .500 or less. Twice during the season, the Browns beat the Dons, Bills, Colts, Dodgers, Rockets, Yankees, and 49ers. They scored 389 points and allowed 190. Browns' fans compare this season to the 17–0 mark of the 1972 Miami Dolphins. Graham passed for 2,713 yards and 25 touchdowns with 15 interceptions. Speedie led the league in receptions with 58 and Motley was the top rusher with 964 yards for an average of 6.1 yards per carry.

About this time, Paul Brown instituted his messenger system—shuttling in guards with plays for the quarterback. Coach Brown believed that this system allowed him to thoughtfully select plays from the sideline. At the time and continuing for some time, quarterbacks on other teams were calling their own plays.

The Browns would face the inconsistent Buffalo Bills for the championship. Buffalo featured George Ratterman a talented quarterback; Chet Mutryn, the league's leading rusher; another gifted rusher Lou Tomasetti; and an excellent receiver in Al Baldwin. However, on defense, the Bills were weak.

1948 AAFC Championship Game

The Browns capped off their perfect season with a brilliant seven-touchdown championship game that had an abundance of highlights on both offense and defense. In the first quarter, Edgar Jones rushed in from the 3-yard line for the first score in a game that featured an awesome Browns' running attack. The Browns scored in the second quarter when George Young picked up a fumble and ran 18 yards into the end zone. Edgar Jones scored his second touchdown on a 9-yard pass from Graham in the third quarter. Motley muscled in his first of three touchdowns on a 29-yard run. Groza was perfect on extra point attempts and the Browns led at 28–0. The Bills finally scored on a pass from Alan Baldwin to Jim Still. In the fourth quarter, Motley rushed for two more TDs. Lou Saban intercepted a pass and scurried 29 yards into the end zone for the final score.

The Browns intercepted five passes and recovered three fumbles. Tommy James snagged two errant balls and Tommy Colella, Tony Adamle, and

Lou Saban had one apiece.[37] The Bills fumbled three times and the Browns recovered all of them. The Browns all-around trouncing of the Bills, 49–7, captured the AAFC championship—the team's third straight.

1949 Season

The 1949 season was the final year for the All-American Football Conference. Prior to the 1949 season, the Brooklyn Dodgers and New York Yankees merged bringing the number of teams down to seven. For the 1949 championship, the top four teams competed in a playoff to determine the championship. Finishing the regular season 9–1–2 gave the Browns the Western Division title. In the extra playoff game the Browns beat the Buffalo Bills, 31–21, to advance to the championship game against the San Francisco 49ers.

San Francisco was coached by Buck Shaw, who like Brown, had a long distinguished coaching career at different levels of play. After his long service to the San Francisco 49ers, he would go on to coach the Philadelphia Eagles and win the NFL Championship in 1960, becoming the only coach to beat Vince Lombardi in an NFL championship game. He would also be remembered for his exemplary sportsmanship. In a late season meeting with the Browns the previous season, Shaw cautioned his defensive players that he would not tolerate anyone taking shots at Otto Graham's injured knee to knock him out the game.[38]

AAFC top-scoring San Francisco had an excellent quarterback named Frankie Albert who had been named league MVP with Graham in 1948. Fullback Joe "the Jet" Perry scored the most rushing TDs that year with 10 and he was the AAFC top rusher with 783 yards. Right end Alyn Beals had 44 receptions for 678 yards. Another notable on the 49ers was Paul T. Salata, a good end with a hall of fame sense of humor. Salata would play a couple seasons in the United States, go to Canada for a couple more, and later in life establish the Mr. Irrelevant Award, a week-long celebration for the last man drafted into professional football each year.[39]

1949 Championship Game

In what would be the last game of the All-American Football Conference, the Browns took on the San Francisco 49ers for the league championship on December 11, 1949 in Cleveland's Municipal Stadium on a cold muddy field. Word of the impending demise of the league kept attendance down to 22,550 hale and hearty fans. Graham got things moving with a 37-yard pass to Mac Speedie. Marion Motley broke through the 49ers line for 10 yards. The drive was finished by Edgar Jones who dove his way into the end zone from the 2-yard line. After Groza's extra point, the Browns led 7–0. In the third quarter, Marion Motley raced off tackle for 63 yards and another touchdown. The only 49er score came in the fourth quarter on a 74-yard drive. On fourth down, Frankie Albert hit Paul Salata for the score on a 23–yard pass play. Joe

Vetrano, who never missed an extra point as the 49ers' kicker, hit another one that made it 14–7. The Browns capped off their scoring with a 69-yard drive that finished with Dub Jones running the ball in from the four. Groza kicked the extra point and he earned the last point in AAFC history. The Browns won their fourth straight championship, this one by a score of 21–7 over San Francisco. The Browns were the only champions that the AAFC had. The league folded that year and the Browns, 49ers, and Colts were absorbed into the NFL for the 1950 season. For the 1949 season, Graham threw for 2,785 yards and 19 touchdowns. Speedie had 62 receptions and Marion Motley rushed for 605 yards and 8 TDs.

Browns in NFL

Surprising to most everyone except perhaps Paul Brown and his team, the Browns were a power in the NFL right from the start. They continued to experience the success that they had in the AAFC.

1950 Season

The solid Browns' defense got a big boost figuratively and literally when they acquired Len Ford in the disbursement draft. The disbursement draft was held in June to place the top players of the AAFC whose teams were not picked up by the NFL. Ford was a 6-foot-4, 245 pound end, who added extra muscle to the Browns' defense. Brown would use the Hall of Famer as a defensive specialist. Ford would be one of the first pass rush specialists in professional football.

The Browns' first game was against the two-time defending league champion Philadelphia Eagles before a huge crowd of 71,237 in Philadelphia. The game was publicized as a true test of the former AAFC Browns against a solid NFL stalwart. The Browns convincingly beat the Eagles, 35–10. The following week, the Browns hammered the Baltimore Colts, 31–0. Many teams had trouble defending against the Browns' powerful offense. They crushed another former AAFC opponent, the San Francisco 49ers, 34–14, later in the year. They would go on to beat the Pittsburgh Steelers, 45–7, and the Washington Redskins, 45–21.

The coach of the Eagles, Alfred Earle "Greasy" Neale, criticized the Browns as a passing-only team after their first meeting. Brown sought retribution by defeating the Eagles, 13–7, in their second meeting of the year without throwing a single pass.[40] The New York Giants were the one team that challenged the Browns. In fact, they beat the Browns 6–0 and 17–13 during the regular season. Three times was the charm for the Browns as they defeated the Giants 8–3 in the divisional playoff game.

1950 NFL Championship Game

The Cleveland Browns and Los Angeles Rams played the title game on Christmas Eve in front of 29,751 screaming fans at Municipal Stadium. The Rams had an awesome offense. They scored 466 points for an average of 38.8 per game; they passed for 3,709 yards for an average of 309 per game.[41] They featured two Hall of Fame receivers in Tom Fears and Elroy "Crazy Legs" Hirsch. The Rams also featured two Hall of Fame quarterbacks, starter Bob Waterfield with Norm Van Brocklin in the wings. College football superstar, Glenn Davis, who had won both the Heisman Trophy and the Maxwell Award while playing at Army, was the Rams leading rusher.[42]

The Browns would mix up their offensive plays to include pitchouts, short sideline passes, and a screen pass when needed. Graham would also run for good yardage when he scrambled away from the rush. A long pass had always been part of the Browns' arsenal as well.

Early in the game, Waterfield hit Davis on an 82-yard pass play for the first score. Graham used a number of intermediate passes and a forced scramble to bring the ball downfield in a hurry. A pass to Dub Jones gave the Browns their first touchdown and with the extra point, tied the game at 7–7. Hoerner scored for the Rams on a 1-yard rush and with the extra point, the Rams took the lead at 14–7. In the second quarter, Dante Lavelli snagged a Graham pass for a 37-yard touchdown, but the Browns missed the point after. Lavelli scored on another reception at the beginning of the second half to put the Browns ahead, 20–14. Hoerner scored again for the Rams on a 1-yard plunge. The extra point was successful. After a Motley fumble, Larry Brink took the ball in from 6 yards out. Another extra point and the Browns were behind by 8 points, 28–20. After Warren Lahr intercepted a Rams' pass, the Browns worked their way downfield and Graham hit Rex Bumgardner in the corner of the end zone for a score.

With the Browns trailing 28–27, Graham fumbled and it looked like the game was over. But the Browns' defense held and with a little under two minutes Cleveland took possession with one last chance to pull out a victory. Graham drove down the field with several precision sideline passes and a critical toss to Bumgardner that got the Browns down to the 19-yard line. A Graham quarterback keeper brought the ball a few yards forward into the center of the field. All business and concentration, Lou "the Toe" Groza kicked a 16-yard field goal. The Rams' Van Brocklin was given his chance at last minute heroics, but another Lahr interception ended the game with the score, Browns 30–Rams 28. When the game ended, exuberant Cleveland fans flooded onto the field to congratulate the players. Both goal posts were triumphantly taken down and carried off outside the stadium. In the locker room, Paul Brown was exuberant:

> *This is the gamest bunch of guys in the world. Next to my wife and family, these guys are my life. What a Merry Christmas they've made it!*[43]

Quarterback Otto Graham touchdowns and passing yards dropped in 1950. Paul Brown was adjusting to the NFL, taking what he was given, and still winning. Marion Motley gained 810 yards on 140 carries. Dub Jones gained 384 yards on 83 carries and he had 31 receptions for 431 yards. Mac Speedie topped the club in receptions with 42 for 548 yards. Groza was 13-of-19 on field-goal tries and led the Browns in scoring with 74 points. The Browns had the second best defense in the league. Each Browns' player received $1,113 for the championship win—about $10,600 in 2013 dollars. After the championship game, Browns' owner Mickey McBride said the Browns would "keep on building and winning."[44]

1951 Season

The 1951 season would mark the first year, the Cleveland Browns did not win it all. Yet, they were a great team. After losing, 24–10, to San Francisco in the opener, they went on an 11-game winning streak to finish the regular season 11–1, winning the American Conference title.

On offense, Dub Jones rushed for 492 yards and 7 TDs. Ken Carpenter rushed for 402 yards and 4 TDs. Lavelli had 43 receptions and 6 TDs. Jones had 30 receptions with 5 TDs. Quarterback Otto Graham, UPI MVP, passed for 2,205 yards and 17 TDs with 16 interceptions. On defense, they served up four shutouts: 45–0 over the Washington Redskins; 17–0 over the Pittsburgh Steelers; 28–0 over the Steelers; and 10–0 over the New York Giants. Cornerback Warren Lahr tied safety Cliff Lewis with five interceptions. Rookie Don Shula, who would play 2 years for the Browns and later go on to a Hall of Fame coaching career, had four interceptions.

1951 NFL Championship Game

The 1951 NFL Championship game was played at Los Angeles Memorial Coliseum in near perfect 70° weather before a crowd of 59,475. Once again, the Browns faced the Rams.

After a scoreless first quarter, the Rams put together a scoring drive by using a variety of passes and runs that featured the solid play of Verda T. "Vitamin" Smith. The drive was aided by a critical pass interference call against the Browns. The Rams continued to drive and Dick Hoerner pushed his way through a very tough Browns' line from the 1-yard line for the first score.

After a Browns' drive stalled, Groza kicked a record-breaking 52-yard field goal for the Browns' first points. Cleveland played tough defense and got the ball in great field position after a punt that landed just shy of midfield. Graham took over from there. First, he hit Mac Speedie for a 14-yard gain. Then he connected with Marion Motley for 23 yards. Dub Jones took his turn on the receiving end of a Graham pass and he made the most of it, scoring from 17 yards out. The Browns were up 10–7 as the first half expired.

In the second half, the Rams' 6-foot-4, 240 pound defensive end, Larry Brink, hit Graham and lodged the ball loose for Andy Robustelli to pick up and run to the 1-yard line. Dan Towler carried it in from there to put the Rams ahead 14–10. When Bob Waterfield chipped in a field goal later in the game, the Rams were up 17–10. From there, Otto Graham went to work and orchestrated a 70-yard drive that was finished off by Ken Carpenter's 2-yard rush.

The Browns' defense was good, but it was not perfect. About a third of the way through the fourth quarter, the Rams had a third and three on their own 27-yard line. Rather than go after a short gain for the first down, Van Brocklin tossed a long pass to Fears who made the grab and outraced Tommy James to the end zone. After a successful point after, the Rams were up, 24–17. The Browns had one more series in which they pushed past midfield, but that's where it ended when they turned the ball over on downs. The proud Browns ended their season with a 24–17 loss.

1952 Season

The Browns almost fell down to earth in 1952, but not quite. Although they finished 8–4, they still made it to the league championship game. The Browns beat out the Giants and Eagles by one game to finish in first place in the American Conference.

Hall of Fame quarterback Otto Graham threw 364 passes about a hundred more than 1951 and connected on 181 for 2,816 yards and a 49.7 completion rate. He would also rack up 24 interceptions—the highest number for his career.

Fullback Marion Motley who was with Brown from the start, was coming to the end of his career, but he was the leading rusher for the Browns with 444 yards. Ken Carpenter was right behind him with 408. Carpenter would have one more year with the Browns and then head up to Canada and play several years for the Saskatchewan Roughriders. Wide receiver Mac Speedie, was the NFL's leading receiver catching 62 passes for 911 yards and five TDs. Dub Jones had 43 receptions for 651 yards. The Browns had the second best defense in the league.

1952 Championship Game

The Detroit Lions were playing for their first championship in 17 years before 50,934 fans in Cleveland. The Browns won in time of possession, passing, and rushing yards, but not the final score. The Lions won with a conservative, mistake-free game.

After a scoreless first quarter, Gillom muffed a punt that went just 22 yards to setup a short Lions' drive in the second quarter. Hall of Fame quarterback

Bobby Layne capped off the drive with a 2-yard keeper for the score. In the third quarter, another Lions' Hall of Famer, Doak Walker, speared Cleveland's heart with a magnificent 67-yard touchdown run off tackle. The Browns responded with an 11-play 67-yard touchdown drive that culminated in a 7-yard touchdown charge by fullback Chick Jagade. The score stood at 14–7 in favor of the Lions. After holding the Lions on their possession, the Browns stormed down the field. Graham passes to Bumgardner and Lavelli helped move the ball into Detroit territory. Graham kept things going with a quarterback keeper and then Motley took a Graham pitchout and drove 41 yards all the way to the Detroit 5-yard line. Then the Lions' defense stiffened and the Browns moved backward. A Motley sweep was stuffed and the Browns were back at the 10-yard line. Graham was sacked way back at the 22-yard line. A Graham run was stopped with no gain and his fourth-down pass fell incomplete. Time was running out, but again, the Browns held. When Detroit's Bob Smith punted the ball, Browns' halfback Ken Carpenter fumbled the punt and the Lions recovered. Pat Harder kicked a 36-yard field goal to cap-off the 17–7 Detroit victory.

1953 Season

After the AAFC was swallowed up by the NFL, players' salaries declined. The AAFC had upped the wages of talented football players in the postwar years, but those wages were not sustained after the new league folded and its financially healthy teams were absorbed into the NFL.

Paul Brown like most everyone coaching in the NFL at the time took a hard line in player salary negotiations. However, it was not unusual for a player to get more money from Brown than another coach. Occasionally, Brown gave a player a bonus for an exceptional performance.

The Browns won their first 11 regular-season games before they fell to the Eagles 42–27 in the final game of the season. Otto Graham was the UPI MVP and he had the best quarterback rating in the NFL at 99.7. He completed 167 passes on 258 attempts for 2,722 yards and a completion percentage of 64.7%. Rushing and receiving yards were scattered around a number of players. Ray Renfro led the team with 352 yards rushing followed by Harry "Chick" Jagade's 344 yards and Billy Reynolds's 313 yards. In receptions, Dante Lavelli had 45 receptions for 783 yards, Ray Renfro had 39 receptions for 722 yards, and Pete Brewster had 32 receptions for 632 yards. The Browns had the best defense in the league. Lou Groza made 23-of-26 field-goal attempts.

Marion Motley would see light duty for the Browns in his final season in Cleveland. An injury would keep him out of the lineup in 1954 and then Brown traded him to Pittsburgh in 1955 where he played linebacker in his final season. Motley would be inducted into the Pro Football Hall of Fame in 1968. Bud Grant who played with Motley on Brown's Great Lakes Naval Station Bluejackets team would call Motley "my all-time hero" when accepting induction into the Pro Football Hall of Fame in 1994.

1953 NFL Championship Game

The 1953 NFL Championship Game was a defensive struggle. The Browns scored four times in the game, but three of those were field goals and only one was a touchdown. The Lions had no easy time of it either, being held to one touchdown and one field goal well into the fourth quarter.

The Browns were leading 16–10 in the waning minutes of the 1953 championship game when Bobby Layne orchestrated an 80-yard touchdown drive that concluded beautifully in a 33-yard pass to Jim Doran in the end zone. Doran, a defensive specialist, played offensive end to replace the injured Leon Hart.[45] But, the difference maker in the game was the versatile Doak Walker. Walker was an offensive halfback, a kick and punt returner, a kicker, a punter, and a defensive back. He rushed for the Lions' first score and kicked the point after in the first quarter. He kicked a 23-yard field goal in the second. And following a Layne pass to Doran for the Lions' second touchdown, Walker kicked the extra point for the one-point win: Lions 17–Browns–16.

1954 Season

Prior to the 1954 season, two of the greatest Cleveland Browns, Marion Motley and Bill Willis, said their goodbyes. Their relationship with Paul Brown predated the Browns' professional debut. On the positive side of the ledger, Paul Brown was excited about acquiring Mike McCormack in a huge trade with the Colts.[46]

The Browns started off losing to Philadelphia 28–10. After they handled the Cardinals, 31–7, without any problems, they lost to the Steelers, 55–27. They corrected their course and won the next 8 games in a row including an impressive victory over the Steelers, 42–7. Their last regular season game was a 14–7 loss to Detroit, whom they would play in the championship.

Otto Graham completed 142 passes on 240 attempts for 2,092 yards with a 59.2% completion rate. Graham had 11 TDs passing and 8 rushing. He threw 17 interceptions. Dante Lavelli snagged 47 receptions for 802 yards. Rookie fullback Maurice Bassett rushed for 588 yards and had another 205 yards in receptions and 6 TDs. The Browns had the best defense in the league.

1954 Championship Game

The Browns had lost the 1952 and 1953 championships to the Detroit Lions. They had also lost their last meeting, 14–10, one week earlier. Now they were facing the Lions again.

The Lions scored first on a 36-yard field goal by Doak Walker. Graham countered with a 35-yard touchdown pass to Ray Renfro. Graham tossed another TD pass to Pete Brewster and then took it in himself for another score. Bill Bowman scored next on a short run for Detroit, but it was lights out for the Lions the rest of the way. Graham would pass for one more score and the

Browns would rush for four more scores including two from Graham himself. For the Lions, Layne had six interceptions in the game after having only 12 during the regular season. The Browns' 56–10 pasting of the Lions would be one for the ages and one that the Lions would not forget. The win over the Lions gave the Browns their second NFL crown in the 5 years they competed in the NFL.

Brown was running out of superlatives to describe his championship teams. He described his 1954 team in this way:

The finest football team I've ever coached on a given day.[47]

1955 Season

The Browns' training camp must have seemed strange without Otto Graham. But his retirement did not last long. Graham was lured out of retirement when the Browns had problems at the quarterback position. The Browns lost their first game to the Washington Redskins, 27–17, but then won 9 of their last 11. Their 9–2–1 record put them in the championship game.

Darrel Brewster had 34 receptions for 622 yards and six touchdowns. Ray Renfro had 29 receptions for 603 yards and eight touchdowns. Fred Morrison rushed for 824 yards surpassing Marion Motley's splendid 1950 season total of 810.

The Browns had the best defense in the league. Linebacker and future Steelers' head coach Chuck Noll, Warren Lahr, and Ken Konz collected five interceptions each.

1955 NFL Championship Game

In the 1955 NFL Championship, the Browns showed the record-breaking crowd of 87,695 that they were the best in the world. The game would pit Paul Brown against Sid Gillman, who like Brown, was a former Ohio State coach and a lover of the pass. Gillman would quip:

God bless those runners because they get you the first down, give you ball control and keep your defense off the field. But if you want to ring the cash register, you have to pass.[48]

In addition to the coaching matchup, two Hall of Fame quarterbacks squared off. For Otto Graham of the Browns, it would be his swan song. For the great "Dutchman," Norm Van Brocklin of the Rams, the song would not be so sweet.

The first quarter was a defensive battle with Lou Groza kicking a 26-yard field goal for the only score. In the second quarter, Van Brocklin threw the first of his six interceptions. This one bounced off the Rams' Skeets Quinlan into the hands of Don Paul who ran 65 yards down the line to the end zone.[49] Groza followed with his first of many extra point kicks that day. Skeets Quinlin made reparations for the interception when he snagged a Van Brocklin pass that was good for 67 yards and the Rams first score. After the extra point, the game looked respectable at 10–7, Browns.

Graham hit Dante Lavelli for the next strike, a 50-yard pass play that was followed by another Groza extra point. Starting from midfield after a solid punt return, Browns' fullback Maurice Bassett, playing for the injured Ed Modzelewski, plowed his way towards another score. Graham himself carried the ball in for the final 15 yards needed for the touchdown. After Groza's point after, the Browns were ahead, 24–7. Van Brocklin threw another errant pass and within a few minutes Graham was back in the end zone on a keeper. In the fourth quarter, Graham hit Renfro for the Browns' last touchdown of the day. Ron Waller finished off the Rams' scoring with an end around from 4 yards out for a touchdown. The Browns won handily 38–14.

Graham-Brown Tandem

Graham ended his career after the 1955 season. Few quarterbacks come close to Graham's success record. He and Brown had won seven titles and competed in 10 championship games in a row. In his last season, Graham completed 98 passes on 185 attempts for 1,721 yards with a completion rate of 53% and 15 touchdowns. With just eight interceptions, Graham had a quarterback rating of 94.0—his second best NFL mark. Graham would be lauded by teammates as a quarterback nonpareil. He had a beautiful touch on the ball—he could throw soft short ones, intermediate bullets down the middle, and loft the long balls. He was a leader. He brought his team to victory in so many games it became routine in Cleveland.

Graham completed 55.8% of his passes for 23,584 yards and 174 touchdowns. He played for 10 years nonstop while taking a beating in an era where there were no special rules to protect the QB. He had great vision and found the open man. And perhaps his greatest quality was his honest focus on his own culpability in losses—focusing on what he could have done better. Graham's teammates responded and made protecting him a priority. Brown was lucky to have such a man lead his team for a decade. Likewise Graham was lucky to have a coach who would work very hard to use Graham's skills and surround Graham with great players. Coach and quarterback, Brown and Graham, would be one of the best football combinations of all time. Graham would be inducted into the Hall of Fame in 1965 and Brown would follow in 1967.

1956 Season

After winning the NFL Championship in 1955, Otto Graham stuck around to help Paul Brown settle his quarterback problem. The Browns tried three different quarterbacks: Tom O'Connell, Babe Parilli, and George Ratterman. O'Connell would finish after Parilli and Ratterman were injured in the first half of the disastrous season when the Browns went 1–4. Ratterman had come to the Browns as a free agent in 1952 and was an excellent backup to Otto Graham. His injury ended his career. O'Connell had played briefly for the Chicago Bears and would give the Browns a modest 4–3 finish the rest of the way. The Brown's 5–7 record gave them their first losing season. It is hard to imagine what the locker room must have been like during a losing season with Paul Brown. Although the 1956 season was an abomination for the Browns, it would not set a trend.

Johnny Unitas

In the annals of sports there are many stories about the "one who got away"— the great player who for any number of reasons did not get picked up by teams that had the early chance. Johnny Unitas was "one who got away" for several NFL teams.

Following his release by the Pittsburgh Steelers after the 1955 training camp, Johnny Unitas asked Paul Brown for a tryout. The coach told Unitas to see him at training camp 1956. Unitas tried out and signed with the Colts under Brown's former assistant coach, Weeb Ewbank, so there was no need for that preseason tryout.[50] Unitas would have given Brown another Hall of Fame quarterback to lead his team for a long time. Unitas would go on to have an extraordinary 17-year career.

But the Browns' disastrous season gave them a high draft choice—number seven. Brown found that Syracuse running back Jim Brown was inexplicably available when it was his pick in the first round. He snatched Brown and picked quarterback Milt Plum in round two.

1957 Season

Paul Brown had not solved the long-term problem of obtaining a franchise quarterback in the 1957 season. Tommy O'Connell and Milt Plum were the quarterbacks for the Browns that year. Both would play well in their careers, but they were no long term replacement for Otto Graham. Jim Brown's Rookie of the Year and leading rusher performance helped Cleveland win the NFL East Division.

Jim Brown would go on to play for the Browns from 1957 through 1965 all at the highest level— retiring when he was still on top of his game. Brown would rush for over 1,000 yards every year except for his first in 1957 and in 1962. He was also a good receiver and his combined yards tallied 2,131 yards in 1963. He was inducted into the Hall of Fame in 1971.

1957 NFL Championship Game

Going into the championship game, both the Lions and the Browns had their issues. The Lions had a new coach, George Wilson, who found himself in the league championship game in his first season. Detroit's veteran quarterback, Bobby Layne, who had led the Lions to back-to-back championships in 1952 and 1953, was out with a broken leg. Backup quarterback Tobin Rote had finished the season off and would start for the Lions. The Browns had their share of problems as well. A few days before the championship game, Milt Plum injured his hamstring as he was leaving the practice field.[51] Brown's other quarterback, Tommy O'Connell, had played well that year with a 93.3 rating, but he had been out since December 1 with a severely sprained ankle and a hairline fracture of the fibula.[52]

O'Connell was rusty and he played poorly. Detroit jumped ahead, 17–0, in the first quarter after taking advantage of two turnovers. Jim Brown ran for a 29-yard touchdown run in the early going of the second quarter, but Rote struck back with a 26-yard touchdown pass to Steve Junker. Terry Barr intercepted an O'Connell pass for a pick six. The half ended with the Lions on top, 31–7.

O'Connell was replaced by the injured Plum right before the half. The Browns got rolling early in the second half with an 80-yard touchdown drive that ended with a 5-yard Carpenter rush for a score. The Lions responded with one of their own featuring just one play—a 78-yard pass play from Rote to Jim Doran. The Lions didn't stop there, Rote would toss three more touchdown passes before the day ended. The Browns would cough the ball up six times: four interceptions and two lost fumbles.[53] When the Lions got turnovers, they made the most of them. When the Browns snagged a Lions' fumble back towards their own goal, it was followed by an interception that was run back for a Lions' score. When the Lions tried a fake field goal, they scored. When the Browns tried a halfback pass, it was intercepted. The Browns were mauled by the Lions, 59–14.

1958 Season

In 1958, Jim Brown had 257 rushes for 1,527 yards and 17 touchdowns. He also had 16 receptions for 138 yards for a total of 1,665 yards from scrimmage. Jim Brown's stellar performance would not be enough for Cleveland. The New York Giants would beat the Browns three times to capture the Eastern Conference. The Giants had a tremendous coaching staff. The Giants' head coach was Jim Lee Howell with Tom Landry as defensive coordinator and Vince Lombardi as offensive coordinator.

After beating the Browns in two regular season games, the Giants and Browns tied for the season, requiring a one game playoff to determine the Eastern Conference Championship. The Giants beat the Browns, 10–0, holding Jim Brown to 8 yards rushing for the entire game. Brown had a 20-yard gain, but had lost yardage on other plays giving him a net 8 yards rushing. According to Giants' linebacker Sam Huff, he had hit Jim Brown "the hardest that I ever hit anyone" in that game.[54]   The Giants would go on to lose to the Baltimore Colts on December 28, 1958, in a back and forth battle in the NFL League Championship game in Yankee Stadium that has been called the Greatest Game Ever Played.

1959 Season

The Browns were 7–5 in 1959. They still did not have their franchise quarterback, their defense was on the decline, and other teams could focus on Jim Brown. Late in the season, they would also lose to the 49ers and Pittsburgh by one point and then get clobbered once again by the Giants 48–7.   In the game against the Giants, Jim Brown was kicked in the head on the first play from scrimmage and was held out for the first half. When he got back in the game in the second half, it was not going to change the outcome. With a little less than two minutes to go in the game, Giants' fans stormed onto the field and took down one of the goal posts. The Browns were forced to run through the mob to get to the locker room. Giants' officials finally restored order by threatening a forfeit. Twenty minutes later, the Browns returned to the field and killed the final minutes of the game. When Brown was questioned if he had considered asking for a Giants' forfeit for the melee during the game, he said, "We didn't even belong on the same field with them today."[55]

The game against the Giants was one of the low points in Paul Brown's long career.   But in sports it is often the low points that say more about a person's character than the highs. In his own words:

A victory at any price had no value for me, nor did I put down our team if we played well and lost.[56]

1960 Season

The Browns could play with any team in the league in 1960, but they did not win consistently enough to make it to the championship game. They split with the Giants, the Eagles, and the Steelers. They beat the Cardinals once and then tied them in their second meeting.

There were some high points. Quarterback Milt Plum notched a 110.4 quarterback rating. He completed 151 passes on 250 attempts for a 60.4% completion rate. He had passed for 21 touchdowns with only five interceptions. Jim Brown was the league rushing leader with 1,257 yards and 9 TDs. Teammate Bobby Mitchell rushed for 506 yards and 5 TDs.

The Browns finished in second place in the Eastern Conference to the Philadelphia Eagles with an 8–3–1 record. Paul Brown had lost some aging veterans to retirement including place kicker and tackle Lou Groza who would return in 1961 as a place kicker only. The Browns would lose other players to the Dallas Cowboys in the expansion draft. Brown was looking forward to the coming year with his new invigorated team.[57]

1961 Season

For the 1961 season, the Browns went 8–5–1 and failed to qualify for the postseason. The Browns lost to the Eagles 27–20, to Green Bay 49–17, to the Pittsburgh Steelers 17–13, to the New York Giants 37–21, and to the Chicago Bears 17–14. They ended the season by tying with the Giants.

The Browns' offense was led by Hall of Fame running back Jim Brown who rushed for 1,408 yards to lead the NFL for the fifth consecutive time. Bobby Mitchell had 548 yards rushing. Quarterback Milt Plum threw for 18 touchdowns with 10 interceptions for a 90.3 passing rating. Receiver Ray Renfro had 48 receptions for 834 yards and 6 TDs.

Len Dawson: Another One that Got Away

In 1957, Len Dawson broke into the NFL, but sputtered in Pittsburgh for the Steelers. He was picked up by the Browns. Paul Brown and others did not think Dawson had a strong enough arm and used him sparingly. In his first 5 years in the pros, he started only 2 games. But in 1962, Dawson would head over to the American Football League, playing for Lamar Hunt's Dallas Texans franchise that would become the Kansas City Chiefs the following year. In Dallas and Kansas City, Dawson would play for the stout, dapper, and animated Hall of Fame coach, Hank Stram. In Stram, Dawson would find a believer. Stram featured the play-action pass that suited Dawson's ability to throw accurately while on the move. And Dawson would keep moving in professional football until 1975. Dawson would play in two Super Bowls with the Chiefs. He and the Chiefs would lose Super Bowl I to the Green Bay Packers in January 1967 by a score of 35–10 and then beat the Minnesota Vikings in Super Bowl IV in January 1970 by a score of 23–7. Dawson would be Super Bowl IV MVP.

1962 Season

Paul Brown wanted to develop a second big back who could compliment Jim Brown. Perhaps to emulate the Green Bay Packers rushing tandem of Jim Taylor and Paul Hornung that had run over Cleveland in 1961. With two big backs in the same backfield, it would make it more difficult for teams to key on Brown and it might also make a championship run more likely without a Graham-caliber quarterback. Brown had been limited to 69 yards rushing in the 1957 NFL Championship game against the Lions and he was held to just 8 yards in the 1958 conference match against the Giants.

The Browns' season was punctuated by tragedy. Paul Brown had his sights set on Ernie Davis, to play the second big back who might make it more difficult for teams to key on Jim Brown. Davis broke many of Jim Brown's rushing records at Syracuse. Davis was by all accounts a stand up young man who was the first African American to win the Heisman Trophy. Davis would be available in the draft, but was expected to be taken earlier than the Browns' picks.

Acquiring the larger back Ernie Davis would make the Browns' second running back, Bobby Mitchell, expendable. Meanwhile, Washington Redskins' owner George Preston Marshall was late to "break the color barrier" that had existed for a 13 year period from 1933-1946. Secretary of the Interior Stewart Udall wrote to Marshall noting that his stadium was built on public land and threatened to create problems if such discrimination continued. Marshall liked the Browns' second running back Bobby Mitchell who was a smaller back and known as someone who would likely handle the stress and celebrity of breaking into the Redskins' all-white lineup. A deal was worked out with the Redskins to pick Davis and then trade him to the Browns for one of their first round picks and Bobby Mitchell.

The deal was consummated, but before Davis could even run a down for Cleveland, he was diagnosed with leukemia. Brown's plan to create the dynamic running tandem of Jim Brown and Ernie Davis never materialized. The Browns finished just 7–6–1.

Wisdom Amidst the Criticism

When the Browns fell from the top echelon in football and ownership changed, criticism increased. The coach's penchant for tough criticism of players and his rigid authority did not suit everyone. His string of championships set expectations so high in Cleveland that no coach could have lived up to them.

Early in the 1962 season, when Brown was responding to criticism when being interviewed for a *Sports Illustrated* article, he said, "They ding you all the time. They don't understand and I don't have time to explain the details to them."[58] Brown would go on to talk about the talents that are needed by a modern quarterback at the time. According to Brown, a quarterback has to be able to "throw long or short, pick up late-opening receivers, and run."[59]

Brown Dealt with Weaknesses

Brown kept working out player personnel moves that would help resolve the team's deficiencies. Brown would later write that quarterback Milt Plum had his limitations and that Brown carefully choreographed plays that would help Plum succeed to the best of his abilities. Brown was criticized for how he handled Plum who was traded to Detroit where he played from 1962-1967, from age 27-32. Under Brown's system, Plum would have an average quarterback rating of 90.3 and while at Detroit, his average rating would be 53.15.[60]

Criticism can extend beyond the bounds of reason. The Ernie Davis trade that sent Hall of Famer Bobby Mitchell to Washington was also a source of continued criticism. Mitchell was a gifted runner and an excellent receiver, even if he was too light to run between the tackles. In Washington, Mitchell would stand out on a team without the Browns' cast of stars. He would develop into a flanker and with two huge years to start, his receptions would average out over 1,000 yards per season in his next 6 years. Those numbers would not likely be ignored by critics.

But the Browns' offensive limitations that kept them from winning championships were real with a team led by running back Jim Brown rather than the all-purpose quarterback Otto Graham who seemingly had no weaknesses for opposing teams on which to concentrate. Tex Maule summarized the 1961 offensive dilemma for the Browns when they played archrival New York Giants: "Ignoring Mitchell's faking inside and conceding the deep receivers (because of Plum's limitation with the long ball), the Giants knew that the area they had to cover was radically decreased."[61] In other words, the Giants could focus on Jim Brown.

Plum was replaced by two quarterbacks, Jim Ninowski and Frank Ryan. Jim Ninowski, who returned to the Browns from the Lions, was a good backup quarterback. He would have a long career in that capacity. For the 3 years in which he had over 100 pass attempts, 1960-1962, his QB rating would average 53.5.[62]

Ryan was acquired by trade from the Los Angeles Rams. He and Ninowski shared quarterback duties in 1962. Ninowski would start most of the games in the first half of the season and about midway, Ryan took over. After Ryan's year of split duty with Ninowski, he would be the Browns' starting quarterback for the following 6 years in which he would post a QB rating of 88.6 on average. Ryan may not have been an exact duplicate of Otto Graham, but he was a credible replacement for him. Brown would not be around to get credit for Ryan's contributions to Cleveland.

The Cleveland record under Paul Brown after the retirement of Otto Graham was 53–30–3. Only the Giants in the NFL East Division had a better record for the period 1956-1962. Yet, Brown was fired after the 1962 season. The fallout from the Brown firing was somewhat abated by a newspaper strike that affected the media coverage.

Cincinnati Bengals

After his firing, Paul Brown and his family spent time away from Cleveland. Although his contract settlement that provided a continuing salary required some scouting-reporting related work, Paul could live most anywhere and still manage his responsibilities. The Browns initially traveled extensively and then they settled down in LaJolla, California in a home by the ocean where Paul and his wife found solace in new friends and athletic activities. Yet, Brown was not ready to quit the game just yet. He longed to be coaching again, but in a place where he could control every aspect of a team. He did not express it in his biography, but perhaps Brown wanted to prove more than anything else that he was a winner, not just in the 30s, the 40s, the 50s, but at any time.

While in retirement, Paul Brown was contacted by several teams who seemed interested in a new coach. Some had sincere interests, others did not. None of them worked out. It occurred to the Brown family that it might be possible to obtain a new football franchise. Brown's son Mike had worked up a study to determine the best franchise location and found that Cincinnati had plenty to offer. Atlanta had been recently added as the fifteenth NFL franchise and one more was planned.

Brown talked about his interest in an NFL franchise with William Hackett, an old friend who had played at Ohio State for Brown. Hackett was a veterinarian who had wealthy influential acquaintances. Hackett started a chain of events that brought Brown into company with people who could partner with him to buy a new professional football franchise in Cincinnati. Chief among these contacts was John Sawyer, President of Orelton Farms and son of Charles Sawyer who had been Truman's Secretary of Commerce. Brown had also contracted NFL Commissioner Pete Rozelle who was willing to support Brown to NFL owners. Another connection that Brown and Hackett sought out successfully was Ohio Governor James Rhodes. With this powerful group behind them, a Cincinnati franchise was front and center. At the same time, Rozelle and others were trying to create a relationship between the NFL and the competing AFL. Unlike the old AAFC, the AFL was a stronger league that had more resources due to a television contract.

In order to achieve a merger, Congressional approval was required and such approval seemed within reach with the support of Louisiana Senator Russell Long and Louisiana Representative Hale Boggs. The logical move for the NFL was to provide the franchise to New Orleans, which had been in the running along with Cincinnati and a few other cities. The awarding of the franchise to Louisiana was made and the legislation was passed. Brown's group lost out, but only temporarily.

Fortunately for Brown and his group, the merger of the NFL-AFL into one league to be completed in 1970 made an AFL franchise much more attractive. Although Brown and his group originally had an NFL team in mind, they began efforts at getting an AFL franchise. One huge hurdle stood in the way— Brown's group needed a stadium that could support the NFL seating capacity requirements. A new stadium would need to be built.

A public stadium could be built in Cincinnati, but it had to be a new dual-purpose public stadium. Everything seemed to hinge on getting Bill DeWitt owner of the Cincinnati Reds to sign on to the stadium plan. DeWitt had been associated with a number of different major league teams in his long career. His Reds were using the venerable Crosley Field, which was beloved and the home of the Reds for 58 years although the seating capacity was under 30,000. DeWitt was in a quandary. On the one hand, he faced the wrath of all of Cincinnati if he did not agree to a new stadium, but on the other hand, he did not believe a dual purpose stadium was in the interest of his organization and team. Rather than doing something he was opposed to do or keeping Cincinnati from getting its new team, he took a third path and sold the Reds to a group of investors who included some of the future owners of the Cincinnati football franchise.

Things got a little more complicated with a second Cincinnati group looking to compete for the AFL franchise. Even more troubling, were the "franchise" terms including TV revenues offered by the AFL for the expansion team. Essentially, the AFL teams would be allowed to protect many more players than the previous AFL expansion in Miami and no TV revenue would be forthcoming for the first 2 years. Brown complained, but he was told to take it or leave it. He swallowed hard and accepted the conditions. A new AFL Cincinnati franchise was approved and it began operating in 1968—it would be merged with the rest of the AFL into the new expanded NFL in 1970.

Brown Establishes the Bengals

Brown found a spot for his training camp in small Wilmington College. He hired Tom Bass, Bill Johnson, Rick Forzano, Bill Walsh, and Jack Donaldson. The expansion draft that gave Brown 40 players only yielded about 17 players that Brown kept. The existing AFL Teams did not want to give Brown much of anything that year because they would be merging into the NFL in 2 years. The Bengals would need to develop from the regular college draft. The college draft picks allocated to the Bengals were more generous and 19 college players made the Browns' 1968 roster.[63]

Brown's Players in Cincinnati

Although the expansion draft would be a disappointment to Brown, the Bengals started building a quality roster with good results from the regular college draft. The first Bengals' draft would include some significant players. Three that contributed from the start were Paul "Robbie" Robinson, Essex Johnson, and Bob Johnson. Others followed soon thereafter.

Bill Bergey

The Bengals snatched up an outstanding defensive player in linebacker Bill Bergey in the second round of the 1969 draft. Bergey would play 12 very intense seasons in the pros, the first five with the Bengals.

Bob Johnson

Bob Johnson, a 6-foot-5, 262 pound center from Tennessee, was Brown's first draft pick for the new Cincinnati Bengals football team. Johnson would captain the team and play for Cincinnati for 12 years.

Bob Trumpy

Bob Trumpy, a solid tight end who would one day be a sportscaster, TV analyst, and radio show host, would also join the team in its first year. Trumpy would play for 10 seasons for the Bengals.

Charles "Boobie" Clark

Acquired in the 12th round of the 1973 draft, fullback Boobie Clark was 6-foot-2, and 245 pounds and would play for six seasons in Cincinnati. He would lead the team in rushing in 1975 and 1976.

Essex Johnson

Essex Johnson was another draft choice from the Bengals inaugural 1968 draft. Johnson would return kickoffs and punts his first few years, but his contributions grew in the following seasons when he would become one of the leading running backs on the team. He also contributed as a receiver.

Isaac Curtis

A gifted wide receiver who was drafted in the first round in 1973. Curtis haunted opposing defenses with his finesse and speed. He was targeted with heavy physical coverage throughout his entire pass routes in an attempt to neutralize his play.

Jess Phillips

Running back Jess Phillips, a former Michigan State player who had been serving time for passing bad checks, got a second chance at life and was paroled from prison to play for the Bengals. He would play five seasons for the Bengals.

Ken Anderson

In 1971, the Bengals picked up quarterback Ken Anderson in the third round of the draft. Anderson would be the starting quarterback for 13 of 16 seasons.

Ken Riley

Ken Riley was a mainstay on the Bengals' defense for 15 seasons. He was drafted in 1969 and played cornerback.

Paul Robbie Robinson

Paul Robinson was a running back drafted prior to the inaugural Cincinnati season. Robinson would play for just over four seasons for the Bengals, but he would start out very strong with a 1,000 plus season in 1968.

Bengals' Inaugural Season: 1968

The Bengals played their first and second seasons in Nippert Stadium, home to the University of Cincinnati, while the new Riverfront Stadium was being built. The Bengals scored 215 points and allowed 329. Cincinnati would end the season with 3 wins and 11 losses, but Paul Brown would express satisfaction with his team's progress. According to the coach, this team of young players would have to be developed slowly. Their three wins were against the Broncos, Bills, and the Dolphins.

1969 Season

In 1969, the Bengals drafted a local, University of Cincinnati quarterback Greg Cook, who reminded Brown in some ways of Otto Graham.

The Bengals would finish 4–9–1, but the season was highlighted by the excellent play of Greg Cook. Cook was a very accurate long ball thrower who averaged an incredible 17.5 yards per pass completion. He completed 106 passes on 197 attempts for a 53.8% completion rate scoring 15 touchdowns with 11 interceptions. Tragically, Cook's injury or subsequent injuries resulting from the first injury in game three, proved to be career ending. Just what Walsh and Cook could have accomplished for the Cincinnati Bengals had the injury never occurred is one of those questions that many fans and analysts have asked themselves over the past 40 years.

Another young Bengal, Bob Trumpy, would make an unexpected contribution to the Bengals. Bill Walsh, who was an assistant coach when Trumpy played with the Bengals, remembered a particular play. During a game against Oakland, Trumpy positioned himself on the wrong side of the line, but discovering his mistake, moved to other side before the ball was snapped. Bill Johnson, the Cincinnati offensive line coach, ran the play over and over again on film and suggested that maybe there was something that could be done with this move. It would become the "end in motion."[64]

1970 Season

In 1970, the Bengals would play for the first time as a member of the National Football League. They would also play in the new Riverfront Stadium. They would win their first game in their new home and they would make their first playoff appearance there as well. For the season, the Bengals won one, lost six, and then won seven for an 8–6 record. With Cook sidelined with his injury, Brown would have to find that elusive franchise quarterback another year. Virgil Carter started 11 games and Sam Wyche started 3 games. Walsh worked extensively with Virgil Carter to make the maximum use of his talents using essentially the precursor to what would be called the West Coast Offense. Paul Brown would give Carter high marks for his performance especially in the last game of the season when he played injured, but managed to lead the Bengals past the Patriots 45–7. The Bengals were first in the AFC Central. In the franchise's first playoff game, they were beaten by the Baltimore Colts and Johnny Unitas, 17–0, in a divisional playoff game.

1971-1975 Seasons

In 1971, the Bengals picked up quarterback Ken Anderson in the third round of the draft. Anderson would play for the Bengals for 16 seasons, 13 of those as the team's starter. He was a 4-year pro bowler and MVP in 1981. Anderson was Brown's kind of QB—he ran a 4.7 in the 40-yard dash, he could throw the ball 70 yards, and he was highly intelligent. However, Anderson came from small Augustana College. Schools like Augustana did not have programs that mirrored pro football the way larger schools did. More work was required to acclimate players from smaller programs, but Bill Walsh was willing to spend the time needed to developing Anderson's skills so he could perform well as a pro quarterback.

Anderson would not make an immediate impact. The 1971 season was an embarrassment. After a season opening win, Cincinnati went into a seven game skid before they finally won another game. They ended the season at 4–10. In 1972, the Bengals finished with a respectable 8–6 finish, but they lost two games that year to the Cleveland Browns, which could not have made Brown happy. The 1973 season would be a different story altogether.

In 1973, the Bengals drafted Charles "Boobie" Clark and Isaac Curtis. Clark would be converted from tight end to fullback. Curtis was a quiet unassuming track star in college who was blazing fast and had soft hands as a receiver. The Bengals finished first in the AFC Central Division with a 10–4 record and went on to play Miami in a divisional playoff game. Miami won 34–16. The Bengals' leading rusher, Essex Johnson, was injured early in the game and the Dolphins neutralized Isaac Curtis by double-teaming him—blocking and shoving him around right from the line of scrimmage well into his pass patterns. Brown made a case in the offseason that the NFL rules needed to change to allow talented receivers like Curtis to play their game. Brown's input resulted in the rule that made contact with a receiver illegal after five yards. More rule changes would follow that would help promote the passing game to what it is today.

Brown would also find himself immersed into some of the more unpleasant aspects of managing a football team. The newest football organization, the World Football League, would start to seek out NFL players. The WFL claimed rights to NFL players in a draft they devised and the Washington Ambassadors contracted Bill Bergey, the great Bengal linebacker. Bergey signed a "future" contract with the Ambassadors that would call for his services once his existing contract with the Bengals expired. Brown and others questioned the ability of a player with such a future relationship to effectively perform his current contract and pursued the case in court. The WFL prevailed in court. The NFL Players Association would also be very active during this period.

In 1974, although the Bengals would defeat the Cleveland Browns in both their games that season, they ended with a disappointing 7–7 year. In 1975, the Bengals' record would improve to 11–3, for second in the AFC Central and good enough for a wildcard spot in the playoffs. The Raiders beat up on the Bengals to take a 24–7 lead in the third quarter. But the Bengals would come back and just miss catching the Raiders in a 31–28 squeaker. It was as close as Brown would come to another league championship as a coach.

Brown Focuses on Front Office

Brown retired from coaching after the 1975 season, but maintained a leading role in the Cincinnati Bengals' front office as part owner, vice president, and general manager. Bill "Tiger" Johnson took over as the Bengals' coach for 2 years, 1976-1977, and then the first five games of 1978. He compiled an 18–15 record. Johnson had played center for the San Francisco 49ers and was nicknamed "Tiger" for his tenacity on the field. Homer Rice finished the 1978 season and returned for 1979, attaining an 8–19 record. For 1980-1983, Forrest Gregg took over in the mold of Paul Brown, a no nonsense, command and control coach. In 1981, Gregg's second year in Cincinnati, the Bengals won the AFC Central and then knocked off the Bills in their first playoff game, 28–21. They had little problem beating the San Diego Chargers in the AFC Championship game, 27–7.

Super Bowl XVI

The Bengals' opponent was the San Francisco 49ers in Super Bowl XVI. Former Cincinnati coach and Brown protégé, Bill Walsh, had taken over the 49ers in 1979. In 1981, Walsh had a contender with "Joe Cool" Montana under center. Gregg's Bengals made it interesting. Behind 20–0 at the half, Ken Anderson led the Bengals back with two touchdown drives. A 49ers' goal line stand in the third quarter froze the Bengals' momentum and San Francisco created some distance with two field goals. The Bengals put one last drive together in the waning minutes of the game to close in, 26–21, but they could not recover an onside kick for one last chance.

In 1982, a strike shortened 7–2 record was good enough to earn a playoff spot for the Bengals, but they were knocked off in the first round by the New York Jets. In 1983, the Bengals battled back from a very poor start to garner a 7–9 record, but after the season, Forrest Gregg left Cincinnati to coach his old team, the Green Bay Packers.

Brown turned next to Sam Wyche who would serve as head coach for the 1984 through 1991 seasons. Wyche was a good fit with Brown and was an excellent intelligent coach similar to Brown in some ways, but with a bit of a free-spirit personality. Wyche would post a 61–66 record with Cincinnati.

Under Wyche, the Bengals posted a 12–4 record in the 1988 regular season and won the AFC Championship by beating Buffalo, 21–10. They faced the 49ers in Super Bowl XXIII—certainly one of the most memorable championships in NFL history. Neither offense scored a touchdown in the first three quarters of play. Both teams had matched each other with two field goals apiece. Stanford Jennings scored the game's first touchdown when he ran back a 49ers kickoff for 93 yards, giving the Bengals a 13–6 lead. In the fourth quarter, Joe Montana led a four play, 85-yard drive, that ended with a Jerry Rice touchdown grab to tie the game at 13–13. The Bengals countered with a 40-yard field goal to set the 49ers back on their ear chasing a 16–13 Cincinnati lead. The clock was down to 3:10 when Montana stood on his 8-yard line. Montana artfully moved the 49ers down the field and tossed the winning score to John Taylor with just 34 seconds to spare. The 49ers won, 20–16.

In 1989, the Bengals had a difficult post-Super Bowl season and fell back to an 8–8 record. But in 1990, they snapped back into shape with a 9–7 finish that was followed with a divisional playoff game in which the Los Angeles Raiders beat them, 20–10.[65] Paul Brown's health deteriorated after the 1990 season and a few different maladies kept him from the camp. He died just as the preseason was getting underway on August 5, 1991.

Brown's Contributions to the Game

As Cleveland Browns' head coach, Brown achieved 167–53–8 record including playoff games. His teams won four AAFC titles and three NFL crowns while competing in ten consecutive championship games. Brown had only one losing season at Cleveland in 17 years. In Cincinnati where Brown started up the Bengals under a highly restrictive expansion draft, his record was 55–56–1 including playoff games. Under Brown, Cincinnati would go to the playoffs in 1970 when they were first in the AFC Central Division in only their third year. They would be back in 1973 and in Brown's last season in 1975.

Most everything Paul Brown did in football was done in Ohio, but his impact has been felt throughout the country. He coached high school in the

1930s, college in the early 40s, a military team during the war, and after the war he coached the pros until the mid-70s. At each level, he was successful, innovative, and demanding. He is the only professional football coach to have a team named after him—the Cleveland Browns. He would be the inaugural coach of both the Browns and the Cincinnati Bengals where he would also serve as general manager.

Brown's coaching approach was developed at the high school level. Brown wanted his players to be thinking Spartans. He did not like hype, but he wanted the desire to win to be viscerally felt—like the "hungry she-lion." He would teach and promote discipline and dedication to becoming stronger, faster, quicker, leaner, and tougher. He demanded that his players be smart when they played and studious about football. As players developed their strengths and skills, they would be drilled to deliver near perfect execution as members of a team. Brown began with player development and ended with a team that was often better conditioned, faster, hungrier, smarter, and more driven than his competition. Brown and his staff focused energy on individual skills and small groups of position players that he wanted to become parts into the whole. Everything the team did was orchestrated to perfection and organized to the last detail.

For his part, Brown would not waste his players' time. He and his staff planned and executed every practice with precision. He did not want his players practicing too many hours and he did want his staff to be up all night either. He not only promoted his ways, but he worked to eliminate bad habits and practices from his players. In the pros, players who did not fit his program were eliminated from it. He saw to every detail. He made sure that his program's funds were spent wisely. Players and their families were educated on his expectations. Those in the school and community understood his program and were invited to become part of it. Brown's football teams were more than a group that got together for a sporting activity; they were part of a movement, a passion, a direction, and an identity. They were not just a part of the community; they were seared into every fabric of it. In this way, Brown elevated football and his supreme confidence and organization skills allowed him to do the same wherever he went at whatever level. Brown would be the same man in the college game and in the professional game. Some would come to say that his system was old-fashioned and out of date. But those who followed Brown into the modern game with much of the same approach, like Bill Belichick, have proven those critics wrong. There are different ways to manage and lead a football team to success; Brown's highly organized, highly disciplined method was used with astonishing results.

In professional football, Brown sequestered players in a hotel before all games—including home games. He timed players on the 40-yard dash because he thought it more indicative of how long a player might run at full speed during a game. He gave his players intelligence and personality tests to

153

Paul Brown Signing Autographs

help develop the best methods for training each individual. He used complete film clip statistical studies and graded his own players based on them.

Brown was inducted into the National Football League's Hall of Fame in 1967. Paul Brown Tiger Stadium was renamed in his honor in 1976. The home of the Cincinnati Bengals, which opened in 2000, was named Paul Brown Stadium in honor of the coach. At Miami University where Brown played, he is honored with a statue, the ninth one in the "Cradle of Coaches" Plaza that memorializes highly successful coaches with Miami roots. Brown was named Sporting News NFL Coach of the Year for 1951 and 1953. He was named UPI NFL Coach of the Year for 1957, UPI AFL for 1969 and 1970.[66] Coaches who worked with Brown were highly recruited and successful.

One testament to Paul Brown's legacy is especially remarkable. Although it is most visible in the professional rank, Brown's influence continues today in football programs at every level.

Paul Brown Timeline

1908

- September 7, 1908, Paul Brown is born in Norwalk, Ohio.

1922

- Brown attends Washington High School in Massillon.

1924

- Brown becomes starting quarterback in his junior year, playing for Coach Dave Stewart.

1926

- Brown enrolls at Ohio State, but he is told that he is too small to play football.

1927

- Brown transfers to Miami University of Ohio.

1928-1929

- Brown plays quarterback for Coach Chester Pittser.

1930

- Brown teaches and coaches at Severn Prep in Maryland.

1932

- Brown returns to teach and coach at Washington High School in Massillon.

1938

- WPA funds are used to build a new 16,600 seat stadium that serves Brown's Washington High School programs and supports school improvements.

1940

- Brown's program at Washington High School amasses a record of 80–8–2, which is good for six consecutive state championships and builds Brown's reputation throughout the state as one of its greatest coaches.

1941

- January 14, 1941, Paul Brown is named head football coach at Ohio State University.

1942

- Brown's Ohio State team is the National Champion based on its number one ranking in the final AP Poll.

1944

- Brown joins the Navy and receives a commission as a Lieutenant assigned to the Great Lakes Naval Station. He is the head coach of the football team.

1946

- Brown begins his professional coaching career with the Cleveland Browns in the new eight-team All-America Football Conference.
- December 22, 1946, the Browns defeat the New York Yankees, 14-9, to win their first AAFC title.

1947

- December 14, 1947, the Browns defeat the New York Yankees, 14-3, to win their second AAFC title.

1948

- December 19, 1948, the Browns defeat the Bills, 49-7, to win their third AAFC title.

1949

- December 11, 1949, the Browns defeat the 49ers, 21-7, to win their fourth AAFC title.
- The AAFC league folds and the Browns, 49ers, and Colts are absorbed into the NFL for the 1950 season.

1950

- December 17, 1950, the Cleveland Browns defeat the New York Giants, 8–3, to win the American Conference of the NFL.
- December 24, 1950, the Cleveland Browns defeat the Los Angeles Rams, 30–28, to win the NFL Championship.

1951

- December 23, 1951, the Los Angeles Rams defeat the Cleveland Browns, 24–17, to win the NFL Championship. It is the first time Brown's team has not won a league championship since the Browns were formed in 1946.

1952

- December 28, 1952, the Detroit Lions defeat the Cleveland Browns, 17–7, to win the NFL Championship.

1953

- December 27, 1953, the Detroit Lions defeat the Cleveland Browns, 17–16, to win the NFL Championship. It's the second year in a row that the Browns lose the championship game to the Lions.

1954

- December 26, 1954, the Cleveland Browns defeat the Detroit Lions, 56–10, to win the NFL Championship.

1955

- December 26, 1955, the Cleveland Browns defeat the Los Angeles Rams, 38–14, to win the NFL Championship.

1957

- December 28, 1957, the Detroit Lions defeat the Cleveland Browns, 59–14, to win the NFL Championship.
- Cleveland's Jim Brown is Rookie of the Year.

1958

- December 21, 1958, the New York Giants defeat the Cleveland Browns, 10–0, to win the Eastern Conference Championship.

1962

- Paul Brown is fired after the 1962 season.

1968

- Brown starts up a new AFL Cincinnati Bengals franchise in 1968.
- The Cincinnati Bengals end their first season with a 3–11 record .

1970

- Brown's Bengals and other AFL teams merge into the expanded NFL in 1970.
- Brown's assistant coach, Bill Walsh, refines an offensive system that "spreads the field" horizontally and makes extensive use of short passes—a precursor to the West Coast Offense.

1976

- January 1, 1976, Paul Brown retires from coaching, but maintains a leading role in the Cincinnati Bengals' front office as part owner, vice president, and general manager.

1982

- January 10, 1982, Coach Forrest Gregg's 1981 Cincinnati Bengals defeat the San Diego Chargers, 27-7, to win the AFC Championship.
- January 24, 1982, the 1981 San Francisco 49ers defeat the Cincinnati Bengals, 26–21, to win Super Bowl XVI.

1989

- January 8, 1989, Coach San Wyche's 1988 Bengals defeat the Buffalo Bills, 21-10, to win the AFC Championship.
- January 22, 1989, the San Francisco 49ers defeat Coach San Wyche's 1988 Bengals, 20-16, to win Super Bowl XXIII.

1991

- August 5, 1991, Paul Brown dies at age 82.

Highlights

Brown's Cleveland teams won four AAFC titles and three NFL crowns while competing in ten consecutive championship games. Brown had only one losing season at Cleveland in 17 years. In Cincinnati where Brown started up the Bengals under a highly restrictive expansion draft, his team was atop the AFC Central Division in its third year. The Bengals were atop their division in 1973 and in Brown's last season in 1975. Brown holds an overall NFL/AAFC head coaching record of 222–112–9.

The only coach to have an NFL team named after him, Brown was inducted into the Pro Football Hall of Fame in 1967. Masillon's Tiger Stadium was renamed Paul Brown Tiger Stadium in honor of the coach in 1976. The home of the Cincinnati Bengals, which opened in 2000, was also named Paul Brown Stadium. At Miami University where Brown played, he is honored with a statue, the ninth one in the "Cradle of Coaches" Plaza that honors the highly successful coaches with Miami roots. Brown was named Sporting News NFL Coach of the Year for 1951 and 1953. He was named UPI NFL Coach of the Year for 1957; UPI AFL Coach of the Year for 1969 and 1970.

Endnotes

1 Paul Brown with Jack Clary, *PB: The Paul Brown Story* (New York: Atheneum, 1979), 14.

2 For a concise discussion on Brown's innovations and program see Jack Clary, "Paul Brown," *The Coffin Corner*, Vol. 14. No. 1, 1992, viewed at http://www.profootballresearchers.org/coffin_corner/14-01-446.pdf on August 21, 2013.

3 The Northern Ohio Data and Information Service (NODIS) of the Maxine Goodman Levin College of Urban Affairs, Cleveland State University. http://urban.csuohio.edu/nodis/historic/pop_place19002000.pdf

4 The Northern Ohio Data and Information Service information at: http://urban.csuohio.edu/nodis/historic/pop_place19002000.pdf

5 Brown with Clary, *PB: The Paul Brown Story*, 31.

6 "Men of Bronze," *Miamian* Feature Story viewed at http://www.miamialum.org/s/916/interior-3-col.aspx?sid=916&gid=1&pgid=4987&cid=9627&ecid=9627&crid=0&calpgid=4983&calcid=9622 on January 6, 2014. .

7 Brown with Clary, *PB: The Paul Brown Story*, 39.

8 Brown with Clary, *PB: The Paul Brown Story*, 43.

9 Brown with Clary, *PB: The Paul Brown Story*, 45.

10 For list of National Champions see http://www.hsfdatabase.com/nationalchampions.htm. For Massillon high school stats sheet on Brown, see http://massillontigers.com/past_coaches/coach_brown.pdf.

11 Andrew O'Toole, *Paul Brown: The Rise and Fall and Rise Again of Football's Most Innovative Coach* (Cincinnati, Clerisy Press, 2008) 46-49.

12 Steve White, *One Game Season: 92 Games of College Football's Greatest Rivalry Ohio State Versus Michigan* (Collegeville, MN: One Game Season, 1995) 133.

13 Western Conference was the common name at that time that was precursor to the Big Ten—the official name given the Conference in 1987. At times the Big Ten would also be referred to as the Big Nine.

14 Jack L. Park, *The Ohio State Football Encyclopedia*, National Championship Edition (Champaign, IL., Sports Publishing LLC, 2003), 192.

15 The AP Poll rankings were made at the time at the end of the regular season. In 1968, the final AP Poll would be made after the bowl games. Ohio State did not play a bowl game in 1942. The University of George defeated UCLA in the Rose Bowl in 1942. Some suggest that Georgia should be the National Champion that year.

16 Brown with Clary, *PB: The Paul Brown Story*, 101.

17 Brown with Clary, *PB: The Paul Brown Story*, 116.

18 Brown with Clary, *PB: The Paul Brown Story*, 117.

19 Brown with Clary, *PB: The Paul Brown Story*, 119.

20 Frank M. Henkel, *Cleveland Brown's History* (Mount Pleasant, SC, Arcadia, 2005), 9.

21 Andy Piascik, *Best Show in Football: The 1946-1955 Cleveland Browns* (Lantham, MD, Taylor Trade, 2007) 18.

22 Piascik, *Best Show in Football: The 1946-1955 Cleveland Browns* ,18-19.

23 George Halas with Gwen Morgan and Arthur Veysey, *Halas by Halas* (New York, McGraw Hill, 1979) 221.

24 Brown with Clary, *PB: The Paul Brown Story*, 16.

25 July 1998 interview with football Hall of Famer Lou Groza conducted by Bruce Janowsky and Greg Peterson at the Sportsmen's Club on Chautauqua Lake NY. http://www.firstpost.com/topic/person/lou-groza-lou-groza-remembers-the-browns-video-RnxWnq_IH_E-35420-4.html

26 George Canton, *Paul Brown: The Man Who Invented Modern Football* (Chicago, Triumph

Books, 2008) 94.

27 Andy Piascik, *Best Show in Football: The 1946-1955 Cleveland Browns*, 269.

28 July 1998 interview with football Hall of Famer Lou Groza conducted by Bruce Janowsky and Greg Peterson at the Sportsmen's Club on Chautauqua Lake NY. http://www.firstpost.com/topic/person/lou-groza-lou-groza-remembers-the-browns-video-RnxWnq_IH_E-35420-4.html

29 Andy Piascik, *Best Show in Football: The 1946-1955 Cleveland Browns*, 154.

30 Tony Grossi, *Tales from the Cleveland Brown's Sidelines* (Champaign, IL., Sports Publishing LLC, 2004)12.

31 Some credit Brown with inventing the draw play.

32 The Baltimore Colts joined the AAFC East in 1947, replacing the Miami Seahawks.

33 Readers might be interested in an analysis and evaluation of the AAFC teams and a comparison with the NFL teams found in Andy Piascik's, *The Best Show in Football: The 1946-1955 Cleveland Browns*, Taylor Trade, 2007. See pages 187-235.

34 Andy Piascik, *Best Show in Football: The 1946-1955 Cleveland Browns*, 66.

35 Andy Piascik, *Best Show in Football: The 1946-1955 Cleveland Browns*, 70.

36 Mike Adamle played for the Kansas City Chiefs, New York Jets, and Chicago Bears. He became a popular sportscaster and co-host of American Gladiators among many other pursuits.

37 Harold Sauerbrei, "Browns Win Third Title, 49-7," *Cleveland Plain Dealer*, December 19, 1948. Viewed at http://www.cleveland.com/brownshistory/plaindealer/index.ssf?/browns/more/history/19481219BROWNS.html viewed on 1/21/2013.

38 Andy Piascik, *Best Show in Football: The 1946-1955 Cleveland Browns*, 118.

39 Salata invited the last pick in the draft to a week of celebrations and fun in Newport Beach. It has become a very popular event in itself. See http://www.irrelevantweek.com/about/.

40 Neale said many things about the Browns and some of those were very positive and even generous, but he also had a sharp tongue that an opposing team might focus on to motivate. The Browns were put down by others in the NFL before the merger, but it was to be expected when coaches and owners in established leagues look at teams from a new start-up league.

41 Andy Piascik, *Best Show in Football: The 1946-1955 Cleveland Browns*, 176.

42 Davis hit .403 for Army's baseball team; he was Army's fastest freestyle swimmer; a basketball guard; and a potential Olympic-level sprinter according to David Ramsey,"Remembering the Legend of Army's Glenn Davis Who Might Be College Football's All-Time Best Running Back," Colorado Spring Gazette, November 4, 2011 viewed at http://daveramseysez.freedomblogging.com/2011/11/04/remember-armys-glenn-davis-who-might-have-been-college-footballs-all-time-best-running-back/7043/ on January 22, 2013.

43 Harry Jones, "Groza Field Goal is Signal for Celebration," *Cleveland Plain Dealer*, December 24, 1950. Viewed at http://www.cleveland.com/brownshistory/plaindealer/index.ssf?/browns/more/history/19501224BROWNS.html on 1/22/2013.

44 AP, "McBride Says Brown Will Stay with Pros," *Toledo Blade*, December 16, 1951.

45 Harold Sauerbrei, "Browns Lose Title Game 17-16," *Cleveland Plain Dealer*, December 27, 1953. Viewed at http://www.cleveland.com/brownshistory/plaindealer/index.ssf?/browns/more/history/19531227BROWNS.html on 1/18/2012.

46 Andy Piascik, *Best Show in Football: The 1946-1955 Cleveland Browns*, 306.

47 Chuck Heaton, "Browns Regain Title, 56-10," *Cleveland Plain Dealer*, December 26, 1954. Viewed at http://www.cleveland.com/brownshistory/plaindealer/index.ssf?/browns/more/history/19541226BROWNS.html on 1/18/2012.

48   Quote from Pro Football Hall of Fame page on Gilman at http://www.profootballhof.com/hof/member.aspx?PLAYER_ID=76, viewed on 1/19/13.

49   Chuck Heaton, "87,695 See Browns Keep Title," *Cleveland Plain Dealer*, December 26, 1955. Viewed at http://www.cleveland.com/brownshistory/plaindealer/index.ssf?/browns/more/history/19551226BROWNS.html on 1/18/2012.

50   Frank M. Henkel, *Cleveland Brown's History* (Mount Pleasant, SC, Arcadia, 2005), 35.

51   Brown with Clary, *PB: The Paul Brown Story*, 249.

52   Http://www.cleveland.com/brownshistory/plaindealer/index.ssf?/browns/more/history/19571229BROWNS.html

53   Pro-Football Reference shows an interception by halfback Chet Hanulak, which would increase the interceptions to five, but other sources do not show this.

54   Dave Buscema, *100 Things Giants Fans Should Know and Do Before They Die* (Chicago, Triumph Books, 2012).32.

55   Andrew O'Toole, *Paul Brown: The Rise and Fall and Rise Again of Football's Most Innovative Coach* (Cincinnati, Clerisy Press, 2008) 213-214.

56   Brown with Clary, *PB: The Paul Brown Story*, 19.

57   Brown with Clary, *PB: The Paul Brown Story*, 261.

58   Tex Maule, "A Man for This Season: Since 1958 Meticulous Paul Brown Has Won Battles and Lost Wars. This May Be His Year," *Sports Illustrated*, September 10, 1962, viewed at http://sportsillustrated.cnn.com/vault/article/magazine/MAG1135048/1/index.htm

59   Tex Maule, "A Man for This Season: Since 1958 Meticulous Paul Brown Has Won Battles and Lost Wars. This May Be His Year," *Sports Illustrated*, September 10, 1962, viewed at http://sportsillustrated.cnn.com/vault/article/magazine/MAG1135048/1/index.htm

60   Pro-Football-Reference at http://www.pro-football-reference.com/players/P/PlumMi00.htm

61   Tex Maule, "A Man for This Season: Since 1958 Meticulous Paul Brown Has Won Battles and Lost Wars. This May Be His Year," *Sports Illustrated*, September 10, 1962, viewed at http://sportsillustrated.cnn.com/vault/article/magazine/MAG1135048/1/index.htm

62   Pro-Football-Reference http://www.pro-football-reference.com/players/N/NinoJi00.htm

63   Brown with Clary, *PB: The Paul Brown Story*, 305.

64   Bill Walsh, Steve Jamison, Craig Walsh, *The Score Takes Care of Itself* (New York, Pengiun, 2010).

65   From 1982-1994, the Raiders were the Los Angeles Raiders.

66   http://en.wikipedia.org/wiki/National_Football_League_Coach_of_the_Year_Award

Weeb Ewbank

New York Jets Coach Weeb Ewbank hangs up the phone. Ewbank has had another conversation with John Riggins's mother. Ewbank's star running back is camping and fishing in the vicinity of his family farm in Kansas. It is before cell phones; Riggins is currently unreachable. Riggins is late to camp— holding out for a higher salary that both he and Ewbank know is unreasonable.

Training camp has started and most of Ewbank's players are getting ready for another morning workout at Hofstra University. In addition to Riggins, he has two other veteran stars whose common agent seems to be stalling with what the old coach and general manager deems to be exorbitant money demands. Ewbank is patient—perhaps more than in his younger days—and perhaps more patient than many people believe wise. But he considers himself a good judge of people, someone who understands human nature. He also understands himself. He is under tremendous pressure, but he is mentally, emotionally, and physically sturdy.

Ewbank is a spark plug of a man. At 5-foot-6, he lives amidst taller men, but he is an outstanding competitor. He can coach a team successfully at the highest level in professional sports and he can take on sports agents with aplomb. Unlike many coaches, he finds pleasure in the challenges of negotiating contracts. Many people underestimate this man. Opponents do so at their own peril.

Incredibly, many football fans do not understand the critical role played by Ewbank in his teams' successes. Many associate his teams with their quarterbacks not their coach. But it was Ewbank who has taken two fledgling teams to the pinnacle of professional football. First it was the "Colts of Johnny Unitas" and then the "Jets of Joe Namath." Perhaps it is the Quaker in Ewbank that makes him more interested in results than recognition.[1]

Weeb Ewbank reflects on Riggins, his young holdout. He wonders what it must be like to be a young man fishing someplace in rural Kansas. The coach puts on his cap as he glances at himself in the mirror. He smiles to himself as he gets ready to head out to the football field with his men. Regardless of what happens, he will treat his men as adults; he will keep his cool with the press; and he will maintain his confidence. Most importantly, today will be another excellent day in the long life of Weeb Ewbank.

Weeb Ewbank at Miami University

Early Life

Wilbur Charles "Weeb" Ewbank was born on May 6, 1907, in Richmond, Indiana, to Charles Clifford Ewbank and Estella Dickerson Ewbank. Charles owned a grocery store in Richmond, which is in Wayne County in the east central portion of Indiana, a short distance from the Ohio border. Early settlers to the area were Quakers moving west immediately after the American Revolution. The Ewbanks were Quakers and the family had come over from England several generations before Weeb's parents were born.

Wilbur Charles had three siblings, Vernon C., Helen Emily, and Myron.[2] The name "Weeb" is thought to have come from younger brother Myron struggling to pronounce Wilbur. Weeb Ewbank attended Oliver P. Morton High School where he played football, basketball, and baseball. He was captain of the basketball and football teams in his senior year. As a sophomore, he started playing for a semipro baseball team making a few dollars a game at the time. He graduated in 1924.

Miami University

In 1924, Ewbank entered Miami University of Ohio, a school that would go on to achieve fame as the "Cradle of Coaches." Miami produced many noted football coaches such as Bill Arnsparger, Earl Blaik, Paul Brown, Carmen Cozza, Dick Crum, Paul Dietzel, Sid Gillman, John Harbaugh, Woody Hayes, Terry Hoeppner, George Little, Bill Mallory, Gary Moeller, William Narduzzi, Joe Novak, Ara Parseghian, Sean Payton, John Pont, Bo Schembechler, Larry Smith, Dick Tomey, Jim Tressel, Randy Walker, and Ron Zook.

At Miami, Weeb Ewbank played quarterback on the football team; was captain of the baseball team; and he played forward on the basketball team. He married his childhood sweetheart, Lucy Keller Massey, in 1926. He continued his semipro career in baseball and would play under the assumed name of Carl "Shorty" Thomas.[3] He coupled his "unofficial" baseball career with semipro football to help support his young family. He graduated with a degree in Physical Education in 1928.[4] Another legendary NFL coach, Paul Brown, who would play a role in Ewbank's life, graduated from Miami University in 1930.

High School Coaching

After graduation from Miami University, Ewbank taught at Van Wert High School in 1928 where he served as Athletic Director and coached several sports. He moved back to Miami University in 1930 where he taught in the College of Education and coached at the University's demonstration school called McGuffey High School. He would remain there for 13 years until 1943. He continued his education and received an MA in Education from Columbia University in 1932. Like many coaches, he enjoyed the teaching aspect of his work. He was good at it.

Miami University 1927 Football Team

World War II Service

Ewbank enlisted in the Navy in 1943 and was assigned to Great Lakes Naval Station where he worked as assistant football coach to Head Coach Paul Brown. Another coach who worked there with Brown and Ewbank was Blanton Collier. Brown, Collier, and Ewbank would once again work together in professional football. Ewbank and Brown would be friends throughout their careers.[5]

College Coaching

In 1946, Ewbank joined the football staff at Brown University where he coached the backfield for one year. He also served as head basketball coach. Ewbank became head coach of football at Washington University in St. Louis in 1947. He did especially well in 1948, his second year at the University when the team went 8–1 for the season.[6] Ewbank took the job knowing that the GI Bill attracted a number of players to the school right after the war although the University administration was deemphasizing football.[7] Ewbank stayed 2 years. One of Ewbank's running backs at Washington University, Charley Winner, went on to a long career in football as both a coach and player personnel director. For much of Winner's career, he worked with Ewbank and in 1950, he married Ewbank's daughter, Nancy.

While at Washington, Ewbank continued to study and improve his understanding of Paul Brown's methods and the modern T Formation of Clark Shaughnessy and George Halas. He taught physical education courses and he kept tabs on his players' grades.[8]

Professional Football

Weeb Ewbank joined the professional football ranks in 1949 when he took a job working for Paul Brown as his line coach. He worked for Brown during one of the Cleveland Browns' most successful periods: 1949-1953. After leaving the Browns, he moved on to the Colts and then the Jets.

Cleveland Browns

As an assistant coach with Cleveland, Ewbank had an opportunity to learn from the master, Paul Brown. Ewbank coached the Browns' line and spent time researching promising college players. Corresponding extensively with college coaches, he devised ways to improve the scouting process. Ewbank brought something of the college professor with him wherever he went. Like Brown, Ewbank combined organizational development and intelligence gathering skills with his own intuitive people skills to develop emergent football teams.

Baltimore Colts

Baltimore entrepreneur Carroll Rosenbloom was persuaded by NFL Commissioner Bert Bell to take ownership of a new franchise to replace the Dallas Texans expansion team that folded after a single season in 1952. Professional football was not new to Baltimore. A former Baltimore Colts team started its life in the old All-American Football Conference (AAFC), but only survived one season in the NFL before it was disbanded late in 1949.

Paul Brown had developed a remarkable system for winning football. Naturally, Brown's success drew the attention of many professional and college teams to his staff. Brown was already losing his closest assistant, Blanton Collier, to the University of Kentucky when Rosenbloom tapped Ewbank for the 1954 season as his new head coach. Collier had been a candidate for the Colts' job as well before he decided upon Kentucky. Losing a second assistant in the same year was unsettling to the feisty Brown. Ewbank's departure was also contentious because he had knowledge of the upcoming draft from the Cleveland Browns' perspective and he would be working for a competitor. Commissioner Bell interceded on Paul Brown's behalf by doing what he could to limit Ewbank's involvement in that draft.

Ewbank replaced Keith Molesworth who had acted as the Colts' head coach for the inaugural 1953 season and was slated to direct player personnel. Molesworth had played for the Chicago Bears during the 1930s and had coached the backfield for the Naval Academy and the Pittsburgh Steelers.

Ewbank's Colts

Needing players badly, owner Carroll Rosenbloom was involved in a huge trade in 1953. The Colts swapped 5 of their players for 10 players of the Cleveland Browns. Ewbank had been with the Browns at the time of the trade. Ewbank kept just four of those men for his first year in 1954. Of the 39 men on the 1953 Colts roster, Ewbank kept 19 players.[9] But the Colts were not without talent in Ewbank's first few years. Ewbank was also skilled at moving players to new positions to suit the players' talents or fulfill a team need.

In addition to his other coaching skills, Ewbank was an exceptional teacher. According to Raymond Berry, Ewbank "was one of the most tremendous coaches ever, a man who could recognize talent and teach football, and there have been very few coaches who can do both well."[10]

Alan "the Horse" Ameche

Heisman trophy winner, Alan Ameche, was a tough fullback who was very difficult to take down. He was the Colts' first draft choice in 1955. He played 6 years in Baltimore.

Alex Sandusky

Alex Sandusky was a 16th-round selection in the 1954 draft. He played right offensive guard for 13 seasons with the Colts.

Art "Bulldog" Donovan

Art Donovan was a Hall of Fame tackle who like Marchetti was already on the Colts when Ewbank got his start. The coach considered Donovan the best tackle in the league when he was at his peak playing on the left side. Donovan got a late start in professional football because of his military service during World War II. Donovan who played smart and tough on the field, was also known for his expansive sense of humor.

Art Spinney

Art Spinney was an intense, intelligent, left offensive guard from Boston College who mastered blocking techniques that made him a formidable foe. He played nine seasons for the Colts.

Buzz Nutter

Buzz Nutter was the starting center for the Colts throughout much of Ewbank's stay in Baltimore, including the championship seasons. Similar to Johnny Unitas, he was not an instant success. He failed to make the Washington Redskins who had drafted him in 1953. After returning to his native West Virginia and working in the steel mills, he tried out and made the Colts in 1954.

Don Joyce

Don Joyce played right defensive end for the Colts with a ferocity that gave him a reputation throughout professional football. He would play for Baltimore for seven seasons and during the off season work as a professional wrestler.

Don Shula

Don Shula was an excellent defensive back on the Colts for four seasons. Smart and skillful, Shula would go on to become a legendary NFL coach.

George Preas

George Preas played tackle for 11 seasons throughout Ewbank's stay in Baltimore. His blocking helped the Colts become a formidable offensive power in the NFL.

Gino Marchetti

Ewbank converted Gino Marchetti from offensive lineman to a defensive end. Ewbank called Marchetti the best defensive end he had ever seen. Hall of Famer Marchetti played 14 years in the big leagues. Playing left defensive end, Gino Marchetti, along with Art Donovan, Don Joyce, and "Big Daddy" Lipscomb, would develop into one of the best defensive lines in football.

Gene "Big Daddy" Lipscomb

Gene Lipscomb played right defensive tackle for Baltimore for 5 years and he was the biggest man on the vaunted Colts' defensive line at 6-foot-6 and 284 pounds. Lipscomb matured as a football player under Ewbank. A showman on the football field, Lipscomb would famously help up opposing tackled quarterbacks and theatrically send them back to the huddle to the delight and amusement of TV viewers.

Jerry Richardson

Jerry Richardson was drafted by the Colts in 1958. He played flanker, offensive end, and halfback for the Colts 1959-1960. Now he owns the Carolina Panthers.

Jim Mutscheller

Jim Mutscheller was drafted by the Dallas Texans in the 12th round of the 1952 draft and made the Colts when the franchise began. Mutscheller played right end for eight seasons for the Colts and had 5 years of 500+ yards receiving.

Johnny Unitas

Johnny Unitas joined the Colts in 1956. The Pittsburgh Steelers drafted him in 1955 and released him before he had a chance to shows his skills. The Hall of Famer was one of the best football players. Unitas was also a game-manager, who tirelessly worked with his teammates to improve their game. He played with the Colts from 1956-1972.

Lenny Moore

Halfback Lenny Moore was a Penn State graduate and the Colts' first round pick in 1956. Moore had a sensational 12-year career with the Colts that led to his induction in the Hall of Fame. He was hailed as an excellent rusher and receiver who could score on any play.

L. G. Duprey

L. G. Duprey from Baylor was a third round draft choice in 1955. He played left halfback for the Colts until he was snagged by Dallas in the 1960 expansion draft. A nifty runner, Duprey was nicknamed "Long Gone" in college.[11]

Raymond Berry

Raymond Berry was a Hall of Fame end who was a perfect match to Johnny Unitas. Berry joined the Colts in 1955 after being selected by the team in the 20th round of the draft. Berry had sure hands and was excellent under pressure throughout his 13-year Colts' career.

Memorial Stadium

Baltimore's second Memorial Stadium was completed in 1950—a huge benefit for the new Colts franchise. Originally, the stadium held 31,000 fans and consisted of a single, horseshoe-shaped deck, with the open end facing north. The stadium was designed to host football as well as baseball. Many modifications would be made over time to increase capacity. The Colts held their training camp at McDaniel College in Westminster, Maryland.

1954 Season

By the time Ewbank got his first head-coaching job in the NFL, he could recognize professional-grade talent and identify weaknesses. Like many coaches, he also believed in building a championship team through excellence in drafting. Succeeding would require holding onto his job long enough to build a winner. Ewbank would say many years later: "I could not have started off with a greater challenge."[12]

Ewbank's job was daunting, but he applied a steady consistent effort that eventually produced excellent results. The Colts finished 3–9 in 1954. They scored 131 points and allowed 279 points. Improvements came one game at a time. Remarkably, they beat the Rams towards the end of the season, 22–21, after being embarrassed by them in the opener, 48–0. They also managed to beat good 49ers' and Giants' teams.

1955-1957 Seasons

The Colts improved to 5–6–1 in 1955. They scored 214 points and allowed 239. They began the season by beating the Bears, the Lions, and the Packers. But they managed only two more wins that season: one against the 49ers, another against the Packers.

Alan "the Horse" Ameche helped the Colts earn some respect on offense in 1955. He gained 961 yards on 213 attempts. He was the league-leading yard gainer with the most yards from scrimmage; he was also the top in rushing touchdowns with nine to his credit.

In 1956, a new quarterback with tremendous possibilities and an excellent new halfback were working themselves into the lineup. Underappreciated by the Steelers' coaching staff, native son Johnny Unitas was cut by the Steel City club. Unitas impressed the Colts in a tryout and he was signed. In the fourth game of the season against the Chicago Bears, the Colts starting quarterback, George Shaw, broke his leg and Unitas stepped in for him. The Bears won 58–27, but Johnny U's professional career was launched. The Colts' new halfback, Lenny Moore, added a powerful scoring threat to the team's developing offense. At season's end, the Colts had managed a 5–7 record, scoring 270 points, and allowing 322.

The 1957 season was a turnaround for the Colts. They were 7–5 for the season. They scored 303 points and allowed 235. In the 1957 draft, Ewbank acquired as his first pick, Hall of Famer Jim Parker, an All-American from Ohio State. "Big Jim," who stood 6-foot-3 and weighed in at 273 pounds, was the Outland Award winner as the nation's top lineman. Ewbank wanted Parker to focus on one thing—protecting Johnny Unitas. Parker did it very well.

The Colts beat the Lions 34–14 in the 1957 opener and then followed with wins against the Bears and Packers. They had an up and down season the rest of the way, but one accomplishment stood above all else. In only his second year, Unitas was the top-rated quarterback, who threw a league leading 24 touchdown passes, and was named league MVP.

1958 Season

The Baltimore Colts whipped the Lions, Packers, and Bears twice in 1958. Their 56–0 slaughter of the Green Bay Packers likely had something to do with the Packers' Board seeking out a new coach after the season. They "settled on" Vincent Lombardi.

Ewbank's team would often reflect his calm, steadfast confidence. The Colts won the Western Conference with two games remaining. After losing the last two games of the season to the Rams and the 49ers, the Colts ended the regular season with a 9–3 mark. They scored 381 points and allowed 203.

1958 NFL Championship Game Background

The Baltimore Colts played the New York Giants for the NFL Championship on December 28, 1958 in Yankee Stadium in front of 70,000 fans with 40 million TV viewers. The Colts did not seem anxious. Nor were they affected by the millions that would view the game on television.

For many growing up in the 1950s and 1960s, Unitas would come to be the archetype for the quarterback. With his clean cut looks and brush cut hairstyle, he would also be the face of football. After his father died when Unitas was a boy, Johnny U. helped support his family by working before and after school. He went to church regularly. He toughed-out injuries. He practiced harder than most players. He commanded attention in the huddle.[13] He gave the game everything he had. He wanted to win them all. Personal honor and glory took a back seat to his team's accomplishments. Even his Lithuanian family name, "Janaitis," had been hammered out in translation to "Unitas" many years before as if to fit the destiny of an "All-American" quarterback of the era.

The Giants had won the championship in 1956 and had a cadre of excellent players who would challenge Unitas and the Colts. New York included the superb Hall of Famers Frank Gifford, Sam Huff, Rosey Brown, Andy Robustelli, and Emlen Tunnell. Gifford was a versatile receiver, rusher, and defensive back. Middle linebacker Sam Huff was a force in the Giants' defense. He loved to play tough and stuff the best running backs in the NFL. Tackle Rosey Brown was a big man whose quickness gave opposing teams fits. Tunnell was in the later part of his career in 1958, but he was a talented defensive back and punt returner who was known as an "offense on defense."

The Giants were directed by Jim Lee Howell who took over as head coach in 1954. Howell was a good head coach with two great assistants: offensive coordinator Vince Lombardi and defensive coordinator Tom Landry.

At quarterback, the Giants had one of the best, Charley Conerly from Ole Miss. Conerly started out at Ole Miss in 1941; he went into the Marines and fought in the Pacific in World War II; and returned to Ole Miss afterward and graduated in 1948.[14] He was a 27-year old rookie when he began his pro career in the days before facemasks and he would play into the modern era of television. Conerly took a beating on some Giants' teams that offered him little protection. Enough was enough and after the 1953 season, he went back to his home in Clarksville, Mississippi, to farm. When Howell was made head coach, he went down to Clarksville and talked Conerly into returning. Howell and his assistants got to work and created a team that could protect their quarterback. Conerly would lead the Giants to the NFL Championship in 1956 and to the Championship game again in 1958 and 1959. He played sparingly in the Giants' 1961 season, his last.

Although Conerly was clearly the number-one quarterback for the Giants, Howell always started Don Heinrich for the first offensive series of each game. Ostensibly, this was done so that Conerly would have the opportunity to view the defense before going into the game.

When Conerly and the Giants had beaten the Colts in the regular season, Conerly wrote that his team "outgutted" the opposition.[15] It was a sentiment that a hundred newspaper writers may have had after such a game, but because it came from Conerly, Ewbank used it to rile his players in the days leading up to the championship. Unitas had not played in the Giants' 24–21 victory that inspired Conerly's words.

The Giants knew something about guts; they had to defeat an excellent Cleveland Browns team in the last game of the season and then beat them again in a divisional playoff game. The Giants featured a well-balanced offense and a tough defense that could grind out wins on other team's mistakes. They shut out the Browns, 10–0, in the conference playoff game to get to the championship game against the Colts.

The Colts won the West Conference outright just ahead of the Bears and the Rams. Ewbank's team had a high octane offense that averaged over 30 points a game.

The Greatest Game

The 1958 NFL Championship Game would come to be known as "the Greatest Game." It was a seminal contest of two of the best NFL teams ever assembled and it delivered incredible drama to an expectant, bourgeoning TV audience.

After several miscues on the first series, Unitas drove the Colts down to the 25-yard line on the strength of a long pass to Moore. The Giants' defense stalled the drive. Kicker Steve Myhra attempted a modest field goal, but the Giants' defensive standout, Sam Huff, charged in and blocked the kick. When the Giants got the ball, quarterback Conerly immediately connected with Triplett. Frank Gifford moved the ball down into Colts' territory on a long run. When the Giants' drive stalled, Pat Summerall kicked a 36-yard field goal.

In the second quarter, Gifford fumbled and the Colts' jumbo-sized tackle, Big Daddy Lipscomb, recovered the ball on the Giants' 20-yard line. After a series of hard-fought short gains, Alan Ameche was able to score from the 2-yard line and the Colts took the lead, 7–3. Unitas led another scoring drive that featured mostly running plays, but he hit pay dirt with a toss to his top receiver and fellow-perfectionist, Raymond Berry. As the half wound down with the Colts leading 14–3, Huff tackled Berry out of bounds right near Ewbank. The Colts' coach did not like it. Words were exchanged and the short stout coach was said to take a swing at Huff who was one of the toughest men in the league. In Ewbank's *Goal to Go* book, he writes that he pushed Huff rather than hit him. Regardless of what exactly happened between the two, there were plenty of players and coaches to keep the David and Goliath apart, and the half ended with all parties still in one piece. Commissioner Bert Bell did not levy any fines over the play.

The second half began with a Colts' drive that brought them to the 3-yard line. Four attempts to score failed. The goal-line stand invigorated the Giants. On a Giants' drive, Conerly threw a bomb to Kyle Rote who lost possession of the ball when he was tackled at the Colts' 25-yard line, but his teammate Alex Webster picked it up and carried it all the way to the 1-yard line. After Triplett scored on a 1-yard plunge, it was Colts 14–Giants 10.

The Giants came at the Colts again in the fourth quarter. A strike from Conerly to Bob Schnelker took the ball down to the Colts' 15-yard line. A toss to Gifford gave the Giants another score and after the extra point, the Giants led, 17–14.

The Colts did not give up, but they did not have much success either—at least for a while. They missed a field goal. They took over on a fumble only to have another drive stall on the Giants' 27-yard line. New York had the ball and a 3-point lead with less than three minutes to go. Gifford was stopped a yard shy on a third-and-three play that could have iced the game if it had resulted in a first down. The Colts were back in business after a Giants' punt from their marksman Chandler brought the ball down to the Colts 14-yard line with a few ticks more than two minutes to go. Unitas managed the clock perfectly by throwing high-percentage passes to Berry that brought the ball down to the 13-yard line with seconds left on the clock. It was just enough time for Myhra to kick a field goal to push the game into sudden death overtime.

The Giants got the ball first in overtime and went three and out; they missed a first down by only inches. Chandler pushed the Colts back to their 20-yard line with a perfect punt. Unitas orchestrated a drive that was perfect football drama. On almost every down, Unitas called a play that ran counter to what was expected. Instead of a pass, the Giants' defense faced a run around end or a draw play. When possession would seem to call for the conservative play, Unitas threw it across the middle. When the Colts were in short field goal range at the 9-yard line, Unitas surprised everyone including Ewbank when he threw another pass that brought the ball down to the 1-yard line. Unitas gave the ball to his fullback Alan Ameche who ran in for the winning touchdown. The Colts won the "Greatest Game", 23–17.

On some plays Unitas had gone against his coach's wishes based on adjustments that the Giants made on the field that gave the Colts an opportunity. That was OK with Ewbank. Ewbank was honored as UPI NFL Coach of the Year for 1958.

1959 Season

The Colts ended the 1959 season with another 9–3 mark that gave them the top spot in the Western Conference. Ewbank's assistant coaches were Don McCafferty, Herman Ball, and John Sandusky who would all stay with Ewbank for the remainder of his Colts' career. The Colts scored 374 points and allowed 251. Most of their games were fairly tight matches, but they picked up steam late in the season, beating both the 49ers and Rams twice while scoring 159 points and allowing just 75 in those contests. Once again, they would play the New York Giants, who had the top spot in the Eastern Conference for the NFL Championship.

1959 Championship Game

In the 1958 Championship game, Moore was more often than not, the focus of the Giants' pass defense giving Unitas more room to work towards Raymond Berry. It was different in 1959. On the Colts' first drive, Unitas faked to Berry and threw a 25-yard strike to Moore who ran it another 35 yards for a score.

The Giants responded with a drive that stalled, but Pat Summerall kicked a 23-yard field goal. Summerall followed with field goals of 37 and 22 yards on two more series when the Giants moved the ball, but they ran out of downs.

Another Giants' drive was stalled when Alex Webster was stopped on fourth and one. Unitas drove the Colts 70 yards downfield including another long pass play to Moore that left Baltimore just 4 yards shy of the goal. Unitas ran the ball in for the score and the Colts pulled ahead 14–9.

The Giants had a difficult time protecting Conerly from the pass rush. Under tremendous pressure, the Giants' quarterback misfired. Andy Nelson intercepted Conerly in the fourth quarter and gave the ball back to Unitas at the Giants' 14. Unitas hit Jerry Richardson for the score and the Colts moved ahead 21–9. The Colts victimized Gifford next. Gifford tossed an option pass that was snagged by cornerback Johnny Sample who ran it 41 yards into the end zone. The Colts led 28–9. Sample picked off Conerly next and returned it to the Giants' 24. Myhra was called on to kick a field goal from the 25-yard line and the Colts led 31–9. The Giants did not quit. Conerly orchestrated a drive in the last two minutes that culminated in a 32-yard touchdown pass to Schnelker. The final score stood at 31–16 when the gun sounded.

1960-1961 Seasons

The Colts looked like contenders again in 1960. They had essentially the same team that had won two championships in a row. But the NFL West Conference would go to the Green Bay Packers and Vince Lombardi who had more staying power. Nevertheless, the Colts gave Green Bay a battle. In the first Baltimore-Green Bay matchup, the Packers won 35–21. Unitas threw four interceptions. In the second meeting, the Colts turned the tables and intercepted Bart Starr four times. The Colts won the second game, 38–24. After the Colts' promising 6–2 start, they fell apart and lost the last four games of the season. They ended the season with a disappointing 6–6 mark. They scored 288 points and allowed 234. Unitas threw 24 interceptions—up from 14 in 1959.

One potential trouble spot for the Colts was their storied-but-aging defensive line. In 1961 before the season started, the Colts traded Big Daddy Lipscomb and Buzz Nutter to the Steelers for end Jimmy Orr. The Colts improved to 8–6 for the 1961 season. They scored 302 points and allowed 307. But Unitas threw 24 interceptions for the second year in a row. His quarterback rating sunk to 66.1. The Packers won the NFL Championship, but they split with the Colts. In their first meeting, the Packers slaughtered the Colts, 45–7, when Ewbank's team turned the ball over eight times. In their second match, the Colts beat the Packers, 45–21, limiting Starr to 6 completions on 17 attempts for 64 yards and no touchdowns.

1962 Season

In Weeb Ewbank's last season with the Colts, they tallied a 7–7 record. They scored 293 points and allowed 288. NFL Western Conference rivals Green Bay, Detroit, and Chicago beat them twice that season. Unitas was still throwing too many interceptions. Although the Colts had a corps of talented athletes, both the offense and the defense seemed to slip towards mediocrity. Ewbank had built a winner in four seasons and his team was still at .500, but the team had not made the playoffs in three seasons. The team looked like it needed some rebuilding and there were several older players who would need to move on. On November 25, when the Bears slaughtered the Colts, 57–0, some believed it was a signal to management that they needed to replace Ewbank. After the end of the season, Ewbank was fired.

Ewbank and his Colts had established a proud fan base in historic Baltimore. Baltimore had always shown spirit. After the Battle of Baltimore in the midst of the War of 1812, Frances Scott Key was inspired to write the words to the "Star Spangled Banner." Baltimore is also known as a city with a large population of medical professionals. Ewbank's Colts became part of the fabric of the city and certainly won over their share of fans. Poet Ogden Nash once described the city's love of the Colts in his own unique way:

My Colts, verses and reverses[16]

The lucky city of Baltimore
Is famed for its medicos galore.
It's simply teeming with fine physicians,
With surgeons, oculists, obstetricians,
All dedicated men in white,
All at your service, day and night
Except—and here's the fly in the ointment—
When with the Colts they
                    have an appointment,
And the vast Memorial Stadium rocks
With the cheers of fifty thousand docs.

They've caught the disease fate
                    holds in store
For the population of Baltimore—
A disease more virulent than rabies,
Felling men, women and even babies.
The cynic becomes a true believer
When caught in the grip of that
                    old Colt fever.

They recall this year that red-letter date,
That day in December of '58
And a drama more violent than MacBeth,
The drama that ended in Sudden Death.
And this year each Sunday they awake,
With another championship at stake.
But ten years later the memory lingers,
Of Raymond Berry's flypaper fingers,
Of Johnny Unitas in the pocket—
Third and long, he launches the rocket—
Of Sandusky and Parker at their pinnacle,
And Shinnick the deadly
                              never more Shinnickal,
Big Daddy, Donovan, Braase, Marchetti,
Scattering Giants like confetti—
Now their bowl-bent juggernaut slams
Into an obstacle called the Rams.
And back in Baltimore, cold with sweat,
I'll be yelling at my TV set,
"Rack'em Sullivan, rock 'em Miller,
Sock 'em Curtis, you Giant-Killer!
Pearson, all the way with the kick-off!
Boyd you're due for another pickoff!"
And here at the height of my exhortation
There's pause for station identification.
While the sponsor is panhandling
Let's look at some manhandling.

—Ogden Nash

New York Jets

Weeb Ewbank had established a reputation as a steady coach who could build a winner from the ground up. He was exactly what the New York Jets needed. When Ewbank won his first NFL Championship as the Colts' head coach in the NFL, there were 12 professional football teams seeking the honor.

At the time of Ewbank's championship run with the Jets in 1968, the AFL-NFL merger was still a few years away, but the two leagues had agreed to a playoff system that led to the Super Bowl. Along with subsequent expansion, the involvement of two leagues greatly increased the difficulty of winning the professional football championship. Ewbank's Jets would essentially be competing with 9 AFL teams and 16 NFL teams. Winning the Super Bowl in 1968 meant that your team was the best of 26 teams.

The American Football League New York Titans that started up in 1960 was a financial failure and the league had to assume its debts. A syndicate of five men purchased the team, changed the name to the Jets, and hired Weeb Ewbank as coach and general manager. The syndicate included David A. "Sonny" Werblin, Townsend B. Martin, Leon Hess, Donald C. Lillis, and Philip H. Iselin.

Ewbank's Jets

Ewbank faced a tremendous challenge building the Jets into a contending team, but he was certainly up to the challenge—in fact he enjoyed it. Continuing his team building philosophy from his days with the Colts, Ewbank would focus on draft choices to create his team of the future, although he was able to pick up a number of players he already knew as well from his work with the Colts.

Al Atkinson

Al Atkinson played for Villanova and was picked up by the Jets in 1965. He played middle linebacker for 10 seasons in New York. He was especially adept at pass defense.

Bill Baird

Bill Baird had played at San Francisco State. He was a defensive back who labored seven seasons for the Jets beginning in 1963.

Bill Mathis

Bill Mathis was an original New York Titan who played halfback. He was a good runner and receiver who would play for the Jets through the 1969 season.

Curley Johnson

Curley Johnson was a punter who played on the original Titans team and then with the Jets through 1968.

Dave Herman

In 1963, Ewbank drafted Dave Herman from Michigan State in the 27th round of the AFL draft. Herman was a right guard who would have a 10-year career. He was especially important to the Jets' Super Bowl season of 1968.

Don Maynard

Hall of Famer Don Maynard was an exceptional athlete with great speed and good hands at the wide receiver position. He was one of Namath's favorite receivers.

Emerson Boozer

Coming from Maryland State College in 1966, Emerson Boozer was an excellent running and blocking back who was a key to the Jets' offense.[17]

George Sauer

George Sauer was a teammate of Jim Hudson at the University of Texas. Sauer played wide receiver for the Jets for six seasons. In the 1965-1968 seasons, he gained over 1,000 yards.[18]

Gerry Philbin

Third round AFL draft choice out of the University of Buffalo, Gerry Philbin would play nine seasons for the Jets at defensive end. He was an excellent pass rusher, fast and strong, who kept things lively for opposing quarterbacks with his relentless efforts.

Jim Hudson

Defensive back Jim Hudson had played at the University of Texas. He was signed as a free agent and would play six seasons for the Jets beginning in 1965. Ewbank praised him for being a smart, fast defensive leader.[19]

Joe Namath

Joe Namath was born on May 31, 1943, in Beaver Falls, Pennsylvania, a steel-mill town outside of Pittsburgh. His father and grandfather worked in the mills. Namath was an excellent baseball and football player. He turned down offers from professional baseball teams and decided to take a college scholarship. Namath played at the University of Alabama under Coach Paul "Bear" Bryant. He was the first overall pick in the 1965 draft by the AFL New York Jets. Ewbank traded away draft rights to quarterback Jerry Rhome to the Houston Oilers in 1964 for their first round pick in 1965, which was used to snag Namath.

On January 2, 1965, the Jets' President Sonny Werblin signed Joe Namath to a 3-year no-cut contract that paid a reported $387,000 and a brand new Lincoln Continental. Ewbank would say that the Jets would be the laughing stock of the NFL if Namath did not produce.[20] Namath was at the center of a number of highly visible competitions. He was the star player who might give a big popularity boost to the Jets versus the Giants in New York. He was the AFL star who would give recognition to the new league that was dwarfed in so many ways by the NFL. He was one of the big names that would help drive TV viewership under a big television contract that had been doled out by CBS.[21]

John Riggins

John Riggins was a big running back who throughout his career was able to get tough yards when practically everyone in the stadium knew he was getting the ball. Ewbank would have his services for 3 years.

John Schmitt

Ewbank signed free agent John Schmitt, a 297 pound tackle from Hosftra. Schmitt would later say that "nobody in pro football wanted me," but Ewbank picked him up and converted him to center.[22] He was good at it. Schmitt would start from 1966-1973.

Larry Grantham

Larry Grantham played end at Ole Miss and became an outside linebacker when he came to play in the pros. He was with the original New York Titans team and continued on with the Jets until 1972. He was consistently one of the best tacklers on the team, one of the most knowledgeable defensive players, and a leader.

Mark Smolinski

Mark Smolinski was a sturdy, steady running back and special teams captain who had played for Ewbank at Baltimore.

Matt Snell

In 1964, running back Matt Snell out of Ohio State was drafted by the Jets in the first round of the AFL draft. He would play for the Jets for 9 years and play a key role through most of Ewbank's years with the team. He was a good runner and blocker. In 1964, he was Rookie of the Year.

Pete Lammons

Tight end Pete Lammons was another University of Texas player whom Ewbank acquired. He began his Jets' career in 1966 and played six seasons with the team.

Ralph Baker

In 1964, linebacker Ralph Baker was drafted by the Jets in the sixth round of the AFL draft. He was a steady, dependable linebacker who would play for the Jets for 11 years.

Robert Hardy "Bake" Turner

Bake Turner was cut by the Colts and Ewbank swooped in and added him to the Jets' roster where he performed as one of the top receivers.

Winston Hill

Winston Hill was acquired for the Jets although he had been drafted by the Colts. The 6-foot-4 and 270 pound left offensive tackle anchored the Jets' protection of their quarterback and helped spell their rushing game.

Coaches

Ewbank's staff included offensive backfield coach Clive Rush, former head coach of the University of Toledo; offensive line coach Chuck Knox, former assistant coach at Kentucky; defensive line coach Walt Michaels, who had been an assistant coach for the Oakland Raiders; and defensive backfield coach Jack Donaldson, who had been an assistant coach at the University of Toledo. Buddy Ryan was added to the Jets staff in 1968 and stayed through 1975.

1963-1965 Seasons

Ewbank was a team builder not a miracle worker. While Ewbank began a building program, the Jets notched identical 5–8–1 records for each season from 1963-1965. Early on, it would be the defense that kept Jets' fans up at night. Wide receiver, Don Maynard who started for the New York Titans in the early days, and stuck with the Jets through the 1972 season, would say:

> *We had a pretty good offense the first three years, but every year we wound up with ten new starters on defense ... We scored a lot of points, but our defense didn't stop many people.*

Ewbank's Jets established Peekskill (N.Y.) Military Academy for their training camp in preparation for the 1963 season. The military influence did not seem to help. The team that would win the AFL Championship, the San Diego Chargers, had a more austere camp: the Rough Acres Ranch, a desert patch about 70 miles east of San Diego along the Mexican border complete with snakes and oppressive heat.

For the season, the Jets scored 249 points and allowed 399 points by their opponents. The San Diego Chargers beat the Jets twice; the second game was a 53–7 humiliation. Three other teams scored more than 40 points in contests against the Jets that season. Ewbank's team was the worst team in the AFL East.

In 1964, the Jets moved into Shea Stadium for their first home game on September 12. Helping to solidify AFL finances, the league and NBC announced a five-year, $36 million TV contract starting with the 1965 season. As a temporary home, the Jets had played in the historic, but crumbling Polo Grounds. Shea was designed as an all-purpose facility that could host baseball and football games. It could hold more than 60,000 fans. In the opener, the Jets beat the Denver Broncos, 30–6.

In 1964, the Jets scored 278 points and allowed 315 points by their opponents. The Buffalo Bills won the AFL Championship. The 1964 Jets played competitively in almost every game with the exception of a 38–3 drubbing at the hands of the Chargers on December 6. The Jets moved up out of the cellar to third place in the AFL East. Fullback Matt Snell rushed for 948 yards, caught 56 passes for 393 yards, and was named the AFL's Rookie of the Year.

In 1965, Joe Namath signed a Jets' contract and beat out Heisman Trophy winner John Huarte of Notre Dame who was also signed for the upcoming Jets' season. The Jets scored 285 points and allowed 303 points by their opponents. The Buffalo Bills won the AFL Championship in 1965. Once again some improvement was made and the Jets moved up to second place in the AFL East. Namath would play well—completing 164 passes on 340 attempts, giving him a 48.2% completion rate with 18 touchdowns and 15 interceptions. With a quarterback rating of 68.7, Namath was named the AFL's Rookie of the Year.

Statistics would never accurately reflect Namath's value to the Jets. He would excel in big games and draw attention to his team in a town that was rich in sports teams. Incredibly, some thought Namath lacked the intelligence to play in the big leagues. Ewbank would say: "Our quarterback doesn't have to be Phi Beta Kappa, but he has to be a thinker and a worker."[23] Namath fit the bill on both counts.

1966 Season

The Jets improved modestly to 6–6–2 in 1966. Ewbank acquired running back Emerson Boozer in the 6th round of the AFL draft. He would play 10 seasons for the Jets. Boozer had a high regard for Ewbank:

The man was a great teacher and knew how to put you in a relaxed state, but he was tough with money.[24]

The Jets scored 322 points and allowed 312 points by their opponents. Buffalo was atop the AFL East, but got beat up by the Chiefs in the Conference Championship, 31–7. The Chiefs in turn, went to the first Super Bowl and were clobbered by the Green Bay Packers of Vince Lombardi, 35–10. The

Jets also had some new competition in the AFL East, the Miami Dolphins, an expansion team that played their inaugural season in 1966. The season ended on a high point with the Jets beating the Boston Patriots in the final game of the season, 38–28.

1967 Season

The 1967 season marked the first winning season in Jet franchise history. The Jets challenged the contenders in 1967. In Ewbank's 5th year in New York, the Jets 8–5–1 record got them second place in the AFL East. They scored 371 points and allowed 329 points by their opponents. The 13–1 Oakland Raiders were the best team in the AFL that year, but they suffered a single loss at the hands of the Jets.

For the season, Namath completed 258 passes on 491 attempts for an incredible 4,007 yards. It was the first time a quarterback would pass for over 4,000 yards. Namath managed a 52.5% completion rate, 26 touchdowns, and 28 interceptions. The New York offense was pass-heavy with the Jets rushing for 1,307 yards out of their 5,152 yards of total offense. On October 1, Joe Namath passed for 415 yards in the Jets' win against the Miami Dolphins. Unfortunately, the Jets' new star running back Emerson Boozer was lost for the season on November 5 after tearing knee ligaments during a 42–18 loss to the Chiefs at Kansas City.

1968 Season

The Jets moved their training camp to Hofstra University in Hempstead, New York. The Jets scored 419 points and allowed 280 points by their opponents.

The Jets started out the season by squeaking past the Chiefs on September 15, at Municipal Stadium in Kansas City. In the first quarter, Namath hit Maynard on a 57-yard touchdown pass. The duo followed with a 30-yard touchdown pass play in the second quarter. The Chiefs only score in the first half was a 33-yard field goal by Norwegian born Hall of Fame kicker, Jan Stenerud. Jim Turner hit a 22-yard strike on behalf of the Jets. The Jets led, 17–3, when the teams took their mid-game rest. In the second half, the Jets were especially anemic on offense and scored just 3 points on one Jim Turner field goal. The Chiefs 5-foot-5 kick returner Noland "Super Gnat" Smith scored on an 80-yard punt return in the third quarter, but the rest of the Chiefs' scoring was accomplished by Jan Stenerud's additional three field goals. When the game ended, the Jets prevailed, 20–19.

In week two, the Jets beat the Patriots, 47–31, in a sloppy game in which each team scored two touchdowns on defense. In the third week, the Jets luck ran out when the Bills beat them, 37–35. Namath helped the Bills' cause by throwing five interceptions, which the Bills ran back for 235 yards and three touchdowns. Tom Janik ran one of those back for 100 yards. The Jets came back and beat a very good Chargers team, 23–20, the following week—Namath threw no interceptions. A relapse followed. Namath passed for 341 yards, but tossed in five interceptions contributing to the Broncos 21–13 victory. Namath would later describe his bad game experience: "I went out in one of those games, convinced I was ready, and went out there and threw five interceptions."[25] The Jets won the next four games in a row and then lost to the Raiders, 43–32, in a wild game that Namath passed for 381 yards with no interceptions.

Heidi Game

The Jets played the Raiders on November 17, 1968, in a game that would later be called the "Heidi Game." It was another famous game in pro football history that featured a Weeb Ewbank team. The game was famous for the last minute of the game that TV fans did not get a chance to see and for what they did get to see instead. The Raiders featured household names in quarterback Daryle Lamonica, kicker and backup quarterback George Blanda, halfback Pete Banaszak, wide receiver Fred Belitnikoff, and tackle Art Shell. Many of these players forever represent "Raiders football" to American fans. Likewise, given the cast of players on the 1968 Jets, any Jets-Raiders contest that year was likely to be memorable.

Daryle Lamonica hit Warren Wells for a Raiders' touchdown and the Jets' Jim Turner kicked two field goals in the first quarter making the score: Raiders 7–Jets 6. Billy Cannon caught a 48-yard touchdown pass from Lamonica and Joe Namath rushed one in from the one in the second quarter. After the Jets missed a two-point conversion, the score stood at 14–12 in favor of the Raiders at the half. In the third quarter, Jets' Bill Mathis rushed one in from the 4-yard line for a touchdown. Weeb Ewbank opted to kick the extra point rather than risk another missed two point conversion. When the Raiders' Charlie Smith rushed for a touchdown from the 3-yard line, the Raiders made a statement with a two point conversion to give them a 22–19 lead. In the fourth quarter, Namath connected with Maynard on a 50-yard scoring play. When Turner followed with a field goal, the Jets were ahead 29–22. Lamonica responded with a touchdown toss to Biletnikoff, but Turner hit another field goal to maintain the lead for New York, 32–29, with a minute and change to go. It was at this time that network television opted to end coverage of the game and go to the regularly scheduled program, which in this case was the movie "Heidi."

While viewers were frustrated, and perhaps most thinking that the Jets had come away with a victory, the Raiders' Charlie Smith caught a Daryle Lamonica pass to give the Raiders the lead with seconds left. Amazingly, the Raiders scored again when the ensuing kickoff was fumbled, recovered by the Raiders' Preston Ridlehuber at the 2-yard line, and run in for the score. Oddly enough, the Raiders won a very tight game, but by a convincing 43–32 margin.

The Jets won their last four games of the season by wide margins. The last minute loss to the Raiders in the Heidi Game was a good exercise leading up to the Conference Championship match with Oakland.

Conference Championship

The Raiders came to Shea for the showdown. It was another boxing match for the contenders. The Jets came out ahead, 10–0, in the first quarter when Namath hit Maynard for a score and Jim Turner followed with a field goal. The Raiders struck twice in the second quarter when Lamonica hit Bilitnikoff for a 29-yard touchdown. Turner and Blanda hit field goals for their respective teams and the first half ended with the Jets ahead, 13–10. When Blanda kicked a 9-yard field goal in the second half, he tied the game at 13–13. Namath hit Pete Lammons to put the Jets ahead, 20–13, heading into the fourth quarter. Another Blanda field goal and Banaszak's 5-yard touchdown rush gave the Raiders new life and a 23–20 lead. Fittingly, it was another Namath to Maynard strike that put the Jets up again, 27–23, for the win. The Jets had won the AFL championship before 62,627 fans at home. Maynard had six catches on the day and two touchdowns. Namath's numbers were not stellar. He connected on 19 passes on 49 attempts for 266 yards, but he had three touchdown passes and only one interception.

Super Bowl III

The media reported extensively on the Super Bowl and followed the stars around before the big game looking for sound bites and lead stories. Few doubted Broadway Joe's ability to provide great copy. When talking to the press, Joe Namath guaranteed that the Jets were going to win Super Bowl III against the favored Baltimore Colts.

The Jets will win. I guarantee it.

Many people thought this was a ridiculous statement. Ewbank was not happy that it was made certainly. "It nearly killed me when Namath told everyone we were going to win."[26] Ewbank had concerns about playing the Colts, but he certainly did not believe they were invincible. In jest, he said:

I'm not showing our people the Colt films until we get to Florida... I'm afraid if they do see them, they won't get off the airplane.[27]

As it turned out, Ewbank showed the films repeatedly to his team. And the more the Jets watched, the more confident they became. According to Ewbank, the Colts were being hyped as the greatest team of all time, and his opinion was that they were a good team, but not that good. Ewbank understood two things that were key. First, the odds makers were putting all the pressure on the Colts, not the Jets. And second, the more the media berated the Jets, the more motivated his players became. The media was helping the Jets' efforts as long as the Jets' players did not believe the stories.

Ewbank told his players, "Fellas, we're not going to change anything. You're going to conduct yourselves like you have throughout the season."[28] Ewbank brought his team out early, a full ten days before the game, and he allowed the players to bring their wives and families as well.

Ewbank made one strategic change before the game. He moved veteran guard Dave Herman to tackle so he could block the monstrous 6-foot-7 Bubba Smith. After the game, Ewbank congratulated Herman on a job well done: "How many guys could I ask to do that?"[29] Herman never forgot his coach's comment.

The Jets received the kick to start the game and managed a drive led by very conservative play calling. The Jets were just shy of the their 40-yard line when they punted to the Colts. The Colts looked impressive on offense for the first part of the series. Earl Morrall hit John Mackey on a 19-yard pass play that was followed by a 10-yard run by Tom Matte and a 7-yard scamper by Jerry Hill. When Morall hit Tom Mitchell for 15 yards for another first down, the Colts looked like they were about to score. A few plays later the drive stalled. The Colts teed it up and missed a field goal.

When the Jets gave up the ball deep in their own territory on a fumble late in the first quarter, the Colts returned the favor when a tipped ball thrown by Morrall careened off tight end Tom Mitchell and into the hands of the Jets' Randy Beverly. At that point in the game, neither team was playing winning football.

The Jets found success on the ground with Snell and kept after it. Namath passed a few times to force the Colts' defense to defend against the pass, but the Jets managed a long drive featuring their ground game. The drive was capped off by a 4-yard touchdown run by Snell.

After the Colts and Jets exchanged possessions, the Colts came down the field in a hurry. On the strength of a 58-yard run by Matte and a couple of Morrall completions, the Colts were on the Jets' 15-yard line. Morrall threw another interception and the Jets took over at their own 2-yard line.

The Jets were once again anemic on offense and punted back to the Colts. As time was running out in the half, the Colts tried a flea flicker in which Morrall handed off to Matte who turned and gave the ball back to Morrall to pass. Morrall did not see a wide open Jimmy Orr in the end zone and tossed an interception to Jets' safety Jim Hudson ending the drive and the half with the Jets ahead 7–0. The Colts had been in the red zone three times and came away with no points.

Early in the second half, the Jets did not move the ball, but were able to kick a field goal. On the next Jets' series, they were able to drive to field goal range and kick another one to put them up 13–0. Namath injured his thumb on the drive and was replaced by Babe Parilli.

Shula pulled Morrall and put Unitas in, but the Colts remained listless on Unitas's first series and had to punt without gaining a first down. Namath came back on the following Jets' possession; he completed a 39-yard toss to Sauer. Sauer was aided by the Colts' attention to Maynard. After the Jets moved down to the Colts' 2-yard line, the Colts held and Jim Turner kicked another field goal putting the Jets ahead 16–0.

Later in the quarter, the Jets used running plays exclusively to use up time and push the ball down field where their drive stalled at the Colts' 35-yard line. After a missed field goal, the Colts took over. Unitas was able to lead a scrappy drive downfield that scored the Colts' first touchdown, but left them with barely three minutes to play and a 9 point deficit. But the Colts kept things interesting. After a successful onside kick, the Colts were able to move down field again, but they ran out of time and downs on the Jets' 19-yard line. The Jets beat the Colts, 16–7.

Super Bowl III was a surprise. Neither team played particularly well on offense. Essentially what won the day was Weeb Ewbank's conservative game plan, the Jets' execution of it, and some uncharacteristic flops on the part of the Colts. Namath to his great credit, played well within himself. The Colts' offense succumbed to the tremendous pressure and turned the ball over five times. Both Namath and Morrall had thrown 17 interceptions for the regular season, but Morrall had three interceptions on the day and Namath had none.

Matt Snell ran for 121 yards on 30 carries. Maynard, who featured so prominently in the conference championship, had a hamstring injury and played decoy much of the day. Sauer caught 8 passes for 133 yards. Eleven Jets were named to the AFL's All-Star team. Namath was selected Super Bowl MVP.

1969 Season

The Jets finished on top in the AFC East with a 10–4 record. They scored 353 points and allowed 269 by their opponents. Namath completed 185 passes out of 361 attempts for 2,734 yards and 19 touchdowns with 17 interceptions and a 74.3 rating. On paper it looked like a promising year, but they were outclassed by two AFC rivals: Oakland and Kansas City. The Raiders looked to be the class of the AFL in 1969 with a season record of 12–1–1. The Raiders roughed up the Jets 27–14 on November 30th, in a game in which Namath went 10 for 30 for 169 yards. But Kansas City was Oakland's undoing in the Conference Championship beating them, 17–7. It was also Kansas City that knocked the Jets out in the division playoff game. The Chiefs' defense could make most offenses look sick if not feeble. They led in practically every defensive category in the AFL and it showed when they beat the Jets on December 20, 1969, by a score of 13–6. Namath threw 14 completions on 40 attempts for 164 yards with no touchdowns and three interceptions. The Jets' running game was held to 87 yards on 22 rushes.

The 1969 season was the end of the road for a Ewbank Jets' team that would contend for a championship. In fact, it would be 1981 before the Jets had another winning season. Ewbank, the championship builder, was working with aging starters and a tight purse string.

1970-1972 Seasons

Namath was the most critical man on the Jets' offense and the early 70s would see Namath struggle to stay healthy. While he had more than his share of injuries, he would play for 13 seasons. In his 12 seasons with the Jets he would play roughly 80% of the games with injury riddled seasons mostly in 1970, 1971, and 1973.

In 1970, the AFL-NFL merger was in place and the Jets' division, the AFC East, included their previous AFL competitors: the Dolphins, Bills, and Patriots along with Ewbank's former team, the Baltimore Colts. The Oilers who had played in the AFL East were now in the AFC Central with the Bengals, Browns, and Steelers. The Raiders, Chiefs, Chargers, and Broncos formed the AFC West.

Going into the season, Ewbank thought the 1970 Jets were perhaps the best of his New York teams. Unfortunately, Namath broke his wrist in the fifth game of the 1970 season against the Colts and missed the remainder of the season. Several other Jets suffered injuries as well. The Jets ended the 1970 season with a 4–10 record. They scored 255 points and allowed 286 points from their opposition.

In the AFC East in 1971, the Jets finished in third place with a 6–8 record for the season, well behind the Dolphins and Colts who had 10 wins. The Jets scored 212 points and allowed 229 points by their opponents. Joe Namath returned after his broken wrist suffered in the 1970 season, but he injured a knee in preseason that kept him out of the first 10 games. The Jets drafted John Riggins, a running back from the University of Kansas, as their first round selection. Riggins would prove to be a remarkable workhouse over his long career, but he needed some coaxing with salary and other issues to keep him on board. He would play 5 years with the Jets and then move on to the Redskins for another nine.

The Jets went 7–7 for the 1972 season. They scored 367 points and opponents scored 324 points against them. They took a second place finish in the AFC East, a mile and a half behind the perfect 14–0 Miami Dolphins. The Jets were one of the teams that made Miami's trip to perfection a struggle. Going into the fourth quarter in the Jets-Dolphins game on November 19, the Jets were ahead, 24–21. Miami's fourth quarter score on a 14-yard run by Mercury Morris gave them a 28–24 lead that they held for the win.

Jets' quarterback Joe Namath had an excellent season completing 162 of 324 attempts for 2,816 yards with 19 touchdowns and a quarterback rating of 72.5. The Jets' rushing game exceeded 2,000 yards for the first time with the addition of fullback Riggins now in full bloom playing with halfback Emerson Boozer.

Ewbank Decides to Retire

Managing Joe Namath, his fragile but exceptionally talented football star, was one of the things that defined Ewbank's career in New York. Although Namath may well be remembered for his cavorting off the field, he was a game changer—a great fit for the Big Apple—a town where any new professional team must compete with any number of entrenched teams in several sports for headlines, TV/radio audiences, and ticket sales. Ewbank worked with Namath to get the best out of him and see his career extended as long as possible. During the time in which Ewbank coached in New York, there were many distractions faced by professional sports—some were important developments—some were trivial, but sports teams will always need to focus on the job at hand to build winning programs.

Threats to a common brotherhood of teammates can harm team performance. The late 1960s and 1970s were filled with such threats. Working through issues of race is especially awkward, uncomfortable, and difficult. In those difficult times, Ewbank and others learned that there was much more to Joe Namath than his quarterback skills and his night life. Namath's childhood neighborhood was predominantly black. He was raised with African American boys who like Namath had a keen interest in sports and accomplishment through sports. In his own way, Namath would help build bridges on the Jets.

During the same period, greater individual freedom and expression was cultivated leading to more challenges to organizations of any kind. Teams require great sacrifices on the part of individuals for a greater good. On top of everything else, the Jets had severe financial problems for which Ewbank was held responsible. Remarkably, Weeb Ewbank was able to keep his team together during this most challenging period. He did this by making difficult personnel decisions on one hand and showing a great deal of patience and tolerance on the other. But the many adjustments made during a time of great change, created a team that was perhaps a little too loose for its own good in the long term. Towards the end of Ewbank's management of the Jets, it was time to restore a more disciplined approach and Ewbank decided to step down as coach—effective after the 1973 season. He continued as General Manager for 1974. He was seeing more challenges ahead that seemed to be the making of a changing world. "It's a rat race" he would give as a reason for retiring.[30] Concerning changes in athletes' customs, he would also say in comical Ewbank fashion:

I never thought I'd see a hair dryer in a locker room—but I did.[31]

1973 Season

The 1973 season, Ewbank's eleventh at the helm of the Jets, would be another one in which Joe Namath would miss many games. The Jets would suffer. The 4–10 season tied Ewbank's previous low point with the Jets in 1970. Only his first season with the Colts would be worse at 3–9. The Jets scored 240 points and allowed 306 points by their opponents. The Jets played their first six games on the road because fellow Shea tenants, the New York Mets, were still playing in the post-season.

Ewbank was an extraordinary team builder, but sustaining a championship caliber club is perhaps the rarest of skills in professional football coaching. In many organizations, it is almost impossible due to financial constraints. Once players become stars on a winning ball club, their salaries rise, leaving less for the rest of the team; draft choices become choice selections not premium grade; and camaraderie and team work become more difficult. After the 1969 season, the Jets went into a decline that would be very difficult for Ewbank to reverse. Namath was injured in three of the four seasons during this period. Riggins had two stellar seasons—1,000 yards from scrimmage in 1971 and 1,174 yards from scrimmage in 1972—then he fell off to 640 combined yards in 1973. Don Maynard's receptions dropped the last few years of his Jets career and in 1973, he snagged his last catch for the St. Louis Cardinals before his career ended. John Schmitt and Dave Herman finished off their Jets careers with Ewbank. Larry Grantham's career ended in 1972. Ralph Baker and Al Atkinson lasted one year past Ewbank.

After Football

Weeb and his wife Lucy retired to Oxford, Ohio, after he left coaching. He attended various football functions and spent time over at Miami University watching practices. He also spent time gardening and with his family—one of his daughters and her family lived in the area. He was active in corresponding with fans and friends. He enjoyed his status as an elder statesman of football and appreciated the interest others took in his teams and his accomplishments. He was inducted into the Pro Football Hall of Fame on July 29, 1978 and he lived another 23 years after his retirement in 1975. Ewbank died in Oxford, Ohio on November 17, 1998 at the age of 91.

Ewbank's Contributions to the Game

Ewbank calmly and methodically turned two fledgling teams into champions. Ewbank's teams accumulated 134 wins and 130 losses with 7 ties overall. He won three NFL Championships including one Super Bowl victory.

Ewbank's teams are thought of as the Colts of Johnny "the Golden Arm" Unitas and the Jets of "Broadway Joe" Namath. Interestingly enough, the two quarterbacks could not be more different, yet Ewbank managed each of them with skill. Ewbank was lauded for his work with players that focused on their talents rather than his own genius. Having worked under Paul Brown twice, he was like him in some ways, but very different in others. Like Paul Brown, he was confident in his own skills and abilities. He put an emphasis on the playbook, kept meticulous records, and graded his athletes on each play. But he was much more at ease with his players than his mentor. Colts and Jets players under Ewbank were allowed to express their opinions and he was not predisposed to try to control their lives off the field. He believed that he could not "treat a player like a child off the field" and expect them to "do a man's job" on the field.[32]

He would be described by longtime Jets' linebacker Larry Grantham as a tireless coach who would be out on the practice field most of the day; hold lengthy meetings after practice; catch up on phone calls, and manage negotiations in the evening; and then when most people would be sound asleep, go out for a drink.[33] The next day, he would be up at the crack of dawn to repeat the same pattern.

Ewbank was also able to juggle the work of general manager with his coaching responsibilities—no small accomplishment according to many who have tried it. Ewbank was the rarest of men in that he was magnanimous. He could go a full ten rounds in a negotiation in which he himself, his player, and his player's agent might go after each other tooth and nail, but all would be forgotten the following day.

The indefatigable Ewbank was the only coach to win championships in both the AFL and the NFL. In his first Colts' Championship win in 1958, the game went into sudden death overtime and was considered a game that won over millions of fans to the NFL. When his Jets beat the Colts in Super Bowl III, the game was another blockbuster event for a different reason. It was a "David and Goliath" story; the upstart Jets of the AFL defeating the mighty Colts.

Ewbank was the team builder who did it with hard work, patience, and player development. He was skilled at managing players, preparing his team for games, and developing strategies to win. He approached the game with discipline, but he approached his players with an eye towards understanding them as men and human beings.

Weeb Ewbank Timeline

1907

- May 6, 1907, Wilbur Charles "Weeb" Ewbank is born in Richmond, Indiana

1924

- Ewbank graduates from Oliver P. Morton High School where he played football, basketball, and baseball.
- Ewbank enters Miami University of Ohio.

1928

- Ewbank graduates from Miami University with a degree in Physical Education after playing football, basketball, and baseball.
- Ewbank teaches at Van Wert High School where he serves as Athletic Director and coaches several sports.

1930

- Ewbank moves back to Miami University where he teaches in the College of Education and coaches at the University's demonstration school called McGuffey High School. He also assists with Miami University's football team.

1932

- Ewbank receives an MA in Education from Columbia University.

1943

- Ewbank leaves McGuffey High School.
- Ewbank enlists in the Navy and is assigned to Great Lakes Naval Station where he works as an assistant football coach to Head Coach Paul Brown.

1946

- Ewbank joins the football staff at Brown University where he coaches the backfield—he also serves as head basketball coach.

1947

- Ewbank becomes head football coach at Washington University in St. Louis.

1949

- Ewbank takes a job as line coach for Paul Brown with the Cleveland Browns.

1954

- Baltimore Colts owner, Carroll Rosenbloom, taps Ewbank for his new head coach.

1956

- Johnny Unitas joins Ewbank's Colts.

1958

- December 14, 1958, the Colts finish their regular season with a 9–3 mark to win the Western Conference.
- December 28, 1958, the Baltimore Colts defeat the New York Giants, 23–17, in the NFL Championship game in Yankee Stadium in front of 70,000 fans with 40 million TV viewers. It is called "The Greatest Game."
- Ewbank is named UPI NFL Coach of the Year and the AP NFL Coach of the year for 1958.

1959

- The Colts end the 1959 season with another 9–3 mark to win the Western Conference.
- December 27, 1959, the Baltimore Colts defeat the New York Giants, 31–16, in the NFL Championship game. It is Ewbank's second NFL Championship.

1962

- Ewbank is fired by the Colts at the end of the season.

1963

- Ewbank becomes head coach of the New York Jets.

1965

- Joe Namath signs on with the Jets.

1968

- December 28, 1968, Ewbank's Jets defeat the Oakland Raiders, 27–23, in the AFL Championship game.

1969

- January 12, 1969, Ewbank's 1968 Jets defeat the Baltimore Colts, 16–7, in Super Bowl III. It is Ewbank's third NFL Championship.

1973

- Ewbank retires as Jets' coach after the 1973 season, but continues as General Manager.

1974

- January 19, 1974, Ewbank is inducted into the Indiana Football Hall of Fame.
- November 12, 1974, Ewbank retires as General Manager of the Jets.

1978

- Ewbank is enshrined into the Pro Football Hall of Fame as a member of the Class of 1978.

1998

- November 17, 1998, Ewbank dies in Oxford, Ohio, at the age of 91.

Highlights

The indefatigable Weeb Ewbank was the only coach to win championships in both the AFL and the NFL. He was a tremendous team-builder who took two fledgling teams, the Colts and the Jets, to the pinnacle of professional football. He successfully coached two of the most talented quarterbacks of their time: Johnny Unitas and Joe Namath. Ewbank holds an overall NFL head-coaching record of 134–130–7.

Ewbank won three NFL Championships. His first Colts' Championship win in 1958, went into sudden death overtime and won over millions of fans to the NFL. When his Jets beat the Colts in Super Bowl III, it was a "David and Goliath" story; the upstart Jets of the AFL defeating the mighty Colts of the NFL. Ewbank was named UPI NFL Coach of the Year for 1958. He was inducted into the Indiana Football Hall of Fame in 1974 and the Pro Football Hall of Fame in 1978.

Endnotes

1 Founder of the Quakers, George Fox wrote: "So let your lives preach, let your light shine, that your works may be seen, that your Father may be glorified; that your fruits may be unto holiness, and that your end may be everlasting life."

2 Ancestry.com records viewed at http://records.ancestry.com/Charles_Clifford_Ewbank_ records.ashx?pid=26311406 on April 20, 2013.

3 Paul Zimmerman, *The Last Season of Weeb Ewbank* (New York: Farrar, Straus, Giroux, 1974) 23.

4 *American National Biography Supplement Number 2*, Mark C. Carnes, Editor (New York: Oxford University Press, 2005) 161.

5 Although Ewbank and Brown would have a temporary falling out at one point, they reconnected. Ewbank visited Brown after Brown had been fired by Cleveland and before he began his career with the Cincinnati Bengals.

6 *American National Biography Supplement Number 2*, Carnes, 161.

7 Bob Broeg, *One Hundred Greatest Moments in St. Louis Sports* (St. Louis: Missouri Historical Society Press, 2000) 78.

8 Cradle of Coaches Collection, Weeb Ewbank Collection and The Walter Havighurst Special Collections, Miami University Libraries.

9 Weeb Ewbank as told to Neil Roiter, *Goal to Go: The Greatest Football Games I Have Coached* (New York: Hawthorne Books, 1972) 2.

10 Mike Towle, *Johnny Unitas: Mister Quarterback* (Nashville, Cumberland House, 2003) 81.

11 Duprey died in 2001. His nickname was etched into his tombstone, see: http://www.findagrave.com/cgi-bin/fg.cgi?page=gr&GRid=5860417

12 Ewbank and Roiter, *Goal to Go: The Greatest Football Games I Have Coached*, 1.

13 Towle, *Johnny Unitas: Mister Quarterback*, ix.

14 For a concise look at Conley and his Old Miss connection see http://www.coachwyatt.com/CharlieConerly.pdf

15 Ewbank and Roiter, *Goal to Go: The Greatest Football Games I Have Coached*, 38.

16 Nash's "My Colts, verses and reverses," Copyright 1968 by Ogden Nash. First Appeared in *Life Magazine*. Reprinted by permission of Curtis Brown, Ltd.)

17 Maryland State College is now called University of Maryland Eastern Shore.

18 Sauer's father, George Sauer, Sr., played with the Green Bay Packers from 1935-1937.

19 Ewbank and Roiter, *Goal to Go, The Greatest Football Games I Have Coached*, 115.

20 W.C. Heintz, "Countdown for Joe Namath," *Life Magazine*, August 20, 1965.

21 Heintz, "Countdown for Joe Namath."

22 Frank Litsky, "Farewell to Ewbank: Vignettes of a True Coach and Friend," *New York Times*, November 19, 1998. Viewed at http://www.nytimes.com/1998/11/19/sports/pro-football-farewell-to-ewbank-vignettes-of-a-true-coach-and-friend.html?n=Top%2fReference%2fTimes%20Topics%2fSubjects%2fF%2fFootball on April 30, 2013.

23 W.C. Heintz, "Countdown for Joe Namath."

24 Frank Litsky, "Farewell to Ewbank: Vignettes of a True Coach and Friend," *New York Times*.

25 Joe Namath, NFL Shutdown Corner blog, posted at http://sports.yahoo.com/blogs/nfl-shutdown-corner/joe-namath-nfl-blog-super-bowl-prediction-191250983.html viewed on May, 1, 2013.

26 Ewbank and Roiter, *Goal to Go, The Greatest Football Games I Have Coached*, 136.

27 Doug Brown, "Looking Back at Namath's Prediction, *The Baltimore Evening Sun*, January

12, 1989." Viewed at http://articles.latimes.com/1989-01-12/sports/sp-376_1_joe-namath viewed on May 1, 2013.

[28] Joe Namath, NFL Shutdown Corner blog.

[29] Frank Litsky, "Farewell to Ewbank: Vignettes of a True Coach and Friend," *New York Times*.

[30] Zimmerman, *The Last Season of Weeb Ewbank*, 96.

[31] Zimmerman, *The Last Season of Weeb Ewbank*, 96.

[32] Zimmerman, *The Last Season of Weeb Ewbank*, 99.

[33] Zimmerman, *The Last Season of Weeb Ewbank*,135.

Vince Lombardi

"They call it coaching, but it is teaching."

Standing on the sidelines at St. Norbert College in De Pere, Wisconsin, is the human lightning bolt that struck Green Bay 9 years ago and has kept the city in lights ever since. His name is Vince Lombardi. He stands looking out in his sunglasses, white football pants with black belt, and white cotton shirt. As the sun beats down, he takes his Green Bay Packers cap off, wipes his forehead, and puts his cap back on. It is the second week of the Green Bay Packers' 1967 training camp. The Packers are preparing for a run at a third NFL Championship in a row.

Lombardi moves out on the parched field; he is hot, frustrated, and angry. He bellows out to one of his linemen: "You turkey. Look at that sloppy stance." Attention is focused on this one raw player. Lombardi criticizes the player repeatedly. Lombardi's face gets darker as he gets angrier. The minutes pass; the drill continues mercilessly. Finally, the coach sees some improvement. He shakes his head to himself and his mood changes. He turns away and chuckles quietly. A smile spreads across his face as he looks up towards the blue sky away from his players for a moment.

It is getting hotter. But for Lombardi, this is when games are won or lost. No one is as demanding as Lombardi. No one wins like him either. A few minutes pass and there is more sloppy play to squash. Lombardi is serious again. The drill instructor is back in the midst of his men "instructing."

Over the course of training camp, Lombardi will beat down his players. He will constantly challenge their endurance. He will drill them a thousand times on every play, instruct them on every move they must make. And just when his players are ready to explode, he will praise them and acknowledge their achievements.

Lombardi is the ultimate disciplinarian. Players love Lombardi. Players hate Lombardi. Players fear Lombardi. For most of them, there is nothing as important as succeeding—bringing pride and honor to their team, their city, and themselves. They are from different races, different social backgrounds, and different parts of the country. Personalities differ as well. Some are quiet and self controlled. Some are rambunctious. Lombardi hones them all into a team—from the playboys to the altar boys, from the rookies to the oldest veterans. Lombardi's Packers seek perfection as a unit. For Lombardi, camp preparation is not just understanding and performing difficult drills. Preparation is repetitive. Preparation is painful.

Players line up for a routine Lombardi drill. Men smash each other. They strike each other with forearms, shoulders, fists, and helmets. They collide and crash to the ground. The coach smiles at their efforts. Lombardi, like his father, and his grandfather, has the greatest respect for making a living in arduous physical work. For Lombardi, football exemplifies such work.

Early Years

Vincent Thomas Lombardi was born on June 11, 1913, in New York City. He was named after his grandfather who emigrated from southern Italy and started a delivery business in New York, using horse-drawn wagons. The Lombardi family originally lived in a New York tenement. Lombardi's father, Harry, became a butcher and opened up a shop with his brother Edward. The business provided a livelihood right through the Great Depression and beyond. A friend, Frank Izzo, introduced Harry to his sister Matilda. Harry and Matilda became a couple and they were married in 1912. The Izzo family was a village unto themselves. Harry Lombardi's father-in-law Anthony Izzo and mother-in-law, Loretta Izzo, had 13 children. Most would grow up, marry, and like Harry and Matilda, live close to their parents in Sheepshead Bay in Brooklyn.[1]

Sheepshead Bay included a small inlet connected to the Atlantic. Sheepshead Bay was a hospitable area known for large hotels, restaurants, and fishing. Inland from the bay, Sheepshead was almost rural when Harry and Matilda settled in to raise their own family. Harry and Matilda had four more children after Vincent: Madeline, Harold, Claire, and Joe spread out over a 17-year period.

Harry was stout at 5-foot-5, covered in tattoos, and strong as an ox. He was also a perfectionist who insisted on doing everything his way. Vince would often work with his father handling huge slabs of meat and developing muscles on his 5-foot-8 frame.

Vince Lombardi's father would be remembered as a strict disciplinarian. His mother would be remembered as affectionate. Vince would grow up in a huge extended family, living with the constant social interactions, warmth, and conflicts that such a family provides. And by living in Sheepshead, he would also share experiences with many friends from immigrant families from all over Europe.

Vince developed a love of the Catholic faith early in his life and he attended Mass regularly. He served with some distinction as an altar boy. Vince attended Cathedral College of the Immaculate Conception, a Prep School that educated students who expressed an interest in the Priesthood. The school did not offer a football program. After deciding that he did not want to become a Priest, Lombardi transferred to St. Francis Catholic for what would be his fifth year of high school. St. Francis gave Lombardi a single year of experience in football.

St. Francis lost only one game when Lombardi played and the loss came at the hands of public school power, Erasmus Hall. The Erasmus Hall game provided Lombardi with the opportunity to play against future Chicago Bears' quarterback sensation, Sid Luckman.[2]

Learning Years

Lombardi obtained a scholarship to play football at Fordham University. Fordham and its Jesuit tradition would have a great impact on him. In this tradition, individuals are highly valued along with their potential. The "cura personalis" (care for the entire person) is central. Jesuits value each individual and his or her potential. Jesuit teachers direct and encourage students to pursue great personal excellence in all aspects of life. This principle of excellence, called "magis," comes from the Latin phrase "Ad majorem Dei gloriam" (for the greater glory of God), which is the motto of the Jesuits dating back to the order's founder, St. Ignatius Loyola. The idea of hard work and achievement is something that was fostered in both Lombardi's home and at Fordham. He passed it on as well. Lombardi often displayed a concern for his players and their potential well beyond the lines of the football field. He drove players to excel not just for their own good, but to give honor to something greater.

Fordham and Crowley

Coach James Crowley had played for Curly Lambeau at Green Bay East High School and then played at Notre Dame under Knute Rockne, where he and three others in the backfield were immortalized by Grantland Rice as the famous "Four Horsemen of the Apocalypse."[3] As a lineman, Lombardi would have to clear his head of any "four horsemen" images, if he ever had them. However, he would become an official member of the Fordham's famous offensive line called the "Seven Blocks of Granite."[4]

Fordham was a national power when Lombardi joined the team. He came to Fordham as a fullback, but he was too slow for the backfield and Coach Crowley moved him to guard. Lombardi was challenged in many ways at Fordham. Early on, there were injuries. As a small 180-pound lineman, he had to compete with much bigger more powerful players. Crowley moved players around to get the best men on the field. As a senior, Lombardi would be included in that number.

Right from the start of his Fordham football career, much of Lombardi's instruction would come from Fordham line coach and future football legend, Frank Leahy. Leahy, who would provide a "masters class" on line play for Lombardi, would later serve as head coach at Boston College and then Notre Dame. Coach Crowley was no slouch either in the college game. He compiled an 86–23–11 college record at Michigan State, Fordham, and North Carolina Pre-Flight.

At Fordham, Lombardi's roommate Jim Lawlor helped Lombardi in many ways, including his love life. Lombardi was introduced to Marie Planitz

Vince Lombardi at Fordham

through a Lawlor connection. Marie was Lombardi's first and last girlfriend. They would date throughout college and marry afterwards.

St. Cecilia High School

When Lombardi graduated from Fordham, he was not sure of what he wanted to do and employment was not easy to get. The Depression was still chugging along. In 1939, after a brief law school experience at Fordham and a few jobs that did not suit him, Lombardi took a position teaching at St. Cecilia High School in Englewood, New Jersey. At St. Cecilia, Lombardi worked with Andy Palau, a former teammate of his at Fordham who was known as "Handy Andy" in his quarterback playing days. Lombardi served as Palau's assistant coach. Together they developed tremendous teams. And just as important, Lombardi was given a variety of teaching assignments. He would eventually spend most of his time on the sciences. For Lombardi, there would always be a connection between teaching and coaching. He would write:

They call it coaching, but it is teaching. You do not just tell them it is so, but you show them the reasons why it is so and you repeat and repeat until they are convinced, until they know.[5]

While the Palau-Lombardi teams were putting St. Cecilia's football program on the map, Vince and Marie were married and began raising a family. They had a son, Vincent, in 1942 and 5 years later, a daughter Susan was born.

Lombardi and Palau teamed up for 3 successful years with Palau focused on the offense and Lombardi on the defense. Before the 1942 season, Palau took a job with Fordham as the backfield coach.[6] This left Lombardi to run St. Cecilia's with a new assistant, Father Tim Moore. Lombardi did some homework in the offseason studying the T Formation. A new book written and published by Clark Shaughnessy, Ralph Jones, and George Halas called *The Modern T Formation with Man in Motion* was being gobbled up by coaches all over the country. The Shaughnessy-Jones-Halas version of the T Formation was a much improved revision that used the quarterback to handle each snap and direct each play, but it also included man-in-motion plays that kept the defense on edge.[7] Lombardi used the T Formation as well as the Notre Dame Box that he had learned at Fordham.

Back to Fordham

In 1947, Lombardi returned to his alma mater, Fordham University, to coach the freshman football team. He continued to work on the modern T Formation that he brought with him from St. Cecilia and he drilled his players intensely on the smallest of movements. His freshman team became masters at execution. Their skill at the T Formation gave them a great advantage over other teams.

The following season, Lombardi was an assistant coach for the varsity. He worked under Coach Ed Danowski and was able to put to use many of his ideas, but not fast enough to improve the Fordham varsity's performance that season that turned in a 3–6 record. Fordham was heading towards deemphasizing football. Lombardi moved on.

West Point

After the 1948 season ended at Fordham, Lombardi accepted a new position coaching the offensive line at the United States Military Academy at West Point. Here he had the opportunity to work with Colonel Red Blaik, West Point's legendary football coach.

After a long series of excellent coaching experiences at a number of schools, the Colonel signed on as the head coach at West Point where he would stay for 18 seasons. He won national championships in 1944 and 1945. Many of Blaik's innovations and practices would show up in Green Bay. Blaik promoted the platoon system, where players would play on offense or defense, but not both. He would analyze plays in great detail and chart team tendencies. He studied film and graded his players. And he planned practices in detail and used the players' time wisely as cadets had less of it to use for football practice than non-military schools. Blaik promoted fundamentals, perfection in execution, and second effort, while pointing out that football was a game of inches. Unlike Lombardi, Blaik was cool and collected in most every circumstance, but certainly much of Blaik's approach would be picked up by his assistant coach.[8] Lombardi spent 5 years at West Point.

New York Giants

In 1954, the New York Giants had a new head coach, Jim Lee Howell, who had replaced Steve Owen. Owen was an institution with the Giants, a long-time player, and a 23-year coach. Owen was beloved by the Mara family, the team owners.

Howell hired two excellent assistants to help improve and modernize the Giants: Vince Lombardi to manage the offense and Tom Landry to manage the defense. Lombardi was boisterous and excitable. Landry was calm and quiet. Lombardi spent 5 years with the Giants. The new coaching staff did turn things around. The Giants won the NFL Championship in 1956 and in 1958 lost the championship in overtime to the Baltimore Colts.

Lombardi had an opportunity to pick up many great ideas about running an excellent NFL defense from Landry, who was a master at it. The Giants were interested in having Lombardi as a head coach, but there was no precise exit plan for Howell. Lombardi moved on when an offer came from Green Bay. Lombardi and the Mara family however burned no bridges between them, so the family would come courting in the future, but the timing was just never quite right.

Green Bay Packers

Ray "Scooter" McLean resigned after the Packers' 1–10–1 season in 1958. The Packers were looking for a change and decided upon Vince Lombardi. Lombardi was a strong personality who would recapture the success that the franchise had when another larger-than-life coach, Curly Lambeau, had run the team.

Playing for Lombardi

How would it have been to play for Lombardi back in the 1960s in Green Bay? Coach Lombardi demands that all his players understand and practice the fundamentals. He tells everyone "unless you can block and tackle, you don't belong on the team."[9] Lombardi reasons: "...if you block and tackle better than the other team and the breaks are even, you're going to win."[10]

There are no prima donnas on Lombardi's Green Bay Packers. Yet the coach understands reality. Not everyone can knuckle down 24/7. He tries to reform his playboys, but in his heart of hearts, he understands that he cannot change them, so he fines them. A few hundred here and a few hundred there—every player pays a price for indiscretions.

Time is important to Lombardi—so important in fact, that he expects his players to be present at all team meetings 15 minutes before the scheduled start. If you are not early, you are late. It comes to be called "Lombardi time" and eventually the clock out in front of Lambeau Field in Green Bay will be set to Lombardi time.[11]

Teamwork is also fundamental. Lombardi has no tolerance for racism. He tells the team that racism is something that he will not tolerate. Lombardi himself was victim to prejudice due to his dark complexion and his Catholic faith.

Focus is another critical aspect of Lombardi's success formula for his players as exemplified by the famous words: "Winning isn't everything; it's the only thing."[12] He wants his players to put aside most everything that might take away accomplishing the team goal of winning. This does not mean that he wants his players to do anything to win, such as cheating or taking cheap shots at the opposition. It simply points to the personal sacrifice required to succeed and deliver the highest performance on the field.

There is a hard edge to Lombardi and softness too, but his players never know what they are going to get. Lombardi is the father who is hard to please, but who loosens up to praise and joke. He is the school teacher who criticizes everyone, even his star students, but looks out with tears in his eyes on graduation day.

Lombardi believes that all the great ones want to win fiercely and they possess a hunger for glory.[13] Lombardi recruits highly competitive players who want to be the best. And being the best is what Vincent Lombardi is all about.

Lombardi's Players

After Lombardi made his first offseason moves and signings, George Halas was asked about the Packers' prospects. Sizing up Lombardi's efforts before the season began, Halas said:

> *I know that Vince Lombardi is not only a fine football technician, but an excellent shrewd organizer as well. I've been watching the deals he's made and the rookies he's added, and believe me, he is doing a reconstruction job that may cause some revision of forecasts in the Western Conference of our league.*[14]

In Lombardi's first season as head coach of the Green Bay Packers, he traded or released 16 players from the 1958 squad. Among those remaining were many excellent athletes, albeit many in need of Lombardi's "polishing."

Bart Starr

Bart Starr joined the Packers in 1956 from Alabama where he led the Crimson Tide to the Southeastern Conference (SEC) title in 1953. Due to an injury and coaching change, Starr did not see much action his last two college seasons and was a long shot in the draft. Selected in the 17th round, he lived through some rough seasons with the Packers when they went 8–27–1 in his 3 years before Lombardi. Lombardi believed Starr would excel regardless of his *checkered* college and early-professional career. Lombardi encouraged Starr and built up his confidence. Starr became an excellent leader who could play especially well in the big games. Especially revered for his decision-making capabilities, Starr was a smart quarterback. He was also one of the most accurate passers in the league. Because the Packers had such a great rushing game, which Lombardi nurtured, Starr would never have the kind of statistics that he might have had if he had played for a team that focused on the pass. However, the balanced attack was what made the Packers great and Starr was a major player in their achievements. Starr would be counted as one of many Hall of Famers who played for Lombardi.

Bill Forester

Bill "Bubba" Forester was a veteran outside linebacker for the Packers. Drafted by the Packers in the third round of the 1953 draft, he played 11 seasons.

Dan Currie

"Dapper" Dan Currie was an All-American center and linebacker at Michigan State. He was also versatile enough to play every position on the line at one time or another for the Spartans.[15] Currie was the top draft choice of the Green Bay Packers in 1958.

Forrest Gregg

Hall of Famer Forrest Gregg was another veteran lineman in place when Lombardi came to Green Bay. Gregg was an offensive tackle whom Lombardi considered to be one of the finest football players to ever play for him.

Henry Jordan

Henry Jordan came to the Packers from the Cleveland Browns in 1959 and the Hall of Famer stayed for 11 seasons. He was a quick, agile defensive tackle especially skilled at pass rushing. He played a key role in harassing the opposing quarterbacks and swatting at the ball.

Jerry Kramer

Jerry Kramer was an All-American at the University of Idaho where he played guard and served as a kicker. He also competed in track and field where he set shot put records. Kramer was a fourth round draft choice of the Packers in 1958. Kramer developed into one of the best lineman of all time under former lineman Lombardi. He was often called Lombardi's whipping boy, but the extra attention paid off for Kramer and the team.

Jim Ringo

Jim Ringo had played center for the Packers since 1953. He was a key member of the successful line that drove much of the offense in the early Lombardi years. Ringo was another Lombardi player who would be inducted into the Hall of Fame.

Jim Taylor

Jim Taylor was a versatile All-American running back at LSU. He led the SEC in rushing in 1956 and 1957. Taylor was a second round selection of the Packers in 1958. The muscle-bound back loved to initiate contact with defenders. He lifted weights before it was customary for football players. He was tough and he gave everything he had in each football game. He was so competitive that he often grew angry and combative with any defender who dared to tackle him. In almost any situation if the Packer offense was stalled, they could give the ball to Taylor. He was exceptional and another Lombardi-era Packer inducted into the Hall of Fame.

Max McGee

Max McGee played for Tulane where he was the leading rusher for 3 years. The Packers selected him in the 1954 draft, but he served as an Air Force pilot in 1955 and 1956 so his Packers' career was postponed. He was a gifted receiver, kick returner, and punter for the Packers.

Paul Hornung

The "Golden Boy," Paul Hornung, was the 1956 Heisman Trophy winner who played quarterback at Notre Dame. Hornung contributed in many ways to the success of the Packers. He was converted to a halfback under Lombardi and he would run, pass, catch passes, and join a number of his teammates in the Hall of Fame. He returned kickoffs and kicked extra points and field goals. Although Hornung was the king of the late night excursion and Lombardi was perhaps the greatest practitioner of player discipline, they made it work. Hornung succinctly described the relationship between Lombardi and himself: "He was the ultimate disciplinarian and I was the ultimate coach's nightmare."[16]

Ray Nitschke

Ray Nitschke played at the University of Illinois and he was skilled enough to play quarterback, fullback, and linebacker. He was selected in the third round of the NFL draft in 1958. Nitschke would develop into a Hall of Fame linebacker who was both feared and revered.

Coaches

Lombardi started out with four assistant coaches: Phil Bengston, Bill Austin, Red Cochran, and Norb Hecker. Bengston who had seven seasons with the 49ers, would coach the vaunted Packers' defense throughout Lombardi's tenure. Austin coached the offensive line through the 1964 season. Cochran was the offensive backfield coach from 1959-1966. Norb Hecker was Lombardi's defensive backfield coach from 1959-1965. Ray Wietecha was offensive line coach from 1965 and beyond Lombardi's last year. Other coaches such as Jerry Burns, Dave Hanner, Tom McCormick, and Bob Snelker served in Lombardi's later years.[17]

Green Bay Sweep

Lombardi had a signature play that he would use in Green Bay that came to be called the Power Sweep, the Lombardi Sweep, and the Green Bay Sweep.[18]

All 11 men on the field had to perform flawlessly for the play to work well, but the key players leading the play were the two guards. Once the ball was snapped, the guards stepped back and moved in the direction of the play (either right or left) running parallel along the line of scrimmage. When they reached the tackle position, they would cut upfield with the running back and blocking back behind them. The blocking back would block the defensive end. The other players would have their blocking assignments as well. The tight end was assigned the outside linebacker; the center would face the defensive tackle. Everyone would have set responsibilities, but some players had to block according to the movement of the targeted player. Meanwhile, the guards would be pushing up field and hitting the defenders in front of them, in some cases linebackers or the safety and corners.

There were hundreds of potential variations on blocks. The running back would "run to daylight," in other words run where the holes were rather than a predetermined place. The guards pulled, blocks were executed, and the running back decided where to run. There was a lot happening for a simple running play, so Lombardi drilled the play and its variations over and over again. To run the sweep to perfection, it required an almost total commitment to the play from an offense and endless repetition. Most coaches would not spend so much time on one single play and few teams had a guard the caliber of Jerry Kramer who was largely credited with making it work so often in Green Bay.

The Sweep came to fruition in Green Bay, but it was developed by Lombardi over time. Something akin to the play had been developed by Lombardi when he was coaching the Giants and Frank Gifford. According to Father Tim Moore, who assisted Lombardi at St. Cecilia, Lombardi was using the optional blocking schemes and "run to daylight" notion there as well.[19] The Sweep brought attention to the Packers' guards Jerry Kramer and Fuzzy Thurston, who were key to the success of the play. These guards were often featured in photographs that showed them leading Paul Hornung or Jim Taylor to "daylight" on scoring plays. Lombardi would bring credit to the Packer guards the way Fordham brought credit to the Seven Blocks of Granite.

1959 Season

The Packers' first game in 1959 was against their archenemy, the Chicago Bears. It was played in front of 28,286 at new City Stadium in Green Bay. The scoring highlights for the Bears came from kicker John Aveni who managed to kick two long field goals—one from 46 yards out in the first half and a second from 42 yards in the fourth quarter. The Packers' defense was stifling all day. Likewise, the Bears held the Packers' offense to "wishing and hoping" for most of the game until a Bears' fumble was recovered by Jim Ringo on the Bears' 26-yard line. The Packers advanced to the 5-yard line where Taylor ran around end for the score. The extra point gave the Packers the lead, 7–6. Later in the fourth quarter, when the Bears were pinned back by their own end zone,

Chicago quarterback Ed Brown was tackled in the end zone by Dave Hanner for a safety. The Packers beat the Bears, 9–6.

Next up were the pesky Detroit Lions who more often than not, played the Packers tough. Packers' quarterback Lamar McHan would have a fine day going 7 for 16 for four touchdowns while gaining 146 yards in the air with one interception. The Lions' highlights included a monstrous 50-yard field goal from Jim Martin and the NFL Rookie of the Year Nick Pietrosante's touchdown run from 1-yard out.[20] The Packers won, 28–10.

The Packers faced the 49ers in the third game of the season at home. The Packers ran out ahead at the half, 14–6. San Francisco quarterback, Yelberton Abraham (Y.A.) Tittle shook up the Packers, but he came up short. In the second half, Tittle connected with Billy Wilson on a 14-yard pass for a touchdown. Then he connected with R.C. Owens on a huge 75-yard touchdown pass that put San Francisco ahead, 20–14. The Packers rallied and McHan came back with a 21-yard touchdown toss to Gary Knafelc in the fourth quarter for the 21–20 win.

Losing came in one big clump for Lombardi in 1959. On October 18, the Packers were blown out by the Rams, 45–6. Green Bay took it on the chin from Baltimore, 38–21, on October 25. Then the Giants beat them, 20–3, on November 1. The Bears beat up the Packers, 28–17, in the next contest and Bart Starr took over for an injured Lamar McHan in the second half of that game. When Baltimore beat the Packers, 28–24, in game 8, it was the last loss of the season. At 3–5, perhaps the Packers' organization was wondering if they made the best choice in coaches. Any doubts would not last long.

On November 22, the Packers blanked the Redskins 21–0 in front of 31,853 fans at new City Stadium for the Packers' last home game. Four days later on Thanksgiving, the Packers scored three times off of turnovers to edge the Lions, 24–17, in Detroit. Before a crowd of 61,044 in Los Angeles, the Packers were able to turn the tables on the Rams, 38–20. The last game of the season was a 36–14 rout of the 49ers. It gave Lombardi a winning season—the first one for the Packers since Curly Lambeau's 1947 season. Lombardi's 7–5 finish was a huge improvement over the 1–10–1 record the previous year.

1960 Season

Joining the Packers in 1960 were two Hall of Famers, Willie Wood and Willie Davis. Wood was an undrafted free agent quarterback from the University of Southern California (USC). Wood played 12 excellent seasons at free safety. Willie Davis would play defensive end for the Packers. Davis was drafted by the Browns and came over to the Packers in a trade. He was a team leader who would never miss a game in his 12-year career. Lombardi valued him for his "speed, agility, and size."[21] Both Davis and Wood were critical contributors to the Lombardi-Era Packers.

Football is simple in one way—the team that scores the most points wins. During the Lombardi years, Green Bay typically scored 100 points more per season than their oppositions scored against them. Green Bay scored 332 points and allowed 209 in the 1960 season. In the early Lombardi years, the Packers' great running game defined the offense. Hornung and Taylor were a big part of that game. Before the 1960 season began, in talking about Paul Hornung, Lombardi said:

Let's face it. He's the guy who makes us go. Hornung is a key player and much of our success will depend upon him.[22]

During the 1960 season, Hornung ran for 13 touchdowns, caught 2 touchdown passes, made 41 extra points, and kicked 15 field goals for a record-breaking 176 point total.[23] Jim Taylor more than doubled his rushing yards from the previous season to 1,101. It was the first of 5-straight 1,000-yard rushing seasons for Taylor. About midway through the season, Starr would take over as starting quarterback, but he would still be developing at the position.

In the season opener against the Chicago Bears, a Packers' score by Taylor in the second quarter and another by Paul Hornung in the third put Green Bay ahead, 14–0. Touchdown runs by the Bears' tandem of Willie Galimore and Rick Casares in the fourth quarter evened up the score at 14–14. With less than a minute to go, the Bears' John Aveni kicked a 16-yard field goal for a 17–14 Bears win. A brutal start, but Lombardi would often show a talent for picking his team up after a loss.

The Packers rebounded and beat the Lions, 28–9. Green Bay limited the Lions to three field goals while scoring four touchdowns themselves. The Baltimore Colts fell apart in the face of Lombardi's defense the following week when the Packers intercepted four passes and recovered two fumbles. The final score was Packers 35–Colts 21.[24]

On October 23, 1960, the Packers' offense sparked a 41–14 rout of San Francisco. Hornung rushed for two touchdowns, kicked two field goals, and made five extra points for a total of 23 points on the day. One ongoing concern about the offense was the up and down play of McHan, the Packers' quarterback. When Green Bay played Pittsburgh on October 30, it was Hornung doing all the Packers' scoring in the first half. He hit four field goals in a row. A Bobby Layne pass to Tom "the Bomb" Tracy gave the Steelers their first score in the second quarter. The 13-year veteran Layne hit Buddy Dial for another Steelers' score in the fourth quarter. The score stood at 13–12 in Pittsburgh's favor. Lombardi had replaced McHan with Starr in the second half and with Starr at the helm, the Packers mounted a successful touchdown drive. Taylor ran the ball in from the 1-yard line to cap off the drive. Hornung's extra point gave the Packers a 19–13 win.[25]

On November 6, 1960, in Baltimore, two Hall of Famers, Johnny Unitas and Raymond Berry, played pitch and catch. The duo connected for three scores to help defeat the Packers, 38–24. Starr completed 23 of 32 passes, but tossed four interceptions. Taylor rushed for one touchdown; Hornung rushed for two and kicked a field goal. Next, Green Bay walloped Dallas, 41–7, in a game that featured a Ray Nitschke interception that the 235 pound linebacker carried 41 yards to the end zone. Fans were also treated to three touchdown runs by Taylor. Two losses followed that might have easily derailed the season: A 33–31 loss to the Rams and a 23–10 loss to the Lions. But on December 4, Lombardi's Packers were able to right themselves with a 41–13 win over the Bears. They followed up with victories over the 49ers and the Rams.

1960 NFL Championship Game

The Packers played the Philadelphia Eagles for the NFL Championship on December 26, 1960, in Franklin Field in Philadelphia before a huge crowd of 67,325.[26] It was a game that would try any coach's soul. The Packers' Bill Quinlan intercepted a pass on the Philadelphia 13-yard line and Green Bay took over from there. Lombardi looked on as the Packers were stuffed on four downs. No attempt at a field goal was made. The Packers turned the ball over to the Eagles on downs at the 6-yard line. The Eagles turned the ball over again, this time on a fumble on their 20-yard line. After three plays, the Packers had advanced the ball 7 yards. This time, a Paul Hornung field goal gave the Packers 3 points. In the second quarter, Hornung kicked another field goal— this one from 20 yards out. Later in the quarter, two Hall of Famers delivered for the Eagles when quarterback Norm Van Brocklin connected with Tommy McDonald on a 35-yard touchdown pass. The Eagles led, 7–6, after the extra point. The Eagles had another successful drive that ended with a field goal by Bobby Walston. And just before the end of the first half, Hornung had a chance to match Walston, but missed. The Eagles nested on a 10–6 lead at the half.

The Packers drove down the field on their opening possession of the second half, but stalled at the Eagles' 26-yard line. Lombardi decided against a field goal once again on fourth down and the Eagles' defense stopped the Packers. After an Eagles' drive into Green Bay territory, Johnny Symank intercepted a pass for Green Bay, but the Green Bay offense sputtered to another stall. Later in the quarter, after another lackluster possession, Max McGee was sent in to punt on fourth down deep in Packers' territory. When the Eagles pulled back at the snap with no one to cover McGee, he took off running past midfield keeping the drive alive. The drive continued and Starr hit McGee for the score on a 7-yard pass. The Packers led, 13–10.

Ted Dean gave the Eagles great field position for their next possession when he took the Green Bay kickoff 58 yards. A short Eagles' drive ensued and a few plays later, running back Dean punched the ball in from the 5-yard line for the score. After the extra point, the Eagles led, 17–13. Late in the waning moments of the game, Starr directed a last minute drive towards the Eagle goal line. On the last play of the game from 22 yards out, Starr hit Taylor with a short pass. With the entire Franklin Field crowd holding their breath, Taylor struggled to make his way into the end zone with everything he had, but he was stopped by the last defender at the 9-yard line.[27] The championship was lost, but Lombardi vowed never to lose another one.

1961 Season

The Packers' number one draft choice for 1961 was Herb Adderley, a running back from Duffy Daugherty's Michigan State team. Lombardi knew that in Adderley he had a great athlete although two great running backs in Hornung and Taylor were already well entrenched with the Packers. He switched Adderley to defensive back and used him on kick returns. The Hall of Famer excelled at both.

In 1961, the Packers were a tremendous power. Bart Starr passed for 2,418 yards with a completion rate of 58.3 for 16 touchdowns and 16 interceptions. Paul Hornung was called up for active duty in the army reserve that year, but he received weekend passes to play. Hornung rushed for 597 yards and eight touchdowns and had 15 receptions for 145 yards and two touchdowns. His 10 touchdowns, 41 extra points, and 15 field goals added up to an amazing 146 points that made him the leading NFL scorer for the third season in a row. Fullback Jim Taylor had 1,307 yards rushing and 15 rushing touchdowns with 25 receptions for 175 yards and one touchdown receiving. The Packers scored 391 points while only allowing 223. They had the top offense and the second highest ranked defense.

Despite their awesome power, the Packers lost their first game in a poor performance against Detroit. The Packers drove the ball downfield and scored on a Taylor run in their first possession. A few series later, the Lions mounted a 52-yard drive to score with fullback Nick Pietrosante taking it in from the 1-yard line. In the second quarter, Detroit's Howard "Hopalong" Cassady returned a punt to the Packers' 46. When the Packers' defense stiffened, Yale Lary faked a punt and rushed to the Packers' 28-yard line on fourth down. A few plays later, as Detroit quarterback Earl Morrall was being hit, he tossed a lateral to Pietrosante who took it in for another score. After Hornung kicked a field goal to close out the half, it was Lions 14–Packers 10. In the second half, the Packers' Johnny Symank intercepted a Morrall pass and the Packers drove downfield to the Lions' 2-yard line, but could not score. After the teams swapped field goals, the scoring ended. When the gun sounded, the final score was Lions 17–Packers 13.[28]

After the loss to the Lions, Lombardi's Packers went on a six-game winning streak in which no opposing team got within 10 points. The streak included a 45–7 romp of the Colts at home, but proving professional football unpredictable, when the Packers traveled to play the Colts in Baltimore's Memorial Stadium on November 5, the Colts won 45–21. Johnny Unitas threw four touchdowns that day.

After rolling off four wins in a row, the Packers lost a 22–21 squeaker to the 49ers, but came right back and beat the Rams, 24–17, in the final regular season game. On top of the NFL Western Conference, the Packers played the Giants for the NFL Championship on the last day of the year, December 31, 1961.

1961 NFL Championship Game

On December 31, 1961, the NFL Championship game featuring the Green Bay Packers and the New York Giants was played in Green Bay at New City Stadium. The Packers had used a variety of large Milwaukee stadiums for previous home championship games. The new City Stadium would be renamed Lambeau Field in 1965 in honor of the Packers' founding father, Curly Lambeau. The temperature hovered just below 20° for the Packers' homecoming against the Giants.

Lombardi knew his foe well having been an assistant with the Giants for five seasons. It had only been three seasons ago when he and Tom Landry worked with Coach Jim Lee Howell. A worn out Howell moved to the front office and Allie Sherman became head coach before the start of the 1961 season.

Although the game was played on New Year's Eve, it was more like Halloween for the Giants. Things began slowly with no score in the first quarter before the nightmare began for the Giants. After a Nitschke interception in the first few minutes of the second quarter, Hornung took the ball in from the 6-yard line. Another Nitschke interception, this one with an assist by Green Bay tackle Henry Jordan who tipped the ball, gave the Packers the ball just 33 yards from the end zone. Flanker Boyd Dowler caught a 15-yard pass from Starr in the end zone a short time later. The next time the Giants had the ball, Hank Gremminger intercepted a pass and the Packers started another drive— this one on the Giants' 36. The Packers excellent tight end, Ron Kramer, caught a Starr pass for the score that punctuated this third drive. Hornung was spot on with the extra point attempts and the Packers led, 21–0.

The Giants' quarterback who was living a nightmare out on the field that day was none other than Y.A. Tittle who had only 12 interceptions that year, but had thrown three in the first half. Tittle was a 13-year veteran before he ever donned a Giants' uniform that year. The Hall of Famer would give the New Yorkers 4 years of excellent play, but December 31, 1961, was not his day.

Tittle was replaced with Charley Conerly, who was in his 14th year with the Giants. Conerly was someone Lombardi knew from his own days with the Giants. In fact, Conerly was one of Lombardi's favorite players according to teammate Frank Gifford.[29] On the Giants' next series, Conerly moved the team downfield where the drive stalled at the six and died there after a fourth down halfback-option pass flew out of the back of the end zone.

The remainder of the game would be good for a Packers' highlight film, but not much of a football contest. Three Hornung field goals and another

Ron Kramer touchdown grab gave the Packers a 37–0 win and the Giants a whopper of a 1961 football hangover. Lombardi and his Packers had won a championship and they made it look easy.

1962 Season

Hornung had finished his active military duty and was available fulltime for the Packers' 1962 season. The Packers scored 415 points that season and only allowed 148 from their competitors. The Packers' first game was against their new neighbors to the West, the Minnesota Vikings. It was the Vikings second season. It was not much of a contest although the packed crowd of 38,669 in Green Bay was not complaining. Hornung made the first four scores of the game with two touchdown runs and two field goals. He kicked both extra points as well. A Starr to Ron Kramer pass gave the Packers a 27–0 lead in the third quarter. Hornung scored again, this time on a 37-yard touchdown run. The "Golden Boy" was perfect on extra points for the day and scored 28 of the team's 34 points. The Vikings' second-year man, Fran "the Scrambler" Tarkenton, hit Jerry Reichow for a touchdown in the fourth quarter to avoid the shutout. The final score was Packers 34–Vikings 7.

The Packers' defense mauled a good Cardinals' offense in the second game of the season. The Cardinals were held to just 16 yards rushing. Taylor led the offense for the Packers with 122 yards rushing, but it was Paul Hornung doing most of the scoring again. Hornung kicked a 13-yard field goal and had a 3-yard rush for the only scores in the first three quarters. Max McGee caught a 19-yard touchdown pass in the last quarter and St. Louis was put to rest, 17–0. Coach Wally Lemm of the Cardinals was impressed by the Packers' balance and summed up his assessment of the team:

Great runners in Taylor and Hornung, excellent passing, at least five dangerous receivers, tremendous defense, outstanding kicking.[30]

Taylor scored three times in a massacre of the Chicago Bears in week three. He would not be the only one to see the end zone. Pitts took it in from 26 yards out and Starr ran one in from 5 yards. Starr also connected with Ron Kramer on a 54-yard pass play for another score. To add insult to injury, in the last quarter, Herb Adderley intercepted a pass that he turned into a 50-yard touchdown play. The final score was 49–0. Bears' linebacker Bill George and elusive halfback Willie Galimore were injured and unavailable.[31]

On October 7, the Lions gave the Packers trouble in the fourth game of the season played in Green Bay. Hornung kicked a first quarter field goal, but the Lions pulled ahead on a 6-yard touchdown run by Dan Lewis. Hornung came back in the third quarter with a 15-yard field goal and the Lions led, 7–6. Just when things looked grim for the Packers, Herb Adderley intercepted a Milt Plum pass in the waning minutes of the game and ran it back 40 yards. As the clock wound down, Hornung kicked a 21-yard field goal for the 9–7 win.

When Green Bay beat Minnesota again, the big story was not the 48–21 score, but the knee injury suffered by Paul Hornung. Hornung was sidelined until the game against the Rams on December 2. Without Hornung, the Packers managed to beat their next five opponents: the 49ers, Colts, Bears, Eagles and Colts again. The Packers outscored their opponents, 152–39. In the second game with the Colts, Baltimore was leading, 13–10, in the fourth quarter when Tom Moore, who was filling in for Paul Hornung, won the game for the Packers on a 23-yard touchdown run.[32]

It would be the Lions who would break the Packers' winning streak on Thanksgiving Day. The Lions not only held the Packers scoreless for the first three quarters, but both the Lions' offense and defense scored. Quarterback Milt Plum tossed touchdown passes to Gail Cogdill for the first two Lions' scores. Then Bart Starr fumbled near his own goal and Sam Williams took it 6 yards for another Lions' score. Things got worse for the Packers when Roger Brown tackled Starr in the end zone for a safety and Milt Plum kicked a 47-yard field goal. The Lions were up 26–0 going into the fourth quarter. The Packers came to life then. First Bill Quinlan intercepted a Milt Plum pass and ran it in from the 4-yard line. Quinlan fumbled the ball in the end zone, but Willie Davis made the recovery for the Packers' first score. Another Detroit fumble deep in its own territory gave the Packers the ball on the 14-yard line. Taylor carried the ball in from the 4-yard line for the last score of the game. Despite the late game comeback by the Packers, the Lions prevailed, 26–14.[33]

Once again, Lombardi turned his team right around from a loss. First, Green Bay beat the Rams, 41–10, and then beat the 49ers, 31–21. They finished out the regular season with a 20–17 win against the Rams. The Packers faced the Giants in the NFL Championship game.

1962 Championship Game

After the crushing 37–0 loss the Giants experienced at the hands of the Packers in the 1961 Championship game, Coach Allie Sherman was looking for a better team performance on December 30, 1962, in a cold and windy Yankee Stadium. The Giants' Y.A. Tittle had a seven-touchdown passing day that season and he was aided by the return of Frank Gifford. Gifford had a lot of mileage in his 9 years as a halfback. He took a year off and returned to play flanker. Gifford's presence at his new position helped Tittle accumulate a whopping 3,446 passing yards. The Giants also had 1,698 rushing yards. The Packers were much better balanced on offense than the Giants with 2,621 passing yards and 2,460 rushing yards. Hornung had a sore knee in midseason and Jerry Kramer took over the field goal kicking duties for the Packers.

The blustery weather favored the rush that day and the bruising fullback Taylor. Both sides found it difficult to score facing both inclement weather and inhospitable defenses. The field was rock hard. The winds gusted up to 40 miles per hour. The temperature dropped to 18°. It was a beautiful day for a football game! About 65,000 fans were in attendance, a few thousand more than the population of Green Bay at the time.

The Packers drove downfield on their first possession with Jim Taylor grabbing up most of the tough yards. When the drive stalled, Jerry Kramer delivered a 26-yard field goal. Responding to the challenge, the Giants drove the ball down to the Packers' 16 with a good mix of runs and passes. Tittle looked sharp, but his arm was whacked by Nitschke while throwing and the resultant wounded-duck pass was intercepted by Dan Currie, killing a promising Giants' drive.

Two of the game's top competitors, Sam Huff, the Giants' great middle linebacker, and Jim Taylor, the Packers' rugged fullback, went toe-to-toe on several plays during the game. Huff always had an extra whack for Taylor on each tackle and Taylor, who was known to take any impediment of his progress personally, was riled up. When Phil King of the Giants fumbled on the Giants' 38 and Green Bay recovered, the Packers were poised to make the most of it. Hornung threw a halfback option pass to Boyd Dowler who ran to the Giants' 7-yard line. Taylor took the ball right up the gut through Huff's turf and into the end zone for a score. The Packers led, 10–0.

In the second half, the Giants' offense stalled, but the defense scored a touchdown when Jim Collier recovered a blocked punt in the end zone. Jerry Kramer kicked his second field goal from 29 yards out and then his third field goal from 30 yards out late in the game. Green Bay won 16–7. Lombardi's Packers had their second championship.

1963 Season

In the 1963 draft, Lombardi made an excellent first round selection in Dave Robinson, a linebacker from Penn State. The 6-foot-3, 245 pound Hall of Famer would become one of those key veterans Lombardi could count on. He played 10 seasons with Green Bay.

The Packers scored 369 points that season and allowed 206, but their championship run came to an end. There were several contributing factors. Paul Hornung was suspended indefinitely for gambling violations by Commissioner Pete Rozelle. The never-humble-but-honest Hornung admitted his mistakes and contritely took his punishment. He was reinstated by the Commissioner in 1964. Bart Starr suffered a hairline fracture on the back of his hand in week six and John Roach capably took over for him. In addition to these setbacks, the Chicago Bears were just better than anyone else that season.

When the Packers took it on the chin 10–3 in their opening match against the Bears, no one in Green Bay was panicking. Lombardi was a master at turning a team around from a loss and this season would be no exception. The Packers rattled off 8 wins in a row and none of those contests were close. The

Packers averaged over 33 points a game in the string and had outscored their opponents 266–116.

The winning streak ended however, when the Packers played the Bears again on November 17. The Bears' defense stymied the Packers' offense that game. The Packers were held to just 7 points and the Bears won, 26–7.

Once again, Lombardi's team finished out the season strong. The Packers beat the 49ers twice, the Rams once, and tied the pesky Lions. By any measure, the Packers turned in an outstanding performance, but their 11–2–1 record was not good enough to win the Conference in 1963. They would not go on to the championship game.

1964 Season

In 1964, the Green Bay Packers scored 342 points and allowed 245 from their competitors. The Packers and other NFL teams lost some top draft picks to the rival American Football League.

Green Bay had a middle-of-the-road season in 1964 with some high points and some low points as well. For high points, the Packers paid back the Bears for the previous season losses. Green Bay beat the Bears 23–12 in their first game of the season and then followed up when the two teams met again on December 3, with a 17–3 victory. The low points were early season heart-break losses. In the second week of the season, the Colts, who would go on to take the Western Division that year, beat the Packers 21–20. After the Packers beat the Lions in week four, they lost again by a single point, 24–23, to the Vikings. After their early stumbles, the Packers won six and lost three. Their final game of the season was a 24–24 tie to the Los Angeles Rams. Lombardi had raised expectations in Green Bay, much like Curly Lambeau had done in the late 1920s and the early 1930s. The 8–5–1 season was a disappointment to the coach and the fans. After two seasons out of the championship hunt, Lombardi would not disappoint again. The drama began anew in 1965.

1965 Season

In 1965, the Packers' ground game would not be the overpowering force that it had been for several years running, but the team excelled in other ways. The Packers scored 316 points and held their competition to 224. In the draft, they picked up Donny Anderson who would become an excellent running and receiving back for the Packers for six seasons starting in 1966. Taylor did not reach 1,000 yards rushing like his five previous seasons. Hornung did less running, but his yards from scrimmage totaled 635, slightly higher than his Green Bay career average. Field goals had been a struggle for Hornung the previous season so Lombardi switched kicking responsibilities to Don Chandler. Starr passed for 2,055 yards with a 55.8% completion rate. The offense was evolving as Taylor's tremendous career was starting to wane. The defense was top ranked and stingy.

In the season opener, the Packers held the Pittsburgh Steelers to three Mike Clark field goals and no touchdowns—all in the first half. The Packers' Herb Adderley had a pick six in the second quarter, but it would take an entire half before the Packers' offense got on track. A 31-yard Starr pass to Marv Fleming in the third quarter was the first score by the Packers' offense. Chandler added two field goals. In the fourth, Starr hit Hornung on a 10-yard touchdown pass and Elijah Pitts rushed for two more touchdowns to close out the game. The Packers won convincingly, 41–9.

The Packers needed another Herb Adderley pick six to get past the Colts in week two. They were also aided by four Colts' fumbles while the Packers coughed up the ball three times. Zeke Bratkowski filled in for Bart Starr who was injured during the game. Taylor did not play due to an ankle injury and Hornung, like Starr, was hurt during the game. It was an ugly 20–17 win with the statistical edge clearly in favor of the Colts.[34]

When the Packers played the Bears in game three, it was more of the same—another statistical loss, but a win. Hornung ran the ball in from the 1-yard line to score first and then like the past two games, a Packers' pick six was the order of the day. This time it was Lee Roy Caffey who intercepted the ball and ran it in from 42 yards out. Starr connected with Bob Long on a 48-yard play, but a blocked extra point gave the Packers a 20–0 lead at half. In the second half, Chandler kicked a field goal to give the Packers a little more cushion and then the Bears snapped out of it, with two touchdowns by Gale Sayers. Sayers ran one in from the six and caught a pass from Rudy Bukich and swallowed up 65 yards on his way to another score. At the gun, the Packers had notched a 23–14 victory.

The Packers beat San Francisco, 27–10, in week four in a game that is remembered for a record-breaking 90-yard punt by Don Chandler. When Green Bay beat Detroit, 31–21, the following week, the Lions dominated in the first half and the Packers cleaned up in the second. Down 21–3 at the half, Starr's arm came alive in the third quarter. He connected on a 62-yard pass play to Bob Long; a 31-yard pass play to Tom Moore; and a 77-yard pass play to Carroll Dale. On the last scoring drive of the day, Starr took it in himself from 4 yards out to seal the 31–21 victory. In week six, the fans witnessed two opposing quarterbacks running for cover from a ferocious pass rush on both sides. The Packers defeated the Cowboys, 13–3, with Green Bay's 63 positive yards of offense. The Packers lost the next two games to teams they had beaten earlier in the season. First, the Bears powered up on a series of offensive strikes to torch the Packers 31–10. A Gale Sayers 62-yard punt return was the media highlight of the day. The Packers' second loss in a row came at the hands of Detroit. After the Packers scored first on a Taylor rush from 1 yard out, the Lions bested the Packers with a Joe Don Looney touchdown plunge from the 1-yard line and a Wayne Walker 13-yard field goal. The scoring ended ignominiously for the Packers when Starr was tackled in the end zone for a safety. The final score was Detroit 12–Green Bay 7. The two losses in a row did not deter the Packers from making the most of what they had—mainly a great defense and a good passing attack.

The Packers snuck past the Rams 6–3, but then walloped the Vikings 38–13. In a bit of déjà vu scheduling, the Packers played the same two teams again. They lost to the Rams, 21-10, but managed to beat the Vikings again, this time in a closer contest, 24-19. Paul Hornung scored five touchdowns in the Packers' 42-27 victory over the Colts at Memorial Stadium in Baltimore. In the final game of the season, the 49ers led by quarterback John Brodie, came back to tie the Packers, 24-24, in the waning moments of the game.

Western Conference Playoff

The Colts and Packers had identical 10–3–1 records at the end of the 1965 season and faced off in a Western Conference playoff game to determine who would advance to the NFL Championship game. The game was played in front of 50,484 fans at the newly renamed Green Bay stadium, Lambeau Field.

The Colts were a very tough team, but they lost superstar Johnny Unitas for the season with a knee injury in a game against the Bears on December 6. The Packers had beaten the Colts twice in the regular season accounting for two of Baltimore's three losses. The game got off to a tough start for the Packers. On the first play from scrimmage, Packers' receiver Bill Anderson caught a Starr pass but then coughed it up when he was hit by Lenny Lyles. The fumble was quickly picked up by Colts' linebacker Don Shinnick who took the ball in for a touchdown. On the play, Starr injured his ribs when he bravely tried to tackle the 230 pound linebacker Shinnick. Starr was out for the rest of the day.

A Colts' drive stalled in Packers' territory and Lou Michaels kicked a field goal to put Baltimore ahead, 10–0. Bratkowski led a Packers' drive that was punctuated by an Anderson catch about a foot from the goal. The Packers could not score on four attempts. It was not until the third quarter that the Packers were finally able to sustain a scoring drive. It was Hornung who finished it off with a 1-yard plunge. A Packers' field goal by Don Chandler tied the score and took the game into overtime. In overtime, the Packers pushed deep into Colts' territory and Chandler kicked a 25-yard field goal to win the game, 13–10.

1965 Championship Game

The Cleveland Browns came to Green Bay to play the 1965 league championship game in front of 50,777 fans. The Browns had one of the finest running backs in NFL history, Jim Brown, whom the Packers needed to stop. They did. Brown was limited to 50 yards rushing that day. The Packers' backfield tandem of Hornung and Taylor proved difficult for the Browns to manage. Halfback Hornung rushed for 105 yards; fullback Taylor ran for 96 yards.

Bart Starr was back at quarterback for the Packers and he quickly led Green Bay to a score. Carroll Dale caught a Starr pass down the sideline and turned it into a 47-yard touchdown play on the Packers' first possession. Chandler kicked the point after and the Packers led 7–0. The Browns responded with quarterback Frank Ryan throwing a 30-yard strike to Jim Brown. Ryan hit Paul Warfield next for 19 yards and then he found Gary Collins in the end zone for a score. A bad snap killed the Browns point after attempt and the score was Green Bay 7–Browns 6. Tough defensive play and turnovers limited the remainder of the first half scoring to two fields goals apiece. The Browns' Lou "the Toe" Groza hit one from 24 and another one from 28 just before the half. Sandwiched in between Groza's strikes were Chandler field goals from 15 and 23 yards out.

In the second half, the Packers stuffed the Cleveland offense. The Packers pushed the ball deep into Browns' territory and Paul Hornung scored on the Packers' sweep from 13 yards out. With Chandler's point after good, the Packers took a 20–12 lead. The final scoring play of the game came on another Chandler field goal from 29 yards out. The final tally was Packers 23–Browns 12. Lombardi had won his third NFL Championship.

1966 Season

Lombardi drafted fullback Jim Grabowski from the University of Illinois as a future replacement for Jim Taylor. Grabowski would give the Packers excellent service, but Taylor was a one of a kind player.

The 1966 Packers were a much improved team over the 1965 championship team. The Packers would score 335 points and only allow 163 points by the competition. On offense, they would continue to focus on the pass with 2,602 yards gained in the air and 1,673 yards gained on the ground. They were not the balanced offense of 1962 and 1963, but they were simply the best team in football.

After 5 years of rushing for over 1,000 yards per season, Taylor was slowing down, but he would still lead the team in total yards from scrimmage with 1,036. Hornung was also coming to the end of his career. Starr on the other hand, had an excellent year with several more in front of him. Carroll Dale was just starting to see his best years as a receiver. Elijah Pitts would have a career year with 853 yards from scrimmage.

In game one, the Packers whipped a good Colts' team in Milwaukee's County Stadium. The Packers frustrated Johnny Unitas and the Baltimore offense limiting them to just one field goal. In the second quarter after intercepting a Unitas pass, Lee Roy Caffey ran 52 yards into the end zone. That was followed by a Packers' 46-yard pick six by Bob Jeter. After a Starr touchdown run from the 8-yard line in the third quarter along with a Don Chandler field goal, the Packers notched a 24–3 victory.

The Packers squeaked by the Cleveland Browns next. Two Frank Ryan passes to 6-foot-5 receiver Gary Collins in the first quarter put the Browns ahead, 14–0. The Packers charged back. Starr tossed a 44-yard touchdown pass to Hornung, and Taylor ran the ball in from the 1-yard line on another drive. Lou

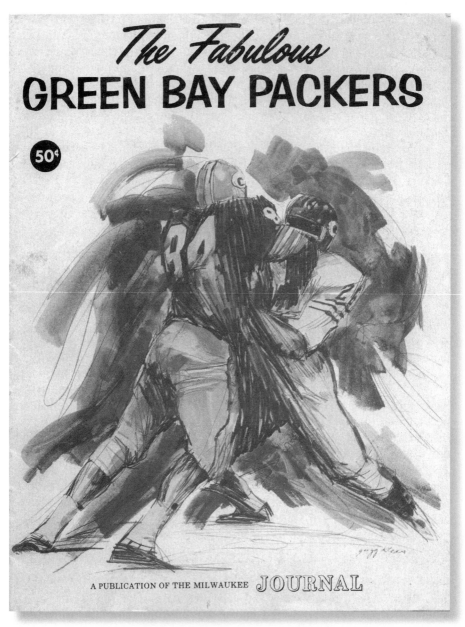

The Fabulous Green Bay Packers

Groza had field goals from 42 and 46 yards that had the Browns ahead, 20–14, as the clock was winding down in the fourth quarter. The Packers put together one final attack, but found themselves at the 8-yard line on fourth down. Starr tossed a short pass to Taylor and the tough fullback eluded two defenders for a touchdown and a Packers' 21–20 win after Chandler's extra point.

After beating the Rams, 24–13, and the Lions, 23–14, the Packers lost a close match to the 49ers, 21–20. In week six, the Packers had an easy time beating the Bears, 17–0, and an easier time beating the Falcons, 56–3, the following week. The Packers-Falcons game featured several plays worthy of an NFL highlight film. Carroll Dale caught a Starr bomb that bagged 51 yards and a touchdown. Herb Adderley snagged an interception that he returned for 68 yards and a touchdown. Donny Anderson returned a punt for 77 yards to score. And Doug Hart picked off another pass and ran it back 40 yards for yet another touchdown.

Detroit was battered next. Green Bay's meddlesome defense and five Motor City turnovers fueled a 31–7 Packers' rout. In week nine at Lambeau Field, the Vikings kept the Packers from getting overconfident as they handed Green Bay their second loss of the season—this one, Vikings 20–Green Bay 17. Scoring had a certain "small-ball" quality to it. Although there were four rushing touchdowns that game, the longest was a 2-yard run. Taylor scored first on a 1-yard run, which was followed by the Vikings' Bill Brown's 1-yard score. Packers' kicker Don Chandler and Vikings' kicker, Fred Cox, traded field goals. Then Pitts ran in from 2 yards out, the longest touchdown run of the day, which was followed by another 1-yard bash by Brown in the last two minutes of the game.

The Packers and Bears met again in week 10 to slug it out. Starr threw two touchdown strikes. Gale Sayers scored once for the Bears. Both teams missed one extra point attempt making the final score: Packers 13–Chicago 6. The Packers continued their winning ways by besting Minnesota, 28–16; San Francisco, 20–7; and Baltimore, 14–10. The Colts gave the Packers a tough game and outgained Green Bay on a muddy, sloppy field. Johnny Unitas fumbled 5 yards from the goal line in the closing minutes of the game. In the final regular season game, Green Bay beat Los Angeles, 27–23.

NFL Championship Game

On January 1, 1967, the Green Bay Packers battled the Dallas Cowboys for the National Football League Championship in the Cotton Bowl before 74,152 fans. Starr hit Elijah Pitts on a 17-yard touchdown pass for the game's first score. Jim Grabowski picked up a fumble and ran it into the end zone for another. The Cowboys struck back on two successive scores. Dan Reeves ran it in from the 3-yard line and Don Perkins ran one in from 23 yards out. In the second quarter, a 51-yard Starr touchdown pass to Dale for Green Bay, was followed by a Villanueva 11-yard field goal for Dallas, to make the score, 21–17, at the half.

In the second half, Villanueva started the scoring out with a 32-yard field goal. The Packers came back with a 16-yard touchdown pass from Starr to Boyd Dowler. In the fourth quarter when McGee snagged a 28-yard touchdown pass from Starr, the Packers looked like winners taking the lead 34–20. But Dallas was not finished. Don Meredith threw his first touchdown pass of the day—a 68-yard bomb to Frank Clarke. In the waning seconds of the game, Meredith and the Cowboys were at the 2-yard line with one last down and one last chance. On the snap, Dave Robinson came storming in on Meredith who was forced to rush a desperation pass that was intercepted in the end zone by Tom Brown. The gun sounded; the final score was Packers 34—Cowboys 27.

Super Bowl I

The National Football League Champion Green Bay Packers played the American Football League Champion Kansas City Chiefs in a game that was called the AFL-NFL World Championship Game and later, it was known as Super Bowl I. The meeting of the two league champions had been suggested in prior years and this game was the result of those efforts. The leagues agreed in 1966 that they would merge and in 1970 the merger would be consummated. As has been the case in such mergers, the teams, their fans, and the press were interested in knowing how the best teams in one league would fare against the best in the other.

The Chiefs had one of the strongest coach-quarterback duos in professional football history. The Chiefs were coached by the animated and dapper Hank Stram, who was an assistant coach at Purdue University when Len Dawson was their quarterback. Stram was coaching the AFL Dallas Texans when they signed Dawson who had been dismissed by both Pittsburgh and Cleveland. The Texans moved to Kansas City in Dawson's second year. Stram recognized that Dawson was best suited as a quarterback in constant motion and built his offense around that scheme. Dawson was a very accurate passer when on the move. Dawson would play an incredible 14 seasons for the team–13 seasons alongside Hank Stram. Dawson would be inducted into the Pro Football Hall of Fame on the strength of his great career in Kansas City.

Lombardi and the NFL community considered it important for the Packers to beat the upstart AFL champions. At the same time, the Chiefs were out to prove themselves to the NFL. But the Chiefs were not just playing the NFL Champion, they were playing a team that some would call one of the best professional football teams of all time.

On a drive that began on the Green Bay 20, Starr directed the Packers downfield into Chiefs' territory. Max McGee caught a Starr pass down the middle for a 37-yard gain and the first score. Chandler kicked the extra point. After a 31-yard bomb to Otis Taylor, Len Dawson followed with a 7-yard strike to Curtis McClinton for the first Kansas City score. Mike Mercer hit the extra point. Jim Taylor swept around left end for 14 yards and another Green Bay score. The Chiefs' Mike Mercer kicked a 31-yard field goal to keep the game close. The Packers were ahead, 14–10, at the half.

In the third quarter, the Chiefs advanced the ball to midfield. A Packers' blitz rushed a Dawson pass that Wood intercepted at midfield and ran back to the Chiefs' 5-yard line. Pitts took it in from there for a Packers' touchdown. After the extra point, the Packers led, 21–10. The Packers' defense smelled blood. Late in the quarter, two Dawson sacks forced the Chiefs to punt from deep in their own territory, giving the Packers the ball on the Green Bay 44-yard line. Starr connected with Max McGee for 11 yards and again for 16 more while giving Jim Taylor the ball a few times to keep the Chiefs' defense honest. Starr went to McGee again from 13 yards out for another Packers' touchdown. As the game moved into the fourth quarter, the Packers continued to stymie the Chiefs' offense with excellent pass coverage. After the Chiefs' punted into the end zone resulting in a touchback, the Packers put together another scoring drive. Quick completions to Carroll Dale and Max McGee took the Packers 62 yards downfield to the Chiefs' 18-yard line. After a 7-yard completion to Dale, the Packers pounded the ball in with four running plays— Pitts getting the touchdown from 1 yard out. In the final few Chiefs' offensive series, Hank Stram put Pete Beathard in at quarterback, but he could do no better than Dawson against the Packers' defense. The Packers won, 35–10.

1967 Season

On offense, the go-to guy for Lombardi's Packers had been Jim Taylor from the start. Taylor would have more than twice as many carries over his career as his halfback running mate Paul Hornung. Taylor got the ball in the tightest of spots and delivered with remarkable consistency often when the defense knew he was going to be carrying the ball. At 6-foot and 215 pounds, he rushed 1,941 times for 8,597 yards and had 225 receptions for 1,756 yards. Hall of Famer Jim Taylor is honored among the top fullbacks of all time: Bronko Nagurski, Jim Brown, Clarke Hinkle, Marion Motley, Larry Csonka, John Riggins, Daryl Johnston, Tom Rathman, Franco Harris, Earl Campbell, Ernie Nevers, Joe Perry, and Cookie Gilchrist. He will famously be remembered for playing with both his "heart and his head" as he liked to say.[35] Going into the 1967 season with Taylor's career coming to an end and with Jim Grabowski waiting in the wings, he was traded to New Orleans where the Saints were willing to pay top dollar.

Like Taylor, Hornung did not play for the Packers in 1967. Hornung will always be remembered as one of the greatest Packers and one who had a "nose for the end zone." As a converted quarterback, Hornung was always a passing threat in addition to his great running skills. He was also an excellent kicker. Slowed by injuries in 1966, he was selected by New Orleans in the expansion draft, but he decided to retire before the season.

Fullback Jim Grabowski and halfback Donny Anderson would play well in 1967. Statistically, the late career contributions of Taylor and Hornung would not be missed in 1967. It would be something intangible, yet magnificent that the Packers lost when these two players cleaned out their lockers.

With the addition of New Orleans to the NFL, four divisions were created. The Eastern Conference included the Capitol and Century Divisions. The Western Conference included the Central and Coastal Divisions. Green Bay would compete with Detroit, Chicago, and Minnesota in the Central Division.

The top team in each division squared off with the top team of the other division within its conference to determine the conference winner. The Western Conference winner played the Eastern Conference winner to determine the NFL Championship. The winner moved on to the Super Bowl. Becoming a world champion football team included a more forgiving path during the regular season in that more teams went to the playoffs, but it also required teams to traverse a more arduous path once the regular season ended.

The Packers opened the season against Detroit. Starr threw four interceptions causing the Packers to struggle mightily to tie the Lions and avoid a loss. Trailing 17–0 at the half, Pitts scored two rushing touchdowns and was on the receiving end of an 84-yard Starr pass play that brought the Packers within field goal range in the final minutes of the game. Chandler hit a 28-yard field goal to tie the game, 17–17.

Game two saw more of the same drama. Again, Starr struggled. The Packers would have to overcome five interceptions and three fumbles against the defense-minded Bears. But the Packers' defense was even stingier than the Bears'. The Packers marched ahead, 10–0, on a Grabowski touchdown run and a Chandler field goal scored in the first half. In the second half, the Bears came out of hibernation with a 22-yard Mac Percival field goal and a 13-yard touchdown run by Gale Sayers. The game was decided by a 46-yard field goal from Chandler in the fourth quarter. The Packers won, 13–10.

On October 1, the Packers played Atlanta and a struggling Bart Starr was injured and replaced by Zeke Bratkowski. Bratkowski connected with Carroll Dale on two touchdown passes in the first half. Willie Davis tackled quarterback Randy Johnson in the end zone for a safety. Packers' fullback Ben Wilson ran one in from 11 yards out for another score. Linebacker Dave Robinson and defensive back Bob Jeter had interceptions that helped stall the Falcons offense, which was held to a meager 58 yards. The Packers won, 23–0.

When the Packers played Detroit for the second time that season on October 8, the game had a familiar come-from-behind theme. The Packers trailed 10–0 in the first quarter after Wayne Walker kicked a field goal and Larry Hand had a pick six off Zeke Bratkowski. From then on, it was almost all Packers. Bratkowski hit Anderson for a touchdown and Chandler kicked two field goals. Nitschke had a pick six with an assist from Dave Robinson who tipped a Milt Plum pass. Dowler caught another Bratkowski ball for the final Packer touchdown. Detroit's Bill Malinchak was on the receiving end of a Karl Sweetan pass that provided one last growl for the Lions on their way out of the stadium. The Packers won 27–17.

When the Packers played the Minnesota Vikings, Lombardi faced Bud Grant in Grant's first of 18 seasons as head coach. Grant's Vikings would win this one. The Packers scored first on an 86-yard pass play from Zeke Bratkowski to Carroll Dale in the second quarter. In the third quarter, Viking defensive back Ed Sharockman intercepted a Bratkowski pass and returned it to the Green Bay 37. The Vikings' Quarterback, Joe Kapp, carefully drove his team downfield and Bill Brown carried the ball in from the 1-yard line for the Vikings one touchdown. Fred Cox's 12-yard field goal in the fourth quarter sealed the game in favor of the Vikings, 10–7.

When Starr returned to play the Giants in Yankee Stadium, the Packers' offense made a statement with a 48–21 victory. Grabowski and Anderson each rushed for a touchdown and Pitts ran for three. Grabowski also scored on a Starr pass and Chandler kicked two field goals. For the Giants, Fran Tarkenton threw three touchdown strikes: two to Homer Jones and one to Joe Morrison.

After facing the "Scrambler," Fran Tarkenton, the Packers' defense stood up to another NFL great, Jim Hart of the St. Louis Cardinals. Hart threw two touchdown passes and Jim Bakken kicked three field goals for the Cardinals. For the Packers, Adderley had a pick six, Pitts rushed for a touchdown, and Chandler kicked a 43-yard field goal. When Travis Williams ran back a kickoff 93 yards, the Packers jumped ahead, 24–23. Dowler scored on a Starr pass for insurance, which made the final score, Green Bay 31–St. Louis 23.

The Packers' next opponent was the Baltimore Colts, an excellent team that would end the season with an 11–3–1 record. A Chandler field goal was the only score in the first three quarters. A Starr 31-yard touchdown pass to Donny Anderson gave the Packers a 10–0 lead in the fourth quarter. Unitas broke the ice late for Baltimore with a 10-yard scoring pass to Alex Hawkins with a measly 2:29 remaining to play. After missing the extra point, kicker Lou Michaels sliced the kickoff and Baltimore rookie defensive Rick Volk fell on the ball at the Green Bay 34-yard line giving the Colts a successful onside kick. Less than a minute later, Unitas hit Willie Richardson on a 23-yard touchdown pass for the 13–10 Colts victory.

At 5–2–1, in an average season, Lombardi and the Packers would be wondering about their chances for even making the playoffs, but the Lions, Bears, and Vikings were all nursing losing records. The Packers rallied to win the next four games in a row. They destroyed the Browns, 55–7, and blanked the 49ers, 13–0.

When the Packers battled past the Bears on November 26, they won a playoff spot. The Bears' defense gave the Packers a tough game and held Green Bay to only 71 yards rushing with one rushing touchdown. Starr did better in the air and he completed 11 passes for 202 yards and scored a second Packer touchdown passing. Don Chandler kicked a third quarter field goal to give the Packers 17 points. The Packers' pass defense stunned the Bears with two interceptions. Chicago did better with their rushing game, but not good enough. The Bears tallied 193 yards on the ground, but only one touchdown run by Gale Sayers. The Bears' Mac Percival kicked two field goals when the Bears' drives stalled deep in Packer territory: the first one from 10 yards out and the second one from 15 yards. The Packers won, 17–13.

To finish out their playoff-bound season, the Packers beat the Vikings, 30–27, and then lost to the Rams, 27–24, and the Steelers, 24–17.

Western Conference Championship

The Packers played the Rams for the Western Conference Championship at County Stadium in Milwaukee with the winner going on to the NFL Championship game. After losing to the Rams, 27–24, just two weeks prior to the game, Packers' fans were apprehensive about this game. When Roman Gabriel hit Bernie Casey to score on a 29-yard pass play, the worry was heightened. When the Packers' Travis Williams rushed for 46 yards and a touchdown, the fans' concerns started to ease up. When Starr hit Carroll Dale on a 26-yard touchdown pass, the worry started to dissipate altogether. And when Chuck Mercein, who had been acquired late in the season, scored from 6 yards out, the fans wondered why they had worried at all. When Travis Williams scored his second touchdown of the game in the fourth quarter, the fans were already looking forward to the NFL Championship. The Packers won, 28–7.

NFL Championship Game

The Packers played the Dallas Cowboys for the NFL Championship on the last day of the year in 1967. The Packers had a secret weapon—Mother Nature. Few NFL games have been so well celebrated and memorialized. The Packers had seen plenty of cold weather before this game, but the so-called "Ice Bowl" was the start of much of the lore and legend surrounding Lambeau Field. From this game forward, Green Bay fans would not just tolerate the cold at Lambeau, they would relish their "frozen tundra."

There were six scoring plays in this game played in front of 50,861 fans on a day when the mercury dipped to -13°. The Packers' leading receiver in 1967 was Boyd Dowler, who at 6-foot-5 and 224 pounds, displayed remarkable skills. Starr targeted Dowler on an 8-yard touchdown pass for the Packers' first score—the 16th play in an 82-yard drive. He followed up with a 46-yard touchdown strike to leading-man Dowler again in the second quarter. Starr was harassed all game by the Dallas defense. The Cowboys struck back when George Andrie gobbled up a Starr fumble and returned it 7 yards for a touchdown. The Packers flirted with disaster when Willie Wood dropped a punt on the Green Bay 17-yard line just before half. After Danny Villanueva kicked a 21-yard field goal, the Packers clung to a 14–10 lead at the half.

After a scoreless third quarter, Green Bay was rocked when the Cowboys' Lance Rentzel snatched a 50-yard touchdown pass from halfback Dan Reeves. The Cowboys were leading, 17–14, on the Packers' frigid home field in the fourth quarter. With only 4:50 on the clock, Lombardi's offense looked 68 yards downfield to the goal and began a 12-play drive for the win. They would need almost every second. A determined Starr completed a pass out in the flat to Donny Anderson for a 6-yard gain. Chuck Mercein found enough running room outside for a first down. Starr tossed one down the middle to Dowler over the 50-yard line and Cornell Green who was struggling with his footing was able to grab and throw Dowler down hard on the tackle to the frozen ground. It was nip and tuck all the way. Anderson received a handoff from Starr, but was tackled in the backfield. It was second down and 19 yards to go for a first on a field that was quickly becoming an ice skating rink. Starr looked around and tossed Anderson an outlet pass that the halfback turned into another 12-yard gain. Starr followed with another short pass to Anderson who gained the first down. Chuck Mercein was targeted next and after the catch he ran the ball down to the Dallas 11-yard line. Landry would call the Mercein strike the most important play of the game because it would give the Packers a chance to score. Landry also said that at about that time during the game, the field had frozen over.[36] Mercein had the hot hand and took a handoff from Starr and ran it up the middle to the 2-yard line. Anderson rushed to within inches of the goal and a first down. The tough, determined Cowboys' defense stuffed two Donny Anderson drives. Starr went to the sideline and told Lombardi since the backs were slipping, he would take the ball himself on a wedge play, which normally goes to the fullback. Lombardi famously responded, "Then do it and let's get the hell out of here."[37] As Starr jogged back on the field, the tension in the stands was almost unbearable.

Starr stood behind center with 13 seconds remaining at the 1-yard line with no time outs. He raised his hands to quiet the crowd and the ball was snapped on a quick count. Jerry Kramer jumped out at Jethro Pugh, hitting him low, followed by Packer center Ken Bowman hitting Pugh high. Cleats scratched on ice and Pugh was driven backwards. Starr shadowed Kramer and plunged into the end zone for the score. Mercein, who thought Starr was going to hand off to him, trailed the play and raised his arms in the air so the officials knew he was not pushing Starr into the end zone—an infraction that might have cost the Packers the game. Millions watching thought Mercein was signaling a score! The fans realized that Starr had scored and in the midst of an arctic field of dreams came the deafening roar of the crowd. Chandler kicked the extra point.

Dallas received the kickoff, but the game ended after Meredith threw two long bombs that failed to connect. The final score was Packers 21–Cowboys 17. The Packers won their third NFL Championship in a row. The frigid but appreciative crowd was one with the team in both suffering from the cold and jubilation from the win. When players and fans alike recall the game decades later, they point to limbs and patches of skin that have never quite recovered from that day.

Super Bowl II

On January 14, 1968, the Green Bay Packers faced the Oakland Raiders in the Orange Bowl in Miami for Super Bowl II. Oakland amassed 13 wins and only one loss. They were led by Daryle Lamonica, who had passed for 3,228 yards

Fr. Dennis Burke (President of St. Norbert College), Bishop Aloysius Wycislo, and Vince Lombardi at St. Norbert College in 1968.

and 30 touchdowns. Hall of Fame center Jim Otto, kicker George Blanda, guard Gene Upshaw, cornerback Willie Brown, and receiver Fred Biletnikoff stood ready.

The Raiders found it difficult to get much traction against the Packers' defense. Initially, the Raiders were tough on the Packers as well. The only first quarter score was a Packers' 39-yard field goal by Chandler. In the second quarter, the scoring started with a Chandler 20-yard field goal. The Packers struck again when Starr threw a perfect strike to Boyd Dowler for a 62-yard touchdown. When Daryl Lamonica hit Bill Miller on a 23-yard pass to make the score 13–7, the Raiders remained optimistic. Later in the half, Donny Anderson kicked a high towering punt that was muffed by Oakland defensive back, Roger Bird, and Green Bay recovered. The Packers moved downfield where Chandler kicked a 43-yard field goal. At the half, the Packers led 16–7.

In the second half, the Packers methodically drove downfield as Starr connected with several different receivers. A 35-yard pass play to McGee accelerated the Packers' drive and the play was followed by a score on an Anderson 2-yard run. The Packers played ball control and kept the Raiders offense from getting on track. Another Packer drive resulted in a Chandler 31-yard field goal and the Packers looked unstoppable with the lead extended to 26–7. A Herb Adderley pick six seemed to say it all in the fourth quarter, but the Raiders did not give up. Lamonica connected on a 41-yard pass to Pete Banaszak and followed with another toss to Miller from 23 yards out for a score. When the gun sounded, the final score was 33–14. Lombardi and his Packers had won their second Super Bowl.

Lombardi Retires as Coach

After the 1967 season Lombardi gave up his coaching responsibilities and concentrated on the general manager position. Some suggested that this was necessary due to health concerns that resulted from Lombardi's own intense nature and the concentrated pressure he was under after his ultra-successful run. Nevertheless, Lombardi regretted this decision soon afterward. Like other coaches of his era, he did not like the complexities of new player-agent-team relationships and by retiring as coach, he had left his favorite part of the game—football and competition—only to concentrate on his least favorite duties. Phil Bengston, a Lombardi assistant coach, took over the Packers for the 1968 season. The 1968 Packers went through Lombardi withdrawals and dropped to a 6–7–1 season.

Lombardi created a dynasty in Green Bay, but for him to come back to coach the Packers after he had relinquished the job, would have been blatantly unfair to Bengston. It was time to break from Green Bay. Lombardi also had ambitions of being an NFL owner, something that the Green Bay directors believed they could not offer him. Lombardi had been courted by Wellington Mara of the Giants very soon after he left New York, but he had turned down the Giants' overtures as he was building the Packers. Celebrated attorney and

President of the Washington Redskins, Edward Bennett Williams, offered Lombardi a job that included an ownership interest. Lombardi snatched it up and he moved back east.

1969 Redskins' Season

Lombardi was back in training camp with great enthusiasm. Happily, he had an excellent, but underperforming quarterback in Sonny Jurgensen. Jurgensen had played 12 years before he had the Lombardi experience. Under Lombardi, he rid himself of some bad habits and became a much better player. Lombardi taught him how to read defenses and to stop forcing the ball.[38] His completion rate jumped up from 57% to 62%. According to Jurgensen, Lombardi was the only coach he had ever had who tried to simplify the game instead of complicate it.

Lombardi would work with some notable veterans and new talent as well in 1969. Legendary linebacker and Hall of Famer, Sam Huff, came out of retirement to play for Lombardi in 1969. In his sixth year in Washington, Hall of Fame receiver Charley Taylor would have 71 receptions for 883 yards and eight touchdowns playing for Lombardi. Rookie running back Larry Brown would begin his 8-year stellar career with the Redskins running for 888 yards.

As he had done in Green Bay, Lombardi began to teach the Redskins what it took to win his way, encourage teamwork over individual accomplishment, and promote confidence. It took only three games for the Redskins to experience the entire range of competitive experiences. The Redskins beat the New Orleans Saints in game one, lost to the Cleveland Browns in game two, and tied the San Francisco 49ers in game three. Next came the most hopeful part of the season when the Redskins went on a three game winning streak in which they beat the Cardinals, Giants, and Steelers. It would be an up and down season without any miracles, but as the season was coming to a close, the Redskins managed a 17–14 win over the Saints that insured them of a winning season—something the Redskins hadn't seen in a long time. It looked like Lombardi would do in Washington, what he had done in Green Bay. In the last game of the season, the Redskins lost to Tom Landry's Dallas Cowboys, 20–10. In Lombardi's first and last year in Washington, the Redskins achieved a 7–5–2 record.

In the offseason, Lombardi was diagnosed with a fast spreading form of colon cancer. He would gallantly hang on to life during the summer months, but he succumbed to the disease on September 3, 1970. The human lightning bolt that had come into Green Bay and lit up the town just a little more than a decade ago, was gone. His funeral Mass took place at St. Patrick's Cathedral in New York on September 7. The crowd that attended the Mass made up a small percentage of the people who had come to love and appreciate him. Those who knew him have held a kind of Irish wake ever since that day. Telling stories, sharing memories, having a good laugh, and expressing their appreciation for the man and what he meant to them. It continues to this day.

Lombardi's Contributions to the Game

In a time when individuals seemed paramount, Lombardi renewed a sense of teamwork and showed how the individual could both sacrifice and achieve for the good of the team. His plays were simple. His players executed them as near perfect as humanly possible. They understood the minutiae of the power sweep and they kept "running for daylight."

Compared to many football legends, Lombardi was in the NFL for a short time. He came and left in 16 years, but his legacy is strong today many years after his death. Lombardi was intelligent and articulate. A boatload of Lombardi quotes helps keep his memory alive. Certainly, the five NFL championships in 9 years; the first two Super Bowl wins; and his 89–29–4 record in Green Bay; remain a source of great pride for Packer fans. His 96–34–6 overall professional head-coaching record and the manner in which he achieved it brings honor to the NFL. The films, tributes, and books remind fans of what he accomplished.

Aside from Lombardi's great achievements, he was a flesh and blood human being who seldom hid his feelings. In many ways, it was Lombardi the person, rather than Lombardi the coach, who made his legacy so strong. Lombardi's ambitions and values were imprinted on those around him. Those affected personally, regardless of their own accomplishments, have been generous in promoting his legacy.

Some of Lombardi's influence is subtle. There is a photograph of Lombardi on a football field in Washington, DC. He is talking to a group of young boys during the summer before his last season in football. Attentive, with eyes wide open, Lombardi is deeply interested in what these kids are feeling, thinking, and saying—and they no doubt are deeply interested in what this coach has to say to them. Those boys were given something of Lombardi in a smile, a handshake, or a word on that day that would last a lifetime.

Much of Lombari's influence is not so subtle. He defined professional football in a new way. He combined the discipline of Colonel Blaik of West Point with the motivational skills of Knute Rockne of Notre Dame in a time when many people thought that the world was too cynical for either of them. Lombardi also elevated the game by making his players approach it as a pursuit towards perfection. Under Lombardi's philosophy, by working to excel at football, a football player excels at life—he seeks to achieve his potential. By becoming the best football player possible, the player contributes to the greater good. For Lombardi, football was not a metaphor for life, it was an integral part of it—not just for him, but for his players and fans.

Lombardi was a New Yorker, but Green Bay was the perfect place for him. In a tradition that had started long before Lambeau, the people of Green Bay had a special affinity for football. And under Lambeau, it became a source of pride for them. Under Lombardi, football and Green Bay became inseparable.

Vince Lombardi Timeline

1913

- June 11, 1913, Vincent Thomas Lombardi is born in New York City.

1928-1933

- Lombardi attends Cathedral College of the Immaculate Conception in Queens in preparation for the priesthood. He transfers to St. Francis Prep in Brooklyn where he plays football and graduates in 1933.

1933-1937

- Lombardi attends Fordham University and plays football on the famous offensive line called the Seven Blocks of Granite. He graduates as a member of the Class of 1937.

1939-1947

- Lombardi teaches and coaches at St. Cecilia High School in Englewood, New Jersey.

1947-1948

- Lombardi returns to his alma mater, Fordham University, to coach the freshman football team and in his second year, he becomes assistant coach for the varsity.

1948-1953

- Lombardi coaches the offensive line at the United States Military Academy at West Point working with Colonel Red Blaik.

1954-1958

- Lombardi serves as offensive coordinator of the New York Giants.

1956

- December 30, 1956, the New York Giants win the NFL Championship.

1959-1967

- Lombardi serves as head coach of the Green Bay Packers.

1959

- Lombardi is named both the AP and UPI NFL Coach of the Year for 1959.

1960

- December 26, 1960, Philadelphia Eagles defeat the Green Bay Packers, 17–13, to win the NFL Championship.

1961

- December 31, 1961, Green Bay Packers defeat the New York Giants, 37–0, to win the NFL Championship.
- Lombardi is named the Sporting News Coach of the year for 1961,

1962

- On December 30, 1962, Green Bay Packers defeat the New York Giants, 16–7, to win the NFL Championship. It is Lombardi's second championship in a row.

1966

- January 2, 1966, the 1965 Green Bay Packers defeat the Cleveland Browns, 23–12, to win the NFL Championship. It is Lombardi's third NFL Championship.

1967

- January 1, 1967, Lombardi's 1966 Green Bay Packers defeat the Dallas Cowboys, 34–27, to win the NFL Conference Championship.
- January 15, 1967, 1966 Green Bay Packers win the first Super Bowl by defeating the Kansas City Chiefs, 35-10. It is Lombardi's fourth NFL Championship.
- December 31, 1967, 1967 Green Bay Packers defeat the Dallas Cowboys, 21–17, to win the NFL Conference Championship.

1968

- January 14, 1968, the 1967 Green Bay Packers defeat the Oakland Raiders, 33-14, to win the second Super Bowl. It is Lombardi's third NFL Championship in a row and his fifth overall.
- February 1, 1968, Lombardi retires from his head coaching position with the Packers, but retains his general manager duties in Green Bay.

1969

- Washington Redskins owner, Edward Bennett Williams, hires Lombardi as coach and vice president. Lombardi is also given an ownership interest in the team.
- Lombardi compiles a 7-5-2 record his first season.

1970

- Lombardi is diagnosed with cancer in the offseason.
- September 3, 1970, Lombardi dies at the age of 57.
- Super Bowl trophy is named "Lombardi Trophy" in his honor.

1971

- Lombardi is inducted posthumously into the Pro Football Hall of Fame, Class of 1971.

Highlights

Vince Lombardi won five NFL championships in nine years including the first two Super Bowl crowns. His three championships in a row match the accomplishment of Curly Lambeau and Guy Chamberlin. He holds an overall NFL head coaching record of 105–35–6. Lombardi was named both the AP and UPI NFL Coach of the Year for 1959 and the Sporting News Coach of the year for 1961. He was inducted into the Pro Football Hall of Fame posthumously with the Class of 1971. The Super Bowl trophy is named the "Lombardi Trophy" in his honor.

Lombardi combined the discipline of Colonel Blaik of West Point with the motivational skills of Knute Rockne of Notre Dame in a time when many people thought that the world was too cynical for either of them. Under Lombardi's philosophy, by working to excel at football, a football player excels at life—he seeks to achieve his potential. For Lombardi, football was not a metaphor for life, it was an integral part of it—not just for him, but for his players and fans.

Endnotes

[1] Michael O'Brien, *Vince: A Personal Biography of Vince Lombardi* (New York, William Morrow and Company, 1987) 21.

[2] O'Brien, *Vince: A Personal Biography of Vince Lombardi*, 30.

[3] David Maraniss, *When Pride Still Mattered: A Life of Vince Lombardi* (New York, Simon and Schuster, 1999) 30.

[4] The legacy of the Seven Blocks of Granite is set in stone at Fordham University in a monument to its famed football linemen from the 1929-1930 and 1936-1937 seasons. The monument credits 19 individuals who played the line during the period, including Vince Lombardi.

[5] Vince Lombardi, *Run to Daylight* (Englewood Cliffs, NJ, Prentice Hall, 1963) 109.

[6] Maraniss, *When Pride Still Mattered: A Life of Vince Lombardi*, 77.

[7] Maraniss, *When Pride Still Mattered: A Life of Vince Lombardi*, 78-78

[8] For a pointed discussion of Blaik and Lombardi involvement at West Point, see Jerry Kramer, Editor, *Lombardi: Winning is the Only Thing*, 42–49.

[9] Paul Hornung, *Golden Boy* (New York: Simon and Schuster, 2004) 96.

[10] Lombardi, *Run to Daylight,* 43.

[11] Dale Buss, "Packers' Lambeau Field Clock Reaches Back to Lombardi Time," *Forbes*, December 11, 2012, viewed at http://www.forbes.com/sites/dalebuss/2012/12/11/packers-lambeau-field-clock-reaches-back-to-lombardi-time/ on November 7, 2013

[12] Some attribute this quote to sources that predate Lombardi's use of these words—others suggest that the quote is not exactly what Lombardi said. However, it is certain that Lombardi can be credited with popularizing the saying.

[13] Paul Hornung, *Golden Boy*, 212.

[14] Halas Suspicious of Lombardi's Packers," *Milwaukee Sentinel*, August 9, 1959, c 3, viewed at http://www.jsonline.com/historicarchive/ search/?searchBy=word&searchText=lombardi+1959+packers&dat=&fromDate= &nid=jvrRlaHg2sAC&s.x=0&s.y=0, accessed on February 9, 2013.

[15] Tex Maule, "Green Bay: A Corner on Defense," *Sports Illustrated*, December 18, 1961. Viewed at http://sportsillustrated.cnn.com/vault/article/magazine/MAG1073347/index.htm on January 30, 2013.

[16] Paul Hornung, *Golden Boy*, 13.

[17] See the Official Packers Web Site for a searchable data base of coaches at http://nfl.packers.com/history/all_time_roster/coaches/ .

[18] See Ed Gruver, "The Lombardi Sweep: The Signature Play of the Green Bay Dynasty, It symbolized an Era," *The Coffin Corner*, Volume 19, No. 5 viewed at http://www.profootballresearchers.org/Coffin_Corner/19-05-712.pdf on February 12, 2013. For a full chapter examination of the sweep see Bob Berghaus, *The First America's Team: The 1962 Green Bay Packers* (Cincinnati, OH, Clerisy Press, 2011) Chapter 7, "The Power Sweep," 95-104.

[19] Jerry Kramer, Editor, *Lombardi: Winning is the Only Thing*, 33.

[20] For a short tribute to Pietrosante see http://blog.detroitathletic.com/2010/02/17/remembering-former-detroit-lions-fullback-nick-pietrosante/.

[21] Hall of Fame biography at http://www.profootballhof.com/hof/member.aspx?PLAYER_ID=52 .

[22] Associated Press, "Packers v. Steelers in Opener," *Milwaukee Sentinel*, August 12, 1960, Part 2, page 5. Viewed at http://www.jsonline.com/historicarchive/ search/?searchBy=word&searchText=lombardi+1959+packers&dat=&fromDate=

&nid=jvrRlaHg2sAC&s.x=0&s.y=0 on February 10, 2013.

23 http://www.packershistory.net/1960PACKERS.html

24 http://www.packershistory.net/1960PACKERS.html

25 http://www.packershistory.net/1960PACKERS.html

26 Franklin Field is the University of Pennsylvania's home field. It has been refurbished reducing capacity to 52,593 today. It is the oldest stadium still operating NCAA football games.

27 Joseph S. Page, *Pro Football Championships Before the Super Bowl: A Year by Year History, 1926-1965* (Jefferson, NC, McFarland & Company Inc., 2011) 164-166.

28 Bud Lea, "44,307 See Packers Lose," *Milwaukee Sentinel*, September 18, 1961, 1, 4, viewed at http://www.jsonline.com/historicarchive/ search/?searchBy=word&searchText=1961+packers+detroit&dat=&fromDate=&nid= jvrRlaHg2sAC&s.x=0&s.y=0 on February 5, 2013.

29 Jerry Kramer, Editor, *Winning Is the Only Thing*, 58.

30 Bob Berghaus, *The First America's Team: The 1962 Green Bay Packers*, (Cincinnati, Clerisy Press, 2011) 30.

31 Berghaus, *The First America's Team: The 1962 Green Bay Packers*, 33.

32 Packers History at http://www.packershistory.net/1962PACKERS.html

33 Packers History at http://www.packershistory.net/1962PACKERS.html

34 Packers History at http://www.packershistory.net/1965PACKERS.html

35 Lance Allen, Sports Glance with Lance, "Packers Sitdown with Jim Taylor, TMJ TV, viewed at http://www.todaystmj4.com/blogs/lanceallan/104251404.html on February 8, 2013.

36 NFL Films, "The NFL's Greatest Games: The Ice Bowl," Produced and Directed by David Plaut, Executive Producer Steve Sabol, 1997 video.

37 NFL Films, "The NFL's Greatest Games: The Ice Bowl," Plaut and Sabol, video.

38 Jerry Kramer, Editor, *Winning Is the Only Thing*, 169.

Chuck Noll

It is late in 1959 after the Cleveland Browns have finished their season. Chuck Noll sits with his wife Marianne in their home. At 6-foot-1, 220 pounds, Noll is husky enough for the linebacker position he played in his early career, but he is undersized for an offensive guard, which is the position that he played in his last few seasons. Noll has been one of Coach Paul Brown's messenger guards who carries in the coach's play every other down.

Noll has spent the past seven seasons playing for Paul Brown and the Cleveland Browns. He is in his late 20s and could play for a few more years, but he has had enough. Noll has decided that it is time to move on. It is exactly the right moment to "retire" from playing. And as one of his players would later say, "Chuck Noll was never a person to let a moment go by."[1]

There is no crystal ball in the Noll house. Chuck Noll does not know what the future will bring. He knows that he can make a living in other fields if football does not work out for him. In fact, he has always thought of football as a temporary stop on the way to his life pursuit. It will be many years before he concludes that his life pursuit was football all along. By the time he has finished coaching, he will have devoted 31 years to it.

Noll is attracted to coaching. He has been watching Brown carefully. Like Brown, Noll is smart, tough, and organized. Noll has seen the importance that Brown puts on time management, discipline, and technical details. He will witness other excellent coaches' work as he takes new jobs. In 10 years, Charles Henry Noll will run his own stellar program in Pittsburgh, but before he gets there, he will spend the next nine seasons as an assistant, coaching on two very different teams: the San Diego Chargers and the Baltimore Colts. By the time he takes over the Steelers, he will be well-seasoned.

Early Years

Charles Henry Noll is the son of William Noll and Katherine Steigerwald Noll. His parents married in 1917. They were of German descent. Katherine was the oldest of 13 children. Her father Henry built a house on Cleveland's east side, and the newlywed Nolls lived there with the Steigerwald family through the Depression. On January 5, 1932, Katherine gave birth to her fourth child, Charles Henry Noll. Charles joined an 8-year-old sister, Rita, and a 12-year-old brother, Robert. Katherine and William had another child, Beatrice, who died in infancy in 1928.[2]

The Nolls' original Cleveland neighborhood was residential with a few factories mixed in. It had a large black population at the time and still does today. Many of the area's factories are shuttered now, but were operational when Noll was growing up, giving the area a gritty feel. The east side of the city is also known for its lake-effect snow, which often packs a winter punch the rest of the city does not experience.

Older brother Robert played high school football long before Chuck could even hold a ball. As a kid, Chuck Noll played on a neighborhood football team that included Harold Owens, a nephew of Olympian Jesse Owens, and Burrell Shields, a future half back of the Baltimore Colts.[3] Growing up on Cleveland's east side, Noll adopted a "color-blind" outlook at an early age. He retained the outlook as a coach. Noll sought the best players regardless of race. Longtime Pittsburgh sports reporter, writer, and broadcaster, Myron Cope, would say that when Noll looked at players like L.C. Greenwood, a 10th round draft choice, or Donnie Shell, a free agent, his thinking was simply:

Can this guy play? Can we make him a player?[4]

Chuck's father, William Noll, was a butcher and his mother Katherine worked in a florist shop. William suffered from Parkinson's disease, which came on when he was still a relatively young man. The disease put additional financial burdens on the family, but everyone chipped in and made due. Noll's sister Rita said:

We never had much, but we always thought we didn't have to have those things. We had one another, and that is what really made us a good family.[5]

The family surroundings may have been humble, but clearly Noll grew up confident and determined to make good. He knew education was important and he sought out a good one.

Benedictine High School

During his high school years, Chuck Noll worked at Fisher Brothers meat market on Cedar Road to pay his tuition for the highly regarded Benedictine High School.[6] As a lineman, Noll played on Benedictine's first undefeated untied football team of 1948. Noll's Benedictine Bengals won the city title that year by beating South High, 7–0, in Cleveland Stadium. As a senior in 1949, Noll was named to the All-Catholic Universe Bulletin Team.[7]

University of Dayton

Noll attended the University of Dayton on a football scholarship where he played linebacker after starting as a lineman. Noll was a co-captain of the team that went on to the the the 1952 Salad Bowl in Phoenix, the forerunner of today's Fiesta Bowl. He would later say that at Dayton, the athletes were expected to work hard on academics—there were no free rides from the rigors of study. Noll was a member of the class of 1953.

Learning Years

Coaches come to learn their trade in different ways. Some like Lombardi, spend many years developing their skills as they rise from high school coaching to college and then on to the pros. Some are able to jump right into the pros for their apprenticeship. Noll had a professional football career as a player and then he joined the professional football ranks as a coach immediately after his playing days had ended. Noll had the good fortune to play for one of the pillars of the NFL, Paul Brown.

Cleveland Browns

A 20th round selection of the Cleveland Browns in the 1953 draft, Noll played for Paul Brown on one of the most storied teams in professional football. Cleveland won two NFL Championships when Noll was on the roster. A tough intelligent player, Noll was dedicated, competitive, and hardworking.

In Brown, Noll saw a serious coach with great organizational skills—a man who was a leader in perfect control of his team. Brown led with his mind and was not predisposed to excite his players with motivational talks. Brown was also a coach who would not become pals with his players. He kept his distance. Noll would adopt many of Paul Brown's methods.

There were several differences between Noll and Brown, but one stood out more than others. Brown was a slight man who had a sharp tongue and used it. Brown had played quarterback in college. In Noll, there was more of a physical presence. He was a former lineman and linebacker who had gotten in a few scrapes in professional football.

When Noll was a player, he was companionable. Noll joined his Cleveland "Brownies" teammates in activities such as Dante Lavelli's basketball team that faced off against the Harlem Globetrotters and Wilt Chamberlain on March 12, 1959 in Columbus.[8] But when Noll became a coach, people thought of him as aloof. Respect was more important than friendship.

San Diego Chargers

Noll began coaching with the Los Angeles Chargers in 1960, which became the San Diego Chargers in 1961. Offensive-minded Chargers head coach,

Sid Gillman, hired Noll to assist with the defense. Noll worked with Gillman through the 1965 season. During this period, the Chargers won the division five times and two AFL Championships. Gillman was known for extensive use of film and a scientific approach to coaching. He broke down the fundamentals of each offensive position like a biologist breaks down samples in a Petri dish. Gillman studied small things that might make a big difference. Although Gillman was said to be highly opinionated and stubborn, his practices caught on. According to Dick Vermeil, Gillman's concepts, schemes, and techniques are ingrained in every NFL offense.[9]

Baltimore Colts

Chuck Noll served as a defensive coach for Don Shula of the Colts from 1966-1968. Shula was an Ohio native who played his college ball at John Carroll University in Cleveland. Like Noll, Shula had played for Paul Brown. Shula became one of the most venerated coaches in NFL history—highly successful in four decades. Shula's approach was one of constant steady improvement in all facets of the game. He would say that he wanted each meeting, each practice, and every preseason game to count.[10] Shula was steady and consistent, and he adapted his approach based on the talent he had. In 1968, Noll's and Shula's last season together, the Colts won the NFL Championship and lost to the Jets in the Super Bowl. After the 1969 season, Shula was on his way to the Miami Dolphins and a legendary career.

Pittsburgh Steelers

On January 27, 1969, Chuck Noll became the head coach of the Pittsburgh Steelers. Don Shula recommended him. There was a certain working-class grit about Noll that appealed to the Steelers. But rather than having a taste for boxing and horseracing like Steelers' owner Art Rooney, Noll enjoyed music and wine. Rather than being a storyteller like Rooney, Noll was plain speaking and direct. Yet, Noll was always a scrapper—like Rooney.

The interviews for head coach of the Steelers were extensive and Noll held nothing back. Race would not be a consideration. The team would be developed through the draft. Noll would need control. The "Chief," Art Rooney, saw to it that he got it.

When Chuck Noll met with Art Rooney Jr. and Dan Rooney before the first draft he directed, he told them about qualities he liked and thought the Steelers needed in their players. He wanted playing speed and football intelligence. He was looking for players who could play with leverage—gaining the advantage with their legs and delivering a blow not taking one. And Noll was a big advocate of weight training.[11]

When Noll came to the 1969 Steelers' draft, he had one player in his candidate list that he insisted the team acquire that year: Joe Greene. Noll saw

Greene as a leader and someone who embodied the kind of team he wanted to build. The staff agreed.

For the next several years, the Steelers drafted a number of players who would go on to the Hall of Fame: Joe Greene (1969); Terry Bradshaw and Mel Blount (1970); Jack Ham (1971); Franco Harris (1972); Lynn Swann, Jack Lambert, John Stallworth, and Mike Webster (1974).

Noll's Players

The Green Bay Packers had dominated much of the 1960s and in some way Lombardi had redefined the public's view of the great coach as motivator. The Packers' great coach of the era, Vince Lombardi, recalled the brilliant oratory of coaches like Knute Rockne. Noll did not motivate his team by speeches, but he did inspire. He was able to communicate by a few words and example. Like the best coaches, Noll taught young players what it meant to be a good football player as well as a man. He exuded a maturity and toughness that players could understand.

Steelers' running back Rocky Bleier would say that Noll would simply tell the team before a game that they had practiced what they need to do and they need to just do it, to execute. At halftime, Noll would talk about adjustments and basically say the same thing, they now know what they need to do, and they need to just execute. Linebacker Jack Lambert liked Noll's approach because it worked with many different types of players—he was able to keep everyone on the same page.[12] And Noll was able to win without leading cheers in the locker room at halftime.

The Rooneys had made overtures to Bill Nunn, a reporter for the Pittsburgh Sports Courier, who covered black colleges and their talented players. Nunn did some work for the Steelers beginning in 1967 and expanded to fulltime when Noll arrived, looking for players from schools that had been overlooked. Initially, Noll would focus on defense. He would say:

Before you can win a game, you have to not lose it.[13]

Success would come from getting the best players and making sure they had the right preparation.

Andy Russell

Russell was a right linebacker who began his career with the Steelers in 1963 and left the NFL to serve in the U.S. Army in 1964 and 1965. He returned to the Steelers in 1966 and was team captain for 10 years.

Franco Harris

At 6–foot–2, 225 pounds, Franco Harris was a large punishing back who was key to the Steelers' offense for more than a decade. In many ways, he personified Steelers toughness on offense. He gained over 1,000 yards rushing in his first year with the Steelers and gained over 1,000 yards rushing 12 years later in his last year with the team.

Jack Ham

Jack Ham was a cool, calculating outside linebacker known for his diagnostic abilities and his speed. Coming out of Penn State University, Ham ranks with the best outside linebackers of all time. Rarely fooled, Ham provided excellent pass coverage and played extremely well in big games.

Jack Lambert

Jack Lambert was 6–foot–4 and slightly over 200 pounds as a rookie. In later seasons, he bulked up another 20 pounds, but it was Lambert's intensity not his size that made him a great middle linebacker. He was also a leader who challenged everyone on the team to do their job. Opponents feared him and he intimidated the opposition his entire career. Like all great linebackers, Lambert had tremendous football intelligence.

John Stallworth

John Stallworth had an illness that led him to ponder his mortality at a young age. He was also a reader of Westerns and other books that featured those who achieved good things while being underestimated by the world around them. He was determined to make his life memorable in a positive way and he developed into one of the best receivers in football. When playing with Swann, Stallworth was often competing for throws. Later, he was the dominant Steelers' receiver.

Joe Greene

Joe Greene was a defensive tackle who was 6–foot–4, 275 pounds, quick and powerful. His team at North Texas State University was called the Mean Green and he would be called Mean Joe Greene from that association. Noll knew that Greene was the kind of player who could anchor a defense and drive everyone around him to play their best.

Jon Kolb

At 6–foot–2, 225 pounds, Kolb was drafted in the third round as a center from Oklahoma State University. He gained 50 pounds and grew much stronger through a remarkable commitment to conditioning. Kolb was converted to left tackle and played a key role in protecting Bradshaw and opening holes for Franco Harris and other backs.

Lynn Swann

Lynn Swann learned dance at a young age and he was a graceful wide receiver who ran flawless pass patterns. He was also a tremendous athlete who could make incredible catches in tight coverage and take the punishment. He played fearlessly and with artistry and intelligence that helped make watching NFL football a spectacle.

Mel Blount

Mel Blount was a large, tough, quick, durable, and intuitive cornerback who excelled for 14 seasons. Like Bradshaw, it took a few years for him to learn the NFL skills for his position in the pros, but he would become the prototype cornerback by whom all others would be measured. When Blount started out in the pros, league rules allowed a rough bump and run style coverage with physical contact until the pass was thrown. Blount was so good at neutralizing receivers with this coverage that the NFL Competition Committee changed the rules to restrict contact after 5 yards from the line of scrimmage. Blunt adjusted his play and remained on top of his game.[14]

Mike Wagner

Wagner played safety for the Steelers throughout the 1970s championships run. Highly intelligent and a sure tackler, Wagner played a key role in the Steelers' success under Noll.

Mike Webster

"Iron Man" Mike Webster was a muscular hard-nosed offensive center who started in 150 straight games. He anchored the line for every game in a 10-year stretch and played 15 seasons in Pittsburgh. Like several of the Steelers' players from the 1970s, he was the kind of player that the Steelers could count on year after year, enabling the team to focus its acquisition activity on other positions.

Rocky Bleier

Rocky Bleier's story is one of the most inspiring in the history of the NFL. Bleier was a rookie running back on the Steelers in 1968 and then served in Viet Nam where he was wounded with injuries from a bullet and shrapnel in August of 1969. By all accounts, except Bleier's, he would never play much of anything again—certainly not professional football. Against all odds, he worked himself back into playing condition and with the support of the Rooney family, he rejoined the team and he was put on injured reserve in 1971 and 1972. Partnered with Franco Harris, Bleier was a major contributor to the critical ground game from 1974 through 1980 that helped power the Steelers to four championships.

Roy Gerela

Kicker Roy Gerela was acquired in 1971 and played for the Steelers for the next eight seasons. Gerela played on three Super Bowl teams. Fans who established a special rooting section for him at Three Rivers Stadium were called Gerela's Gorillas.

Terry Bradshaw

Terry Bradshaw from Louisiana Tech was athletic and strong-armed—so much so that on sheer ability he eclipsed all rivals. Bradshaw's development would take time and patience. While the media depicted Bradshaw as a slow country boy, Noll thought otherwise. But Bradshaw's development was slowed by criticism that he took to heart.[15] Noll remained confident in Bradshaw, but the coach could often be seen forcefully "instructing" the young man when he performed poorly. Similar to other great quarterback-coach relationships, the Bradshaw-Noll tandem had its share of difficult times while producing Hall of Fame results.

Noll's Coaches

During Noll's tenure he would have a number of assistants who would go on to long coaching careers. His defensive assistant coaches have gotten especially high marks for creating the Steel Curtain defense.

Bud Carson

Carson was hired as defensive backs coach in 1972 and became defensive coordinator in 1973, a position he held until he left following the 1977 season.

George Perles

Perles coached the defensive linemen from 1972-1977. He was defensive coordinator in 1978 and then served as assistant head coach from 1979-1982.

Tony Dungy

Tony Dungy played for the Steelers from 1977-1978. He joined the coaching staff in 1981 working as a defensive assistant and moved up to become defensive coordinator in 1984. Dungy stayed through the 1988 season.

Woody Widenhofer

Widenhofer was an assistant coach with the Steelers from 1973 to 1983. He was the linebacker coach from 1973-1978 and defensive coordinator from 1979 to 1983. Widenhofer taught complex coverages to the Steelers' defense.

Steel Curtain

"Chuck Noll was looking for beef on the line and speed and smarts behind it."[16] He wanted his defensive line to rush the passer —to pressure the quarterback. The front four defensive players of Joe Greene, L.C. Greenwood, Ernie Holmes, and Dwight White made up the core of Pittsburgh's Steel Curtain. In time, some would use the name to describe the entire Steelers' defense.

1969–1973 Seasons

In 1969, Noll's inaugural season, the Steelers won their first game and then lost the remaining 13. The 1969 Steelers scored 218 points and allowed 404 points scored against them. Dick Shiner was the Steelers' quarterback, and rookie Terry Hanratty, a local favorite from Notre Dame, was available if needed. Shiner was a two-year starter in Pittsburgh. In the Steelers' single victory, they beat the Lions with three field goals and one touchdown.

After the season, the Pittsburgh Steelers and the Chicago Bears were tied for dead last in the NFL with identical 1–13 records. Perhaps the highlight of the season for both teams was the coin toss to determine which team was to select first in the draft. The Steelers won and picked the much-coveted Terry Bradshaw from Louisiana Tech. Ironically, the Bears single victory of the season had come when they crushed the Steelers, 38–7, in Chicago.

The Steelers were again inept on offense in 1970, but they went 5–9 and their defense improved. They scored 210 points and gave up 272. Bradshaw threw 24 interceptions and six touchdowns. The Steelers beat the Bills, Oilers, Bengals, Jets, and Browns. Bradshaw started eight games.

In 1971, Noll's third season, the Steelers improved to 6–8. They scored 246 points and allowed their opponents to score 292 points against them. Bradshaw's completion rate was 54.4%, but he threw 22 interceptions and only 13 touchdowns.

Overall progress was slow. Luckily, the Rooneys were patient with their new coach. In time, Art Rooney, Jr. would famously sum up his family's appreciation of Chuck Noll:

Chuck Noll is the best thing to happen to the Rooneys since they got on the boat in Ireland.

Chuck Noll Moments after the Immaculate Reception

Noll for his part would keep repeating his personal mantra:

Whatever it takes.

The Steelers scored 343 points and allowed their opponents to score 175 points against them in the 1972 season. They finished at 11–3 to take the top spot in the AFC Central Division. The offense was coming around. Their first round draft choice running back, Franco Harris, gained 1,055 yards. John Fuqua rushed for 665 yards. A five-game winning streak in midseason was enthusiastically welcomed by fans and the Steelers won the last four games of the season. Joe Greene was recognized as the NFL Defensive Player of the Year.

Defining Moment for Noll's Steelers

The defining moment that ended the string of frustration and put the Steelers into a new winning way came at the very end of the divisional playoff game on December 23, 1972. Pittsburgh had the ball on its own 20-yard line with just 1 minute 20 seconds to go. Bradshaw was no miracle worker in those days and five plays later, the Steelers were still 60 yards from pay dirt with only 22 seconds remaining. Bradshaw threw over the middle to "Frenchy" Fuqua, but Raiders' defensive back Jack Tatum crashed into Fuqua and the ball with such force that the ball flew backward like it had been redirected by some unknown hand. Franco Harris grabbed the ball off his shoelaces in stride and eluded tacklers on his way to the end zone for the score and the win. The play was called the "Immaculate Reception."[17] Although the Steelers went on to lose the AFC Championship to the Dolphins, they made an impression with football fans, their competitors, and most importantly, themselves. They had arrived. Noll's Steelers were winners and now with the Immaculate Reception, it seemed like they had fans in high places.

The Steelers scored 347 points and gave up just 210 in 1973. Improved, but streaky, the Steelers went 8–1 to start, but lost 3 in a row down the stretch making the playoffs at 10–4. They played the Raiders on Oakland turf for the division. The Raiders won easily, 33–14, avenging their loss at the hands of the Steelers in 1972 in the Immaculate Reception game. Despite the score, the Steelers' defense played especially tough. Four times when the Raiders were pressing, the Steelers held, but George Blanda's field goal attempts were right on. Bradshaw was intercepted twice with one of those run back for a touchdown by Raiders' Hall of Fame cornerback, Willie Brown.

1974 Season

The Steelers had a phenomenal draft in 1974. Wide receiver Lynn Swann, who would play for nine seasons, was Noll's first round draft choice. Linebacker Jack Lambert, who was Noll's second round choice, would play for 11 seasons. Another wide receiver, John Stallworth, who would play for 14 seasons, was the third selection. Center Mike Webster was picked in the fifth round and he would play for the Steelers for 15 seasons. Remarkably, all of these players would be inducted into the Pro Football Hall of Fame. With Swan and Stallworth, Bradshaw made tremendous strides in his game, which improved his confidence.

The Steelers scored 305 points and allowed just 189 points in 1974. They racked up a 10–3–1 record in the regular season. Everything came together late in the year, but the journey had its potholes. Bradshaw was slowed by a shoulder injury in 1973 and he had not yet won the starting position at the beginning of the 1974 season.[18] Noll saw Bradshaw's great potential, but he could be hard on him. Bradshaw would later say that he was glad that Noll was tough on him and he is a better man for it.[19]

Backup Quarterback Joe Gilliam had a solid preseason and started the regular season. In the season opener against the Colts, Gilliam led the Steelers to a 30–0 win, connecting on 17 of 31 passes for 257 yards and two touchdowns with only one interception. Gilliam cooled off, however, and Bradshaw got his job back by midseason.

After defeating the Colts, 30–0, in the opener, the Steelers' offense was seemingly able to score at will against the Broncos, but the Broncos did not have much of a problem racking up points against the Steelers either. Gilliam threw for 348 yards, one touchdown and two interceptions in a 35–35 tie. The Raiders shut the Steelers out, 17–0, in the third game of the season. Gilliam struggled, completed only eight passes on 31 attempts for 106 yards, and tossed two interceptions. The Steelers snuck past the Oilers 13–7 in week four scoring on two field goals by Roy Gerela and a rushing touchdown by Preston Pearson. The Steelers beat the Chiefs, 34–24. Gilliam completed 14 of 36 pass attempts for 214 yards and one touchdown and one interception. The Steelers beat the Browns, 20–16, with Gerela making two key field goals in the second half. Bradshaw got the start against the Falcons in week seven, but did not shine in the 24–17 victory. Essentially, it was midseason and Noll's number one quarterback was just loosening up.

When the Steelers beat the Eagles, 27–0, in the 8th game of the season, Bradshaw connected on 12 of 22 passes for 146 yards. A 17–10 loss to the Bengals in week nine was followed by victories against the Browns and the Saints. While the Steelers were moving towards the post season, they were not impressive when they lost to the Oilers, 13–10. But they picked up steam and beat the Patriots, 21–17 and then they repaid the Bengals with a 27–3 Steel City victory in their season closer.

Pittsburgh moved on to the divisional playoff game against Buffalo. The Steelers topped the Bills, 32–14, managing to limit O. J. Simpson to 49 yards on 15 rushes.

AFC Championship

The Pittsburgh Steelers faced the Oakland Raiders for the AFC Championship on December 29, 1974. The game was played at Oakland-Alameda County Coliseum. Oakland's Silver and Black had the best offense in the NFL. Quarterback, Kenny "the Snake" Stabler; two Hall of Fame receivers, Fred Biletnikoff and Cliff Branch; a 47-year-old "Ageless Wonder" kicker, George Blanda; and their remarkable coach, John Madden gave the Raiders a tough-to-beat persona. But regardless of all the Raiders' "California dreamin' designs" on the championship, the Steelers won it on the ground with Franco Harris running for 111 yards and two touchdowns along with Rocky Bleier's 98 yards. Bradshaw had a modest-but-safe day completing 8 of 17 passes for 95 yards and one touchdown with only one interception. Stabler completed 19 passes on 36 attempts for 271 yards and one touchdown, but was intercepted three times. The Steelers stuffed the run, but Branch caught 9 passes for 186 yards and one touchdown. The Steelers 24–13 win gave Art Rooney his first championship game in 42 years of ownership. Next up for Noll's Steelers was Super Bowl IX against a solid Minnesota Vikings team under Bud Grant.

Super Bowl IX

Super Bowl IX featured an all-star cast with two Hall of Fame quarterbacks leading the way: Terry Bradshaw and Fran Tarkenton. The game also spotlighted two vaunted defenses: Pittsburgh's Steel Curtain and Minnesota's Purple People Eaters. The Purple People Eaters were the Vikings front line defense that included Carl Eller, Alan Page, Jim Marshall, and Gary Larsen/Doug Sutherland. The game was played at Tulane Stadium in New Orleans on January 12, 1975.

For the Vikings, Super Bowl IX was the second year in a row they fought their way into the National Football League championship game. In the post season, Minnesota had defeated the St. Louis Cardinals and the Los Angeles Rams on their way to New Orleans.

Offensively, the game started out slowly and never did speed up. The Steel Curtain hung tough and the Purple People Eaters kept the Steelers in check for much of the day. The first half yielded little more than a demonstration on the art of punting. Fran "the Scrambler" Tarkenton was sacked in his own end zone for a safety—the only score in the half. In the opening kickoff of the second half, the Steelers recovered a fumble on the Vikings' 30-yard line. Three Franco Harris runs covered the distance and it was Steelers 9–Vikings 0. More punts followed. The Vikings scored in the fourth quarter when Matt

Blair blocked a Bobby Walden punt that was recovered by Terry Brown in the end zone. The extra point was missed and the score stood Steelers 9–Vikings 6. The Steelers responded by driving 66 yards on the ensuing possession— scoring on a 4-yard Bradshaw pass to Larry Brown. The Steelers won 16–6. Pittsburgh had 333 yards of total offense. Steelers' Fullback Franco Harris, who ran for a Super Bowl record 158 yards and a touchdown, was named the Most Valuable Player. Joe Greene was recognized as the NFL Defensive Player of the Year for the second time.

Noll had delivered. In 5 years, he had put together a dynamic team with outstanding draft selections, an excellent football program, and a patient-yet-prodding coaching staff.

1975 Season

After winning Super Bowl IX, the Steelers would get the best that their opponents had to offer each game of the 1975 season. They were up to the task. The Steelers scored 373 points and gave up just 162 points to opponents. Bud Carson's formidable defense was mature. Bradshaw was firmly established at quarterback. Franco Harris scored more points than any other running back except for O.J. Simpson. The Steel Curtain was intimidating. According to Mike Wagner, the "attitude, optimism, and determination were there."[20]

The Steelers beat the San Diego Chargers 37–0 in the season opener. Noll told the team they had played badly! Their second game, which pitted the Steelers against the Bills, started out badly. O.J. Simpson ran all over the Steelers and scored on an 88-yard touchdown gallop. In the third quarter, the Steelers looked up at the scoreboard after an O. J. Simpson touchdown and saw that they were losing, 23–0. In the remaining time, the Steelers outscored the Bills, 21–7, but it was not enough. Buffalo won, 30–21. Suitably motivated, the Steelers jumped on an 11-game winning streak. In the midst of the streak, they were able to get past division rival Cincinnati Bengals, 30–24 in their first meeting. They followed by beating the Oilers, 24–17, on a fourth quarter Bradshaw touchdown pass to John Stallworth. The string continued until they lost the last regular season game to the Rams, 10–3. They approached the playoffs with a 12–2 record.

On December 27, 1975, the Steelers took on the Baltimore Colts in their divisional playoff game at Three Rivers Stadium. The Steelers powered past the Colts, 28–10, with a strong rushing performance by Franco Harris. The Steelers commanding back ran for 153 yards on 27 carries. Bradshaw passed for 103 yards with 8 completions on only 13 attempts.

In the last scoring play of the game, veteran linebacker Andy Russell, who was not known for blazing speed, recovered a fumble and ran it back for 93 long yards. In recalling the ribbing that came from teammate Ray Mansfield after the play, Russell said:

> *… NBC cut to a commercial during the return and came back to catch me score the touchdown. Nonetheless, it was a memorable play in my career.[21]*

AFC Championship Game

The Steelers played the Raiders for the AFC Championship in Three Rivers Stadium on January 4, 1976. This game would be remembered for miserable field conditions and weather. It was 16° at game time with a sharp wind and a frozen slippery field that was as hard as granite. Ray Gerela kicked a field goal in the second quarter and the rest of the scoring took place in the fourth. Franco Harris had a nifty 25-yard run for a touchdown to give the Steelers a 10–0 lead. Harris looked like he was trapped in the backfield, ran outside and John Stallworth blocked two players to help free him. For the Raiders lone touchdown, Stabler hit Mike Siani on a 14-yard pass. Bradshaw countered with a 20-yard touchdown pass to Stallworth who made the grab in the midst of two defenders in the end zone. The Steelers' extra point failed. Later, George Blanda was able to kick a 41-yard field goal to get Oakland back to within a touchdown, but that is where the scoring ended. The Steelers won, 16–10.

Super Bowl X

The Steelers faced the Cowboys in Super Bowl X on January 18, 1976, in the Orange Bowl in Miami. The Steelers' Roy Gerela kicked off to the former Steeler, now Cowboy, Preston Pearson, just in front of the goal. Pearson handed the ball off on a reverse to Thomas "Hollywood" Henderson, who eluded all the Steelers' players on the field with the exception of the kicker Roy Gerela. The Pittsburgh kicker threw himself at Henderson and knocked him out of bounds at the Pittsburgh 44-yard line. Regardless of the trickery, the Steelers held the Cowboys and forced them to punt. When the Steelers had trouble moving the ball, their punter, Bobby Walden, fumbled the snap and recovered the ball himself, but he did not get the punt off. The Cowboys took over on the Steelers' 30-yard line. Roger Staubach hit Drew Pearson on a touchdown pass right down the middle that looked easy.

On the Pittsburgh possession, Rocky Bleier and Franco Harris ground out the yards early. Then Lynn Swann acrobatically snagged a 32-yard Bradshaw sideline pass that brought the ball to the 16-yard line. A few plays later, Randy Grossman caught a 7-yard touchdown pass to tie the score. When a Cowboys' drive stalled in the second quarter, kicker Toni Fritsch hit a 36-yard field goal to put Dallas ahead, 10–7.

Later in the second quarter, Swann made a second spectacular catch when he leapt in the air for a 50-yard Bradshaw bomb with defender in tow to flick the ball up and catch it on the bobble as he was falling to the turf.

Nevertheless, the Steelers' drive stalled and Gerela came in and missed a 36-yard field goal. Henderson believed that Gerela had hurt his ribs on the tackle he made on the opening kickoff.[22] Some believe the turning point in the game came in the third quarter when Cliff Harris taunted Roy Gerela who had just missed his second field goal. Linebacker Jack Lambert responded to the taunt by throwing Harris to the ground, which seemed to excite and motivate the Steelers. The Steelers' defense did their part throughout the game by sacking the Cowboys' quarterback Roger Staubach an incredible seven times.

The score remained 10–7 with Dallas in the lead into the fourth quarter. On the first full series for the Cowboys in the fourth quarter they started on their own 19-yard line. The Steelers sacked Staubach two of three downs for negative yardage and running back Doug Dennison managed a 1-yard gain. Mitch Hoopes was sent in to punt from the Dallas 16 and Reggie Harrison blocked it in the end zone resulting in a safety making the score Dallas 10–Pittsburgh–9.

When Gerela kicked a 36-yard field goal, the Steelers moved ahead 12–10. A short time later, Mike Wagner intercepted a Staubach pass in Dallas territory and brought it all the way down to the Cowboys' 7-yard line. The Cowboys' defense held, and Roy Gerela kicked an 18-yard field goal to make the score 15–10.

Later in the fourth quarter, the Steelers took possession on their 30-yard line after a Dallas punt. Following two Franco Harris short runs, Bradshaw connected with Swann again on a beautiful 64-yard touchdown strike. Bradshaw was hit after the pass with helmet to helmet contact and knocked out of the game. After missing the extra point, the Steelers led 21–10.

Dallas came right back on an 80-yard drive that took just four passes, the last one being a 34-yard touchdown strike to Percy Howard. Pittsburgh had a precarious 21–17 lead. The Pittsburgh offense was in a predictable run mode especially with Bradshaw out. Backup quarterback Terry Hanratty was asked to use up as much clock as possible, but the Cowboys defended the run. After three downs, the Steelers were sitting at their own 42-yard line with 9 yards to go for the first down. Rather than risk any blocked punts or interceptions, Noll settled on another Rocky Bleier run that turned the ball over to the Cowboys and left the Steelers' defense to defend the lead with 1:22 remaining. After driving down to the Pittsburgh 38-yard line with seconds remaining in the game, Staubach threw to Drew Pearson in the end zone, but Mike Wagner got a hand on it and defensive back Glen Edwards intercepted the ball and ran it out to the 30-yard line. The Steelers had won their second Super Bowl under Noll. Mel Blount was named the NFL Defensive Player of the Year.

1976 Season

The Steelers scored 342 points and gave up just 138 in 1976. The season got off to a bad start when the Steelers' playoff nemesis, the Oakland Raiders, beat them, 31–28, in the opener. The Steelers were ahead, 28–14, with five minutes remaining when Oakland turned it around. Oakland scored three times in a hurry while the Steelers were shut out. The first score came when Stabler hit Dave Casper on a 10-yard touchdown pass. Once the Raiders had the ball again, a Stabler to Branch pass gave the Raiders the ball at the 2-yard line. Stabler ran the ball into the end zone to tie the score. A short time later, Fred Steinfort kicked a 21-yard field goal to seal the victory for the Raiders.

Lynn Swann, who had been knocked out the previous season by the Raiders' George Atkinson in the AFC Championship game, was whacked again by the same man with the same result.

John Stallworth caught two touchdown passes as the Steelers handled the Cleveland Browns, 31–14, in the second game of the season. After the Browns' quarterback Brian Sipe threw two touchdown passes in the first quarter, the Steelers' defense shut Cleveland out for the remainder of the game.

The Steelers lost a tight game to the Patriots that featured five field goals in the first half and a Franco Harris touchdown run. The Steelers led, 13–9, at halftime, but in the second half, the Patriots outscored the Steelers, 21–7. Quarterback Steve Grogan hit big tight end Russ Francis for one touchdown and wide receiver Darryl Stingley for another, before he ran one in himself. Franco Harris rushed for his second touchdown of the game in the third quarter, and Bradshaw hit tight end Randy Grossman for a late score, but it was not enough. The Patriots won, 30–27.

The Vikings and their Purple People Eaters chewed up the Steelers, 17–6. When the Steelers lost their fourth game in their second match with the Browns, few would imagine the Steelers would go undefeated the rest of the regular season. Not only did the Browns take away an 18–16 victory on the strength of four Don Cockroft field goals, but the Steelers lost Bradshaw for several games after he suffered a neck injury. Browns' defensive end Joe "Turkey" Jones wrapped his arms around a struggling Bradshaw in the backfield as the Steelers' quarterback was trying to hang onto the ball. Jones pulled him up in the air and flung him down where he landed head-first. Bradshaw flew back to Pittsburgh on a stretcher and would not be at full strength again until the Tampa Bay game on December 5.

In Bradshaw's absence, rookie quarterback Mike Kruczek did everything the Steelers' coaching staff asked him to do—short passes and assisting the running game of Franco Harris and Rocky Bleier.

During the Steelers' nine game winning streak, the defense stepped up by shutting out five opponents and allowing a miserly 28 points from the other four. Pittsburgh ended the regular season with a 10–4 record, which was remarkable considering that they lost four of their first five games.

When the Steelers played the Baltimore Colts in the divisional playoff game, it was more of a tragic play than a football contest. The Steelers won 40–14, but both Pittsburgh starting running backs, Rocky Bleier and Franco Harris, were injured and lost for the AFC Championship game that followed. Roy Gerela was also injured forcing punter Bobby Walden to kickoff and center Ray Mansfield to fill in for him on field goal attempts.

AFC Championship Game

Pittsburgh's fine-tuned defensive squad and injured offense went up against their playoff nemesis, the Oakland Raiders, in the AFC Championship game at Oakland Alameda County Stadium on December 26, 1976. On the Raiders' first possession, Stabler was sacked by Mike Wagner on a third down safety blitz that forced a Ray Guy punt from the end zone. Starting their first possession on the Oakland 45, the Steelers could not move the ball and punted it back to Oakland. In the ensuing series, both teams continued to keep the other from the end zone, but the Raiders were slowly winning the struggle for field position. Eventually, a Steelers' punt from deep in their own territory was tipped, giving Oakland the ball on the Pittsburgh 38-yard line. Oakland was able to drive into field goal range where Errol Mann kicked a 39-yard field goal for the first score. When the Steelers got the ball back, the offense continued to sputter without Bleier and Harris. Bradshaw slipped on one play and Harrison dropped a third down pass. The ball was punted back to the Raiders.

In the second quarter, Willie Hall picked off a Bradshaw pass that bounced off Fuqua's hands and he took it down to the 1-yard line. The Steelers did not make it easy, but Clarence Davis scored on the Raiders third attempt from close in. The Raiders were up 10–0 with 10 minutes to go in the first half when the pace accelerated. The Steelers drove towards midfield on a Bradshaw pass to Frank Lewis. Unbelievably, it was Bradshaw's first completion and it resulted in Pittsburgh's first first down of the game. Fuqua started to gain on the ground and Bradshaw switched things up with a pass to Stallworth down the middle. He followed with a pass to Lynn Swann that moved the Steelers inside the 10-yard line. After a penalty, Reggie Harrison took it in from 3 yards out and Mansfield kicked the extra point. The score was Raiders 10–Steelers 7.

When the Raiders got the ball back after the kickoff, their offensive line opened up huge holes against an overworked Steelers' defense. As the Raiders closed in toward the goal, the Steelers were called on a hold, which resulted in a first down on the 4-yard line. Stabler tossed a touchdown pass to a wide open tight end, Warren Bankston, on the next play. After the 13-play drive and the extra point, the Raiders led 17–7 and that's how it ended less than a minute later at halftime.

Sadly for the Pittsburgh fans, the only scoring in the second half was a Stabler 5-yard touchdown pass to Pete Banaszak. The Steelers lost 24–7. The Steelers only mustered up 72 yards rushing compared to their 196-yard performance against the Raiders earlier in the season. Facing adversity the way they did, Noll's 1976 team is often named as one of the most admired in the Steelers' history. Linebacker Jack Lambert was named the NFL Defensive Player of the Year.

1977 Season

In 1977, the Steelers' team seemed to implode. Jack Lambert held out. There were other distractions as well. It all led to a 9–5 season. Dan Rooney would comment that there were years when the Steelers would have welcomed a 9–5 season record, but things had changed under Noll and expectations were much higher.[23]

The Steelers scored 283 points that season and allowed 243. They started out well enough by shutting out San Francisco 27–0, but lost to Oakland 16–7 in their second game after committing five turnovers. The Steelers beat the Browns, 28–14, who were not a very good team that year, but then lost to the Oilers, 27–10, who were better. After taming the Bengals, 20–14, they topped the Oilers by the same score they had lost to them by two weeks earlier, 27–10. After losing to the Colts and Broncos, the Steelers put together a four game winning streak before they lost to the Bengals, 17–10. They beat the Chargers, 10–9 and limped into the playoffs. The Broncos knocked the Steelers out in the division playoff match. The Steelers matched every score the Broncos put up in the first three quarters and the score stood at 21–21. In the fourth, the Broncos kicked two field goals and Jack Dolbin caught a Craig Morton touchdown pass for a 34–21 Denver win.

1978 Season

Remarkably, the 1978 Steelers' team featured nine players headed for the Hall of Fame. Rule changes favored the passing game, which impacted the Steelers' defense and made Bradshaw's game more important. Noll made adjustments. Bradshaw led the league with 28 touchdown passes and was named NFL MVP. The Steelers scored 356 points and allowed 195. Bradshaw passed for 2,915 yards. Swann had 61 receptions for 880 yards. Stallworth had 41 catches for 798 yards and tight end Randy Grossman had 37 catches for 448 yards. Franco Harris ran for 1,082 yards and Bleier ran for 633. Roy Gerela, who was finishing out his Steelers' career, made 12 of 26 field goal attempts and was almost flawless on extra points, kicking 44 of 45.

Defensive Coordinator Bud Carson had moved on to the Rams after six seasons with the Steelers and was replaced by defensive line coach George Perles. The defense featured Greene, Greenwood, Hamm, Lambert, Blount, and Shell.

During the season the Steelers lost just two games. The Oilers beat the Steelers, 24–17, on the strength of three rushing touchdowns by sensational rookie running back Earl Campbell. The Oilers' success did not come easy; the Steelers made it difficult for Campbell allowing only 89 yards on 21 carries. The Rams beat the Steelers 10–7. Pittsburgh finished with a five game winning streak before they manhandled the Broncos in the division playoff, 33–10, with 425 yards of offense, two rushing touchdowns, two passing touchdowns, and two field goals.

AFC Championship

The Steelers rolled over the Oilers in the AFC Championship game, 34–5. The Steelers scored on runs by Harris and Bleier; Bradshaw passes to Stallworth and Swann; and two Gerela field goals. For the Oilers, Toni Fritsch kicked a 19-yard field goal late in the game; Bleier was tackled in the end zone for a safety. The Steelers' scoring success belied the miserable cold conditions in Three Rivers Stadium.

Super Bowl XIII

The Steelers took on the defending-champion Dallas Cowboys in Super Bowl XIII on a warm day in the Orange Bowl. The game was one of the most dramatic, entertaining Super Bowls, but both teams made many mistakes and both missed opportunities. After a Cowboys' fumble and a Steelers' recovery, Bradshaw orchestrated a successful drive that ended with a 28-yard touchdown pass to Stallworth. A stalled drive by Dallas was followed by a Bradshaw pass that was intercepted by Dallas linebacker D.D. Lewis. Dallas went three and out, but the Steelers gave them another opportunity when Bradshaw fumbled and Ed "Too Tall" Jones recovered. Staubach tossed a 39-yard touchdown strike to Tony Hill. Bradshaw fumbled again on the next series and Mike Hegman recovered the ball and took it 37 yards for a touchdown. The Steelers came right back when Bradshaw hit Stallworth for a 75-yard score. Later in the second quarter, Mel Blount intercepted a Staubach pass and the Steelers capitalized with a drive that culminated in a 7-yard Bradshaw touchdown pass to Rocky Bleier. Pittsburgh led at halftime, 21–14.

In the third quarter, the scoring began with the Cowboys' Rafael Septien's 27-yard field goal to make the score, Pittsburgh 21–Dallas 17. Bradshaw put together a long drive in the fourth quarter that began at the Steelers' 15-yard line and was aided by a 33-yard pass interference infraction. Franco Harris ran for a Steelers' touchdown from 22 yards out. After the extra point, Pittsburgh led, 28–17. Randy White fumbled the ensuing kickoff that Dirt Winston recovered. Quickly, Bradshaw struck pay dirt on an 18-yard touchdown pass to Swann. It was 35–17 when Staubach fought back. With a couple of nifty runs by Tony Dorsett mixed in, Staubach connected with Billy Joe DuPree and Drew Pearson. Staubach went to DuPree again on a 7-yard touchdown strike that tightened the game, Pittsburgh 35–Dallas 24, after the extra point. Time was running out when the Cowboys succeeded on an onside kick, which Dennis Thurman recovered. It was Dallas ball in good field position with just over two minutes to go. The Cowboys did not disappoint. Staubach drove 52 yards in nine plays with a touchdown toss to Butch Johnson to make the score, 35–31. With seconds remaining, the Cowboys tried another onside kick, but Rocky Bleier was able to recover the ball to secure the win.

1979 Season

After winning the Super Bowl the previous season, Chuck Noll told the press that he thought the Steelers had not yet peaked. His players took the statement in good humor, but they knew that their coach was serious about winning another Super Bowl. In 1979, the Steelers scored 416 points and gave up 262.

The Steelers' tremendous season challenged the team's depth. At the start of the season, Joe Greene, Lynn Swann, and Rocky Bleier were out of action. Several reserve players would have to step up and fill in at times for the league's superstars. Undrafted free agent John Banaszak, who made the team in 1975, would fill in at right defensive end in 1979. He had a tremendous season and was beloved by the Steelers' fans for his blue-collar efforts and upbringing. Some of the best Steelers would have to improve their game as well. Stallworth would be Bradshaw's leading target because Swann would be out at times with injuries. Stallworth would have 70 receptions during the regular season. The Steelers would be a powerful team, but not as crisp and disciplined as other Noll Pittsburgh teams. They would lead the league in turnovers with 52 and they would play some of their worst games under Noll. Yet, the Steelers' offense would be top-rated in the NFL and their defense would continue to intimidate other teams.

The Steelers' season opener was a Monday night game against the New England Patriots. Steve Grogan was in his fifth year with New England. Grogan hit big tight end Russ Francis on a 4-yard pass for the first score. Steelers' running back Sidney Thornton rushed for Pittsburgh's first score, but the Steelers missed the extra point. The Patriots' John Smith hit two field goals to end the scoring for the first half. The Patriots led, 13–6. Sidney Thornton caught a Bradshaw touchdown pass and after the extra point, the score was tied, 13–13, at the end of regulation. In overtime, the Steelers' new kicker, Matt Bahr, nailed a 41-yard field goal for the 16–13 win. It was a suspenseful ending for the national audience. In the second game of the season, the Steelers beat the Oilers and Earl Campbell, 38–7. After managing to beat the Cardinals and Colts, they lost their first game to the Eagles, 17–14. Each team scored two touchdowns. The difference in the game was Tony Franklin's 48-yard field goal for the Eagles. The Steelers beat the Browns in a wild high-scoring game, 51–35, that gave witness to a 71-yard rushing touchdown by Franco Harris and a 70-yard rushing touchdown by Rocky Bleier. The Steelers lost to the Bengals, 34–10, when they fumbled an incredible nine times losing possession in seven of those cases. Pittsburgh was able to string out four wins in a row before they got stomped by the Chargers, 35–7. The Steelers committed eight turnovers in that game including five Bradshaw interceptions. After beating the Browns and the Bengals, they lost to the Oilers whom they had beaten badly early in the season. They ended the regular season on a high note by shutting out the Bills, 28–0.

In the divisional playoff game, the Steelers beat the Dolphins, 34–14. The Dolphins had finished first in the AFC East with a 10–6 record.

AFC Championship

Pittsburgh was able to frustrate the Oilers magnificent human battering ram, Earl Campbell, who gained only 15 yards on the day. The Oilers, coached by Bum Phillips, were held to just one touchdown and that was a 75-yard interception return by Vernon Perry. Toni Fritsch added 6 points on two field goals to make the Oilers tally of 13. The Steelers' Terry Bradshaw hit Bennie Cunningham on a 16-yard touchdown pass and connected with John Stallworth for a 20-yard score. Matt Bahr kicked two field goals. Rocky Bleier rushed for a 4-yard score in the fourth quarter. The Steelers took home a 27–13 victory and another AFC Championship.

Super Bowl XIV

On January 20, 1980, the Pittsburgh Steelers took on the Los Angeles Rams in Super Bowl XIV at the Rose Bowl in Pasadena, California, before 103,985 spectators. Matt Bahr kicked a 41-yard field goal for the first score. The Rams charged back. Wendell Tyler broke loose for a 39-yard run and Lawrence McCutcheon powered to the 1-yard line on three rushes. Cullen Bryant took it in from there for a touchdown. On the Rams' kickoff, the Steelers' Larry Anderson gobbled up 45 yards and gave the Steelers excellent field position. Bradshaw moved the ball with short passes and power runs by Bleier and Harris. Harris muscled in to score from the 1-yard line for the Steelers in the second quarter. The Rams' Frank Corral hit 31-yard and 45-yard field goals to give the Rams a 13–10 lead at halftime.

Again, Larry Anderson gave the Steelers excellent field position when he returned the second half opening kickoff 37 yards. Bradshaw hit Lynn Swan on a 47-yard bomb to start the scoring in the third quarter. Lawrence McCutcheon hit Ron Smith on a 20-yard halfback option for a Rams' touchdown, but the extra point was missed, leaving the Rams with a thin 19–17 lead. In the fourth quarter, Bradshaw got to work and connected with Stallworth on a 74-yard bomb that gave the Steelers the lead at 24–19. A few series later, Rams' quarterback Vince Ferragamo threw a pass that was intercepted by Jack Lambert. On third down and seven, Bradshaw hurled a 45-yard bomb to Stallworth that the Steelers' receiver caught in the midst of four Ram defenders. Two plays later, a pass interference call in the end zone brought the ball out to the one, where Franco Harris scored the game's final touchdown. The Steelers held on to win, 31–19. Noll's Steelers had captured four Super Bowls.

End of a Dynasty

Pittsburgh picked up Pennsylvania and Ohio talent going back to the early days of the franchise. Other early NFL teams also focused most on local talent especially for teams that resided in areas that were known as fertile areas for football talent. In time, a local focus could hurt teams when the competition searched larger and larger areas. When the Steelers got serious about picking the best talent available from any part of the country, they were able to build a winner. Still, a momentary lapse that might favor a local boy might have been helpful in the 1979 draft when a quarterback from Monongahela named Joe Montana was not drafted until the 82nd pick. The "lapse" did not take place!

The Steelers of the 1980s were not the mighty Steelers' of the 1970s. Longtime Steelers' broadcaster Myron Cope guessed that more than anything else the Steelers did not have the great assistant coaches that cultivated their 1970s stars. A more obvious reason would be that the Steelers could not duplicate their draft success.

It would be Montana and the San Francisco 49ers not the Steelers who would win four Super Bowls in the 1980s. And like the Steelers, the 49ers would be building a great team from one with a losing tradition. In the seasons of the 1990s, the Dallas Cowboys would come back strong to win three Super Bowls. In the first decade of the 2000s, Bill Belichick's New England Patriots would win three Super Bowls.

Noll built a dynasty from the ground up in his early years and the Steelers of 1980 still had a core group of Hall of Fame players. A start-from-scratch strategy was not an option. Sustaining a winning program is generally deemed a matter of specific acquisitions to fill needs while maintaining the team's strengths. Noll stuck to what he could do to make the Steelers winners. Tony Dungy remembered Noll's simple formula as "let's do things the right way, do them very well, and get them done."[24] Noll would argue that players win games not coaches, but most observers would say that a winning system is really a combination of talent, coaching, and a great program. The Steelers had all three in the 1970s.

On defense, Noll began building his team with Joe Greene who was a tremendous athlete as well as a leader whose presence was felt every down. Built around Greene was a Steel Curtain brotherhood and team culture that demanded toughness and competitive superiority. On offense, Noll chose a quarterback with the greatest athletic skills at the position in Terry Bradshaw. Bradshaw also needed the right players around him. Having Franco Harris and Rocky Bleier meant that when needed, the Steelers' rushing game was going to be top notch. With Swann and Stallworth for Bradshaw's passing game, the Steelers were able to attack other teams in a balanced way. The offensive team that grew out from these key players was one that had firepower on the ground and in the air. The defense was effective and intimidating.

The great players who formed the core of the team that had come together in the early Noll years would trail off into retirement, but it would not happen all at once. As they grew older, some fissures showed up in the Steelers' cast.

Most aging stars would not be replaced by players of the same caliber. The Steelers would remain tough and competitive, but not a dominant championship team. In the 1980s, the Steelers would have four post season opportunities, but there would be no more Super Bowl appearances for Chuck Noll and his team.

Mark Malone

The Steelers selected Mark Malone in the first round in the 1980 draft, the number 28 pick overall. Malone was 6-foot-4 and 220 pounds. He was a magnificent athlete and coveted by many NFL teams, but his career was limited by injuries. In his first season, he filled in as a receiver. According to Malone, "I had developed bursitis in my elbow, so I couldn't throw anyway."[25] Unfortunately, he injured his knee in 1981 and did not play at all in 1982. He would be the Steelers' starting quarterback 1984-1987.

1980 Season

The Steelers were the best team in football in 1979, but they fell like a rock in 1980. In 1980, the Pittsburgh Steelers scored 352 points and gave up 313. It was Rocky Bleier's final season. The Steelers' losses to the AFC Central Division rival Cincinnati Bengals provide a glimpse of their fate for the upcoming decade. In their first game with Cincinnati, they were ahead, 21–13, in the fourth quarter. They could not hold the lead. Although the Steelers scored another touchdown on a Greg Hawthorne rush, the Bengals did better. Jack "the Throwin Somoan" Thompson hit wide receiver Isaac Curtis on an 18-yard score and he hit Don Bass on a 22-yard touchdown strike while Ian Sunter kicked a 21-yard field goal. The Bengals won 30–28. In their second game against the Bengals, the Steelers were behind 17–0 at the halftime. They rallied, but essentially lost the game by missing an extra point. It was Bengals 17–Steelers 16. In their last game of the season, they could not catch the Chargers and lost, 26–17, to mark the end of a respectable, but frustrating 9–7 season.

Who was to blame for the steep drop from 1979 to 1980? Noll would say: "You win as a team and you don't point fingers. Losers point fingers. And we are not losers."[26]

1981-1983 Seasons

In 1981, the Steelers finished 8–8 for the season, scored 356 points, and gave up 297. They finished second in the AFC Central Division and did not make the playoffs. It was the last year that Joe Greene and Randy Grossman played. The Steelers managed a four-game winning streak in the first half of the season that gave them a 5–3 record and some hope for a post season appearance. But the team fell apart at the end of the season with a three-game losing streak that put them at 8–8 for the year. The losing streak began when the Steelers played the Raiders on December 7. Bradshaw suffered a season-ending injury after he whacked his hand against the helmet of Rod Martin, an Oakland linebacker. The Raiders won 30–27. The Steelers lost the next two games without Bradshaw and the season ended without a post-season invitation.

The 1982 draft was a good one. Pittsburgh selected Walter Abercrombie and Mike Merriweather, and picked up Gary Anderson after he was drafted and cut by the Bills. Abercrombie was a good running back who could also catch the ball out of the backfield. Outside linebacker Merriweather would play 11 years in the pros, 6 of those for the Steelers. Kicker Anderson would play for the Steelers for 13 years.

The Steelers scored 204 points and gave up 146 in 1982. It was the Pittsburgh Steelers' 50th Anniversary, but a players' strike shortened the regular season to nine games. A special playoff system was devised for the season. Based on regular season records, 8 teams from each conference were seeded 1 through 8 and a playoff bracket design was created leading to the Super Bowl.

After beating a very good Cowboys' team 36–28 in the opener, the Steelers earned an overtime win against the Bengals, 26–20. The strike began and the Steelers were inactive until their 24–10 win on November 21 against the Oilers. In the game against the Oilers, it was still Bradshaw throwing the ball with touchdown catches made by Greg Hawthorne, Bennie Cunningham, and Jim Smith. For the remainder of the regular season, the Steelers finished 3–3, which gave them a 6–3 finish. That was good enough to make the Wild Card game against the Chargers on January 9, 1983.

When the Steelers played the Chargers, they faced a potent offense that featured Hall of Famers Dan Fouts at quarterback and Kellen Winslow at tight end. The Chargers also had gifted wide receiver Wes Chandler and running back Chuck Muncie who had rushed for 1,144 yards the previous season. The potent offense of the Chargers was capable of scoring fast and they proved it that day. The Steelers were ahead, 28–17, in the fourth quarter, but Fouts led the Chargers to the last two scores making the final: Chargers 31–Steelers 28.

The 1983 draft offered a great opportunity for team-building, featuring six Hall of Famers in the first round: John Elway, Dan Marino, Jim Kelly, Eric Dickerson, Bruce Matthews, and Darrell Green. Pittsburgh fans no doubt think about how Dan Marino from the University of Pittsburgh was available and passed over by the Steelers. Several other teams passed over Marino as well before he was selected by Miami. Yet, for the Steelers, the draft would be an opportunity lost, not due to a poor choice, but a tragic event.

Now with many great Steelers retired, Noll wanted to rebuild his defense first. Noll chose center Gabe Rivera from Texas Tech.[27] Rivera was going to be a new anchor in the future Steelers' defensive line. Tragedy struck when Rivera was seriously injured in a car accident in his rookie season that put him in a wheelchair. Rivera showed Steelers' grit, when he went forward with his life making the best of his situation after many very difficult years.

The Steelers scored 355 points and gave up 303 in 1983. The legendary Steelers of the 1970s continued to take their leave. Lynn Swan and Jack Ham retired after the 1982 season. Terry Bradshaw underwent surgery on his elbow in the off season and was unable to play until late in the season.

The Steelers were playing well right into November. After they beat the Colts, 24–13, on November 13, they had won seven games in a row and stood at 9–2. Quarterback Cliff Stoudt's completion percentage was good and the Steelers were averaging better than 25 points a game. Things changed quickly. In the last five games of the season, they lost to the Vikings, Lions, Bengals, and Browns. When Bradshaw returned against the Jets in the second to last regular game of the season, he threw two touchdown passes early in the game, but reinjured his elbow, never to play again. The Steelers won easily, 34–7. Stoudt threw two touchdowns and Gary Anderson kicked two field goals. The only Jets' score came in the third quarter when Pat Ryan hit wide receiver Lam Jones on a 27-yard strike.

The Steelers finished the season, 10–6, first in the AFC Central Division, but they backed into the playoffs in a slump. They faced their playoff nemesis, the Raiders, in the divisional playoff game.

The Los Angeles Raiders had a powerful offense with veteran quarterback Jim Plunket, wide receiver Cliff Branch, outstanding running back Marcus Allen, and superb tight end Todd Christensen.[28] Christensen caught more passes than any wide receiver in football that year.

The Steelers' Gary Anderson kicked a field goal for the first score of the game, then it was all Raiders. Lester Hayes intercepted a Stoudt pass and ran it in for the score. In the second quarter, Marcus Allen rushed for a touchdown and the Raiders' Chris Bahr kicked a 45-yard field goal. Kenny King and Marcus Allen rushed for touchdowns in the third quarter before John Stallworth got the Steelers on the board again with a 58-yard touchdown reception of a Cliff Stoudt pass. The Raiders' Frank Hawkins scored the final touchdown on a 2-yard rush. The Raiders won 38–10.

1984 Season

The Steelers scored 387 points and gave up 310 in 1984. Tony Dungy was promoted to defensive coordinator. Pittsburgh's first selection in the 1984 draft was Louis Lipps who was named Offensive Rookie of the Year. His presence gave the Steelers a big spark that season. It was time to say goodbye to two great ones: Larry Brown who played both offensive tackle and tight end for 14 years, and Hall of Fame linebacker Jack Lambert, an 11-season veteran.

The Steelers' up and down season started with a loss to the Kansas City Chiefs and then victories over the Jets and the Rams. They lost to the Browns, beat the Bengals, and then lost to the Dolphins. And then they did something significant—they handed the Super Bowl bound San Francisco 49ers their only loss of the season, 20–17. The Steelers finished the season at 9–7.

The Steelers moved on to the divisional playoff game against Denver. Denver had finished with a 13–3 record and their quarterback, Hall of Famer John Elway, had excellent receivers in Butch Johnson and Steve Watson. Broncos' running back Sammy Winder was also having an excellent year having 1,153 yards rushing along with 44 receptions for 288 yards.

The Steelers started sloppily. Quarterback Mark Malone fumbled the ball on the Steelers' first two possessions. John Elway hit tight end James Wright on a 9-yard touchdown pass after the second fumble recovery for the first score of the game. Gary Anderson kicked a 28-yard field goal for the Steelers' first score. After a Steelers' punt was blocked, Elway turned the ball over on an interception made by Gary Dunn. A long Steelers' drive followed with Frank Pollard plunging into the end zone from the 1-yard line to give the Steelers a 10–7 lead. In the third quarter, Denver came back and Rich Karlis kicked a 21-yard field goal that was followed by a 20-yard Elway touchdown pass to Steve Watson. Denver had the lead, 17–10. Malone came back to Lipps on a 10-yard touchdown score to tie the game. The Steelers scored the only points in the fourth quarter on a 2-yard run by Pollard. Elway was suffering from injuries that hindered his mobility and made it very difficult for the Broncos to stage any last minute comeback. Managing to overcome difficulties at the quarterback position along with a poor showing down the regular season stretch, the Steelers beat one of the best teams in football and earned the right to play the Miami Dolphins and Dan Marino in the AFC Championship game.

AFC Championship

Marino had thrown for over 5,000 yards and 48 touchdowns. With two superb wide receivers, Mark Clayton and Mark Duper, Marino was a scoring machine. The Dophins' high octane offense also included Tony Nathan, a nifty running back adept at catching passes, and fullback Woody Bennett who was having a career season.

The game began in earnest when Marino hit Mark Clayton for a 40-yard touchdown pass. The Steelers bounced back when Rich Erenberg rushed for a touchdown from 7 yards out. Berlin born Uwe Detief Walter von Schamann kicked a field goal in the second quarter for the Dolphins. John Stallworth, the NFL Comeback Player of the Year, caught a 65-yard touchdown bomb from Mark Malone. A 41-yard strike from Marino to Duper was followed by a Tony Nathan run from 2 yards out to end the half with Miami on top, 24–14.

Marino tossed a 36-yard pass to Duper for the first touchdown of the second half. Malone hit Stallworth for a 19-yard touchdown pass that kept the Steelers within reach at 31–21. When Woody Bennett cracked the plane of the end zone on a 1-yard run, it started to look grim for the Steelers. In the fourth quarter, Marino tossed a 6-yard scoring pass to hit Nat Moore and it was essentially over at 45–21. The Steelers came back for one more score, a 21-yard pass play from Malone to wide receiver Wayne Capers. When the game ended, the final score was Dolphins 45–Steelers 28.

For Noll, the AFC Championship game for the 1984 season, would be the closest he would come to another championship season. Two weeks later, Marino's Dolphins would get slaughtered, 38–16, by another Pittsburgh area quarterback and his team: Joe Montana and the San Francisco 49ers. Marino would hover around the top of the NFL quarterback ranks for the next two decades.

1985-1990 Seasons

In 1985, the Steelers scored 379 and allowed 355 points from the opposition. Mark Malone had established himself as the top quarterback of the Steelers, but he was injured halfway through the season. David Woodley came off the bench in relief, but the Steelers were up and down. Going into the last game of the season with a chance at .500, they lost convincingly to the Giants, 28–10, and ended the season 7–9.

In the third round of the 1986 draft, the Steelers picked up another quarterback, Bubby Brister, who would be the Steelers' top quarterback for three seasons starting in 1988. Noll kept the team grounded, but the challenges continued to mount with little relief. The Steelers scored 307 and allowed 336 in the regular 1986 season. After winning just two games and losing six in the first half of the season, the Steelers struggled to finish 4–4 in the second half. Their 6–10 season record gave them a finish well outside the playoffs.

In 1987, the players went on strike after the second game of the season, but the season resumed with replacement players for three games. For the 15-game season, the Steelers scored 285 and allowed 299 points. They posted an 8–7 record. In the first half of the season with the strike distractions, the Steelers won five games and lost three. In the second half, they won three and lost four. They finished 3rd in the AFC Central Division and did not make the playoffs. It was Malone's last year on the Steelers. Noll summed up the season this way:

We have lots of needs and we will address them if we can.[29]

Pittsburgh struck pay dirt with their first selection in the 1987 draft, cornerback and kick/punt returner Rod Woodson. Woodson was an All-American track star at Purdue University. He played 10 seasons for the Steelers and is numbered with so many other Steelers of the Noll era in the Hall of Fame.

The 1988 Steelers' 5–11 season was the worst one a Noll team had seen since 1970 when he was building the team of the decade. The Steelers scored 336 points and allowed 421 points from the opposition. Pittsburgh drafted Dermontti Dawson who would play mostly center for 13 seasons and earn Hall of Fame recognition. The Steelers finished 4th in the AFC

Central Division. The AFC Champions were the Bengals who slaughtered the Steelers 42–7 in midseason.

After the 1988 season, the Steelers front office fired four assistant coaches. Preferring to move on himself, Defensive Coordinator Tony Dungy resigned and took a job as defensive backfield coach with Marty Schottenheimer and the Kansas City Chiefs. To show their commitment to Noll, the Steelers extended a lifetime contract to him.

The Steelers scored 265 and allowed 326 in 1989. Rod Rust was Noll's defensive coordinator for the season and John Fox was the defensive backs coach. In the second round of the draft, the Steelers picked up Carnell Lake who would play for 10 productive seasons in Pittsburgh mostly at strong safety. The Steelers' defense was middle of the road and the offense was one of the worst in the NFL, but they finished 2nd in the AFC Central Division. Their 9–7 season gave them a Wild Card slot.

The Steelers played the Houston Oilers in a Wild Card game on December 31, 1989, in the Houston Astrodome. The game featured seven field goals including a 50-yard game winner in overtime by the Steelers' Gary Anderson. The Steelers won 26–23.

In the divisional playoff, the Steelers lost a close game to the Denver Broncos and John Elway. Late in the game, Anderson kicked a 32-yard field goal to put Pittsburgh ahead, 23–17, but the Steelers could not hold the lead and the Broncos came from behind to win 24–23.

In 1990, the Steelers scored 292 and allowed 240. Dave Brazil was Noll's defensive coordinator. Joe Walton was the offensive coordinator in 1990 and 1991. In the draft, the Steelers picked up quarterback Neil O'Donnell who would spend five seasons in Pittsburgh. The 9–7 Pittsburgh Steelers finished in a three-way tie for first in the AFC Central, but they were eliminated from the playoffs by their 2–4 division record.

Bubby Brister had his best year as the Steelers' quarterback that season. He completed 223 passes on 387 attempts for a completion rate of 57.6%. He passed for 20 touchdowns and threw 14 interceptions. His quarterback rating was 81.6. It was a predictable season for Pittsburgh. After losing the season opener to the Browns, the Steelers beat the teams with losing records and lost to those with winning records. On December 9, 1990, the Pittsburgh Steelers beat the New England Patriots 24–3 at Three Rivers Stadium for Chuck Noll's 200th win as a head coach. The New York Giants won the Super Bowl that season with an awesome defense and the careful quarterbacking of Jeff Hostetler.

1991 Season

The 1991 season would be Noll's last as head coach of the Steelers. The Steelers scored 292 and allowed 344 in the regular season. Quarterbacks Neil O'Donnell and Bubby Brister would each start eight games.

Coach Chuck Noll

The season would teeter-totter up and down with the exception of a terrible four game losing streak that knocked the Steelers from any post season hopes. In Noll's last game, his Steelers beat Bill Belichick's Browns, 17-10, in Three Rivers Stadium. The Steelers finished 7–9, good for 2nd in the AFC Central. On December 26, 1991, Chuck Noll announced his retirement in a joint news conference with Steelers' President Dan Rooney. In typical Noll fashion, he said he came to his decision that morning "not easily."[30] Immediately following, the greatest coach in Steelers' history jumped into his car and drove off.

Life after Football

Noll had many hobbies and when he was away from football, he was away from football. He enjoyed fine wine, roses, flying, and sailing. He enjoyed classical music and Jazz. And he was devoted to his family. After all, without interests outside of football, how can you have a good family life? Noll believed that family life was very important and he "was a great family man."[31] In retirement, Noll has lived a quiet life, doing what he enjoyed outside the game.

Noll's Contributions to the Game

Noll's Steelers won four Super Bowls in 6 years. His Steelers beat the Minnesota Vikings 16–6 in Super Bowl IX; the Dallas Cowboys 21–17 in Super Bowl X; the Cowboys 35–31 in Super Bowl XIII; and the Los Angeles Rams 31–19 in Super Bowl XIV.

Noll played under the legendary coach Paul Brown. He coached under Sid Gillman and Don Shula. NFL Head Coaches Bud Carson, Tony Dungy, John Fox, Rod Rust, and Joe Walton all worked for Noll.

Noll was the right man for Pittsburgh. The Steel City was very tough on the Steelers during his early years. Fans and the media had high expectations for top draft choice Terry Bradshaw and when he did not deliver immediately, they booed him mercilessly. When the Steelers drafted Joe Greene, one headline read "Joe Who." They did not like some of Noll's other early acquisitions either. Noll, on the other hand, was supremely confident, but guarded. If the Steelers' fans and media were tough, well, so was the coach.

Noll was pro football's 1970s answer to the winning traditions of Paul Brown and Vince Lombardi. He was organized and focused on teaching like Brown. He wanted his players to be just as disciplined as Brown's men of the late 1940s and 1950s. Noll pushed his Steelers to be fierce like Lombardi's Packers, but he wanted those qualities to be lasting and come from within. Noll was his own man in many ways. He avoided the limelight. He wanted the stories, the interesting interviews, the spectacles, and the celebrations to focus on his players. Noll is the rare man who has a rock-solid ego, but has no desire to call attention to himself. When people try to analyze his public persona, he has said:

> *I've never been good copy at any stage in my life. It's just not my nature. I've always avoided publicity. I've never strived for it because I don't think it's important whether I am good copy or not. The two can go together, if that's your personality. But every person is unique. I've never patterned myself after anybody. You have to be what you are. This is what I am.*[32]

Noll never bought into the philosophy that the public needs to know everything about everyone. Football was his life's pursuit, but he never warmed up to giving his thoughts and ideas on the game outside of coaching. Outside the game, he has been described as a very caring individual, but he never mixed that person with the tough demanding coaching persona.

Noll brought the Pittsburgh Steelers their first championship in over 40 years. Noll's Steelers won nine AFC Central Division Championships. His teams won four Super Bowls in 6 years. His career record stands at 209–156–1. Noll received the inaugural Earle "Greasy" Neale Award for Professional Coach of the Year in 1989 from the Maxwell Football Club. He was named the UPI Coach of the Year Award in 1972. He and 11 of his players are in the Hall of Fame.

Like many other legendary NFL coaches, Noll educated his players on football. "I'm a teacher," he said. "Players win, coaches teach them. I teach."[33] Noll believed in building a team through the draft. And once he had the right people, he challenged other teams to beat his best—his key performers.

Pat Livingston, sports editor and pro football reporter for The Pittsburgh Press during the Noll years, wrote that there are three qualities that marked Noll as a successful coach: "his perception, pedagogy, and patience."[34] The Steelers were the best drafting team in the NFL during Noll's early years. Some of the most talented players came from small programs and needed instruction. They got it with Noll and his staff. Noll also had patience enough to see his talent develop. Before Noll, the Steelers ran off rookies before they could develop.[35] Noll also worked for patient owners: The Rooney family.

But Noll's players and colleagues knew him as more than a team-builder. When asked about Chuck Noll's legacy, Pittsburgh Head Coach Mike Tomlin replied:

> *I think it's the men that he instructed… The men that he nurtured and raised, if you will…he was influential in those people's lives when they were young people and probably in a lot of ways helped mold them into the people that they are…what it is they do and have done inside our game and out.*[36]

A forward focus on football was one thing that led to Noll's success. He did not take on endorsements with the exception of a bank commercial for a friend. He did not have a TV show. He did not even like to dwell on team history. Steelers' equipment manger, Tony Paris put it this way:

I've been around him for 20 years and I have never heard him talk about the past. It's always today and tomorrow.[37]

Noll was also consistent. He had the same message to his players in 1990 that he had in 1970. He told his players to "be a tomorrow person."[38] He was always well prepared, but like Paul Brown, he did not spend outrageous hours at the office. This helped him avoid burnout in all the years he coached.

In the summer of 1989, the Steelers got a glimpse of their coach that many had not seen before. Chuck Noll conducted the Pittsburgh Symphony Orchestra performing John Phillip Sousa's "Stars and Stripes Forever" at the Steelers' training camp at St. Vincent College in Latrobe, Pennsylvania, on August 9, 1989, in honor of Art Rooney who had died the previous year. For Steelers' fans, it was a fitting tribute to the team founder and who better to conduct than the man who led the storied franchise to its greatest success.

Chuck Noll Timeline

1932

- January 5, 1932, Charles Henry Noll is born in Cleveland.

1945-1949

- Noll attends Benedictine High School, plays lineman on the football team, and graduates in the Class of 1949.

1949-1953

- Noll attends the University of Dayton as a member of the Class of 1953. He serves as co-captain and plays linebacker and guard on the football team.

1953-1959

- After graduating from Dayton, Noll plays for Paul Brown's Cleveland Browns. He plays linebacker and offensive lineman on teams that win two NFL Championships.

1960-1965

- Noll works for Sid Gillman as a defensive coach for the Los Angeles/San Diego Chargers. The Chargers top their division five times and win the AFL championship twice while Noll is there.

1966-1968

- Noll serves as defensive coach for Don Shula's Baltimore Colts. In 1968, the Colts win the NFL Championship and go on to the Super Bowl where they are defeated by the New York Jets.

1969-1991

- January 27, 1969, Noll is named head coach of the Pittsburgh Steelers and remains in the position until 1991.

1972

- December 23, 1972, Steelers defeat the Raiders, 13–7, in the divisional playoff game.
- December 31, 1972, the Dolphins defeat Steelers, 21–17, to win the AFC Championship. Noll awarded UPI coach of the year

1974

- December 29, 1974, Pittsburgh Steelers defeat the Oakland Raiders, 24–13, in the AFC Championship game.

1975

- January 12, 1975, Noll's 1974 Pittsburgh Steelers defeat the Minnesota Vikings, 16–6, in Super Bowl IX. It is Noll's first NFL Championship as a head coach.

1976

- January 4, 1976, the 1975 Pittsburgh Steelers beat the Raiders, 16–10, in the AFC Championship game.
- January 18, 1976, the 1975 Pittsburgh Steelers beat the Dallas Cowboys, 21–17, in Super Bowl X. It is Noll's second NFL Championship as a head coach.
- December 26, 1976, the Oakland Raiders defeat Noll's 1976 Steelers, 24-7, in the AFC Championship game.

1979

- January 7, 1979, the 1978 Pittsburgh Steelers defeat the Houston Oilers, 34–5, in the AFC Championship game.
- January 21, 1979, the 1978 Pittsburgh Steelers beat the Dallas Cowboys, 35–31, in Super Bowl XIII. It is Noll's third NFL Championship as head coach.

1980

- January 6, 1980, the 1979 Pittsburgh Steelers beat the Houston Oilers, 27–13, in the AFC Championship game.
- January 20, 1980, the 1979 Pittsburgh Steelers defeat the Los Angeles Rams, 31–19, in Super Bowl XIV. It is Noll's fourth NFL Championship as head coach.

1989

- Noll is named AFC Coach of the Year by the Professional Football Writers of America.

1991

- December 26, 1991, Chuck Noll announces his retirement from coaching.

1993

- Noll is inducted into the Pro Football Hall of Fame, Class of 1993.

Highlights

Chuck Noll's Steelers won four Super Bowls in 6 years and nine AFC Central Division Championships. Over his 23 seasons as head coach of the Steelers, Noll holds an overall NFL head coaching record of 209–156–1. Noll received the inaugural Earle "Greasy" Neale Award for Professional Coach of the Year from the Maxwell Football Club. He was named the UPI Coach of the Year Award in 1972. He was inducted in the Pro Football Hall of Fame in 1993.

Noll was pro football's 1970s answer to the winning traditions of Paul Brown and Vince Lombardi. He was organized and focused on teaching like Brown. He wanted his players to be just as disciplined as Brown's men of the late 1940s and 1950s. Noll pushed his Steelers to be fierce like Lombardi's Packers, but he wanted those qualities to be lasting and come from within.

Endnotes

[1]   America's Game, The Super Bowl Champions Series, "Super Bowl X: The Story of the 1975 Pittsburgh Steelers," NFL Films.

[2]   http://familytreemaker.genealogy.com/users/n/o/l/Dave-Noll-OH/WEBSITE-0001/UHP-0019.html

[3]   Paul Zimmerman, "Man Not Myth," *Sports Illustrated*, January 7, 1975, viewed at http://sportsillustrated.cnn.com/vault/article/magazine/MAG1123620/1/index.htm on February 15, 2013.

[4]   Myron Cope, *Double Yoi!*, (Champaign, IL, Sports Publishing LLC, 2002) 70.

[5]   Jody Valade, "The Invisible Legend, A Near Recluse in Retirement, Chuck Noll Brought Steelers Brown's Rivalry to Life, " *Cleveland Plain Dealer*, December 28, 2008, viewed at http://www.cleveland.com/browns/index.ssf/2008/12/the_invisible_legend_a_nearrec.html on February 18, 2013.

[6]   Jody Valade, "The Superman of Steel," *Cleveland Plain Dealer*, December 28, 2008, viewed at http://www.cleveland.com/browns/index.ssf/2008/12/the_invisible_legend_a_nearrec.html on February 18, 2013.

[7]   Bill Livingston and Greg Brinda, *The Great Book of Cleveland Sports* (Philadelphia, Running Press, 2008) 26.

[8]   "Globetrotters Here March 12," *Ohio Jewish Chronicle*, Friday March 6, 1959, viewed at http://www.ohiomemory.org/cdm/compoundobject/collection/ojc/id/17923/rec/2 on February 21, 2013.

[9]   Josh Katzowitz, *Sid Gillman Father of the Passing Game* (Covington, KY, Clerisy Press, 2012) xiv.

[10] Ken Blanchard and Don Shula, *The Little Book of Coaching: Motivating People to Be Winners* (NY, HarperBusiness, 2001) 17.

[11] Rooney with McHugh, *Ruanaidh: The Story of Art Rooney and His Clan*, 244.

[12] ESPN Greatest Coaches Series viewed at http://espn.go.com/nfl/story/_/page/greatestcoach5/greatest-coaches-nfl-history-chuck-noll on June 11, 2013.

[13] Chuck Noll. BrainyQuote.com, Xplore Inc, 2013. http://www.brainyquote.com/quotes/authors/c/chuck_noll.html, accessed March 12, 2013.

[14] Don Smith, "Mel Blount," *Coffin Corner*, Vol. 11, No.2, 1989, viewed at http://www.profootballresearchers.org/Coffin_Corner/11-02-366.pdf on March 11, 2013.

[15] Larry Fox,"Terry Bradshaw, Steel Driv'in Man," *Boys Life*, November 1979, 10.

[16] Paul Zimmerman, "The Best Athletes on the Field," *Sports Illustrated*, September 4, 1985 viewed at http://sportsillustrated.cnn.com/vault/article/magazine/MAG1119853/7/index.htm on March 5, 2013.

[17] The Immaculate Reception is a word play on the Christian doctrine called the Immaculate Conception. The Immaculate Conception states that Mary (the mother of Jesus) was conceived without original sin or its stain.

[18] Don Smith, "Terry Bradshaw," *The Coffin Corner*, Volume 11, No. 2, 1989. Viewed at http://www.profootballresearchers.org/coffin_corner/11-02-367.pdf on February 27, 2013.

[19] ESPN Greatest Coaches Series viewed at http://espn.go.com/nfl/story/_/page/greatestcoach5/greatest-coaches-nfl-history-chuck-noll on June 11, 2013.

[20] America's Game, The Super Bowl Champions Series, "Super Bowl X: The Story of the 1975 Pittsburgh Steelers," NFL Films.

[21] "Seventh Greatest Play at Three Rivers Stadium," Steelers.com, Official web site of the Pittsburgh Steelers, viewed at http://www.steelers.com/history/three-rivers/7th-great-game-and-play.html on June 12, 2013.

[22] Bob McGinn, *The Ultimate Super Bowl Book* (Minneapolis: MPI Books, 2012) 80.

23 Rooney with Masich and Halaas, *Dan Rooney: My 75 Years with the Pittsburgh Steelers and the NFL*, 200.

24 "Tony Dungy's Championship Life", *Success Magazine*, viewed at http://www.success.com/articles/1370-tony-dungy-s-championship-life on June 19, 2013.

25 Sam Toperoff, "Open Season in Pittsburgh," *Sports Illustrated*, September 9, 1987, viewed at http://sportsillustrated.cnn.com/vault/article/magazine/MAG1066431/index.htm on March 5, 2013.

26 Robert Dvorchak, "In the 80s the Steelers Greats Fade Away," *Pittsburgh Post Gazette*, Oct. 14, 2007, viewed at http://www.post-gazette.com/stories/sports/steelers/in-the-80s-the-steelers-greats-fade-away-505980/#ixzz2NF0VjOit, on March 11, 2013.

27 Rooney with Masich and Halaas, *Dan Rooney: My 75 Years with the Pittsburgh Steelers and the NFL*, 215.

28 The Raiders were the Los Angeles Raiders from 1982-1994.

29 Tom Rose, "Steelers Season Ends with Frustrating Loss Against Browns," *Observer Reporter*, December 27, 1987.

30 AP, "Steelers' Noll Calls It Quits—Coach Resigns After 23 Years," Seattle Times, December 26, 1991 viewed at http://community.seattletimes.nwsource.com/archive/?date=19911226&slug=1325033 on July 29, 2013.

31 "Tony Dungy's Championship Life," *Success Magazine*, viewed at http://www.success.com/articles/1370-tony-dungy-s-championship-life on June 19, 2013.

32 "Chuck Noll, the Teacher Who Is Nobody's Pet," *Miami News*, October 12, 1985. Viewed at http://news.google.com/newspapers?id=IqEmAAAAIBAJ&sjid=wAEGAAAAIBAJ&pg=2616,3721393&dq=chuck+noll&hl=en on February 18, 2013.

33 Paul Zimmerman, "Man Not Myth," *Sports Illustrated*, January 7, 1975, viewed at http://sportsillustrated.cnn.com/vault/article/magazine/MAG1123620/1/index.htm on February 18, 2013.

34 Pat Livingston, "The Coaches: Steelers' Noll or Pitt's Majors,Whose Shoes Would You Like to Be In Coach Noll." *Pittsburgh Press*, September 16, 1973, viewed at http://news.google.com/newspapers?id=jakbAAAAIBAJ&sjid=hVQEAAAAIBAJ&pg=5675,1252722&dq=chuck+noll&hl=en on February 18, 2013.

35 Paul Zimmerman, "Teacher, Scientist, Innovator, Coach: For Chuck Noll Winning Was Simply a Bi-Product of His Team Learning How to Play," *Sports Illustrated* August 23, 2007, viewed at http://sportsillustrated.cnn.com/vault/article/magazine/MAG1115639/index.htm on February 18, 2013.

36 Greatest Coaches in NFL History, ESPN Series article, Greg Garber, "Great Futures Ahead of Them," viewed at http://espn.go.com/nfl/story/_/page/greatestcoachfuture130611/nfl-greatest-coaches-coaches-make-future-list on June 19, 2013.

37 Ron Cook, "Noll's Longevity Secret: Separate Lives," *Pittsburgh Press*, August 28, 1988 viewed at http://news.google.com/newspapers?id=KKkcAAAAIBAJ&sjid=e2MEAAAAIBAJ&pg=5598,7798122&dq=chuck+noll&hl=en on February 18, 2013.

38 America's Game, The Super Bowl Champions Series, "Super Bowl X: The Story of the 1975 Pittsburgh Steelers," NFL Films.

Bill Walsh

For Super Bowl spectators a kind of temporary numbness comes from the sensory overload before the game begins. The place is awash in the continuous motion of coaches, referees, photographers, television camera operators, dignitaries, cheerleaders, and hundreds of others who swarm around the sideline. But the fog lifts at game time as the noise level begins to rise. Once the game begins, the crowd's emotions ebb and flow—the cheers, shouts, screams, and clapping are there one minute at unimaginable levels and then taper off and then return again. In the close games, the intensity is electric as the fourth quarter winds down...

It is January 22, 1989. The venue is Joe Robbie Stadium in Miami, Florida. Three minutes and ten seconds remain in Super Bowl XXIII. White-haired, professorial Bill Walsh stands on the sidelines and looks out onto the football field where the greatest contest of his coaching career is at its most critical point. Moments ago, the Cincinnati Bengals kicked a field goal to give them a 16–13 lead and put San Francisco fans into shock. As if that wasn't bad enough, the 49ers were called for a penalty on the kickoff that followed and they are starting at their own 8-yard line. But the crowd senses something exciting about to happen and the noise picks up.

A whistle is blown and the refs call a television time out. Quarterback Joe Montana comes to the sideline. It's a long three minutes. The noise level falls.

For Walsh, this game is not just the end of the season; it is the end of his head-coaching career with the 49ers. He has told owner Edward DeBartolo, Jr. that he's retiring as head coach and there is no going back. It will be Assistant Coach George Seifert's show after this.

Regardless of what Bill Walsh has accomplished before today, he aches for this win. For Walsh his second Super Bowl was more important than the first and this game is right off the charts for him.

It's been difficult to be head coach of the 49ers. A Super Bowl victory in his third year in San Francisco was followed by a horrific season. It prompted some critics to call the first 49ers' Super Bowl win a fluke. Such comments ate at Walsh. When the 49ers won the Super Bowl after the 1984 season, it silenced many of the critics, at least for a while. But quick exits from the playoffs that followed 1984 brought out the doubters again. However, the 49ers are back to the big dance and Walsh is still the orchestra leader. In recent days, Walsh wondered if a victory will be enough for his critics, but right now he doesn't care so much about them. He only cares about this game and this team. For Walsh personally, this game is about making the top rung of the

Hall of Fame, about having his name mentioned in the same group with the likes of Paul Brown and Vince Lombardi—of George Halas, Chuck Noll, and Curly Lambeau. For his team, he knows with a victory they will never be the same men. Each one of them will have achieved something that every boy who picks up a football comes to dream about and every football fan comes to respect as the ultimate accomplishment.

The time out ends and the TV cameras are back on and the crowd seems to speak in a single voice that swells to new heights. Montana is back in the huddle. Walsh's face hardens with the pressure of the moment. He looks more like a prize fighter than the dapper coach the TV cameras love to focus on. His offense is ready to settle into their role as world beaters one more time. The coach looks out at Montana. The whistle sounds and it is time for the 49ers to start play. The coach maintains his focus. "Keep them off balance—give them the unexpected," Walsh thinks to himself.

As Walsh looks on, Montana throws complete to Roger Craig over the middle to the 16-yard line…

Early Life

The Walshes were hardworking people and like most Americans of the time, they struggled through the Depression and the prewar years to make ends meet. Bill's father found employment at a Chrysler plant. A modest house in central Los Angeles located a few miles from the Coliseum served as the family home. William "Bill" Ernest Walsh was born on November 30, 1931. A sister, Maureen, was born a few years later. His father, William Archibald Walsh, was of Irish descent and his mother Ruth's ancestors were German, but both families had moved from a hard life in Colorado rather than across the ocean like earlier generations.

Once young Bill was old enough, he helped his father with automobile body and fender work that the elder Walsh took on for extra income.[1] His father was remembered like many other men of the era as a hard man who demanded perfection from his son very early on.

Bill was athletic and especially smitten with football at an early age although there were no organized sports for boys until high school. He attended a talent-laden Washington High School in Englewood as a skinny kid with aspirations to play quarterback.[2] Before he had the chance, the family moved to Oregon for a short time where his father opened up a body shop business. The family came back to California when the business failed, but the economy was improving in post World War II California. The family relocated to Hayward, an East Bay town in an area around San Francisco that was especially fertile and surrounded by beautiful farms. It was a time before California housing would spread from city to city creating an endless chain of population centers. Bill's father went to work at a nearby Chrysler plant and the family was able to settle in on firmer financial ground. Bill settled in as a senior at Hayward High School in 1949 and played halfback for the Fighting

Farmers. In addition to displaying some talent on the football field, he was known to be good with his fists.

Walsh enrolled at San Mateo Community College in 1950 and he was All Conference at quarterback his second year under coach Herb Hudson.[3] Walsh transferred to San Jose State College in 1952 where he played end on the 1952 and 1953 football teams coached by Bob Bronzan. He received some scholarship money, but would sometimes live out of his car or at friends when money ran out. He developed a close group of like-minded athletic friends that he would maintain the rest of his life.

Like many young men of his generation, Walsh's early life was marked by insecurity, struggle, and a perceived lack of affection and approval by his father. Under these influences, it's not surprising that Walsh would display great enthusiasm for his work one minute and then face gut-wrenching doubts about his own abilities the next. Millions of football fans remember the handsome distinguished coach on the sidelines, but few understand the anxieties that also defined him. Yet, he was a great advocate of advancing confidence in his own players and understood the importance of maintaining confidence in one's work.

San Jose State Football coach Bob Bronzan greatly influenced Walsh's life. Bronzan was a tough, disciplined coach who ardently developed his players' skills in a superbly organized program. At the same time, he taught an expanded understanding of the game, which was scientific and detailed. Bronzan's approach opened up possibilities for Walsh and others who were intrigued by strategies and planning. Many coaches at the time, and some today, define football as a contest of brute force. Coach Bronzan's expanded vision of the game was passed on to his players, many of whom went on to coach themselves.

The 6-foot-2, 205 pound Walsh also boxed at San Jose State. He was intramural heavyweight champion in 1952 at a time when boxing was extremely popular.

After graduation from San Jose State, Walsh served in the U.S. Army at Fort Ord on Monterey Bay for 2 years. In the service, he would box for extra income, but ultimately, he decided against pursuing a boxing career.

Learning Years

Walsh came back to San Jose State in 1956 and he began working towards a graduate degree. He worked for his old coach, Bob Bronzan, as an assistant.

High School Coaching

Walsh coached football and swimming at Washington High School in Fremont, California, from 1957 to 1959. At Washington High School, Walsh turned around the football program from doormat to contender. In addition to his coaching responsibilities, Walsh drove the school bus to take his players to games.[4]

Bill Walsh at San Jose State

Walsh finished his graduate studies and received his master's degree from San Jose State in 1959.[5] His thesis was entitled: *Flank Formation Football -- Stress: Defense.*

College Coaching

From Fremont Walsh moved on to an assistant-coaching job at the University of California, Berkeley in 1960. He worked for Coach Marv Levy. Levy would enjoy a long successful career with the Buffalo Bills and induction into the Pro Football Hall of Fame. Following his work at the University of California, Walsh served as an assistant coach under John Ralston at Stanford from 1963 to 1965.

Professional Football

Bill Walsh was a student of football. Through his long career assisting other professional coaches and his work at the college and high school levels, his knowledge of the game was professorial—his experiences broad and deep. He studied the game's history, its coaches, and players. He used stories of military generals and battles to make his points. He absorbed knowledge. He assimilated the work of others. Then he contributed his life's work to the evolution of the game. His magnum opus was the San Francisco 49ers of the 1980s.

Based on his cerebral approach to the game, Walsh was called "Genius." It was a mixed blessing. When his team did well, the media and the public would concur that Walsh certainly was a genius. But when the team did not live up to expectations, the term genius was voiced with cynicism and used mean spiritedly.

Walsh served as assistant coach for two seasons under John Rauch of the Oakland Raiders, eight seasons under Paul Brown with the Cincinnati Bengals, and one season for Tommy Prothro of the San Diego Chargers.

Oakland Raiders

In 1966, Walsh began his pro coaching career in Oakland working under John Rauch for Al Davis's Raiders. In Oakland, Walsh was exposed to the organization, strategies, and idiosyncrasies of Al Davis and the excellent coaching talents of John Rauch.

San Jose Apaches

After Walsh left the Raiders, he coached the San Jose Apaches in 1967. The Apaches were a minor league football team that played in the Continental League.

Cincinnati Bengals

In 1968, Bill Walsh was hired by Paul Brown as an assistant coach for the Cincinnati Bengals. While in Cincinnati, Paul Brown gave Bill Walsh a football master class on organization, development, direction, and discipline. Walsh developed many habits from Paul Brown. He held closely-timed practices, he used psychological testing of players, he practiced plays until perfected, and he focused on precision. During Walsh's long "apprenticeship," he amalgamated ideas from several passing game innovators. Walsh attacked defenses using a passing game that spread the field. But unlike many before him, Walsh spread the field horizontally and vertically. He created a ball control passing game. Contrary to most coaches, he set up the running game with passes rather than set up the passing game with runs. Walsh also quickened the pace of professional football strategy. For Walsh, winning was about constantly changing his game plans so the opposition was always chasing him, but never catching up.

Walsh's creativity was born out of necessity. After a remarkably talented Bengals' quarterback named Greg Cook was severely injured, Walsh worked with Virgil Carter who was not a prototype strong armed quarterback. Carter came from Brigham Young University, played 2 years in Chicago, and then came to Cincinnati. Carter was smart, quick on his feet, and accurate, but he was not a long-ball thrower. Walsh created a game plan to maximize strengths that Carter had. He attacked defenses at perceived weak points and he devised a plan of short passes, multiple receivers, and precise patterns. Walsh advocated strictly defined movements for receivers so they could maximize each catch with long gains afterward. It was not just important for the quarterback to throw accurately for the catch; the quarterback needed to lead the receiver so he could catch the ball in stride. There was little room for error and Walsh gave his quarterback many targets. His program relied more on art than sheer muscle. His offense could win ball games against more talented teams. His program would come to be called the West Coast Offense although most of it had been developed in Ohio.

But just as important as the concept of the West Coast Offense was Walsh's philosophy of attacking the other team, keeping them off balance, and constantly evolving plans and plays that could achieve these ends. Walsh changed his teams to stay ahead of competition.

Walsh helped develop the raw talents of Ken Anderson of the Cincinnati Bengals. Anderson came from a small school, Augustana College, whose football program was not dialed in to train professional quarterbacks in the same way larger school programs were set up. While a Bengals' assistant, Bill Walsh spent time developing Anderson's skills so he could perform well as a pro-quarterback.

San Diego Chargers

In 1976, Walsh became the offensive coordinator for Coach Tommy Prothro. Walsh helped develop another talented quarterback, Dan Fouts. Walsh worked to recast Fouts's mechanics after the young man had spent a few underachieving years in the league. According to Fouts:

> *He broke me down and then he built me back up.*[6]

Walsh was especially knowledgeable in quarterback fundamentals. He spent many hours promoting techniques and skills of the position in others that he himself had studied, but did not have a chance to use.

Stanford Head Coach

Walsh took his "West Coast" offense to Stanford in 1977-1978 where he believed his players were able to understand and develop its complexities quickly. After all, Clark Shaughnessy had taught his complex modified T Formation to the Cardinal players in 1940; they went on to an undefeated season and a Rose Bowl win. At Stanford, Walsh added college transfers and new recruits to build a competitive team. Walsh's players featured future NFL players: quarterbacks Steve Dils, Guy Benjamin, and Turk Schonert; wide receivers James Lofton and Ken Margerum; and running back Darrin Nelson. At Stanford, Walsh also hired his future 49ers' colleague and head coach, George Seifert.[7]

In 1977, Walsh's first year at Stanford as head coach, the team went 9–3, took second place in the Pac 10, and beat Louisiana State University in the Sun Bowl. In 1978, Walsh's team slipped to 8–4 for a fourth place finish in the Pac 10, but beat Georgia in the Bluebonnet Bowl.

San Francisco Head Coach

At the age of 47, Walsh became head coach and general manager of the San Francisco 49ers on January 9, 1979. The 49ers were 2–14 the previous season and they had several poor seasons prior to that. Walsh constantly developed his roster and built his team with draft choices. He was very selective and he was not afraid to trade several draft choices to put him in a position to get the one or two players he wanted.[8] Walsh also earned a reputation for making the most of his players' talent. His teams were disciplined and well trained—often thought to be overachievers.

Walsh's Players

Walsh wanted to construct an advanced football system that used a large playbook and precise movements and contingencies. He needed players who were physically skilled and had the intellect to carry out his plans. He acquired many remarkable players over his seasons in San Francisco.

Bill Romanowski

Linebacker Bill Romanowski was a San Francisco third round selection in 1988. Romanowski played the first six seasons of his 16-year career with the 49ers.

Bubba Paris

In 1982, Walsh drafted Bubba Paris. A monstrous 300 pound offensive tackle, Paris was a University of Michigan All-American who the 49ers drafted in the first round in 1982. Paris played 9 years in San Francisco.

Carlton Williamson

Carlton Williamson was an exceptional defensive player selected in the 1981 draft. He played strong safety for seven seasons for the 49ers.

Charles Haley

Charles Haley was the San Francisco 49ers' fourth round draft choice in 1986. The 6-foot-5, 252 pound defensive end and linebacker from James Madison was a versatile defensive force who played on 5 different Super Bowl teams.

Dwight Clark

Dwight Clark was drafted by the 49ers out of Clemson in the 10th round of the 1979 draft. He played wide receiver nine seasons for the 49ers.

Eric Wright

An excellent coverage man, Eric Wright was selected in the second round of the 1981 draft and played 10 seasons for the 49ers. Wright and Ronnie Lott are considered one of the best cornerback tandems of all time.

Fred Dean

Hall of Fame defensive end Fred Dean came over from San Diego to the 49ers in a trade in midseason 1981 right before a crucial game with the

Dallas Cowboys. Known as a tremendous pass rusher, Dean applied heat to opposing quarterbacks.

Fred Solomon

Fred Solomon was a wide receiver who came over from the Dolphins and played from 1978 through 1985 with the 49ers. He returned kicks during the first 2 years of Walsh's time in San Francisco. Solomon accumulated over 6,000 yards in receptions, rushing, and returns for the 49ers.

Guy McIntyre

Guy McIntyre was an offensive guard from the University of Georgia. He was drafted by the 49ers in the third round in 1984. The stout 6-foot-3, 275 pound guard would eventually be used by Walsh as a blocking back in special short yardage situations. He played 10 seasons in San Francisco.

Harris Barton

Harris Barton was a first round draft pick in 1987 and he played offensive tackle for most of 10 seasons for the 49ers.

Jack "Hacksaw" Reynolds

Intense and extremely studious, Jack Reynolds was a veteran linebacker who came over from the Rams in 1981. Excellent at stopping the run, Reynolds's superb work ethic made him an immediate leader and helped shape young 49ers by example.

Jerry Rice

The 49ers' first round draft pick in 1985, Jerry Rice is considered by many to be the NFL's best wide receiver. He played in San Francisco for 16 years of his incredibly productive 20 seasons.

Jesse Sapolu

Jesse Sapolu was a 6-foot-4, 270 pound rock who would play both center and guard for the 49ers for 13 seasons beginning in 1983. Sapolu hailed from Samoa and played for the University of Hawaii.

Jim Stuckey

Jim Stuckey was drafted in the first round of the 1980 draft by the 49ers. He played left defensive end in San Francisco from 1980-1986.

Joe Montana

When Walsh began building the 49ers, he wanted a mobile quarterback who could make good decisions and throw accurately. In the third round of the 1979 draft, Bill Walsh drafted Joe Montana. Montana was a superb quarterback for Notre Dame, but he was thin and he was inconsistent. Scouts ranked several quarterbacks ahead of Montana in the draft and Walsh was able to snag the Hall of Famer in the third round.

John Taylor

John Taylor played wide receiver and returned punts for the San Francisco 49ers from 1987-1995. He was acquired in the third round of the 1986 draft and played well on a team that featured many gifted receivers.

Keena Turner

A gifted linebacker from Purdue, Keena Turner was drafted by the Dolphins in 1980, but he was traded to the 49ers on draft day. Turner played for the 49ers from 1980-1990.

Kevin Fagan

Kevin Fagan was a strong defensive end who was drafted in the fourth round of the 1986 draft. He played for the 49ers from 1987 to 1994.

Michael Carter

Michael Carter was a 1984 Olympic Silver Medalist in the shotput. The 6-foot-2, 285 pound nose tackle from Southern Methodist University was a fifth round draft choice in 1984. He played for the 49ers from 1984-1992 and was considered one of the league's premier nose tackles.

Pete Kugler

Defensive lineman Pete Kugler was a 1981 draft choice for the 49ers. He played for eight seasons in San Francisco.

Randy Cross

Randy Cross was an offensive lineman who had joined the 49ers in 1976. Walsh moved him from center to guard. Cross was an excellent athlete who had set shot put records in high school.

Riki Ellison

In 1982, Riki Ellison was drafted out of USC in the fifth round by San Francisco. He was a New Zealander and a Maori who played linebacker for the 49ers for six seasons.

Roger Craig

University of Nebraska standout Roger Craig was selected in the second round by the 49ers in the 1983 draft. He played mostly fullback in his 8 years in San Francisco.

Ronnie Lott

Hall of Fame defensive back Ronnie Lott was the 49ers' first round selection in the 1981 draft. He made an impact immediately. He was a superb passionate athlete who was one of the hardest-hitting defenders to play professional football. He started out as the 49ers' left cornerback, but he also played safety in his career.

Russ Francis

Russ Francis was drafted by the New England Patriots in the first round in 1975 and played for the Patriots through the 1980 season. The gifted receiver and great blocker was picked up by Walsh prior to the 1982 season after being out of football for a season.

Steve Wallace

Offensive tackle Steve Wallace was drafted in the fourth round of the 1986 draft by San Francisco. He did much to protect Joe Montana.

Steve Young

Steve Young played for Walsh in 1987-1988 and then continued with the 49ers until 1999. Although he played a backup role to Joe Montana during Walsh's time, his contribution to Walsh's 49ers was significant and helped the team make the playoffs. He is the only left-handed quarterback in the Pro Football Hall of Fame.

Tom Rathman

Tom Rathman was a tough fullback from Nebraska whom Walsh picked up in the 1986 draft. He was a powerful blocker, runner, and receiver who was known for his unselfish play. John Madden described Rathman as "everything that's basic about football."

1979 Season

In Walsh's first season as head coach, the 49ers maintained their basement position after another 2–14 finish. Record aside, few people who saw the 1979 49ers believed they were watching the team that played in San Francisco the previous season. Walsh's 1979 49ers were exciting, creative, and entertaining—win or lose. Walsh's system was the evolution of passing game enthusiasts who had come before him. In 1979, the 49ers scored 308 points and allowed 416, giving them a point differential of -108. They managed to beat the Tampa Bay Buccaneers and the Atlanta Falcons. Walsh was happy to see the season come to an end.

1980 Season

When Walsh's 49ers improved to 6–10 in 1980, "dynasty" was not likely a word that fans thought they would be using for the team any time soon. For the season, their opponents scored 95 points more against them than the 49ers put out themselves. The 49ers looked great right out of the gate with three wins in a row including a tight overtime win against the Cardinals. But any tide of euphoria in the City by the Bay soon ebbed. In what would be remembered by Walsh as one of the lowest points in his career, the 49ers lost the next eight games in a row—including drubbings such as a 59–14 loss to the Cowboys and a 48–26 loss to the Rams. The final loss in the eight game string came in Miami against the Dolphins that Walsh took particularly hard. On the plane flight home, Walsh remembered:

I broke down emotionally. I conceded I could not get the job done—14 losses the first year, 8 straight the next year.[9]

The 49ers recovered along with Walsh's confidence and they won the next three games. They beat the Giants and Patriots before clawing their way to their second overtime win of the season – this one a 38–35 victory against the Saints. In the game against the Saints, the 49ers dug themselves into a 35–7 hole at half. Walsh calmly challenged his team during the intermission to fight back rather than roll over.[10] Amazingly, the 49ers came back to win the game in overtime, 38–35. Montana was outstanding in the second half and gave San Francisco fans a glimpse into the future. The season ended with two final losses that demonstrated the vulnerability of Walsh's young football team. Yet, the overall 6–10 record was promising.

1981 Season

Walsh had made obvious improvements, but the eight game losing streak in 1980 suggested that something around a .500 finish with more consistency might be within reach in 1981. But the 49ers would do much better.

Quarterback Steve DeBerg had moved on to Denver leaving Joe Montana as the clear starter. DeBerg was a good quarterback; Montana was better. Montana had fewer interceptions and a better completion percentage. The come-from-behind heroics and intangibles in Montana's game had only partially surfaced in 1980 when the 49ers won two and lost five with "Joe Cool" starting under center.

The 49ers' defense went from doormat to door buster in one season. Three gifted rookies started in the much improved defensive backfield: Ronnie Lott, Eric Wright, and Carlton Williamson. New acquisitions, Jack "Hacksaw" Reynolds at linebacker along with pass rush specialist and former member of the Chargers' "Bruise Brothers," Fred Dean, pumped up the defense as well. Dwight Hicks and Keena Turner were making a greater contribution.

The 49ers lost two of their first three games in 1981 and then started a 7-game winning streak. After beating the Saints 21–14 in the first game of the streak, they took on the Redskins at Robert F. Kennedy Stadium. Montana led long time-consuming drives that kept the ball out of the Redskins' hands. The defense scored when Ronnie Lott induced a fumble that popped into the hands of Dwight Hicks who ran it in for a touchdown. Later, Hicks snagged an interception that he ran in for his second touchdown of the day. When the game ended, the 49ers had a feel-good confidence-building 30–17 victory with plenty of TV highlights.

Next up for the 49ers was a very good Dallas Cowboys' team. The 49ers bushwhacked "America's Team" 45–14. Montana and his offense ran all over the Cowboys, while newly acquired Fred Dean and the defense harassed Danny White. White passed for only 60 yards and the Cowboys' great running back Tony Dorsett had a mere 21 yards on 9 rushes. As the San Francisco winning streak extended, each new victory improved the 49ers' confidence and their fans view of the Walsh-led team.

After losing to the Browns 15–12 in week 11, the 49ers won their last five games. For the season, the 49ers outscored their opponents by 107 points. They entered the playoffs as one of the top teams—albeit in Cinderella fashion. Were the 49ers contenders or was the fairy tale soon to end?

In the divisional playoff game, the 49ers faced the New York Giants. The Giants had Hall of Famers, along with others whose full potential would not be felt around the league until the mid 1980s. They also had a remarkable coaching staff. The Giants were led by Ray Perkins who had young assistants—Bill Parcells, Bill Belichick, and Romeo Crennel. It was the first time in 18 years that the Giants qualified for the playoffs, but they got there with a pedestrian 9–7 record.

Montana hit Charle Young on a touchdown pass in the first quarter. Giants' quarterback Scott Brunner responded with a pass to Ernest Gray for 72 yards and a score. But the 49ers pulled away in the second quarter. A Wersching field goal was followed by a Montana to Solomon 58-yard touchdown pass. Ricky Patton rushed in for another 49ers' touchdown. The Giants scored on a 48-yard field goal by kicker Joe Danelo. At the half, the 49ers led, 24–10.

In the third quarter, Brunner hit Johnny Perkins from 59 yards out to tighten the game up at 24–17. The game moved into the fourth quarter, before the 49ers responded with two more scores. Bill Ring rushed in from 3 yards out and Ronnie Lott made a 20-yard interception return to put the game out of reach. The Giants scored once more on a Brunner to Perkins 17-yard touchdown pass. The 49ers prevailed 38–24 in San Francisco's Candlestick Park. The win set up another match with the Dallas Cowboys whom the 49ers had humiliated earlier in the season.

NFC Championship Game

The 49ers and Cowboys fought head to head in a close game. At times, the 49ers looked out of sync committing six turnovers, including three interceptions by Montana. The 49ers had the ball late in the game, chasing the Cowboys' 27–21 lead. With time for one last drive, the Cowboys played the pass and Walsh called for the unexpected. The 49ers ran the ball using Lenvil Elliot who had not seen much action that year. Elliot was successful enough bringing the ball downfield to force the defense to respect the rush. Play after play under extreme pressure Montana handed the ball off or tossed a short nerve-wracking pass often in heavy traffic. On third and three from the 6-yard line, Montana danced around in the backfield looking for an open man. The seconds ticked off. Montana escaped to his right from a vigorous rush from his blindside. The Cowboys were closing directly in front of Montana as he tossed an off balance floater toward the back of the end zone to Dwight Clark. As defenders flew behind Clark, the 49ers' receiver leaped high to make a fingertip grab for the touchdown. The crowd at Candlestick Park exploded in cheers. Wersching kicked the extra point for the 28–27 win.

Clark's touchdown grab would come to be called "the catch." The NFC Championship game win signaled a reversal of fortune for the 49ers and the Cowboys. The 49ers were suddenly heading into the top strata of professional football just as the Cowboys were stepping off the championship podium for a long drought.

Super Bowl XVI

Super Bowl XVI was the first Super Bowl for both the 49ers and their opponents, the Cincinnati Bengals. It was an excellent game that featured some of football's greatest competitors. Although the game took place at the first cold-weather venue in Super Bowl history, the Pontiac Silverdome, it was played in comfort indoors.

Walsh famously borrowed a bellman's uniform and upon the teams' arrival at their hotel, he stood out at the curb handling the players' bags. After a tug-of-war over Montana's bag, the players finally recognized their coach. It was Walsh's way to help the players loosen up for the big game.

One marquee matchup was young quarterback Joe Montana facing off against veteran quarterback Ken Anderson who was the league's MVP and comeback player of the year. Walsh's coaching counterpart was Forrest Gregg, who had a storied career playing for the Green Bay Packers under Vince Lombardi. Gregg was an intense coach, who like Walsh, had managed great gains in a short time. The 1981 season was only Gregg's second season with the Bengals.

Both teams played nervously at the start. On the opening kickoff, the 49ers' Amos Lawrence fumbled the ball over to the Bengals deep in San Francisco territory. After Ken Anderson drove the Bengals down to the 5-yard line, he suffered a sack that took the ball back to the 11. Anderson threw an interception to 49ers' safety Dwight Hicks who seemed to be in exactly the right spot to spoil the play while the intended receiver Isaac Curtis looked to be out of position. Years later, Hicks would tell Anderson that he dropped off the man he was supposed to be covering in the slot and went towards Isaac Curtis on a hunch.[11] Anderson would simply describe it as his mistake.

Montana took over for San Francisco and threw three short passes that brought the ball to midfield. The 49ers ran a flea flicker that fooled no one. Montana got the ball back after a couple of handoffs and tossed the ball up field for 11 yards to tight end Charle Young who pulled it down in the midst of three defenders. A couple of running plays were called with the second one reminiscent of something from an old football playbook. The left tackle was pulled to the right of center creating an unbalanced line for a running play that gained seven more critical yards. A pass to Fred Solomon brought the ball down to the 1-yard line where Montana ran in for the score. The 49ers had the important first lead, 7-0.

In the second quarter, Anderson hit rookie receiver Cris Collinsworth at the San Francisco 8-yard line, but Eric Wright stripped the ball to stop the Cincinnati drive. Montana followed with a drive that featured a series of runs to soften up the Bengals' pass coverage. He also passed to receivers Clark and Solomon. The final pass of the drive was to running back Earl Cooper for the touchdown. San Francisco led 14-0. On Cincinnati's next series they failed to move the ball and punted back to the 49ers. Again Montana moved the ball steadily downfield with several passes averaging about 10 yards and a number of modest runs to keep the Bengals' defense honest. The drive stalled at the Bengals' 5-yard line and Ray Wersching kicked a field goal to put the 49ers ahead, 17-0. On the ensuing kickoff, Wersching's squib kick was mishandled by the Bengals for another turnover. The 49ers made it count when Wersching kicked another field goal. Three turnovers had the Bengals chasing the 49ers 20–0 at the half.

Anderson came back on the Bengals' first possession with a successful series of short passes. The veteran quarterback ran the ball in himself from the 5-yard line for Cincinnati's first score. The Bengals' defense completely shut down the 49ers in the third quarter. Picking up steam again in large part on a 49-yard bomb to Collinsworth, the Bengals drove to the 3-yard line. With four plays to score, the Bengals seemed on the verge of comeback. Anderson gave the ball to big 255 pound fullback Pete Johnson for a 2-yard gain on first down. Johnson was stuffed for no gain on second. Anderson hit Charles Alexander with a pass on third, but he was tackled on the line of scrimmage. Pete Johnson got the carry on fourth down, but he came up short by a few inches. The man doing much of the "stuffing" was veteran linebacker Hacksaw Reynolds whom Walsh had picked up prior to the season.

The Bengals did not give up. Once again the 49ers' offense was held in check and the Bengals took over about midfield a few minutes into the fourth quarter. Anderson drove down the field with a 12-yard pass to Collinsworth and two short passes to tight end Chris Ross. A 4-yard toss to Ross gave Cincinnati another touchdown. The lead was now, 20–14.

The 49ers responded to the Bengals' score with a drive that brought the ball down to the Cincinnati 23-yard line where Wersching kicked a 40-yard field goal. Eric Wright intercepted an Anderson pass on the next series and Wersching kicked his fourth field goal of the day. In six plays, Anderson drove the Bengals 74 yards for a touchdown. The Bengals failed on an onside kick with seconds remaining in the game. San Francisco won, 26–21.

According to Walsh after his first Super Bowl win, there were three keys to the 49ers' passing game: "I think we're willing to settle for a little less yardage on passes than some teams are. Two, our willingness to throw to the second and third receivers. And three, to look downfield for the great individual play."[12]

Ken Anderson, Walsh's old protégé with the Bengals, was chosen the NFL Most Valuable Player for 1981. Anderson threw for 3,754 yards, 29 touchdowns for a 62.6% completion rate with only 10 interceptions. Montana threw for 3,565 yards, 19 touchdowns for a 63.7% completion rate and 12 interceptions. Receiving the Associated Press Coach of the Year Award was Bill Walsh who had taken the league's top loser to the pinnacle of NFL success in just three seasons.

1982 Season

The 49ers' 1982 campaign was marred by a players' strike that shortened the regular season to nine games and created friction among teammates. The 49ers' efforts fell short of a championship team. Their 3–6 record gave them a third place finish in the NFC West.

1983 Season

The 49ers regained some confidence with a 10–6 finish for first position in the NFC West in 1983. They scored 432 points and allowed 293 from competition to give them a point differential of 139. George Seifert became the 49ers' defensive coordinator and like Walsh, he advanced more complex plans.

Roger Craig, an excellent fullback from Nebraska, was obtained through the draft. Walsh acquired Rams' running back Wendell Tyler who gave the 49ers a running game that demanded much more attention from opposing defenses. Jesse Sapolu, who would play 13 seasons for the 49ers as offensive guard and center, was also selected in the draft.

During the 1983 season, the 49ers fared well, but they suffered four losses in one month, from October 30, to November 27. They came back strong winning their last three regular season games on the road to the playoffs.

In the division match, the 49ers faced an excellent Detroit Lions' team that featured a strong defense to counter Walsh's innovative offense. The Lions' offense featured a great running back, Billy Sims, who was exciting to watch and difficult for tacklers to bring down. The Lions' starting quarterback, Eric Hipple, was injured and replaced by veteran Gary Danielson. A rusty Danielson threw five interceptions that day, but the Lions battled right up to the end. Craig and Tyler rushed for San Francisco scores and Wersching kicked a field goal. Lions' kicker, Eddie Murray, kicked three field goals in the first half and Sims ran for two touchdowns in the fourth quarter to put the Lions ahead, 23–17. Late in the fourth quarter, Montana tossed a touchdown pass to Solomon that put the 49ers ahead. San Francisco squeaked past Detroit, 24–23.

NFC Championship

In the NFC Championship game, San Francisco faced a well coached, veteran Washington Redskins team. San Francisco was out of sync for much of the game. It was all-Washington for the first three quarters. John Riggins scored two touchdowns on short runs. Theismann hit Charlie Brown on a 70-yard touchdown pass play and going into the fourth quarter Washington was comfortably ahead 21–0.

Then Montana got busy. He drove the 49ers downfield in a little over a minute and tossed a short touchdown pass to Mike Wilson. On San Francisco's next possession, the game's greatest come-back quarterback heaved a 76-yard touchdown bomb to Fred Solomon. After the extra point, the score was 21–14. The 49ers got the ball again after the Redskins did not score on their third possession of the quarter. Montana drove the 49ers downfield and hit Wilson for a 12-yard score for a 21–21 tie after the extra point. On the ensuing Redskin drive, two penalties on the 49ers helped the Redskins keep their drive alive. In the final minute of the game, Mark Mosely kicked a 25-yard field goal. Montana had 36 seconds of playing time remaining, but he had no final miracle that day. The Redskins won, 24–21, and advanced to the Super Bowl.

1984 Season

The 49ers were terrific in 1984 when they tallied a 15–1 record. For the season, the 49ers had an incredible score differential of 248. They lost to the Steelers in week seven by a score of 20–17, but dominated the opposition in most of their remaining games. In the playoffs, no one got within 10 points of them.

In the divisional match, Walsh's 49ers beat Parcells' Giants, 21–10. George Seifert's defense held the Giants' offense to a field goal. The Giants managed a touchdown on an interception by linebacker Harry Carson. Montana threw touchdown passes to Clark, Francis, and Solomon.

NFC Championship Game

The NFC Championship game against the Chicago Bears on January 6, 1985, in Candlestick Park began as a defensive struggle. The 49ers shutout the Bears and managed just two field goals themselves in the first half. Tyler ran for a score in the third quarter and Montana hit Solomon on a touchdown pass in the fourth quarter. A Wersching 35-yard field goal capped off the 23–0 San Francisco win. The San Francisco 49ers received the first George Halas trophy for the NFC Championship.

Super Bowl XIX

Super Bowl XIX was a "home game" for Bill Walsh because it was played at Stanford University Stadium in Palo Alto where Walsh had coached. On January 20, 1985, Walsh faced Don Shula's Dolphins with Dan Marino at quarterback.

Super Bowl games have plenty of pomp and circumstance. They are, after all, the world championship of football. Super Bowl XIX had tremendous appeal. Both Marino of the Dolphins and Montana of the 49ers were top quarterbacks—not just for the 1984 season, but for all time. Both hailed from the Pittsburgh area and both remain as top 10 NFL quarterbacks in wins. Walsh and Shula were interesting combatants as well. Shula had played under Paul Brown in Cleveland and took over the reins of the Baltimore Colts at age 33. He was a veteran coach in every way when he faced Bill Walsh in Super Bowl XIX. In fact, his Dolphins were 2–2 in Super Bowl contests and heading into their fifth championship game under Shula. Shula was also wily and super competitive. Walsh had coached under Brown in Cincinnati. Walsh was also a Super Bowl winner. Walsh had a reputation for intelligent planning and innovative strategy.

The 49ers received the opening kickoff and had some success in their first series moving the ball toward midfield. Two short runs and an incomplete pass forced a punt from their own 41-yard line. Marino was able to move the ball towards the 49ers' goal, but the Dolphins' offense stalled at the San Francisco 19, where Uwe von Schamann kicked a field goal to put Miami ahead. Montana charged right back with a mix of short passes and runs to midfield. Then he took it himself for 15 yards and followed with a 33-yard touchdown strike to Carl Monroe. After the extra point, the 49ers led 7–3. It only took Marino six plays to take back the lead, 10–7, throwing passes to the usual Dolphins' suspects: wide receivers Mark Duper and Mark Clayton, along with tight end Dan Johnson. In the second quarter, the 49ers got the ball in good field position after pinning the Dolphins back towards their own goal. Starting at the Miami 47, Montana scored on the fourth play of the series, an 8-yard toss to Craig giving the 49ers a 14–10 lead. After the Dolphins went three and out, Montana started at his 45-yard line. He made the Dolphins pay with a quick drive that included two Russ Francis catches and a touchdown run by Montana. The 49ers pulled ahead, 21–10.

The Dolphins' running game was not giving Marino any relief on pass coverage. Three and out for Marino and the ball was once again in Montana's hands. He followed with another drive, another score. Marino orchestrated a long scrappy drive that brought the ball down to the San Francisco 13, before it stalled. Uwe von Schamann kicked a field goal to put the score at 28–13. After Guy McIntyre fumbled the ensuing kickoff, von Schamann kicked another field goal to the put the score at 28–16 at the half.

In the second half the Dolphins' defense stiffened, but the Miami offense could not get on track. Wersching kicked a 27-yard field goal and Montana managed a 16-yard touchdown pass to Craig. The 49ers won, 38–16.

1985 Season

Walsh knew that a Super Bowl champion could fall like a rock the following season. In 1985, the 49ers returned to earth with a 10–6 record, but they did not repeat the 1982 season of humiliation. They scored 148 points more than their opponents that season. They finished second in the NFC West and faced the NFC East leader, the New York Giants, in the Wild Card game. Bill Parcell's Giants were able to frustrate the 49ers' offense and allow only one Wersching field goal the entire game. On the other side of the ball, Eric Schubert opened the Giants' scoring with a 47-yard field goal in the first quarter. Phil Simms threw an 18-yard touchdown pass to Mark Bavaro in the second quarter and followed it with a 3-yard touchdown pass to Don Hasselbeck in the third. The Giants won 17–3 and San Francisco was out of the playoffs. The Chicago Bears beat the Giants the following week in the division matchup.

1986 Season

Mike Holmgren joined the 49ers' staff as the quarterback coach in 1986. Holmgren was known as a coach who was highly competitive, but one with self deprecating humor and humility.

Walsh determined that the 1986 draft offered few exceptional players on top, but a deeper group of talent than usual. He determined that it was a draft that called for trading down for more picks. He picked up defensive end Larry

Roberts from Alabama, fullback Tom Rathman from Nebraska, cornerback Tim McKyer from the University of Texas at Arlington, defensive tackle Kevin Fagan from the University of Miami, offensive tackle Steve Wallace from Auburn, linebacker Charles Haley from James Madison, and cornerback Don Griffin from Middle Tennessee State—all became contributing members of the team. He also traded backup quarterback Matt Cavanaugh, but picked up another backup, Jeff Kemp.

Montana's Woes

In 1986, Montana, who had shoulder surgery in the offseason, was nursing a sore back and ankle in the 49ers' start against the Tampa Bay Buccaneers. He played exceptionally well, but he severely injured his back. Montana was slated for back surgery and Jeff Kemp became the starting quarterback for the 49ers. Kemp played well, but he injured his hip against the Falcons in week seven. Mike Morowski took over against the Green Bay Packers and led the 49ers to a 31–17 victory on October 26. The 49ers faced New Orleans a week later.

Going into the game against the Saints on November 2, the 49ers were 5–2–1 on the season. They had several key starters out with injuries. Against the Saints, the team played poorly and turned the ball over four times. After two Saints' touchdowns in the first quarter, the 49ers scored on a Wersching 50-yard field goal, which was followed by a Morowski touchdown pass to tight end John Frank. It was Saints 14–49ers 10 at the half. In the second half, San Francisco could do little right other than keep the Saints from the end zone. Saints' kicker Morten Andersen kept the scoring going with field goals of 45, 50, and 23 yards. The Saints prevailed 23–10.

For Walsh, the New Orleans loss was crushing, but on the heels of the defeat came news that Montana had recovered enough to play the following week. With Montana under center, the 49ers finished the season with five more wins and two losses. Despite Montana's surgery and several key injuries, the 49ers finished 10-5-1, which gave them a first place finish in the NFC West. They scored 374 points and allowed 247. Montana's stats were not bad for the eight games he played, except that for the first time in his career, his interceptions (9) outnumbered his touchdown passes (8). He was also slowed by his injuries and he was not the running threat that he had been in past.

Walsh must have known that the 49ers were very vulnerable going into the divisional playoff game. But he certainly would not have anticipated the game that his team played when they faced the Giants in the Meadowlands on January 4, 1987. The San Francisco scoring began and ended with a Wersching field goal in the first quarter. The Giants' offense fared much better. Phil Simms threw four touchdown passes. Joe Morris ran for two touchdowns. To add insult to injury, Montana was literally knocked out of the game on a helmet to chin hit that led to a Lawrence Taylor interception and runback for another score. The Giants humiliated the 49ers, 49-3, and went on to win the Super Bowl.

1987 Season

Walsh drafted an offensive lineman from North Carolina, Harris Barton, in the 1987 draft. Barton would provide 10 years of service to the 49ers. The 49ers' quarterback duties would be problematic even with Montana whom some consider one of the greatest. Montana suffered many injuries and the 49ers added Brigham Young star Steve Young to their roster in 1987. Young was acquired in a trade with the Tampa Bay Buccaneers. Young had not played particularly well for the struggling Tampa team, but this move would delight 49ers' fans long after Walsh had retired. Young became expendable in 1987 when the Buccaneers picked up Vinny Testaverde as a number one draft pick.

San Francisco's quarterback coach Mike Holmgren was a former coach at BYU where Young had played. Holmgren would find himself in the midst of the quarterback controversy involving Montana and Young during his tenure. Young would be called in to substitute for an injured Montana, perform admirably, and then sit on the bench when Joe Cool returned. Competition between the two great quarterbacks would result in conflict that would stir up on occasion, but one most NFL coaches would have loved to have.

In 1987, a strike was called after the second game of the season by the players union. Team owners cancelled the third game and set up camps to gather and train replacement players. The season continued with replacement players filling in for most positions in a three game string. The strike was effectively over after the second game in the replacement series. Montana was back in at quarterback against the Falcons on October 11.

The 49ers continued to earn a reputation as one of the best teams in the league. They finished with a 13-2 record, which gave them a first place finish in the NFC West. They scored 459 points and allowed 253. Montana was having a superb year. He had completed 266 passes on 398 attempts for 3,054 yards and a 66.8% completion rate. He threw an incredible 31 touchdown passes while tossing 13 interceptions. His quarterback rating was 102.1. With Montana playing well, his backup, Steve Young, had been used sparingly, but Walsh had Young start the last three games. Montana played in the second half of the 49ers-Rams contest in the last game of the season as a warm up for the playoffs. It would not be enough.

Going into their division match against the Vikings in Candlestick Park on January 9, 1988, most observers thought the 49ers would win easily. Montana had problems with his footing on the wet soggy field that day and his top receiver Jerry Rice seemed to be affected as well. On the other side of the ball, the Vikings' wide receiver, Anthony Carter, had a tremendous day.

Montana had 12 completions on 26 attempts for 109 yards, and no touchdowns. Najee Mustaffa had intercepted a Montana pass and returned it 45 yards for a Viking touchdown. The 49ers had managed a Wersching field goal and a defensive score by Jeff Fuller who ran back an interception. Montana was yanked by Walsh and replaced by Young in the third quarter.

Before Young could make a difference, the Vikings' Wade Wilson had thrown two touchdown passes and Chuck Nelson had kicked two field goals in addition to the interception run back for a score. The Vikings were ahead 27-10 when Steve Young rushed for a touchdown in the third quarter. Nelson kicked two more field goals before Young tossed a touchdown pass to tight end John Frank in the fourth. Nelson finished the day with another field goal and the 49ers were upset by the Vikings, 36–24. Carter had 10 receptions for 227 yards.

In addition to what many considered a subpar performance by Montana, there were other 49ers who played poorly in the post season. Jerry Rice had a superb season, but he caught only 3 passes for 28 yards in the defeat to the Vikings. With Young essentially in relief in the last three regular season games, Montana had only thrown 17 passes total in the four games preceding the playoffs.

1988 Season

In Walsh's last season of coaching, the 49ers won their third Super Bowl. For the 1988 Season, the 49ers finished 10-6, scoring 369 points and allowing 294 points from opponents.

In the first game of the season, the 49ers battled with the New Orleans Saints who were led by Bobby Hebert at quarterback. The 49ers orchestrated a successful drive that was capped off by a short Roger Craig run for the first score of the game. Three Montana touchdown passes and two field goals from the 49ers' new kicker, Mike Cofer, were just enough to defeat the Saints, 34-33. Montana had been beaten up in the game against the Saints and Steve Young started the following week against the Giants. Young struggled and Montana won the game in relief when he tossed a long bomb to Jerry Rice for the winning 78-yard touchdown strike with less than a minute remaining to play. The 49ers beat the Giants, 20-17. Upset by the Falcons in week three, the 49ers regrouped—beating the Seahawks and Lions in the following two games. They lost to John Elway's Denver Broncos in overtime, 16-13. The 49ers continued an up and down season.

Montana was taking a beating as the season progressed. After the 49ers beat the Rams, they succumbed to a good Chicago Bears' team 10-9 and then beat the Vikings with Steve Young in relief. Walsh's team lost to the Cardinals and the Raiders. In the Cardinals' game, the 49ers looked to have the game easily in hand with a 23-0 lead, but they collapsed in the second half and lost 24-23. They lost to the Raiders, 9–3, when Montana returned. From that low point, the 49ers rallied to string four wins in a row. The 49ers took on the Rams and lost the final game of the season, but they won the NFC West and a spot in the playoffs.

In the division matchup in Candlestick Park against the Vikings, the 49ers rolled on, 34–9. San Francisco avenged their upset loss to the Vikings in the 1987 playoffs. The Vikings were held to one Wade Wilson touchdown pass to Hassan Jones and one Chuck Nelson field goal. With the Vikings held to just 54 yards rushing, Wilson threw 47 passes, but could not get the ball into the end zone enough to counter the 49ers' three Montana to Rice scores and Craig's two touchdown runs. After the game, Montana told his team there would be no letup in the coming weeks.

NFC Championship

The 49ers played the Chicago Bears on a cold windy day at Chicago's Soldier Field for the NFC Championship on January 8, 1989. The Bears had key injuries going into the game. Before the season started, they had lost three of their 1985 Super Bowl marquee players to retirement and one to free agency. Yet, they ended the season 12-4. Pass rushing great Richard Dent and supersized tackle William "the Refrigerator" Perry were sidelined for the game. Jim McMahon, who had been out for several weeks with a knee injury, was given the starting assignment at quarterback over Mike Tomczak. While the 49ers looked to Montana to win their games, the Bears looked to their running backs and defense to win theirs. Mother Nature provided cold inhospitable playing conditions, but Joe Montana from Monongahela, Pennsylvania, was not much affected. In fact, the entire San Francisco squad that played home games in cold and windy Candlestick Park, seemed to be just fine.

Walsh believed when the 49ers lost to the Bears 10–9 during the regular season that he had been too conservative and vowed to come with a much more aggressive game plan. Some teams had tried to limit receiver Jerry Rice's effectiveness by making it hard for him to get a good jump off the line. Walsh put Rice in motion to make it more difficult for the Bears' defenders to hinder his pass patterns.

Walsh's special weapon in big games was quarterback Joe Montana. Montana often came through under the kind of pressure that made many quarterbacks crack. He also was one of the best at throwing in traffic. Over and over again on plays in which most quarterbacks would slip up trying to "force the ball in" to someone who was covered, Montana managed to thread the needle. During the course of a game, he hit several passes in heavy traffic—managing somehow to find the smallest space for the ball to travel or the perfect lead that would allow the catch by a receiver in full stride.

Once the game began, both teams were having a difficult time moving the ball until late in the first quarter when Montana found Rice on the sideline about 22 yards downfield. When two Bears' defenders got in each other's way after the catch, Rice flew past them to the end zone 62 yards from scrimmage. Early in the second quarter, Montana already had over a 100 yards passing in the miserable weather, but the Bears' offense struggled. McMahon tossed one ball that fluttered in the wind before falling into the hands of 49ers' Jeff Fuller for the interception. San Francisco made it pay. Montana sprinkled in passes in the midst of runs by Craig and Rathman to move the ball downfield. The Bears sensed their inability to stop the 49ers' progress. When the Bears came after Montana hard on a second and 10 on the Bears' 28-yard line, Rice came out of the backfield in motion and Montana hit him at about the 15-yard line as he was passing the last Bears' defender. The 49ers were up 14–0 against a Bears' team that was not moving the ball well.

In the next series, the Bears started with good field position after a short kickoff and a good return by Brad Muster to the home team's 45-yard line. Chicago moved the ball well to the 13-yard line, but the drive died just after McMahon got the wind knocked out of him on second down and a third down quarterbacked by Mike Tomczak failed to move the chains. Kevin Butler came in and kicked a 25-yard field goal for the Bears' first and only score. The Bears would have some chances, but San Francisco shut them out the remainder of the game while adding two more touchdowns to win 28-3.

Super Bowl XXIII

When Bill Walsh coached the 49ers, there seemed to be a feeling of destiny that hung about the team—a sense that providence was at work. Often in the history of the NFL, it seems that great teams are destined to play each other repeatedly in big games. The 1988 49ers and Bengals Super Bowl XXIII recalled the two teams' previous Super Bowl meeting. Great quarterbacking and coaching were a common thread.

The Bengals were clearly one of the best teams in football in 1988 with exceptional talent. Their quarterback Boomer Esiason passed for 3,572 yards collecting 28 touchdowns and only 14 interceptions. He was the top rated quarterback in the NFL with a 97.4 rating and was the NFL MVP. Esiason was the master of the play-action pass and he had top talent around him to confound opponents. The Bengals' running back, Ickey Woods, was a 1,000-yard ground gainer and his compatriot, James Brooks, was a multipurpose back who was an excellent receiver. Wide receivers Eddie Brown and Tim McGee along with tight end Rodney Holman gave Esiason very talented targets. Cris Collinsworth, the Bengals' sure-handed veteran receiver, was also a key contributor. The Bengals' offensive line was famously bolstered by Anthony Munoz and Max Montoya. Munoz was a Hall of Famer considered to be one of the best offensive tackles. Montoya was a dominating guard. The Bengals' head coach, Sam Wyche, had played for the Bengals when Walsh was an assistant and had also been an assistant with the 49ers in Walsh's first few years in San Francisco. Wyche received much attention and instruction from the Bengals' founder Paul Brown. Wyche was a creative coach like Walsh and the Bengals' offense was one of the most challenging. Although the Bengals' defense ranked in the middle of the NFL, they had one of the best defensive coaches in Hall of Famer, Dick LeBeau, who would prepare them well for the 49ers.

Regardless of the firepower on the field that day on January 22, 1989 at Joe Robbie Stadium in Miami, Super Bowl XXIII was a defensive battle well into the third quarter. Both teams had kicked two field goals apiece for a 6-6 tie when the pace changed dramatically. When San Francisco kicked off following their second field goal, Bengals' running back, Stanford Jennings, returned the kickoff 93 yards for the first touchdown of the day. After the extra point, Cincinnati led 13-6.

Montana and the 49ers were energized by the Cincinnati score. At the same time, the 49ers caught a few breaks that kept them in the game. Montana threw the ball into the hands of Bengals' cornerback Lewis Billups who dropped it. Following his miscue, Montana threw a touchdown strike to Jerry Rice to tie the game at 13-13. After the ensuing Bengals' drive stalled, John Taylor fumbled a punt, but his 49ers' teammate Darryl Pollard recovered the ball to keep the 49ers out of harm's way again. Montana's next drive stalled at the Bengals' 32 and a 49-yard field goal was missed.

When the Bengals took over, Boomer Esiason drove the ball to the San Francisco 22-yard line as the final period was winding down. Jim Breech kicked a field goal to give the Bengals a 16-13 lead. With 3:10 to go, Montana and the 49ers took over on their own 8-yard line. When the officials called a TV time out, Montana told his nervous offensive tackle Harris Barton to look down towards the other goal—"There's John Candy in the end zone."[13] The entire huddle looked down to see the famous comedian and Montana managed to reduce the pressure. Montana himself was still under duress, but he kept it under wraps. During the drive, Montana attempted to call a time out twice as he was hyperventilating, but Walsh called it off wanting to save the time out and not knowing his quarterback's dilemma.[14]

Joe Cool drove the ball down to the Cincinnati 35, but a penalty pulled the 49ers back to the 45-yard line with a second down and 20 yards to go for a first. Walsh's teams had a play for every situation and the confidence to make it work. Montana hit Rice over the middle and the Bengals' defenders nearly collided allowing Rice to run the ball down to the 18-yard line. The 49ers kept doing the unexpected. While the Bengals were guarding the sidelines, Montana hit Craig down the middle for an 8-yard gain with 39 seconds remaining. Perhaps there was no one in the stadium expecting any less from Montana and Walsh at that moment, when Joe Cool hit a wide open John Taylor for the touchdown and the win. The final score was San Francisco 49ers 20–Cincinnati Bengals 16.

Walsh Retires

Walsh experienced the constant pressure of high expectations throughout his entire pro coaching career. The pressure never diminished after his first Super Bowl win in 1981. After the 1988 Super Bowl, it was time for the 49ers' coach to move on. Always harboring doubts of one kind or another while competing masterfully at the highest level, Walsh no doubt thought that his retirement timing missed the mark, when the 49ers came back for another Super Bowl victory following the 1989 season. Within a few years, Walsh was coaching again.

Return to Stanford

Bill Walsh returned to coach at Stanford in January 1992. He coached for three seasons in his second stint as head coach there. Walsh's team had an excellent first year that was punctuated by a 24–3 win over Penn State in the Blockbuster Bowl on January 1, 1993. During this period, Walsh's Stanford Cardinal teams were 17-17-1. The 1994 Cardinal team struggled at 3-7-1 in Walsh's final year. When Walsh left his Stanford coaching job in November 1994, he said:

> *I love the game of football. It's been my entire life. I've thrived on it and thoroughly enjoyed it.*[15]

Walsh's 5-year record as head coach at Stanford, including his first head coaching term from 1977-1978 and his second from 1992-1994, stands at 34-24-1.

Walsh's Contributions to the Game

Bill Walsh coached San Francisco from 1979-1988 and posted a 102-63-1 record including Super Bowl victories in XVI, XIX, and XXIII. The 49ers won their first NFL Championship in Walsh's third year by defeating the Cincinnati Bengals, 26-21, in Super Bowl XVI on January 24, 1982. They beat the Dolphins, 38-16, in Super Bowl XIX on January 20, 1985. They beat the Bengals, 20-16, in Super Bowl XXIII on January 22, 1989.

Walsh was an excellent team builder. He had an eye for talent. Walsh was especially good at judging quarterback talent. He had great confidence in his abilities to bring out the best in his players. Often he was willing to draft players who may have shown some inconsistency in their college play and help them perform consistently in the NFL. With the support of San Francisco ownership, he was also able to retain his veterans and meet challenging salary demands.

Walsh looked at his position as one that came with certain social responsibilities. Not satisfied with simply getting the best out of his players, he wanted his players to be the best people they could be and he also wanted the NFL to advance in healthy ways within society. He looked at the changing racial makeup of the locker room of the 1980s and worked to have his players from all different races get along. He brought in sports sociologist, Dr. Harry Edwards, in 1985, to help facilitate that and more. With Edwards's help, he created the NFL's Minority Coaches Internship and Outreach Program renamed the Bill Walsh NFL Minority Coaching Fellowship program. This initiative provides an opportunity for young minority coaches to network and get some advance training on NFL coaching. Mike Tomlin, Marvin Lewis, Herm Edwards, Lovie Smith, Raheem Morris, and others have benefited.

Walsh insisted that everyone on the squad and throughout the organization was treated with respect. At times, he struggled with the conflicts that came with coaching men in a game that requires constant review and criticism. He also struggled to keep his distance from his players while still trying to maintain their respect. Like all NFL coaches, Walsh also had the difficult job of cutting veterans—veterans who had given so much to their team. And Walsh also struggled with putting pressure on his players to maintain their peak performance. This proved especially difficult when Walsh had two very capable quarterbacks in Joe Montana and Steve Young.

Walsh took personal responsibility for practically every slip, foible, and failing of the 49ers during his tenure. Walsh set the bar very high, very quickly in San Francisco. By the standards of most of the top NFL coaches, Walsh's tenure was short—just a decade. During that time, Walsh's performance, like a modern player's performance, was judged every year if not every game. Walsh would go from hero to goat in a heartbeat and then back again.

On the surface, Walsh could exude confidence and cool—standing on the sideline, looking like he walked off a golf course after a casual round in a resplendent white sweater. The coach who takes it all to heart the way that Walsh did, does not leave the game without scars of one sort or another. In the end, Walsh won three world championships in 10 years and regardless of how he felt on occasion, he knew that his Super Bowl record would trump all other measures of success.

Walsh was inducted into the Pro Football Hall of Fame in 1993. Among many awards, he was honored as the NFL Coach of the Year in 1981 and the NFC Coach of the Year in 1984. After coaching, he continued to contribute to his schools, his community, and his sport. Bill Walsh died July 30, 2007 at the age of 75.

Bill Walsh Timeline

1931

- November 30, 1931, William Ernest Walsh is born in Los Angeles.

1949

- Walsh plays halfback his senior year for the Fighting Farmers of Hayward High School.

1950

- Walsh enrolls at San Mateo Community College.

1951

- Walsh is All Conference at quarterback under coach Herb Hudson.

1952

- Walsh transfers to San Jose State College and he plays end on the football team for coach Bob Bronzan.

1953

- Walsh is intramural heavyweight boxing champion at San Jose State.

1954-1955

- Wash serves in the Army for two years.

1956

- Walsh returns to San Jose State to work towards a graduate degree and to serve as an assistant to Coach Bob Bronzan.

1957-1959

- Walsh coaches football and swimming at Washington High School in Fremont, California, where he attended high school himself in his first year.

1959

- Walsh receives his master's degree from San Jose State, which is fulfilled in part by his thesis: "Flank Formation Football – Stress: Defense."

1960-1962

- Walsh coaches at the University of California, Berkeley under Marv Levy.

1963-1965

- Walsh serves as assistant coach at Stanford under John Ralston.

1966

- Walsh begins his pro coaching career in Oakland, working under John Rauch for Al Davis's Raiders.

1967

- Walsh coaches the San Jose Apaches minor league football team in the Continental League.

1968-1975

- Bill Walsh works for Paul Brown as an assistant coach for the Cincinnati Bengals.

1976

- Walsh becomes offensive coordinator for the San Diego Chargers where he helps develop the skills of Dan Fouts.

1977-1978

- Walsh returns to Stanford and becomes head coach.
- December 31, 1977, Walsh's Stanford Cardinal team defeats Louisiana State University, 24–14, in the Sun Bowl.
- December 31, 1978, Walsh's Stanford Cardinal team defeats the Georgia Bulldogs, 25–22, in the Bluebonnet Bowl.

1979-1989

- January 9, 1979, Bill Walsh becomes head coach of the San Francisco 49ers and remains until 1989.

1981

- Walsh is honored as the AP, UPI, Sporting News, and Pro Football Weekly NFL Coach of the Year in 1981.

1982

- January 10, 1982, the 1981 San Francisco 49ers defeat the Dallas Cowboys, 28–27, in the NFC Championship game.
- January 24, 1982, the 1981 San Francisco 49ers defeat the Cincinnati Bengals, 26–21, in Super Bowl XVI.

1984

- January 8, 1984, the Washington Redskins defeat the 1983 San Francisco 49ers, 24–21, in the NFC Championship game.

- Walsh is honored as the NFC Coach of the Year in 1984.

1985

- January 6, 1985, the 1984 San Francisco 49ers defeat the Chicago Bears, 23–0, in the NFC Championship game.
- January 20, 1985, the 1984 San Francisco 49ers defeat the Miami Dolphins, 38–16, in Super Bowl XIX.

1989

- January 8, 1989, the 1988 San Francisco 49ers defeat the Chicago Bears, 28–3, in the NFC Championship game.
- January 22, 1989, the 1988 San Francisco 49ers defeat the Cincinnati Bengals, 20–16, in Super Bowl XXIII.
- Walsh retires.

1992-1994

- Walsh returns to Stanford in January 1992 and leaves after the 1994 season.
- January 1, 1993, Walsh's Stanford Cardinal team defeats Penn State, 24–3, in the Blockbuster Bowl.
- Walsh is inducted into the Pro Football Hall of Fame in 1993.

2007

- July 30, 2007, Walsh dies at the age of 75.

Highlights

Bill Walsh coached San Francisco from 1979-1988 and posted a 102-63-1 record including victories in Super Bowl XVI, XIX, and XXIII. Walsh created the NFL's Minority Coaches Internship and Outreach Program to help foster the advancement and success of minority coaches. Walsh was inducted into the Pro Football Hall of Fame in 1993 and he was named the AP, UPI, Sporting News, and Pro Football Weekly NFL Coach of the Year in 1981 and the UPI NFL Coach of the Year in 1984.

Walsh also had an eye for talent that focused on what athletes could do and how to make them more confident and consistent in those efforts. Walsh developed several excellent quarterbacks—work that was coupled with a strategy to spread the field using a more calculated passing game. Borrowing on other innovative offensive-minded strategies that used the pass liberally, he developed what is called the West Coast Offense. Walsh was also intense, determined, and competitive.

Endnotes

1 David Harris, *The Genius: How Bill Walsh Reinvented Football and Created a Football Dynasty* (NY, Random House, 2008), 28.

2 David Harris, *The Genius: How Bill Walsh Reinvented Football and Created a Football Dynasty*, 30.

3 San Jose State News Release, "San Jose State Legend Bill Walsh Dies," July 30, 2007, viewed at http://www.wacsports.com/ViewArticle.dbml?DB_OEM_ID=10100&ATCLID=1139580 on October 5, 2013.

4 Dennis Georgatos, *Stadium Stories: San Francisco 49ers*, (Guilford, CT, Globe Pequot Press, 2005) 54.

5 San Jose State News Release, "San Jose State Legend Bill Walsh Dies," July 30, 2007.

6 Larry Fox, "Father Knew Best," *Boys' Life*, November 1980, 39.

7 "Sports at a Glance," *The News and Courrier*, Dec. 21, 1976 viewed at http://news.google.com/newspapers?id=jQU1AAAAIBAJ&sjid=QU8KAAAAIBAJ&pg=4768,5136072&dq=bill+walsh+stanford&hl=en on June 3, 2013.

8 Don Smith, "Bill Walsh," *The Coffin Corner*, Vol 15, Nov. 6, 1993 viewed at http://www.profootballresearchers.org/Coffin_Corner/15-06-543.pdf on May 20, 2013.

9 Transcript of Bill Walsh's Hall of Fame Acceptance Speech.

10 David Harris, *The Genius: How Bill Walsh Reinvented Football and Created a Football Dynasty*, 121.

11 Cincinnati Bengals' official web site, Jeff Hobson, "Generation XXX," posted September 21, 2001. Viewed at http://www.bengals.com/news/article-1/Generation-XXX/170ffca2-35c3-4825-8734-3687e3475046 on May 20, 2013.

12 Richard Goldstein, "Bill Walsh, Innovator of West Coast Offense, Dies at Age 75," New York Times, July 31, 2007. Viewed at http://www.nytimes.com/2007/07/31/sports/football/31walsh.html?_r=0 on May 31, 2013.

13 Warner Home Video, "America's Game, The Super Bowl Champions, 1988 San Francisco 49ers, Super Bowl XXIII," 2007.

14 Warner Home Video, "America's Game, The Super Bowl Champions, 1988 San Francisco 49ers, Super Bowl XXIII," 2007.

15 Stanford University News Release, "Walsh to Step Down as Stanford Head Coach," November 30, 1994.

Joe Gibbs

Coach Joe Gibbs stands out on the sideline at Jack Murphy Stadium in San Diego. It is Super Bowl XXII—Gibbs's third NFL championship game as the Washington Redskins' head coach. It is 60° and overcast in San Diego—a beautiful day for football, near perfect. Gibbs wears his Redskins' sweater and cap. His oversized glasses give him the look of a Physics teacher, but he is a jock—at least that's how he defines himself.

Gibbs is competitive to the bone and grabs onto games and activities of every kind with the vigor of a kid. He loves football, especially championship football. Gibbs looks out on the field as his players warm up. Everything seems to be in order. But there are two big questions that will be answered during the game. First, will Doug Williams excel today? Gibbs has selected the more experienced Williams over Jay Schroeder to start at quarterback. Schroeder was his starter, but he was injured and Williams played well when he filled in. The coach could have gone with either one today.

Gibbs's second question concerns his running back. Will Timmy Smith give the Redskins a ground game today? They need a first-rate ground game to help open up the passing game. George Rogers, Gibbs's top running back, is banged up and Smith is faster. Rogers replaced John Riggins, the "diesel," who was essentially unstoppable for at least a few yards on every carry. Like Riggins, Rogers was difficult to stop. Smith needs to have a good day for the Redskins to succeed.

Although one of the most successful coaches, outside the beltway Gibbs is under the radar. He does nothing to call attention to himself other than win. Gibbs is not controversial or flashy. Gibbs has a good relationship with the Redskins' owner Jack Kent Cooke and he gets along with the players. He is a devout man and he finds no conflict between his faith and his football. He is tough and innovative in a practical way. His schemes and designs are built with purpose. When called a genius by reporters, he tells them to come back after more seasons have unfolded. He is often serious, but he has a good sense of humor. And like most of the great coaches, he is confident.

Once the game begins, the Redskins are self-destructing. On Washington's first possession, a dropped pass on third down kills a first down. The ball is punted to the Broncos. On his first play, Denver superstar quarterback John Elway burns the Redskins' defense with a touchdown pass. Gibbs looks calm and collected. When the Redskins have the ball again, another third down pass is dropped. Gibbs looks on quietly. The Broncos have the ball again and Denver's head coach Dan Reeves gets creative. After a long completion over the middle, Elway hands the ball off to his running back who starts off on a run, but turns to pass it back to a wide open Elway. But despite the two long gains, the Broncos' drive stalls and they kick a field goal. Gibbs's Redskins are behind 10–0 and the Gatorade has hardly been touched.

Gibbs is behind in the biggest game in football. Yet, he is so calm it looks like he is bird watching on the sidelines. Gibbs knows his team will play on; they always do.

Washington moves the ball, but Doug Williams leaves the game with an injury. Another drive ends. When Washington gets the ball back, Williams returns and connects with Ricky Sanders for an 80-yard touchdown pass. Denver's potent offense is stopped on the next series and Williams leads another scoring drive. The Redskins take the lead and they never relinquish it. When the game ends, Gibbs congratulates those around him. He treks across the field looking for Coach Dan Reeves. A disappointed Reeves congratulates a pensive Gibbs. In the post game interview, Gibbs gives credit to the owner, the coaches, the players, and the fans. Gibbs is completely composed and he says he is humbled by the victory.

Early Years

Joe Jackson Gibbs was born November 25, 1940, in Mocksville, North Carolina, near Asheville in the Blue Ridge Mountains. His father, Jackson Cephas Gibbs, was a county sheriff. His mother, Winnie, worked for the phone company. He and his younger brother, Jim, loved the outdoors and lived outside as much as possible.

When Joe Gibbs was 14 years old, his family moved across the country to Santa Fe, California. He attended Santa Fe High School. Captivated by sports, Gibbs played football, basketball, and baseball. During his senior year in 1959, he was named athlete of the year. Gibbs played quarterback for the football team and he prized hot rods, burger joints, and hanging out with friends. In his junior year, he met a cheerleader named Pat Escobar, whom he would date and marry. Gibbs made friends he would keep a lifetime such as Rennie Simmons who would coach for him in the NFL.

College

Joe Gibbs attended Cerritos Junior College and transferred to San Diego State University where he played football for legendary head coach Don Coryell. At San Diego State, he played tight end, guard, and linebacker. Coryell remembered him as intelligent, versatile, feisty, and hard-nosed. There was something else about Gibbs that stood out. Coryell said, "he could adjust to any change or situation."[1] In a nutshell, Coryell had identified Gibbs's greatest key to success.

Learning Years

Gibbs began his coaching career in the college ranks working for a number of outstanding coaches. When he made it to the pros, he had an exceptional mentor in Don Coryell.

College Coaching

Once Gibbs began coaching, he would share his beliefs and commitments with his players. There are two things that defined Gibbs. First, he was devout in his faith. In every major decision in his life from the earliest of days, he was apt to seek guidance from God. In his success and in his failings, he sought a divine roadmap to not only guide him, but to see where he may have gone off course. Second, Gibbs was thoroughly hooked on competition since he was a boy. He was driven by competition and it never waned as he grew older. Gibbs took up golf, racquetball, cards, hunting, jogging, skiing—both water and snow, and auto racing.[2] This mix of faith and competition defined his life and brought an unflappable strength and effort to coaching his teams.

Gibbs graduated from college in 1964 and went on for a master's degree that he obtained in 1966 while assisting Coach Coryell as a volunteer. Future Raiders' head coach and sportscaster John Madden was serving as an assistant coach to Coryell at the time. Coryell was known for his intensity, but the staff was certainly not devoid of humor. Gibbs joked about the duties he performed as an assistant.

The most important job I had was to go to the local Jack in the Box and get the tacos and hamburgers and bring them back and the only time I really got in trouble was if I left something off John Madden's taco.[3]

In 1966, Gibbs's third year working for the team, he became an offensive line coach on the staff and San Diego State went 11–0. Coryell credited Gibbs with working with all new recruits on the line and helping San Diego State receive the top rating in its division.[4] Coryell thought Gibbs was just too good to let him get away, but he did. Other coaches became aware of Gibbs's coaching talent and recruited him. Gibbs served a who's who of college coaches for several years. Moving on from San Diego State University, he coached the line for Bill Peterson at Florida State from 1967-1968. While Gibbs was working with the Florida State Seminoles, they went 15–4–1. Next stop was University of Southern California assisting John McKay from 1969-1970. While working for McKay at USC, Gibbs's son Jason Dean (J.D.) Gibbs was born. USC was 14–3–1 during the two seasons Gibbs was there. Lastly he moved to Arkansas to work for Frank Broyles from 1971-1972. On the coaching staff at Arkansas was Raymond Berry whom Gibbs would remember as a remarkably good man and an exceptional example to others. Gibbs's second son, Coy, was born during this period.

Professional Football

Joe Gibbs would also spend time as an assistant coach in the NFL before he got a head coaching position. His college coach, Don Coryell, would play a key role in Gibbs's career movements. As he developed his own approach, Gibbs was a tireless coach who expected everyone around him to work until the job was done regardless of the hours. In his coaching rooms, there would be no clocks. Gibbs's assistant coach Joe Bugel once said, "It's like Las Vegas. Time doesn't matter."[5]

St. Louis Cardinals

After Coryell had moved to the St. Louis Cardinals in the pros, he hired Gibbs in 1973, this time as offensive backfield coach. Gibbs stayed in St. Louis through 1977. The Cardinals' record for those years was 42–27–1. During this time, Gibbs became engrossed in competitive racquetball and won the nationals senior title in 1976.

Tampa Bay Buccaneers

Gibbs moved on to help the Tampa Bay Buccaneers' head coach, John McKay, in 1978. Gibbs and McKay had worked together at USC. Gibbs served as offensive coordinator for the Buccaneers.

San Diego Chargers

Once again, Gibbs met up with Don Coryell who had moved to the San Diego Chargers. Gibbs was set to take up the job of backfield coach in 1979, but Ray Perkins, the current offensive coordinator, left for the Giants so Gibbs was given the coordinator position. The Chargers won the AFC West in 1979 and 1980 with Gibbs as offensive coordinator and Coryell as head coach. They lost the AFC Championship in 1980 to the Oakland Raiders who were on their way to win the Super Bowl.

Washington Redskins

Gibbs left San Diego for the head coaching job for the Washington Redskins in 1981. The legendary Washington Redskins' General Manager, Bobby Beathard, supported Gibbs as a candidate when the Redskins were looking for a new coach. Washington Redskins' majority owner, Jack Kent Cooke, considered to be an excellent judge of talent himself, signed Gibbs. Cooke worked out a fairly general contract that Gibbs shook on without counsel and in time Cooke generously rewarded Gibbs financially in a way that perhaps no formal written contract would have stipulated.[6]

Gibbs's Players

Bobby Beathard was one of the exceptional talent experts in professional football. He would work with Gibbs to assemble an incredibly talented team whom Gibbs could mold to succeed. Beathard was instrumental to Gibbs's success in Washington.

Art Monk

Hall of Famer Art Monk from Syracuse University was selected by the Redskins in the first round in 1980 and became a top Redskins' receiver. Monk was a member of Washington's "Posse," three receivers (Art Monk, Gary Clark, and Ricky Sanders) who would all post 1,000 yard seasons on the same team. He was conspicuously tall at 6-foot-3, especially when compared to the Washington Redskins "Smurfs," a group of receivers so called because of their diminutive size.

Charlie Brown

Charlie Brown was a wide receiver who played for six seasons with the Redskins and was a key offensive talent in Gibbs's early years with the team. He was a member of the Smurfs receiving corps.

Clint Didier

Drafted by the Redskins in 1981, Clint Didier was an excellent tight end who played for six seasons with the Redskins.

Clinton Portis

Drafted by Denver in 2002, Clinton Portis came over to the Redskins in 2004 under Joe Gibbs. Portis was both an excellent runner and receiver. When Portis was healthy and played well, the Redskins were difficult to beat. Despite his small size, Portis's heavy build helped him perform well as a power back who could run up the middle, but he also had the speed to run outside.

Darrell Green

Darrell Green was an amazing, fast, skilled, and tough defensive back who could also return punts. Green was a game-changer, a big-play star who had a prolific career. The Hall of Famer played for an incredible 20 seasons in Washington.

Darryl Grant

Drafted in 1981, Darryl Grant played defensive tackle for the Redskins for 10 seasons. He was another superb defensive star who made big plays in important games.

Dave Butz

Dave Butz was in his ninth season as defensive tackle when Gibbs joined the team. Butz liked it so much he stuck around for another seven seasons. He was one of the largest players of his era at 6-foot-7, 300 pounds.

Dexter Manley

Dexter Manley was a superb pass rusher who is the Redskins' franchise sack leader. Manley was someone opposing teams feared.

Doug Williams

Doug Williams had been drafted in the first round by Tampa Bay in 1978 when Gibbs was serving as offensive coordinator there. After five seasons in Tampa and two seasons in the USFL, he was acquired by the Redskins' as a veteran backup. Williams played a significant role in important victories and was the first African American quarterback to start in an NFL championship game. For Gibbs, Williams was a tough competitor who could play Redskins' ball.

George Rogers

George Rogers was a Heisman Trophy winner from the University of South Carolina. He came from the New Orleans Saints to replace John Riggins—he was identical to Riggins in size. Rogers played in Washington from 1985-1987. Although he was injured in 1987, his contributions enabled the Redskins to achieve an 11–4 season leading to the Super Bowl.

Jeff Bostic

Jeff "Bosco" Bostic came from Clemson as a free agent, stayed for 14 seasons, and he played center as part of the "Hogs" offensive line. He was another key contributor to Gibbs's team and he was the center for Gibbs's three Super Bowl wins.

Joe Jacoby

Joe "Jake" Jacoby was a 6-foot-7, 300 pound free agent when he made the Redskins in 1981. He played left tackle and was a key member of the "Hogs" offensive line.

Joe Theismann

Theismann was drafted by the Miami Dolphins in 1971, but he chose to play for the Toronto Argonauts in the Canadian Football League. Washington signed him in 1974. Oddly enough, he began his Redskins' career as primarily a kick returner until 1976 when he started a 10-year run at quarterback. He was tough, competitive, and assured.

John Riggins

John Riggins was a big fullback who was able to get tough yards—a workhorse who would have a Hall of Fame career. After playing 5 years with the Jets, he joined the Redskins in 1976, but Gibbs had to convince Riggins to return to the NFL after a one-year holdout.

Mark May

Outland Trophy winner from the University of Pittsburgh and a first round draft choice in 1981, Mark May played offensive guard and tackle for nine seasons in Washington. May was an original member of the "Hogs."

Mark Moseley

Mark "the Mose" Moseley was the Redskins' excellent kicker who holds the top scoring position for the franchise. His role was especially important in the years when the team relied heavily on defense, ball control, and a running game that required that the Redskins make the most of every opportunity to score.

Mike Nelms

Mike Nelms was plucked from the Canadian Football League where he played for three seasons after being cut by the Buffalo Bills who had drafted him. He was an excellent kick returner for the Redskins and played for five seasons.

Neil Olkewicz

Middle linebacker Neil "Olky" Olkewicz from the University of Maryland signed with the Redskins as a free agent in 1979 and played for 11 seasons. He was a small middle linebacker, known for his work ethic and determination. Olky was always one of the leading tacklers on the team and helped establish the Redskins' reputation for toughness.

Russ Grimm

Hall of Famer Russ Grimm was drafted in the third round of the 1981 draft by the Redskins. Grimm played offensive guard and epitomized the blue collar spirit and work ethic of the original "Hogs."

Gibbs's Coaches and Administrators

Gibbs was always an honest, simple, straightforward speaker. In looking back at the time of his Redskins start, Gibbs summed up his prospects with his great group of coaches:

Coaches can't make a team win, but we were sure as heck going to do everything we knew to get the team prepared.[7]

Al Saunders

Al Saunders, who like Gibbs had worked under Don Coryell, was assistant coach-offense for the 2006-2007 seasons. Saunders had an extensive complicated play book that provided a high level of sophistication.

Bobby Beathard

Bobby Beathard was the Washington Redskins' General Manager starting in 1978 and continuing into the spring of 1989. No doubt, his great efforts freed up Gibbs to focus more on the team and its games. Beathard had a great eye for talent and developed working strategies to get it.

Don Breaux

Don Breaux was an assistant coach who worked with Gibbs from 1981-1993 and 2004-2007. Don Breaux was one of Gibbs's top advisors.

Gregg Williams

Gregg Williams was the defensive coordinator for the Redskins beginning in 2004 and lasting through 2007. Like Petitbon in Gibbs's first coaching time in Washington, Williams was given autonomy in running the Redskins' defense and his hallmark was using aggressive schemes to put maximum pressure on the quarterback.

Joe Bugel

Joe Bugel served as Gibbs's offensive coordinator in 1981 and then moved up to assistant head coach. Bugel worked extensively on the offensive line and developed the Redskins' "Hogs."

Rennie Simmons

Rennie Simmons was Gibbs's tight end coach who worked with Gibbs from 1981-1993 and 2004-2007. Simmons was an old friend of Gibbs and remained with him throughout his career.

Richie Petitbon

Richie Petitbon was on staff with the Redskins when Gibbs signed on. Gibbs promoted Petitbon to defensive coordinator and he served the Redskins from 1981-1992. Gibbs liked to concentrate on offense so it was important for him to have a master like Petitbon in control of the defense.

Gibbs Solves the Riggins Holdout Problem

Riggins was a free spirit who had made his mark with the Jets, but he seemed less than enthusiastic about coming back to play again after he had taken a year off. Gibbs famously met with Riggins on the Seneca, Kansas native's own turf while the running back was apparently taking a short break from a hunting excursion. When the two met, the running back was sporting camouflage hunting gear and a can of beer at 10 a.m. Gibbs was not impressed. He remembered Riggins telling him that he would make Gibbs famous. Gibbs was not taking the bait and described his thinking:[8] "Oh, my God, he's an egomaniac...I'll get him back and then I'll trade him."

But when Riggins returned his call a few days later, he explained to his prospective coach: "There's only one thing I want in my contract...A no-trade clause.[9]"

Gibbs worked things out with Riggins and the powerful Kansan helped Gibbs achieve great success in Washington. Upon Riggins' return to Washington, he famously explained to the press:

I'm bored, I'm broke, I'm back.

Gibbs not only liked Riggins's performance, he created an offensive scheme that maximized it. After Riggins retired, Gibbs looked for Riggins type players he could use in the same way.

1981 Season

In Gibbs's first season, the Redskins scored 347 points and allowed 349 points from their opponents. They looked remarkably overmatched at the start of the regular season when they lost their first five games by 10 or more points. Owner Jack Kent Cooke gave Gibbs a vote of confidence when the season looked like it was taking a disturbing turn for the worse. Gibbs joked about it:

Now 0 and 5 in Washington is a big deal. I was looking for different ways home at night. I didn't want anyone to know where I was.[10]

It must have been difficult for Gibbs to fathom, but it would be October 11, 1981, before he won his first game as head coach. Gibbs had used Riggins sparingly in the first four games of the season and with emphasis on the pass; the Redskins had 21 turnovers heading into Chicago's Soldier Field. Gibbs decided to make better use of their running game going forward. Riggins ran for 126 yards and scored two touchdowns to contribute mightily to the Redskins 24–7 win.

After their win in Chicago, the Redskins turned things around for an 8–8 finish. After losing to the playoff-bound Dolphins, they won seven of their last nine games. Gibbs would remember the 1981 season as one that brought his coaches and his players together on their way to championships. Gibbs would also refer to the season repeatedly long after his career had ended.

Adjusting for Offensive Success

Riggins was an amazingly strong runner, but regardless of his fullback size at 6-foot-2, 230 pounds, he was not a blocker. In time, the pragmatic Gibbs adjusted by frequently going to a one back set and adding a blocker at the line. When he added an extra tight end, it also helped him provide better protection for his quarterback when facing teams like the Giants and Lawrence Taylor. Most fullbacks were incapable of blocking Taylor. Often Gibbs would have a versatile tight end setback from the line of scrimmage where he would be considered a back—called an "H-back" who might be used to block, run, or catch passes. Gibbs also created the Trips Formation—where he had three wide receivers line up on one side of the field. This disrupted zone defenses and allowed for many play variations.

Gibbs created these offensive strategies and positions to fit needs that he had on his team rather than creating innovations for their own sake. More than anything else, the super competitive Gibbs wanted to win. With Riggins and the Hogs, he built a system of power football. Gibbs's signature running play was the counter trey, a misdirection running play designed for the offense to feign rushing in one direction and attack the defense in the opposite.

Gibbs knew that adjustments were crucial and he did not have problems abandoning elements of a "brilliant" game plan that was not working. He got high marks from his players like quarterback Joe Theismann on his halftime adjustments.[11] If something wasn't working, he threw it out. He listened carefully to his players during a game. He determined exactly what changes would create opportunities and made them.

Although Riggins ran like a deisel, it was the smaller running back Joe Washington who led the team in 1981 with 916 yards rushing and 70 receptions for 558 yards giving him a total of 1,474 yards from scrimmage. The Redskins' third back, Terry Metcalf, had 595 yards receiving. Wide receiver Art Monk had 56 receptions for 894 yards. In a few years, Monk would begin a string of 1,000 yard seasons on his way to the Hall of Fame.

1982 Season

The Washington Redskins story in 1982 was something out of Aesop's Fables. The Redskin defense was troll-like—the most miserly in football. The "hares" at running back burst forward behind the "Hogs"—Washington's fearsome offensive line. When Theismann took to the air, his receivers included the giant 6-foot-3 Art Monk and the "Smurfs," the diminutive trio of Alvin Garrett, Virgil Seay, and Charlie Brown.

The Hogs especially captured the imagination of Redskins' fandom to say nothing of adding a lot of color to the clothing, costumes, and signage found at Robert F. Kennedy Memorial Stadium (RFK Stadium). Gibbs's original Hogs were starting tackles Jacoby and Starke, guards Grimm and May, and center Bostic. Honorary Hog mention went to Fred Dean and Ron Saul along with tight ends Don Warren and Rick Walker.

A players' strike shortened the regular 1982 season to nine games and a special playoff system was devised. Based on regular season records, eight teams from each conference were seeded 1–8 and a playoff bracket design was created leading to the Super Bowl. Although kicker Mark Moseley had to fight off preseason competition in camp, his season performance was a record breaker.

In the season opener, the Redskins had their hands full in a scrappy back-and-forth match against the Philadelphia Eagles. Each quarter reflected a momentum shift with the Eagles winning the first and the third and the Redskins taking the second and fourth. At the end of regulation time, the score was tied, 34–34. The Redskins' Moseley kicked a 26-yard field goal for the 37–34 win in overtime.

The Redskins scored in the air, on defense, and with Moseley's foot to beat the Buccaneers, 21–13. Afterwards, the players' strike put the season on hold until four days before Thanksgiving. The Redskins met the Giants on November 21, 1982. Leading at the half, 21–3, the Redskins would hold on and win, 27–

17. The Eagles gave the Redskins a battle, but Gibbs's team pulled away with a 13–9 win. When the Cowboys came to RFK Stadium to play the Redskins on December 5, the Redskins fell flat and lost, 24–10. A Moseley field goal and a Theismann touchdown pass to Charlie Brown in the fourth quarter kept the score respectable. Moseley hit four field goals the following week when the Redskins beat the Cardinals in an anemic offensive display, 12–7.

The Giants came into town for the second battle of the season with the Redskins on December 19. It was a contest that helped build the NFC East's reputation for toughness. The Redskins displayed relentless aggression that wore out opponents. Many Washington fans look at this trait as the hallmark of Redskins' football.

Moseley kicked three field goals—his third set a record for 21 consecutive field goals without a miss. Joe Washington scored on a 22-yard run. Riggins topped 2,000 career carries in the victory. The Redskins won, 15–14, but it was a brutal day. Gibbs would remember Theismann's gutsy, no-quit play. Theismann was beat up by the Giants' defense. He threw four interceptions and had two teeth broken off. He stayed in and kept playing until he led the Redskins into field goal position for Moseley's final kick and the win.[12]

The Redskins continued their winning ways with a 27–10 victory over the Saints. In the final game of the regular season, the Redskins shut out the Cardinals, 28–0. Moseley was named the Associated Press Most Valuable Player in the NFL.

1982 NFC Championship Game

Washington played the Dallas Cowboys at RFK Stadium for the NFC Championship on January 23, 1983. The Redskins-Cowboys rivalry is considered to be one of the best in the NFL; the conference championship was a defining moment for Redskins football under Gibbs. The Cowboys had come off an incredible string of championships in the 1970s. During the decade, they were NFC Champions five times and Super Bowl Champions twice. They were called America's Team.

The Cowboys were East Division leaders in 1980 and 1981, but lost the conference championship in 1980 to the Eagles and lost the same title in 1981 to the 49ers. In 1982, they were determined to get back up to the top. The Redskins stood in their path.

The Cowboys scored first on a 27-yard Rafael Septien field goal. Washington advanced the ball with Riggins powering his way downfield. After Riggins softened up the defense, Joe Theismann hit Charlie Brown down the middle on a 19-yard touchdown pass. Later in the second quarter, a Cowboys' turnover gave the Redskins the ball on the Dallas 10-yard line. Four plays later, Riggins scored on a 1-yard plunge and the half ended with the Redskins leading, 14–3.

Dexter Manley knocked Cowboys' quarterback Danny White out late in the first half on an explosive sack. The Cowboys' backup, Gary Hogeboom, hit Drew Pearson on a 6-yard touchdown pass in the third quarter—the score stood Redskins 14–Cowboys 10. When Dallas kicked off, Mike Nelms ran the ball back 76 yards to the Dallas 21-yard line. Theismann threw a pass to Brown that covered most of the remaining distance and then Riggins took it in from 4 yards out.

Hogeboom hit Butch Johnson on a 23-yard touchdown pass for another third quarter score. Washington led 21–17. Moseley kicked a field goal in the fourth quarter putting the Redskins ahead, 24–17. The Cowboys had the ball deep in their own territory when a tipped Hogeboom screen pass was intercepted by Redskins' tackle Darryl Grant and run in for a score. The Redskins beat America's Team, 31–17.

Super Bowl XVII

The Redskins played Don Shula's Dolphins on January 30, 1983, at the Rose Bowl in Pasadena, California, in Super Bowl XVII. The Dolphins' David Woodley hit Jimmy Cefalo on a 76-yard touchdown pass for the dramatic first score. On Miami's next possession, Woodley was sacked and gave the ball up to Dave Butz in Miami territory at the 46-yard line. John Riggins's thundering legs moved the Redskins downfield where Moseley kicked a 31-yard field goal for the first Washington points. On the ensuing kickoff, Miami's Fulton Walker ran the ball back to midfield. Woodley moved the ball to the Washington 3-yard line and Uwe von Schamann kicked a 20-yard field goal. On Washington's next possession, Theismann advanced the ball with short passes to his receivers and runs by the unstoppable Riggins before he hit Alvin Garrett from 4 yards out for a score. Walker thrilled the fans with a 98-yard kickoff return for the Dolphins. The half ended with Miami ahead, 17–10.

In the second half, Theismann directed a successful drive that included a 44-yard pass play to Alvin Garrett and concluded with a 20-yard field goal by Moseley. The second half featured tough defense. In the fourth quarter, the Redskins faced a fourth and one from the Miami 43-yard line. Riggins broke through the line and kept running for a touchdown that gave the Redskins the lead, 20–17. Theismann orchestrated another drive—this one featured more Riggins' power runs and a 6-yard touchdown pass to Charlie Brown. The Redskins won, 27–17. Gibbs had a Super Bowl victory in his second year as head coach. His wacky running back John Riggins was Super Bowl MVP after rushing for 166 yards on 38 carries. When the Redskins' plane landed at Dulles, President Ronald Reagan and First Lady Nancy Reagan were there to welcome Gibbs and his team.

1983 Season

The Cowboys beat the Redskins in the opener in a tale of two halves. A Joe Theismann to Charlie Brown touchdown pass, three Moseley field goals, and one Riggins touchdown run gave the Redskins 23 points at the half. Dallas had 3 points from a Rafael Septien field goal. In the second half, Danny White threw two touchdown passes to Tony Hill—the first for 75 yards and the second for 51 yards. White ran one in himself to capture the lead, 24–23, and then he came back one more time to hit Doug Cosbie from 1 yard out. Theismann managed one more score for the Redskins when he hit tight end Don Warren late in the game. The Cowboys won by a paper thin 31–30 margin.

In Veterans Stadium Philadelphia, the Redskins beat the talented Eagles, a team that featured quarterback Ron Jaworski, receivers Mike Quick and Harold Carmichael, and long distance barefoot kicker Tony Franklin. The Eagles' running game was limited to a paltry 35 yards and although Jaworski threw for 326 yards, the Redskins balanced attack won the day, 23–13.

When the Redskins played the Chiefs in game three, Nick Lowery pounded the Redskins in the first half with four field goals including a 58-yard rocket. The second half was all Redskins with two Moseley field goals, a Riggins touchdown run, and Theismann scoring passes to Warren and Didier. The Redskins won by a score of 27–12.

The Redskins handled Seattle's quarterback Jim Zorn to receiver Steve Largent duo and posted a 27–17 win before facing the Raiders. In a wild and woolly one, the Redskins' Theismann and the Raiders' Plunkett each passed for over 300 yards in a close match. The game was settled late in the fourth quarter on a Theismann to Joe Washington touchdown pass. The 37–35 Redskins' win was followed by an easy 38–14 victory over the Cardinals.

Gibbs's team took their 5–1 start to Lambeau Field in Green Bay on a Monday night. Starr's Green Bay Packers were a dangerous inconsistent club that would play five overtime games that season. The Packers and Redskins gave football fans a great game that featured six lead changes. The game included two defensive scores—one by each team in the opening quarter, six field goals, and a pile of touchdowns to keep the newspaper writers hustling to file their stories on time. Lynn Dickey, the Packers' quarterback who hailed from Paola, Kansas, tossed three touchdown passes while Theismann hit two. Riggins had two rushing touchdowns while the Packers' Gary Lewis and Gerry Ellis each had one. The Packers prevailed, 48–47, to give the Redskins their second one-point loss of the season.

After the loss to the Packers, the Redskins went through the rest of the season undefeated, beating the Lions, Chargers, Cardinals, Giants, Rams, Eagles, Falcons, Cowboys, and Giants (again) to close off the regular season at 14–2.

When the Redskins faced the Rams in the divisional playoff game, they slaughtered the Los Angeles foe, 51–7. The Rams were not a strong team that year with a regular season mark of 9–7, but they had beaten Dallas in the Wild Card game.

NFC Championship

Bill Walsh had quickly built a contender in San Francisco. They had won the Super Bowl at the end of the 1981 season, Walsh's third season, but the team fell like a rock in 1982. Walsh was making significant progress in building a much stronger team in 1983 when his 49ers met the Redskins in the NFC Championship.

The Washington Redskins owned the game for the first three quarters. John Riggins scored two touchdowns on short runs. Theismann hit Charlie Brown on a 70-yard touchdown pass play. Going into the fourth quarter Washington was comfortably ahead, 21–0.

During the fourth quarter, San Francisco quarterback Joe Montana had one of his patented "in the zone" clutch performances. Montana brought the 49ers downfield in a little over a minute and tossed a short touchdown pass to Mike Wilson. Next possession, he threw a 76-yard bomb to Fred Solomon to make the score, 21–14. When the 49ers got the ball again, Montana drove the 49ers downfield and hit Wilson for a 12-yard score to tie the game at 21–21. In the waning minutes of the game, the Redskins were able to drive the ball downfield. Two penalties helped the Redskins keep their next drive alive. In the final minute of the game, Mark Moseley, who had missed four field goals during the contest, managed to kick a 25-yard field goal for the 24–21 win.

Super Bowl XVIII

On January 22, 1984, the Redskins of Joe Gibbs faced the Raiders of Tom Flores in Super Bowl XVIII. The Raiders' defense stuffed the Redskins early on and errors followed. After a couple of Riggins's rushes on their first possession, Theismann threw three incomplete passes to Monk forcing a punt from the Washington end zone. When the kick was blocked, Derrick Jensen recovered the ball in the end zone for the Raiders' first score. The Raiders led 7–0. When the Redskins got the ball back, Theismann managed to get the Redskins within marginal field goal range. Moseley missed a 47-yard attempt. The Raiders dodged a bullet on their next possession when Marcus Allen fumbled the ball and teammate Charley Hannah recovered.

After several series where the defenses held, Jim Plunkett started to make use of his great offensive stars. First he hit Branch for a 50-yard gain and then mixed it up with a Marcus Allen run before going back to Branch for a 12-yard touchdown pass. After the extra point, the Raiders were up 14–0. The Redskins responded with a long difficult drive that brought the ball down to the Raiders 7-yard line and yielded a Moseley field goal. After the next Raiders' drive stalled, in the waning moments of the half, a Redskins' screen pass from the 10-yard line was intercepted by Jack Squirek who made the short run into the end zone for the score. The Raiders led 21–3 at the half.

On the opening kickoff of the second half, Alvin Garrett ran the ball up to the 30-yard line. Theismann was much more competent on the Redskins' first drive of the second half and after a long drive, Riggins scored from the 1-yard line. Moseley's extra point attempt was blocked. The Raiders led 21–9. Greg Pruitt took the Redskins' kickoff to the 30-yard line and a few plays later, a pass interference penalty brought the ball down another third of the way. Plunkett managed to drive the final 30 yards to the end zone mostly using short passes.

Marcus Allen got the touchdown on a 5-yard run. After the extra point, the Raiders led 28–9. The defenses held for the next several series until Marcus Allen scorched the Redskins on a 74-yard first down run in the final seconds of the third quarter. In the fourth quarter, the Redskins were threatening at the Raiders 8-yard line when Theismann was sacked and he fumbled the ball away. A few series later, the Redskins fought back against another Raiders' drive that provided a first and goal at the 1-yard line. The Redskins held tight to force a field goal. The Raiders were ahead 38–9 and that's where it ended.

1984 Season

Gibbs's Redskins would take a few tumbles in 1984, but they would be back in the playoffs. After losing to the Dolphins and the 49ers in their first two games, they lined up against Bill Parcells's Giants in game three. Parcells was building a winner, but they were not quite there in 1984. The Redskins handled the Giants, 30–14, aided by an interception and a fumble both returned for touchdowns in the second half. The Washington Redskins were on a roll and easily defeated the Patriots, Eagles, Colts, and Cowboys—winning on average by over 18 points per game. They stumbled against the Cardinals and the Giants before righting themselves against Atlanta and Detroit. Leading the Eagles 10–9 after a Moseley field goal in the third quarter, the Eagles' Andre Waters ran the ensuing kickoff back for a touchdown. The Eagles' won, 16–10,—the Redskins' last defeat of the regular season. The Redskins ended the season with victories against the Bills, Vikings, Cowboys, and Cardinals.

In their divisional playoff game against the Chicago Bears, Theismann was sacked an incredible seven times. With Theismann under duress from the Bears' pass rush, Riggins scored two rushing touchdowns and Moseley kicked a field goal. The Bears' scoring started with a Bob Thomas field goal and featured a halfback pass by Walter Payton to tight end Pat Dunsmore, and a 75-yard bomb from quarterback Steve Fuller to speedster Willie Gault. Fuller hit wide receiver Dennis McKinnon for 16 yards and one more score. In the fourth quarter, Chicago punter Dave Finzer stepped out of the end zone on a punt giving the Redskins a safety. The Redskins lost, 23–19, and their season came to an end.

1985 Season

The 1985 season would be a transition year for the Redskins. First, it was Riggins's final season and his contribution would be reduced significantly. The Redskins had picked up George Rogers a Heisman Trophy winner who was identical to Riggins in size. Rogers was acquired in a trade with New Orleans. He would turn in two excellent seasons in the Washington backfield before being slowed by injury. Joe Washington was gone. It was also Joe Theismann's 12th and last season. Gibbs's third round quarterback draftee, Jay Schroeder, would start five games in 1985. Rookie wide receiver Gary

Clark would contribute immediately. The defensive line and backfield along with the offensive line were essentially the same.

In the season opener, Dallas destroyed the Redskins, 44–14, on the strength of seven turnovers. The Redskins came back in week two to nudge past the Oilers, 16–13. The Eagles beat the Redskins, 19–6, the following week in a game that featured six field goals and one touchdown. The Redskins scored 10 points early in their match against the Super Bowl bound Bears, but lost their grip thereafter. The Bears won, 45–10. The Redskins beat the Cardinals and Lions easily, but then lost to the Giants, 17–3. They beat the Browns and Falcons and then lost to the Cowboys, 13–7.

The Redskins beat the Giants in their second meeting, 23–21, but the game would be remembered as Theismann's last. Lawrence Taylor, in hot pursuit of Joe Theismann, leapt to make an extraordinary athletic grab of the quarterback as he was moving forward to avoid the rush. As Taylor was coming down, his lower body swung under Theismann's leg at an angle, breaking it badly. It was a nasty injury memorialized in gruesome detail on television.

With Schroeder starting at quarterback, the Redskins beat the Steelers, 30–23, and were clobbered, 35–8, by the 49ers. They finished the season with a three game win streak by beating the Eagles, Bengals, and Cardinals. Their 10–6 record matched the Cowboys and the Giants for the top spot in the NFC East, but Dallas had the better head-to-head record and the Giants were the NFC Wild Card team based on a better conference record. The Redskins went home.

1986 Season

Gibbs picked up running back Kelvin Bryant in the 1986 draft from North Carolina. An excellent runner and receiver, Bryant added a much-needed punch to the Redskins' offense.

The Redskins were a good team in 1986, but the New York Giants were better. The Giants beat the Redskins twice during the season. In the season opener, the Redskins beat the Eagles, 41–14, and then tallied wins against the Raiders, Chargers, Seahawks, and Saints, before they were thoroughly crushed, 30–6, by the Cowboys. The Cowboys had several marquee players including Tony Dorsett, Herschel Walker, Tony Hill, Doug Cosbie and others, but they were a few years away from their next great quarterback, Troy Aikman.

The following week, the Redskins beat the Cardinals in a come-from-behind win, 28–21. Parcells's Giants beat the Redskins, 27–20, on a Joe Morris touchdown run in the fourth quarter. The Redskins regrouped to win five in a row. An overtime win over the Vikings was followed with wins against the Packers, 49ers, Cowboys, and Cardinals. After defeats to the Giants and Broncos, the Redskins beat the Eagles 21–14 in the season finale.

The Redskins faced the Rams and Eric Dickerson in his prime in the Wild Card game.[13] Dickerson ran for 158 yards on 26 carries, but it was not enough for Los Angeles. Schroeder threw a 14-yard touchdown pass to Kelvin Bryant.

Otherwise, the Rams kept the Redskins out of the end zone, but not far enough away. Jess Atkinson kicked four field goals for Washington and the Redskins won, 19–7.

The Redskins' Wild Card win gave them the right to play the previous year's Super Bowl Champion Chicago Bears for the division. The Bears were favored to win, but Chicago's starting quarterback Jim McMahon had been knocked out for the season in week 12 and Coach Mike Ditka slotted in a young Doug Flutie into the starting role. Flutie had only thrown 46 passes that season.

Schroeder hit Art Monk on a 28-yard pass for the opening score. Flutie hit Willie Gault on a 50-yard bomb to tie things up. The Bears contained the Redskins' offense, while Flutie spent a lot of time running away from the Redskins' pass rush. The Bears' Kevin Butler kicked two field goals and it was Bears 13–Redskins 7 at the half. The Redskins' defense continued to pressure Flutie and force several mistakes from the Bears' offense in the second half. Schroeder tossed a 23-yard touchdown pass to Art Monk and George Rogers ran for another score from 1 yard out. Jess Atkinson kicked two field goals to give the Redskins a convincing, 27–13 win.

1986 NFC Championship Game

The Washington Redskins faced the hungry New York Giants in the NFC Championship game. Under Bill Parcells, the Giants advanced from doormat to top contender in four seasons. They were burned in the NFC divisional playoff game the previous season by the Bears and were no doubt thankful that the Redskins had knocked Chicago from their path. Having beaten the Redskins twice during the regular season, the Giants were familiar with Gibbs's team.

The Giants were the top defensive team against the run and had stopped the Redskins' ground game during the season. George Rogers and Kelvin Bryant were stymied again in the NFC Championship game. Schoeder was called on to make up the difference and he could not. Schroeder completed 20 passes on 50 attempts for 195 yards without a single touchdown. The Giants were surgical in their attack. Phil Simms threw just 14 passes as the Giants favored the ground game. Simms hit Lionel Manuel on an 11-yard touchdown strike and Joe Morris ran one in from 1 yard out for the Giants' two touchdowns. A Raul Allegre field goal was the only other score, giving the Giants a 17–0 win.

1987 Season

The NFL was embroiled in another players' strike in 1987. Joe Gibbs had proven himself to be a master at quick preparation and adjustment in the shortened 1982 season and he would do it again in 1987.

In the offseason, Gibbs picked up veteran quarterback Doug Williams. It would turn out to be a great, timely move. Gibbs also picked up field goal kicker Ali Haji Sheikh for a single season. Defensive back Vernon Dean and tight end Clint Didier would post their last seasons with the club.

In the opener against the Eagles, Schroeder was injured and Doug Williams stepped in to win the game, 34-24. The veteran completed 17 passes on 27 attempts for 272 yards and two touchdowns with no interceptions. On the worrisome side of the ledger, the leading ground gainer was Kelvin Bryant with 7 rushes for 32 yards. The Redskins lost the following week to the Falcons, 21–20, when they missed an extra point.

When the players' strike took place right after game two, substitute players were employed. Gibbs understood the importance of doing well during the "replacement period" and managed to assemble a top team in short order. After a brief training period, the season restarted on October 4, when the Redskins beat the Cardinals, 28–21, with their new crew of players. The following week, the replacement team slaughtered the Giants, 38–12. Gibbs's and his coaches' work was beautifully exhibited when the replacement Redskins managed to beat the Cowboys who had several of their season regulars come back for the contest.

Replacement Redskins' quarterback Ed Rubbert, who had played well in the first two replacement games, was injured early in the Cowboys' contest and replaced by another sub, Tony Robinson. Gibbs was given credit for a tremendous pregame speech extolling the game as a once in a lifetime opportunity. The exuberant players carried Gibbs off on their shoulders after their 13-7 win!

After the game against the Cowboys, the Strike ended, but Washington's success during the period helped inspire a popular movie called "The Replacements" that was loosely (or perhaps very loosely) based on the Washington season. Gibbs would remember his replacement team with great fondness.

The regulars returned to play the Jets on October 25 and won 17–16 and continued winning the following week when they beat the Bills, 27–7. In the second half of the season, they lost to the Eagles, Rams, and Dolphins making their replacement wins critical for making the playoffs. Down the stretch they beat the Lions, Giants, Cardinals, and Cowboys. The last game of the season against the Vikings was played like a championship match with the Redskins winning on a field goal in overtime. Doug Williams came in to spark the Redskins' offense and he was selected as the starter going into the playoffs.

When the Redskins met up with the Bears on January 10, 1988, for the division playoff game, it was a frigid day in Chicago's Soldier Field. The Bears scored the first two touchdowns with Jim McMahon leading the team in what would turn out to be Hall of Fame bound Walter Payton's last game. In the second quarter, Doug Williams brought the Redskins back with two scores.

The decisive play came in the third quarter when the Redskins' gifted cornerback Darrell Green ran a punt back for 52 yards and a touchdown. Green had legendary speed and with a leaping side step hurdle avoided a tackle at the beginning of the run that gave him enough room to accelerate around other tacklers. Bears' quarterback Jim McMahon tried to get back on track, but the best the Bears could accomplish was a Kevin Butler field goal from 25 yards out. McMahon had three interceptions and was sacked five times, but his most painful moment came when he was picked off in the end zone with less than 10 minutes to go in the game. It was the Bears' second post season defeat at the hands of the Gibbs's Redskins and Bears Coach Mike Ditka summed the game up in his usual direct fashion:

> We had numerous opportunities today, but that's old hat. The Redskins just played well and beat us.[14]

The 21–17 Redskins' victory advanced Gibbs team to another National Football Conference Championship game for the fourth time in his career. This time he faced the Vikings.

1987 NFC Championship Game

After eking out a tough overtime victory over the Vikings just a few weeks earlier, Gibbs knew he would have a battle in the NFC Championship game. In fact, Gibbs believed that the Vikings were "playing the best ball in the league."[15] Doug Williams opened up the scoring with a 42-yard touchdown pass to Kelvin Bryant. Vikings' quarterback Wade Wilson spent much of his time peppering passes around the tough Redskins' defense that would not yield much to the running game. He hit Leo Lewis for a 23-yard touchdown pass to tie the game in the second quarter. In the second half, both teams scored field goals and the game was deadlocked into the fourth quarter. In the fourth quarter, Williams led the Redskins downfield in seven plays. On the eighth play of the series, he hit Gary Clark on a 7-yard touchdown pass to take the lead. The Vikings came back. In the waning moments of the game, Wilson drove his team to the Redskins' 7-yard line and faced a fourth down with seconds remaining. The entire season came down to one play. Gibbs fell to his knees and with his hands on his hips watched the action. Wade Wilson dropped back and fired the ball to running back Darrin Nelson who was breaking left towards the sideline at the front edge of the end zone. With Darrell Green in tight coverage, the ball passed through Nelson's hands. The Redskins won, 17–10, and advanced to another Super Bowl.

Super Bowl XXII

The Washington Redskins played the Denver Broncos on January 31, 1988, in Super Bowl XXII at Jack Murphy Stadium in San Diego, California. To insure a good night's rest, Gibbs pulled his team out of their existing hotel and moved them into the Lawrence Welk Resort for a quiet night.[16] Gibbs's starting quarterback, Doug Williams, was a big story—the first African

American signal caller to start in an NFL championship game. Another Redskins' story line was running back Timmy Smith starting in place of George Rogers who was slowed by several injuries during the season. The Broncos were coached by Dan Reeves whose mentor was Tom Landry of the Cowboys. Reeves had quarterback John Elway who could run away from pass rushers for big yards and he could throw a football like Nolan Ryan pitched baseballs.

The Redskins took the opening kickoff, but they went three and out. Wide receiver Gary Clark dropped a soft third down pass that was followed by a Steve Cox punt. The Broncos took over on their own 44-yard line. On first down, Elway hit Ricky Nattiel flying down the sideline for a 56-yard touchdown pass. One more Redskins' series ended quickly after another third down pass was dropped. After Cox's second punt, the Broncos took over on their own 32. Elway passed to Mark Jackson across the middle for a 32-yard gain. On the next snap, running back Steve Sewell took a handoff from Elway and passed it back to his quarterback who caught the ball and made his way to the 13-yard line. In two plays, the Broncos were 55 yards further downfield, but Washington's defense dug in. On third and three, Elway was tackled behind the line at the Washington 7-yard line on a delay designed for Elway to run. The Broncos settled for a field goal.

In addition to the dropped passes, the Redskins were struggling with the Broncos use of a 4–3 defensive alignment rather than their traditional 3–4. Reeves's changeup was causing problems with the Redskins' offensive line. After Gibbs talked to his offensive line, he noted that some adjustments on their part could bottle up the defenders and open things up for the Redskins.[17] The adjustments were made.

Washington dodged a bullet on the ensuing kickoff when the Redskins' Ricky Sanders fumbled the ball and it was picked up by teammate Ravin Caldwell. The Redskins moved the ball up to midfield, but they were not able to get within field goal distance and punted the ball back to Denver. Elway gained 42 yards in three plays, but after a couple of incomplete passes, he was sacked for an 18-yard loss by Alvin Walton. Mike Horan was called in to punt and put the Redskins back at their 16-yard line. Again Washington moved the ball, but another dropped pass on third down killed off a drive. Williams left the game for a few plays when he hurt his knee, but he would be back in for the next series. A few minutes later when Washington had the ball again on the 20-yard line, Doug Williams connected with Ricky Sanders for an 80-yard touchdown pass on first down. After the extra point, the game stood at 10–7.

Elway was under pressure in the second quarter and the Denver offense was sputtering while Williams and the Redskins' offense were at their best. When the Redskins got the ball back after a Denver three and out, Williams hit Don Warren for 9 yards and running backs Smith and Bryant moved the ball up another 28 yards on the ground. Hot handed Williams hit Clark who made a diving catch at the front of the end zone for 27 yards and another touchdown.

The Redskins were up 14–10. Gibbs's offense was effective and his defense was getting a handle on Elway.

On Denver's next possession, Elway tossed a shovel pass to Winder who brought the ball down to the Denver 45-yard line. Elway ran the ball himself to the 26-yard line. A few missed passes stopped the Broncos and a failed field goal attempt followed. With the ball back in Williams's hands, he hit Gary Clark for 16 yards down the middle. A few seconds later, Timmy Smith dashed downfield for a 58-yard score. Washington led, 21–10. It got worse for Denver. On the next Washington possession, Williams hit Sanders for a 50-yard score. Elway was pressing when he tossed an interception to lanky defensive back Barry Wilburn who had smothered a much smaller Ricky Nattiel on the coverage. Washington moved the ball again on their next series and Williams hit his tight end, Clint Didier, for another score. In the second quarter, Williams completed 9 of 11 passes for 228 yards and four touchdowns. The first half ended with Washington in the lead, 35–10.

Mercifully, both defenses dug in for the second half and the Redskins scored just one more touchdown for a 42–10 slaughter.

Doug Williams completed 18 passes on 29 attempts for 340 yards with four touchdowns and one interception. He broke the Super Bowl record for passing yards and touchdowns. The first African American quarterback to start in a championship game was named Super Bowl XXII MVP. Timmy Smith, an unheralded running back, rushed for 204 yards—another Super Bowl record. Ricky Sanders had 9 receptions for 193 yards. On the other side, Elway was pressing after the Redskins had jumped out ahead and the Broncos as a team gained just 97 yards on the ground. Two years later, the Broncos would lose yet another Super Bowl, but Elway would win two in a row with the Broncos in 1998 and 1999.

1988-1990 Seasons

The Redskins suffered from a post Super Bowl Season let down in 1988. Jay Schroeder had moved on to the Raiders. But just as Doug Williams had a clear path to the starting role, he injured his back. As the season wore on, Gibbs prepared for Mark Rypien to be his future starting quarterback.

Bill Parcells's Giants beat the Redskins, 27–20, in the first game of the season. The Redskins beat the Steelers and Eagles only to take it on the chin against the Cardinals, and the Giants again. After beating a weak Cowboys team, Gibbs's team knocked off the Cardinals. They beat the Green Bay Packers with a fourth quarter field goal by new kicker Chip Lohmiller. Jerry Glanville's Oilers took the Redskins to task, 41–17. The Redskins beat a good New Orleans Saints team before losing to the Bears, 49ers, and Browns. They beat the Eagles, but lost to the Cowboys and Bengals. Their 7–9 record marked Gibbs's first losing season

The Redskins bounced back in 1989. Losing to the Giants and Eagles to begin the season, they came back to beat the Cowboys, Saints, and Cardinals. Then the Giants beat them again.

On October 22, 1989, in one of the most exciting games, the Redskins kept the talented Vinny Testaverde of the Tampa Bay Buccaneers frustrated for three quarters. The Redskins held a 29–7 lead going into the fourth quarter. In the opening minute of the fourth quarter, Testaverde hit Lars Tate for a 10-yard touchdown and on their next series he hit Bruce Hill for a 20-yard touchdown pass making the score, Redskins 29–Buccaneers 21. Rypien managed to lead a long time-consuming drive that ended in Lohmiller's third field goal. With Washington up 32–21, Testaverde led one more scoring drive for a close 32–28 finish. The Tampa game illustrated Gibbs's propensity for having his teams jump out to a big lead and then challenge their opponents to attempt to come back.

The Redskins dropped games to the Raiders and Cowboys. After beating the Eagles, the Broncos handed the Redskins their last loss of the season. The Redskins won their last five games, knocking off the Bears, Cardinals, Chargers, Falcons, and Seahawks. They ended the season, 10–6, for third place in the NFC East.

Doug Williams, the Super Bowl XXII MVP, had been banged up badly and although he wanted to continue in Washington, Joe Gibbs would not pick him up for the 1990 season. Rypien was the number one quarterback with 25-year old Stan Humphries as the top backup and veteran Jeff Rutledge the 7-year Giants' veteran as their number three man. The Redskins began the 1990 season by shutting out the Cardinals 31–0. They lost to the 49ers and then beat an improving Cowboys' team before man-handling the Cardinals again. After losing to the Giants, 24–20, the Redskins beat the Eagles, 13–7, and then took their lumps from the Giants again, 21–10. Halfway through the season on November 4, they won a wild overtime shootout with the Detroit Lions, 41–38. The second half of the season produced mixed results. They lost to the Eagles, Cowboys, and Colts while beating the Saints, Dolphins, Bears, Patriots, and Bills.

The Redskins moved past the Eagles, 20–6, in the Wildcard game—their third meeting that year. They faced the San Francisco 49ers in the division match. The Redskins managed a 31-yard Rypien-to-Monk touchdown pass and a Lohmiller 44-yard field goal in the first quarter. After that it was all 49ers who went on to win, 28–10. Gibbs's Redskins were 10–6 for the regular season scoring 381 points and giving up 301. Earnest Byner who had come over from Cleveland in 1989, had gained 1,219 yards rushing and 279 receiving. Rypien had a healthy quarterback rating of 78.4 while passing for over 2,000 yards with 16 touchdowns and 11 interceptions.

1991 Season

In his 11th season, Gibbs and his Redskins would once again work their way into the Super Bowl. Gibbs had three quarterbacks at the helm in his four Super Bowl contests: Theismann in 1982 and 1983, Doug Williams in 1987, and now Rypien in 1991. The Redskins won their first 11 contests. Their first loss came on November 24, when the Cowboys nipped them, 24–21. They got back on track with three straight wins and then stumbled in the last game, losing, 24–22, to the Eagles in essentially what was an exhibition game for them. They beat the Falcons, 24–7, in the divisional match with the Falcons turning the ball over six times.

NFC Championship

The Redskins smashed the Lions, 41–10, in the NFC Championship game. Running back Gerald Riggs, who came to Washington from Atlanta in 1989, ran for two touchdowns and Rypien threw for two more hitting Clark and Monk for one apiece. Redskins' Darrell Green ran an interception back for a touchdown as well. The Lions' Erik Kramer hit Willie Green for one touchdown. Eddie Murray kicked one field goal for the Lions and Lohmiller kicked two field goals for the Redskins.

Super Bowl XXVI

In Super Bowl XXVI, the Redskins played the Buffalo Bills on January 26, 1992, at the Hubert H. Humphrey Metrodome in Minneapolis, Minnesota. Like the Redskins, the Bills piled up the wins in 1991 and finished at 13–3. They beat the Broncos in the AFC Championship Game. They had a no-huddle offense, a fine quarterback in Jim Kelly to run it, and the league leading rusher in Thurman Thomas.

The first quarter was sloppy. After several frustrating series, the Redskins put together a good drive that featured Rypien passes to Monk. But with first and goal at the Buffalo 2-yard line, the Redskins were pushed back and the Bills took over on their own 10-yard line. Jim Kelly threw a pass that was intercepted by Brad Edwards at the 10-yard line, but a subsequent Rypien pass was intercepted by Kirby Jackson that gave the ball back at the Bills' 11-yard line.

The Bills moved the ball to midfield with Jim Kelly passing to Andre Reed and James Lofton, but the drive stalled there. The Redskins moved the ball into field goal range and Lohmiller delivered when the drive stalled. The Bills could not move the ball when they were deep in their own territory and they had a poor punt that gave the ball back to the Redskins at the Washington 49-yard line. Byner ran for 6 yards and Monk and Clark caught passes that brought the ball to the Bills' 21-yard line. When Rypien was roughed, the Redskins had the ball on the 11-yard line. After Byner ran for a yard, he caught a Rypien pass for the first touchdown of the game. The Redskins led, 10–0.

On the next Buffalo series, Kelly was intercepted by Darrell Green. The Redskins took over on the Buffalo 45-yard line. Rypien hit Clark on a 34-yard pass play. Ricky Ervins gained 14 yards on the ground to set up a 1-yard plunge by Riggs for another touchdown. The Redskins were up, 17–0.

Neither team could sustain a drive for the remainder of the first half. When the Bills took over on the 20-yard line after the opening kickoff in the second half, Jim Kelly threw an interception to Kurt Gouveia who brought the ball to the Buffalo 2-yard line. Gerald Riggs ran it in from there and the Redskins were up, 24–0.

After all his frustrations, Kelly finally had an excellent drive that brought the ball down to the Redskins 3-yard line, but it stalled out and the Bills settled for a Scott Norwood field goal. The Bills held the Redskins on their next possession. When the Bills took over, Kelly drove the Bills downfield. A pass interference call against the Redskins gave the Bills a first and goal from the 1-yard line. Thurman Thomas took it in for a score. After the extra point, the Redskins led, 24–10.

After the ensuing kickoff, the Redskins took over on their 21-yard line and Rypien put together another scoring drive. It was not easy. The Redskins had to convert three third downs with the final one yielding a 30-yard touchdown pass from Rypien to Clark. The Redskins led, 31–10.

Kelly was being harassed by the Redskins' defense that had neutralized the Bills running back Thurman Thomas. On second down at the Buffalo 22-yard line, Kelly was sacked and he fumbled the ball to Fred Stokes. As the fourth quarter opened and the Redskins' drive stalled, Lohmiller kicked his second field goal. Kelly continued to press, and he tossed another interception that led to Lohmiller's third field goal. The Redskins led, 37–10.

The Bills did not give up. In a sixteen play drive in which Kelly overcame a big penalty and five incompletions, a pass to tight end Pete Metzelaars gave the Bills another score. It was Redskins 34–Bills 17. A successful onside kick gave Kelly the ball again. A 10-play drive ended in another Buffalo score—this time with Kelly tossing a 4-yard pass to Don Beebe. The score stood at Redskins 37–Buffalo 24 with time running out. Again, Buffalo attempted an onside kick, but this time the Redskins recovered at midfield and used up almost all the clock before Buffalo took over at their own 24-yard line with seconds remaining and a 10-point deficit. Backup quarterback Frank Reich came in for the final play and threw an incomplete pass to Kenneth Davis. Gibbs won his third Super Bowl—this one by a score of 37-24.

Joe Gibbs Racing

Joe Gibbs had built and raced dragsters in college. He had an interest in auto racing for many years and it was a sport that would allow him to work with his sons, J.D. and Coy, and build a different kind of team. Like their father, the sons have football roots. J.D. Gibbs played at William and Mary and Coy Gibbs played at Stanford. Joe Gibbs had friends in racing and he created a NASCAR team in 1992. Gibbs viewed racing as a sport similar to football in that it requires bringing an excellent group of people together and creating the right chemistry to win. His team, Joe Gibbs Racing, has an impressive history of managing several of the best drivers in the business and winning races.

1992 Season

Rypien was back at quarterback for the Redskins in 1992. He performed well, but not nearly as well as the previous Super Bowl MVP season in 1991. The offense slipped from one of the top in the league to middle of the road, while the defense was still good, but not superior. Rypien's touchdowns dropped from 28 to 13 and his interceptions rose from 11 to 17.

In the opener against the Cowboys, the Cowboys scored in many ways. A Washington punt was blocked out of the end zone for a safety. Emmitt Smith scored on a short run; Dallas quarterback Troy Aikman hit Alvin Harper on a 26-yard pass for a score; and Kelvin Martin scored on a 79-yard punt return. For the Redskins, Rypien hit Gary Clark for a 30-yard score and Lohmiller kicked a 49-yard field goal. Dallas beat Washington, 23–10.

The Redskins pulled themselves together and beat the Falcons and the Lions before they had a bye week. When they returned, they lost to the Cardinals and then beat the Broncos, Eagles, and Vikings. When they played the Giants in RFK Stadium, running back Brian Mitchell scored the Redskins' only touchdown of the game on an 84-yard punt return. The Giants won, 24–7. The Redskins beat Seattle and then lost convincingly to the Chiefs and the Saints. Gibbs believed that in order to do well in a season, a team needed to avoid losing streaks. After the Redskins beat the Cardinals, Giants, and Cowboys, they lost close contests to the Eagles and the Raiders.

Their 9–7 record was good enough to get them a Wild Card game with the Vikings. The Vikings scored first on a 1-yard run by Terry Allen, but the Redskins took over from there. A Lohmiller 44-yard field goal was the first strike for the Redskins. Byner and Mitchell rushed for touchdowns and then Rypien hit Clark for the final score of the game. The Redskins advanced by beating the Vikings, 24–7.

In the division playoff game against San Francisco, the Redskins slowed the 49ers, but they could not put up enough points to win. Steve Young hit wide receiver John Taylor for the first score. Then Washington's Lohmiller and San Francisco's Mike Cofer swapped field goals. Young hit Brent Jones for the 49ers second touchdown. Lohmiller kicked another field goal for the Redskins and the score stood at 17–6 in favor of San Francisco at the end of the third quarter. Rypien himself scored on a 1-yard run, but Mike Cofer kicked another field goal to put the 49ers ahead for good at 20–13.

Gibbs's First Retirement

After a difficult season in 1992, an exhausted Joe Gibbs retired. The nucleus of the Super Bowl team was still on the roster, but Gibbs had been diagnosed with diabetes and he decided to call it quits. Richie Petitbon was named the new head coach. But Gibbs never did lose interest in football. He and a group of investors attempted to buy the Washington Redskins in 1998, but were unsuccessful. He ended up owning a 5% stake in the Atlanta Falcons.

Gibbs Returns to Football

Gibbs was still tuned into the Redskins over a decade after his retirement from football. He ached to coach again although he had been somewhat leery of the challenge after his long absence. The current Redskins' owner, Dan Snyder, wanted Gibbs to return and he did not give up. Gibbs agreed to a lucrative 5-year contract with agreement from Snyder that he could bring together his old coaching staff. Gibbs had established a coaching camaraderie that lasted decades. When he came back to coach in 2004, he brought back his old friends and a few new faces as well. His son J.D. joked about the return of Gibbs "Space Cowboys," a reference to a Clint Eastwood movie in which a retired engineer who must rescue a failing satellite brings back his old teammates to accompany him on his mission.[18]

2004 Season

The Redskins had only made the playoffs one season since Gibbs had retired. When Gibbs returned for the 2004 season, Washington fans had high hopes, but the Redskins needed an improved roster. In the draft, they picked up tight end Chris Cooley and defensive back Sean Taylor who would provide some help, but during Gibbs's second stint with the Redskins, he did not have the player acquisition talent that he enjoyed previously. The 2004 season was forgettable or at least it was one that most Washington fans would like to forget. After a 16–10 win over Tampa, the Redskins lost four games in a row. The Giants, Cowboys, Browns, and Ravens collected the wins in this stretch. Gibbs hated losing streaks, but it would not be the last one that painful season. After beating the Bears, 13–10, the Redskins lost to the Packers and beat the Lions in Detroit. Another losing streak followed. The Bengals, Eagles, and Steelers collected wins in this stretch. For the first 12 games, the Redskins had not scored 20 points in a single game. However their defense, coached by Gregg Williams, was one of the top in the league.

The Redskins went on to beat the Giants, 31–7. The Giants were in the middle of an eight-game losing streak. The Redskins lost to the Eagles for the second time that season. They beat the 49ers, lost to the Cowboys and then won their last game of the season over the Vikings. It was a muddle, but Gibbs's 6–10 record was an improvement over the previous season's 5–11 mark. It was also a tough season for two other legendary coaches. Tom Coughlin's Giants went 6–10 as did Bill Parcells's Cowboys.

2005 Season

In the 2005 draft, Washington picked up defensive back Carlos Rogers and a big promising quarterback Jason Campbell. After beating the Chicago Bears to open the season, the Redskins played a Monday night game against their archrival, the Dallas Cowboys. Dallas led, 13–0, into the fourth quarter, but when quarterback Mark Brunell connected with Santana Moss on a 39-yard touchdown pass, the Redskins were back in the game. The Redskins held the Cowboys on the next drive, and Brunell hit Moss on a 70-yard touchdown for a Washington win, 14–13. The following week, when the Redskins beat the Seahawks in overtime, the season looked bright.

The tables turned when the Redskins lost six of eight games giving the fans a mathematical possibility to consider, but little hope of any playoff action. Remarkably, they won the last five games of the season and their 10–6 record was good enough for a Wild Card spot. In the Wild Card game against Tampa Bay, Redskins' running back Clinton Portis dove into the end zone from 6 yards out for the first score. Defensive back Sean Taylor intercepted a pass and scored the second Redskins' touchdown. The Buccaneers grew tougher as the game wore on, but the Redskins outlasted them, 17–10, to move on to the divisional match against the Seahawks.

Seattle's skilled quarterback, Matt Hasselbeck, led the top offense in the league against the Redskins' excellent defense. The first quarter featured defensive stops and punts. Early in the second quarter, the Seahawks' Jimmy Williams muffed a punt and the Redskins got close enough for a field goal by John Hall. Hasselbeck brought the ball downfield 70 yards on a successful drive that culminated in a 29-yard touchdown pass to Darrell Jackson. Seattle led 7–3 at the half.

Early in the third quarter, Hasselbeck led an 81-yard drive that he finished with a quarterback keeper to score from the 6-yard line. Early in the fourth quarter, Seattle's Josh Brown kicked a 33-yard field goal to pad the Seattle lead, 17–3. A 52-yard pass play from Brunell to his tight end, Chris Cooley, helped fire up another Redskins' drive. The drive finished with Mark Brunell hitting Santana Moss on a 20-yard scoring pass. After John Hall's extra point, the Redskins were within a touchdown with the Seahawks ahead, 17–10. Hall recovered a fumble on the kickoff, but the Redskins could not take advantage of the turnover. The final scoring play of the game was a Josh Brown 31-yard field goal. The Seahawks won, 20–10. Absent throughout the two post season games was a solid contribution of Clinton Portis who had played well for the Redskins throughout the regular season, but was injured in the post season. Gibbs found the Seattle loss troubling and determined to take steps to improve his offensive production for the following season.

2006 Season

Al Saunders, who like Gibbs had worked under Don Coryell, was named Assistant Coach-Offense for the 2006 season. Coming from Kansas City, Saunders had established a more complicated modern offense that placed more emphasis on the pass, albeit short passes. Blocking schemes were also different and the players had difficulty making the adjustment. Some considered the new program an abandonment of Gibbs's power football. Gibbs believed his Redskins needed a complete offensive overhaul.[19]

Much was going on that season. Starting quarterback Mark Brunell was under pressure to master a new complex offensive system. An excellent new untested quarterback who cost the Redskins dearly, Jason Campbell, was getting experience. A third quarterback, Todd Collins, knew Saunders's system, but was considered a backup to Brunell and Campbell.

Gibbs had always done things fast. He was not the kind of coach who thought in terms of 4 or 5 year plans. Every year was a new beginning and a new opportunity to win. Although he was plugging in a new complicated offense, he wanted immediate results.

In 2006, Washington fans were looking for a great season based on the strong 2005 finish, but they were disappointed. The defense struggled and the offense did not meet expectations. The 2006 Washington Redskins finished the season 5–11, a drop from 10–6 in 2005. They scored 307 points and allowed 376 from the opposition. They were ranked towards the bottom of the league on defense and on a good day, their offense was average to mediocre. They only won two games against teams with winning records.

Having an excellent new untested quarterback on the roster, Jason Campbell, led to a quarterback controversy in Washington when the offense was underperforming that season.

Opening on Monday night against the Vikings, the Redskins struggled to control the Viking passing game. In the opening drive, Viking quarterback Brad Johnson drove his team 80 yards downfield to score in 11 plays. The Vikings missed a two-point conversion attempt. The Redskins were able to drive downfield on their possession, but they came up 3 yards short of the end zone on a third down and John Hall kicked a field goal. On their second series in the second quarter, the Redskins were able to drive the ball down for a score on a short run by Clinton Portis. Later in the same quarter, Brunell connected on a 43-yard pass play to Santana Moss to the Vikings' 6-yard line, but again he could not get the ball into the end zone and settled for another field goal. Right before the half, the Vikings' kicker, Ryan Longwell, kicked a 46-yard field goal. The Redskins led, 13–9.

Johnson hit wide receiver Marcus Robinson for a Viking touchdown in the third quarter. When another Redskins' drive stalled at the 3-yard line, John Hall kicked another field goal and the game was tied at 16–16. The defenses played tough in the fourth quarter, but the Vikings' Ryan Longwell kicked a 31-yard field goal for the final points of the game. The Vikings won, 19–16.

In an otherwise painful 27–10 loss to Dallas on the following Sunday night, Redskins' fullback Rock Cartwright ran a kick off back 100 yards for a score. The Redskins snagged their first win of the season by defeating the Houston Texans, 31–15. Brunell was 24 of 27 for 261 yards. When Brunell completed his first 22 pass attempts in the game, he set a new record for consecutive completed passes. In assessing Brunell's performance, Gibbs said:

You can't do much better than he did today. He threw everything pinpoint and made some very good plays. You could kind of see in Mark that he's a great competitor.[20]

The Redskins beat the Jaguars, 36–30, the following week in overtime, but their two-game winning streak would be the season high watermark. For the remaining 12 games of the season, they would win three and lose nine. The Redskins displayed weaknesses throughout the season, but for Gibbs, the chief weakness was fundamental.

By mid-season 2006, Gibbs determined that his team had lost its identity. He had supported Al Saunders and his new offensive program, but after the Tampa Bay Buccaneers beat the Redskins on November 19 by a score of 20–17, Gibbs was disturbed. He had put Jason Campbell in at quarterback prior to the Tampa game, but he saw that more was needed. He could see that in the transition to a new offense, the Redskins had lost their identity as a tough hardnosed relentless running team. He called the team, the coaches, and the administrative staff together and he reflected on how the competition saw the Redskins as soft and that they were no longer feared and respected. In response to this, he told the entire Redskins' staff that things were going to change:

If we lose, we're going to lose our way. We're going to play Redskins' football. Redskins' football means being tough. It means if we're on the goal line, we're going to pound it at them four times. And if they stop us, then good for them. They were better than us. But this is how we're going to play.[21]

Gibbs went about toughening up his Redskins with vigorous full contact practices. Adjustments were made and the Redskins began looking more like Gibbs's Redskins as the season came to an end. In the final game of the season, the Redskins gave the Giants everything they had, showing a toughness that was not on display earlier in the season. Nevertheless, Gibbs's team came up short. The Giants won, 34–28.

2007 Season

The Redskins went 9–7 in 2007. They scored 334 and allowed 310 points from the opposition. They were middle of the pack on passing defense and great at stopping the run. On offense, they had improved their rushing game to be one of the best, but they were struggling to improve their passing performance.

Brunell had moved on. Jason Campbell was the number one quarterback with Todd Collins backing him up. Clinton Portis was back at full strength.

The Redskins struggled with the Miami Dolphins in their opener, but managed to win in overtime, 16–13. They beat the Eagles, 20–12, but then lost to the Giants, 24–17. In their game with the Giants, the Redskins led 17–0 at the half, but fell apart in the second half. Yet, they still had a chance to tie the game in the final minute. After Campbell spiked the ball on first down on the 1-yard line to collect his team, the Redskins were stuffed on three downs as the seconds ticked away. On second down, Campbell's pass to Mike Sellers was dropped. Then on two conservative running plays, Ladell Betts went nowhere and the Redskins had the kind of loss that would sting. All through the previous season, they had difficulty getting into the end zone with Saunders's new offense. They had the same problem, but this time playing Gibbs's power football. The Giants on the other hand had a win that would help propel them to a championship season.

Going into Philadelphia on November 11, the Redskins were 5–3 and it looked like they had a chance to make the playoffs, but then they lost four games in a row. Tragedy struck the team on November 27, 2007, when Washington free safety Sean Taylor died from gunshot wounds that he had received in an invasion of his home the day before. Taylor was one of the finest players on the Redskins and his loss was felt deeply on the team. Gibbs stepped in and helped his team come to grips with the death and he necessarily redirected the team's focus so they could finish the season.

When the Redskins played Buffalo on December 2, a special tribute to Taylor was given by the players. As the Bills prepared to run their first play, the man who replaced Taylor, Reed Doughty, stood on the field, but outside the action. It was the Redskins' way of symbolically getting their fallen comrade Sean Taylor back on the field. "We were going to let him ride with us one more time," said Coach Gregg Williams, who described Taylor as being like a son to him.[22]

When Chicago came into town on December 6, Washington was 5–7. Todd Collins came on in relief of an injured Campbell to win the game, 24–16. Collins had played on Saunders's Kansas City Chiefs and he knew the coach's complex system. Collins led the Redskins to three more wins to improve the Redskins' season record to 9–7, which was good enough for the wild card game against Seattle on January 5, 2008.

The Wild Card game began with several uneventful series. About midway through the first quarter, Nate Burleson returned a Redskins' punt that gave Hasselbeck the ball on the Washington 45-yard line. The Seahawks' quarterback completed a few short passes before Leonard Weaver galloped 17 yards for a touchdown. Early in the second quarter, the Seahawks' Josh Brown kicked a 50-yard field goal. Defense prevailed on both sides of the ball until well into the third quarter. It was another field goal by Brown, this one from 33 yards that started the scoring again.

On a 12-play scoring drive, Todd Collins got the Redskins back in the hunt when he hit Antwaan Randle El on a 7-yard touchdown pass early in the fourth quarter. After the extra point, the Seahawks had the lead, 13–7. LaRon Landry intercepted a Hasselbeck pass that gave the Redskins the ball on the Seahawks' 42-yard line. A 30-yard pass from Collins to Santana Moss scored the Redskins' second touchdown. When Shaun Suisham kicked the extra point, the Redskins led, 14–13. The Seahawks scored next after taking over on the 42-yard line of Washington. Hasselbeck hit D.J. Hackett for a 20-yard score. After making the two-point conversion with a Hasselbeck-to-Marcus Pollard pass, the Seahawks were ahead by a touchdown at 21–14. With just under six minutes to go, a long downfield pass by Collins was intercepted by Marcus Trufant who ran it back 78 yards for another score. In three minutes time, the Redskins had lost their one-point lead and found themselves behind, 28–14. With less than a minute to go, Jordan Babineaux intercepted another pass by Collins and returned it 57 yards for another Seattle touchdown. The Seahawks won by a final score of 35–14 in what had been a close game with seven minutes remaining.

Gibbs Retires

Gibbs seemed more inclined to leave coaching as the Redskins' season had wore on. He announced his retirement after the Seattle game. Gibbs felt a tug to a more controlled existence that would allow him to spend more time with his family. Despite the fact that he had set up an outstanding coaching staff with veteran assistant coaches to lead both the offense and defense, he found himself pulled again to long hours and a separation from his family during the season. Gibbs had made progress in developing a team with Saunders's more modern and complex offense. But Gibbs had put his own stamp on it and it was still a work-in-progress. The Redskins had shown themselves to be a contender and Jason Campbell certainly seemed poised to take them further in the future. Gibbs, at owner Dan Snyder's urging, agreed to continue with the club in some limited capacity as a consultant. Gibbs said at the time:

I think we've got a lot of pieces in place. I personally want to be a part of that. I want to see it finished. ... Our fans deserve championships. I want to be a part of seeing that come to fruition.[23]

Life after Football

Gibbs is perhaps the perfect example of someone who leaves a job without abandoning his passion. Always busy with efforts on behalf of his faith and sports interests, Gibbs's life expanded rather than contracted. While in his first

Redskins' coaching stint, he created his NASCAR Team in which he involved family and friends. With a staff of several hundred, his NASCAR team members are just as passionate about racing success as football players, coaches, owners, and their administrators are about their team's success. Gibbs continues to surround himself with exceptional people and extraordinary competition.

Gibbs continues to work with the Youth for Tomorrow program that he developed in 1986. This foster care home and private school for troubled children in Bristow, Virginia, provides safe and healthy residences, high school education, and therapy for boys and girls ages 12-18.

Gibbs's faith has led to other activities as well. His Game Plan for Life program uses books and other media to share Gibbs thoughts on both defining and achieving success. He has also written books on his football and racing careers. He is a speaker known for motivational presentations.

Gibbs's success has brought great wealth, but Gibbs's personal legacy includes an honest assessment of himself as both a coach and man. While Gibbs was succeeding as few have in football, he was also struggling with priorities. Quiet in some ways, serious in others, Gibbs is purposefully devout. His great confidence exudes from a faith that centers and directs most every move in his life. Yet Gibbs also uses a liberal dose of self deprecating humor that casts a passionate human quality to most everything he does.

A self admitted job junkie, who readily admits and regrets his "neglect" of family, Gibbs and his wife have established a wonderful family—although his wife was unduly burdened at times. Upon returning from the hospital after a serious operation, Pat Gibbs found a mountain of dirty clothes. Always able to adjust to changing circumstances, Joe Gibbs kept his boys in clean clothes during his wife's time in the hospital by filling their closets with new purchases rather than running the washing machine and dryer![24]

Joe Gibbs's Contributions to the Game

In Gibbs's first 12-season stretch as Redskins' coach, he led his team to three Super Bowl victories and four NFC Championships. His Redskins made the playoffs an incredible 8 times in 12 years. In Gibbs's second stretch, from 2004-2007, he had two teams make the playoffs. In both cases, the Redskins were eliminated by the Seattle Seahawks.

Gibbs's first record as the Washington head coach was 124–60–0 with a 16–5 mark in post season. His .683 winning percentage was third best behind Vince Lombardi and John Madden. Reflecting his second seasons with the Redskins, he was 154–94–0 and 17–7 in playoff play. His winning percentage is .621. Gibbs was enshrined in the Pro Football Hall of Fame in 1996. He was named AP Coach of the Year twice, Sporting News Coach of the Year three times, Pro Football Weekly Coach of the Year twice, and UPI Coach of the Year once.

Gibbs was a remarkable coach. When he began his job with the Redskins, he had ambitions about mounting an explosive passing attack like Don Coryell's

Joe Gibbs at Ease

at San Diego. When it did not work with the existing Washington personnel, Gibbs took stock of his talent and put together a power running game. He did not have San Diego's tremendous passer Dan Fouts; he had John Riggins. Gibbs was not a theoretical genius; he was a practical one. His innovations were hatched to meet needs.

Gibbs adjusted his offensive attack to take advantage of Riggins's strengths. He also adjusted for Riggins's weakness—he was not a blocker. An extra tight end on the line could help take of care of a superior pass rusher. He worked on various formations that would find open men for his passers. His high-energy, tireless approach to coaching was perhaps most productive in the long hours of the night working out game plans with his tight-knit staff. Gibbs's efforts were most visible on the playing field where his Redskins manhandled the opposition. Gibbs did not put together perfect seasons, but no season was without hope. Some Redskins' teams were written off as failures, only to resurrect at midseason or later. Whether in a season or a game, the Redskins were never done until the final whistle. Gibbs's teams demonstrated this again and again.

Gibbs was able to get along with most everyone including his bosses Jack Kent Cooke and Daniel Snyder. He showed his bosses an honest respect and required the same back. Gibbs was also cognizant of his success being made possible by a superb group of assistant coaches. These men also had Gibbs's respect and appreciation. Gibbs and his coaches created an exciting, competitive, and successful environment for his players. Special attention was given to an offensive line of "Hogs" and tough steamrolling running backs. The teams' 3-yard plunges could create as much excitement as 30-yard runs.

Don Coryell was a key figure in Joe Gibbs's life. He was a passionate committed coach whom players and fellow coaches loved dearly. When Coryell died in 2010, Gibbs was one of the people asked to speak at his memorial service at San Diego State University. This event gave Gibbs pause and he described his feelings now that he is in the "fourth quarter" of his life. Gibbs talked about how we leave an influence on others that extends beyond our lives. He alluded to all those at the service who were influenced by Coryell. And he respectfully implied that everyone needs to consider their own influence in this way.

In Gibbs's case, his influence was not made solely with x's and o's, great schemes, plays or programs, although he does leave brilliant influences in these areas. Gibbs's most important influence comes from his achievements while maintaining a great passion for life, for meaning, and for living right.

Joe Gibbs Timeline

1940

- November 25, 1940, Joe Gibbs is born in Mocksville, North Carolina.

1959

- Gibbs graduates from Santa Fe High School in California after playing football, basketball, and baseball. He is named athlete of the year.

1959-1960

- Gibbs attends Cerritos Junior College.

1961-1964

- Gibbs attends San Diego State University and plays football for legendary coach Don Coryell. He graduates in 1964.

1965-1966

- Gibbs stays on at San Diego State as a graduate assistant for two years working as a volunteer for Coach Don Coryell's program. Gibbs is promoted to offensive line coach for his last year at the school.

1967-1968

- Gibbs coaches with Bill Peterson at Florida State.

1969-1970

- Gibbs serves as assistant coach for John McKay at the University of Southern California.

1971-1972

- Gibbs serves as assistant coach for Frank Broyles at the University of Arkansas.

1973-1977

- Gibbs serves as offensive backfield coach for Don Coryell who is head coach of the St. Louis Cardinals.

1978

- Gibbs serves as assistant coach to John McKay of the Tampa Bay Buccaneers.

1979-1980

- Gibbs is offensive coordinator for Don Coryell's San Diego Chargers.
- January 11, 1980, the San Diego Chargers are defeated by the Oakland Raiders, 34–27, in the AFC Championship.

1981-1993

- January 13, 1981, Washington Redskins owner, Jack Kent Cooke, hires Gibbs as head coach. Gibbs remains until 1993.

1982

- Gibbs is named AP, Sporting News, and Pro Football Weekly NFL Coach of the year for 1982.
- Gibbs is named UPI NFL Coach of the Year for the NFC in 1982.

1983

- January 22, 1983, the 1982 Washington Redskins defeat the Dallas Cowboys, 31–17, in the NFC Championship game.
- January 30, 1983, the 1982 Washington Redskins defeat the Miami Dolphins, 27–17, in Super Bowl XVII.
- Gibbs is named AP, Sporting News, and Pro Football Weekly NFL Coach of the year for 1983.

1984

- January 8, 1984, the 1983 Washington Redskins defeat the San Francisco 49ers, 24–21, in the NFC Championship game.
- January 22, 1984, the Los Angeles Raiders defeat the 1983 Washington Redskins, 38–9, in Super Bowl XVIII.

1987

- January 11, 1987, the New York Giants defeat Gibb's 1986 Redskins, 17–0, in the NFC Championship game.

1988

- January 17, 1988, the 1987 Washington Redskins defeat the Minnesota Vikings, 17–10, in the NFC Championship game.
- January 31, 1988, the 1987 Washington Redskins defeat the Denver Broncos, 42–10, in Super Bowl XXII.

1991-1992

- Gibbs is named Sporting News NFL Coach of the year for 1991.
- January 12, 1992, 1991 Washington Redskins defeat the Detroit Lions, 41–10, in the NFC Championship game.

Highlights

- January 26, 1992, 1991 Washington Redskins defeat the Buffalo Bills, 37–24, in Super Bowl XXVI.
- Gibbs creates a NASCAR team.
- March 5, 1993, Gibbs retires from coaching.

1996

- Gibbs is inducted into the Pro Football Hall of Fame as a member of the Class of 1996.

2004

- January 8, 2004, in a news conference, Gibbs is introduced as the new coach and president of the Washington Redskins.

2005

- In his second year of his second stint in Washington, Gibbs leads his Redskins to a 10–6 season, but the Seahawks defeat them, 20–10 in the division playoff.

2008

- January 8, 2008, Gibbs resigns as head coach and president of the Washington Redskins.

In Gibbs's first 12-season stretch as Redskins' coach, he led his team to three Super Bowl victories and four NFC Championships. His Redskins made the playoffs an incredible 8 times in 12 years. His .683 winning percentage was third best behind Vince Lombardi and John Madden. Gibbs holds an overall NFL head coaching record of 171–101–0. Gibbs was enshrined in the Pro Football Hall of Fame in 1996. He was named AP Coach of the Year twice, Sporting News Coach of the Year three times, Pro Football Weekly Coach of the Year twice, and UPI Coach of the Year once.

Gibbs took stock of his talent and put together a program to win that was based on existing personnel. His high-energy, tireless approach to creating game plans consumed long hours well into the night, but the effort was visible on the playing field. And regardless of his lofty success, Gibbs always respected and appreciated his players, his coaches, his fans, and his owners.

Endnotes

1   Coryell's speech at Gibbs's enshrinement in the Pro Football Hall of Fame.

2   For more on Gibbs competitiveness, see Peter King's article on *SI.Com*, "In His Skin: Times Have Changed, but Joe Gibbs Hasn't and that's Why He Will Win," Jan.12, 2004, viewed at http://sportsillustrated.cnn.com/2004/writers/peter_king/01/09/mmqb/ on June 25, 2013.

3   Life Story Foundation, "Joe Gibbs Life Story," viewed at http://www.joegibbsstory.com on June 24, 2013.

4   Coryell's speech at Gibbs's enshrinement in the Pro Football Hall of Fame.

5   Peter King, "In His Skin: Times Have Changed, but Joe Gibbs Hasn't and that's Why He Will Win," *SI.Com*, Jan.12, 2004, viewed at http://sportsillustrated.cnn.com/2004/writers/peter_king/01/09/mmqb/ on June 25, 2013.

6   Washington Post, *Redskins: A History of Washington's Team*, (Washington, DC., Washington Post Books, 1997) 120. Online version at http://www.washingtonpost.com/wp-srv/sports/redskins/longterm/book/skinbook.htm .

7   Joe Gibbs with Jerry Jenkins, *Joe Gibbs: Fourth and One* (Nashville: Thomas Nelson, Inc., 1991), 19.

8   Washington Post, *Redskins: A History of Washington's Team*, 123.

9   Washington Post, *Redskins: A History of Washington's Team*, 123.

10 Life Story Foundation, Joe Gibbs Life Story, viewed at http://www.joegibbsstory.com on June 24, 2013.

11 Leonard Shapiro, "The Playbook According to Gibbs," *Washington Post*, September 9, 2004, viewed at http://www.washingtonpost.com/wp–dyn/articles/A6713–2004Sep8.html on July 17, 2013.

12 Joe Gibbs with Jerry Jenkins, Joe Gibbs: *Fourth and One*, 157.

13 There are four divisions in each NFL conference (AFC and NFC) and the division winners qualify for the playoffs. Two other teams from each conference qualify as wild card teams based on their win–loss records. The two division winners in each conference with the highest winning percentage do not play in the wild card round and host the next round of the playoffs. The third and fourth division winners host the wild card teams for the first games of the playoffs. The two division winners in each conference with the highest winning percentage host the wildcard game winners in the Divisional Playoff games. The winning teams move on to the conference championship game and the winner of each conference championship moves on to the Super Bowl.

14 Christine Brennan, "Redskins Beat Bears Again, 21–17," *Washington Post*, January 11, 1988, viewed at http://www.washingtonpost.com/wp–srv/sports/redskins/longterm/1997/history/allart/87bears2.htm on July 2, 2013.

15 Christine Brennan, "Redskins Beat Bears Again, 21–17," *Washington Post*, January 11, 1988.

16 Bob Verdi, "Williams Never a Pain to Skins," *Chicago Tribune*, February 2, 1988, viewed at http://articles.chicagotribune.com/1988-02-02/sports/8803270266_1_doug-williams-wunnerful-lawrence-welk-resort on July 20, 2013.

17 Leonard Shapiro, "The Playbook According to Gibbs," *Washington Post*, September 9, 2004.

18 Michael Silver, "Joe and the Space Cowboys," May 31, 2004, *Sports Illustrated*, viewed at SI Vault, http://sportsillustrated.cnn.com/vault/article/magazine/MAG1032156/1/index.htm on July 17, 2013.

19 Howard Bryant, "Of Two Minds on Offense," *Washington Post*, January 2, 2007, viewed at

http://www.washingtonpost.com/wp–dyn/content/article/2007/01/01/AR2007010101001.
html on July 2, 2013.

[20] ESPN News Services, "Brunell Sets Record with 22 Straight Completions in Win," viewed
at http://scores.espn.go.com/nfl/recap?gameId=260924034 on July 16, 2013.

[21] Howard Bryant, "Of Two Minds on Offense," *Washington Post*, January 2, 2007.

[22] Associated Press, "Redskins Remember Slain Taylor, Use 10 Men on First Defensive
Snap," December 3, 2007, Viewed at http://sports.espn.go.com/nfl/news/story?id=3138182
on July 19, 2013.

[23] ESPN News Service, *Gibbs Cites Pull of Family Obligations for Retiring from Redskins*,
January 8, 2008, viewed at http://sports.espn.go.com/nfl/news/story?id=3186165 on July
17, 2013.

[24] Michael Silver, "Joe and the Space Cowboys," May 31, 2004, *Sports Illustrated*, viewed
at SI Vault, http://sportsillustrated.cnn.com/vault/article/magazine/MAG1032156/1/index.
htm on July 17, 2013.

Bill Belichick

Are you with me?

There is Bill Belichick on the practice field, the coach with aging Hollywood looks, and a red-hot intensity that he keeps under wraps. In a calm voice, he minces no words with his players. Even if his message is painfully fundamental, he states it and then states it again. He teaches—he corrects. He believes players have the most respect for a coach who makes them better. They respect the coach's knowledge not the school he attended or the NFL team on which he played.

Belichick walks over to a 300-pound lineman, and like an old schoolmaster, the coach fanatically quizzes his player about a game situation. The coach wants to be sure that the player understands the ramifications of his actions down by the goal line—in a game situation. It is a scene that is repeated hundreds of times during a season to clarify any number of concepts from Belichick's football curriculum. The player nervously tells Belichick what he thinks his coach wants to hear—he is wrong. Belichick's tone remains calm, but his voice gets a little louder as he continues to press for the right answer. Towering over his coach, frustrated and embarrassed, the player takes a deep breath, spits out his second answer—he is correct.

Belichick sums up his lesson, restates his point, and ends with his signature phrase: "Are you with me?" And as all Belichick's players would attest, if you want to play for Belichick, you need to be "with him."

Belichick's Methods

Belichick is demanding. He wants things done his way. He will not tolerate meddling from anyone. He tells players to "just do your job"—to execute. He wants players to play in the moment—no excuses. He demands excellent play in critical circumstances. He instructs and pushes his rookies as well as his seasoned veterans. He is consistent. He is steady. He is competitive every minute. In practice he hounds his players to do things right all the time. He never lets up.

According to Patriots' offensive lineman Matt Light:

He loves the game of football. He probably could recall every single snap that he has ever coached. He'll bring up stuff that happened with the Giants 25 years ago. He'll bring up certain players who burned one of his guys on a play from a long time ago.[1]

Belichick is organized. Organization is key—a big part of his success formula. He leaves little to chance. His system provides an ironclad structure from one year to the next. Roles are understood. Every player and staff member is accountable and under evaluation. He wants his coaches to offer constructive criticism of others. Evaluations need to be honest and understood. Each coach is responsible for his advice and counsel. Mistakes are mistakes. Each loss and victory points to areas that need improvement.

Belichick's consistent treatment of players breeds respect. Because the team is the "highest good," players need to be role players, partners, and peers—not superstars. His expectations are high; his faith in players is strong. He may have a special place in his heart for his Super Bowl quarterback Tom Brady, but his focus is all team. After all, the Patriots posted an 11–5 record in 2008 without Brady.

Players who succeed under Belichick understand his demands and they are willing to work unceasingly towards being better players and improving the team. His team consists of excellent players who can fill in for each other. He loves his defense as well as his offense. New players earn a starting position. No one is ever given anything.

His strategy is to take away the opponents' strengths—something he learned long ago from his father. How can his team neutralize the opposition's strengths? He likes to see his opponents set up for one defense and then give them something unexpected.

His team lives by pressure that he unceasingly provides, but he wants them to understand the only thing that's important is to "do your job." When things get tough, he turns up the pressure on opposing teams and he is confident that his own team can perform under it. After all, they experience it every day at practice. For Belichick, a reputation for toughness and excellence within the NFL is important. Success builds reputation. Reputation gives you an edge.

Early Years and Learning Years

Bill Belichick was born to coach football. He was raised under the football tutelage of his father, Steve Belichick. The elder Belichick had the look of a man whose face was chiseled from mines and mills. Steve Belichick came from hard-working parents who lived in Croatia before they immigrated to the

United States. Steve's father, John Belichick (originally Bilicic), came first and then his wife Mary followed.

Steel Valley

Five children, the first generation of American Belichicks, were all born just outside of Pittsburgh in Monessen, Pennsylvania. As a young family, the Belichicks moved to Struthers, Ohio, south of Youngstown. John found work at Youngstown Sheet and Tube Factory where he made wire.[2] The immigrant family survived tough times during the Depression by each family member chipping in and doing everything possible to help. They grew their own vegetables, took in boarders, and wasted nothing. The older Belichick children went to work early and helped pave the way for the younger ones. They lived a rugged life in a region called "Steel Valley" that would prove to be a fertile area for football.

Steve Belichick took to football at an early age and played well during high school and college although he was not a big man. Like many other boys from the region, he took to the game with a passion. He played at Case Western Reserve and then briefly for the Detroit Lions before serving in the Navy during World War II. Upon his return, he sought out a coaching position.

A life of football must have seemed like heaven to Steve Belichick coming from his Youngstown industrial roots. But the insecurity of growing up during the Great Depression in one of the most unforgiving industrial areas in the country made its mark. He would always strive towards excellence, but his career path would reflect more caution than ambition.

It looked like Steve Belichick could follow the path of highly successful football coaches: starting out in minor roles and small schools, working up to bigger schools in various assistant jobs, and then taking on head coaching responsibilities at a major university. However, Steve Belichick moved a few times as a young coach and decided that he didn't want to face the uncertain lifestyle of a head coach. Once he took a job as an assistant coach and football scout for the Naval Academy, he was determined to stay in Annapolis.[3] He secured his long-term livelihood at the Academy by becoming a physical education instructor as well as an assistant coach. He was offered several head coaching jobs while at the Academy, but he wanted stability—he didn't want to move around. He focused most of his energy and considerable football intelligence on scouting—he was one of the best.

Scouting is a special skill and a good scout is someone any good coach would want to retain. Belichick was better than a good scout; he was a great one who wrote a book about it. Steve Belichick's *Football Scouting Methods* is considered by many to be the classic text on the topic.[4] A large network of football coaches came to know and admire Steve Belichick. While no one gave Bill Belichick anything that he did not earn, his father's standing in the coaching community would help establish his son's reputation as well.

As a player in high school and college, Bill Belichick had already acquired a coach's understanding of the game. Like Steve Belichick, Bill's mother, Jeannette Belichick, was a teacher. Bill Belichick was not just learning about life from his parents, he was also learning to teach.

Hardest Working Boy Wonder in the NFL

Bill Belichick got his "undergraduate degree" in coaching from his father, Steve. He began his graduate work in earnest working for a series of talented, and in some cases, visionary coaches. Once he graduated from Wesleyan University in Middletown, Connecticut, Bill Belichick began his pro career working as a special assistant on Ted Marchibroda's Baltimore Colts staff.

Baltimore Colts

In 1975, lured by a free room at the Howard Johnson hotel and a $25-a-week salary that doubled after training camp, Belichick meticulously broke down film for the Colts.[5] The young "apprentice" spent endless hours talking football with Marchibroda and his assistants. Part of Belichick's duties included chauffeuring the coaching staff back and forth between the hotel and practice.

While in Baltimore, his talents and energy were quickly apparent. Defensive coach Maxie Baughan, who played linebacker for the Los Angeles Rams and learned complicated defensive schemes from George Allen, thought that Belichick was wise beyond his years—different in several key ways from other coaches. According to Baughan, Belichick supported the coaches' program completely. The young coach also understood that each game might have to be played differently because the game was always changing. Baughan noticed that Belichick worked at his job with an unmatched work ethic. Belichick could break down film to the point of not just understanding each play, but he could understand the thinking of the opposing coach in calling each play. According to Baughan, young Belichick was thoroughly professional in his approach.[6]

Belichick was in a sense a perfect candidate to learn and follow George Allen's defensive philosophy. Allen focused on understanding the opposing team's offensive strategies and tendencies to a point where his defense could predict the offense's moves. Alert defenders could position and play proactively rather than reactively. This philosophy would require meticulous study of film and intense game preparation—work that is a given today. Belichick put his own measure of intensity and professionalism on these practices early in his career.

Belichick would develop an understanding of every aspect of the game and a defensive persona that is centered on the mantra "give up nothing." According to Vic Carucci of NFL.com, "Give up nothing means exactly that. No yards. No points. No injury information about your players. No personal information about yourself. No deep insights about anyone or anything connected to your club."[7]

Belichick would remember the long camps at the time he started out and working with great coaches;

> *We went to camp July 5. The first game was September 21...a whole two and a half months of training camp... a long, long preseason. Squads were small so, I snapped a lot to help the timing for the offense...It was great experience with Coach Marchibroda and Maxie Baughan and the rest of the defensive staff, George Boutselis, the special teams coach.*[8]

Detroit Lions

Belichick's meager salary with the financially troubled Baltimore Colts could not provide a living during the off-season so he found work with Rick Forzano and the Detroit Lions in 1976. Belichick served as a personal assistant to Forzano, scouted and coached tight ends, and broke down film in Detroit as he absorbed football wisdom from a number of excellent coaches including Jerry Glanville, Fritz Shurmur, Jim Carr, Floyd Reese, Joe Bugel, and Ken Ship.

Ship ran the offense in Detroit and famously quizzed Belichick on the playbook a few weeks after his arrival only to find that the young coach had mastered it. Ship's offense included a myriad of adjustments to counter defensive moves.

Belichick was also exposed to another phenomenal football coach in offensive line coach, Joe Bugel. Bugel would go on to build the famous "Hogs" of the Washington Redskins. Bugel's Hogs were regularly featured as the strongest part of the Redskins' team. Bugel was also a master at patching up a line after key injuries—an idea that would have fed into Belichick's tendency to build teams with players who can fill in for each other. In Detroit, Belichick became known as a boy wonder, a football genius, and one of the hardest working young coaches in the game.

Denver Broncos

Belichick moved on to the Denver Broncos for one year, assisting special teams and defense. He broke down film for defensive coordinator, Joe Collier, and talked football continuously with another coach, Richie McCabe, who had coached for Al Davis in Oakland. McCabe schooled Belichick on Davis's seemingly maverick, yet highly successful methods. Under Davis, no player was secure in his position—everyone was regularly evaluated including coaches.[9] Players and coaches were constantly challenged.

In Denver, players were expected to know exactly what they were supposed to do in each circumstance and execute. Both the Davis system and the Denver emphasis on role responsibilities are threads that have run through the Belichick system.

New York Giants

In 1963 the Giants lost the NFL Championship to the Chicago Bears. The Giants had won a league championship and five conference championships in 8 years. But between 1964 and 1980, the best the Giants could do was to earn a second place finish in the NFC East in 1970. However, a new General Manager, George Young, was hired in 1979. He would begin a series of personnel moves that would right the Giants. In 1979, Bill Belichick moved on to the New York Giants where he would stay until 1990.

When Belichick was originally hired, the head coach was Ray Perkins who held that position through 1982. Perkins's staff included Bill Parcells as defensive coordinator. He joined the team at the same time as Belichick. Perkins was a very tough, hard-nosed old fashioned coach. His best year was 1981 when he led the Giants to a 9–7 season. Perkins left the Giants after the strike-shortened 1982 season to take over the University of Alabama head coaching position that had been vacated with the retirement of Paul "Bear" Bryant, the celebrated Crimson Tide coach.

Parcells replaced Perkins as head coach in 1983. Belichick worked with special teams, then linebackers, and finally in 1985 he took over as defensive coordinator. Belichick played a crucial part in the Giants' two Super Bowl titles under Parcells.

Belichick and Parcells

Belichick and Parcells were miles apart in their personalities and coaching styles. Parcells exuded a physical toughness and presence that was matched by a sharp tongue that he used liberally to cut his "adversaries" off at the knees. He was intimidating and he could motivate men to play at their best regardless of how modern or pampered they might have been. He was an explosion of biting humor and folksy quotes. Parcells used the nickname "Doom" for Belichick—saying that when it came to Belichick: "His glass was usually half-empty."[10]

Belichick matches mind-power with physical preparation and practice that melds into his team's psyche. His players buy into his team-first system, know their place, and play their part. By being in control of his emotions, Belichick is also able to coolly coach his team during a game and make adjustments.

Parcells worked at the emotional center of coaching, relied heavily on those around him, and attracted much attention. Belichick hides his emotions and logically instructs his players to play their roles flawlessly. Belichick relinquishes control in most areas reluctantly and he has developed a consistent program that varies little from year to year. He hides from the spotlight in oversized sweatshirts. He conducts "close to the vest" news conferences. However, like Parcells, Belichick insists that everyone respect his position as head coach and for him that means that he is the primary contact for team information. In New York with Parcells, Belichick coached a gifted group of athletes that included Pro Football Hall of Famers Lawrence Taylor and Harry Carson.

Cleveland Browns

Cleveland is a storied NFL franchise that has the stamp of legendary coach Paul Brown all over it. On February 5, 1991, Belichick was hired as head coach of the Cleveland Browns.

Belichick's Players in Cleveland

During Belichick's years with the Browns, there were several notable players.[11]

Eric Metcalf

Eric Metcalf was an excellent versatile running back who returned kicks and punts. He averaged over 1,500 all-purpose yards a year for the Browns.[12]

Eric Turner

Eric Turner was an All-American from UCLA who was a first round draft choice of the Browns in 1991. Turner was an excellent safety with the Browns from 1991-1995. In 1994, he had a league-high 9 interceptions.

Leroy Hoard

Leroy Hoard played five seasons at running back for the Browns under Belichick. Hoard was an excellent short yardage runner especially at the goal line. One of the most famous quotes about a short-yardage specialist is attributed to Hoard: "Coach, if you need one yard, I'll get you three yards. If you need five yards, I'll get you three yards."

Michael Jackson

Wide receiver Michael Jackson played five seasons under Belichick in Cleveland. Jackson had 170 receptions for 2,797 yards and 28 touchdowns.

Michael Dean Perry

Michael Dean Perry played defensive tackle for Belichick for four seasons at 6-foot-1 and 285 pounds. Like his older brother, William "the Refrigerator" Perry of the Bears, Michael was a fan favorite. The popular Perry had a

McDonald's sandwich named after him, the MDP. Perry was named AFC Defensive Player of the Year in 1989.

Vinny Testaverde

Vinny Testaverde had an incredible 21-year career in the NFL. During the three seasons he played for Belichick's Browns, he started in 31 games, completed 578 passes, and passed for 7,255 yards.

Cleveland Years

Belichick developed the Browns' roster and put a tough no-nonsense program in place. The team grew stronger. Belichick's Browns improved to 11–5 in 1994 and made the playoffs. The Browns' season ended when the Pittsburgh Steelers beat them, 29–9, in the divisional playoff game.

The 1995 season was Belichick's final one with the Browns. After the season, the NFL franchise was moved to Baltimore to begin anew as the Ravens. Much has been written and spoken about the uprooting of the team.[13] When the former Browns' franchise was moved to Baltimore, the city of Cleveland retained the name, colors, history, and records.[14] A new Browns' franchise was back in Cleveland in 1999.

The Browns showed improvement each year that Belichick coached in Cleveland until his last season in 1995 when his team lost seven of its last eight games and finished 5–11. Under Belichick, the Browns were 6–10 in 1991, 7–5 in 1992 and 1993, and 11–5 in 1994. The young coach learned much from his experiences that helped him develop his successful program that he would use at his next head coaching job.

Brief Stay in New England

After leaving Cleveland, Belichick joined Parcells again, this time at New England as an assistant and defensive backs coach for the 1996 season. Parcells had been hired in New England in 1993 by owner James Busch Orthwein who gave him full control of the team. In Parcells's second year, the Patriots' 10–6 record got them to the playoffs, but Orthwein sold the team to long-time fan, Robert Kraft.

Under Parcells in 1996, the Patriots fought their way to the Super Bowl where they lost to the Green Bay Packers and Bret Favre, 35–21. Immediately after the loss, although still under contract to the Patriots, Parcells took off to New York where he signed with the Jets. The Jets paid New England compensation for Parcells.

New York Jets

Belichick followed Parcells to the Jets in 1997 and stayed through 1999 as defensive coordinator. Parcells was asked to resuscitate the team with the worst record in the NFL. With Belichick as his defensive coordinator, Parcells's Jets improved to 9–7 in 1997 and 12–4 in 1998—good enough for a playoff berth. After beating the Jacksonville Jaguars in a division playoff, 34–24, they advanced to the conference championship game against the Denver Broncos. In the conference matchup, the Jets scored the first 10 points, but failed to score again for the duration of the game. Belichick's defense held John Elway in check with just 13 completions in 34 attempts for 173 yards. Elway did connect with Howard Griffith for an 11-yard touchdown pass. Terrell Davis ran for 167 yards and one touchdown. The Broncos made the most of good field position with Jason Elam kicking three field goals on the day. The Jets' Vinny Testaverde passed for 356 yards, but no touchdowns. The Broncos beat the Jets, 23–10.

In a disastrous 1999, the Jets saw their quarterback Testaverde go down early in the season. After accumulating a number of early-season losses, the Jets picked up the pieces towards the season's end to finish at .500. Parcells called it quits as coach and served as Director of Football Operations thinking that Belichick would take over as head coach. Belichick's Jets' contract stipulated that he would serve as head coach should Parcells leave that position. When Belichick was introduced in a press conference as the new head coach, he resigned the job after holding it for just one day.

Return to New England

Belichick's next move was to take over as head coach of New England, a move that created legal controversy. The Jets' organization was in flux at the time of Parcells's coaching retirement. Jets' owner Leon Hess had passed away several months before and the team was being sold. A legal battle over Belichick's new position ensued, but it was settled when Parcells called Patriots' owner Robert Kraft and worked out an arrangement. Thus, in an odd twist of events, the Jets had to compensate New England in 1997 when they acquired Parcells's services and 3 years later in 2000, New England had to return the "favor" and compensate the Jets when they acquired Belichick's services.

The Jets were subsequently purchased by Robert Wood "Woody" Johnson IV who is the great-grandson of Robert Wood Johnson I, the founder of Johnson & Johnson.

Patriots' Dynasty

In sports, a dynasty is a team that establishes a position of leadership and holds it for several years. In the modern NFL, revenue-sharing, the draft, and salary caps create healthy competition throughout the league and a system that makes it very difficult to create dynasties. Yet, Belichick has been at the helm of New

England for over 13 years and has won three Super Bowl titles, five conference championships, and 11 division titles.

Belichick's Players in New England

Good fortune smiled on Belichick early in 2000 when he drafted Tom Brady in the sixth round of the draft, pick number 199. Belichick had liked Brady, but he really had no idea just how good Brady would become. He was looking for a backup to Drew Bledsoe. Scott Pioli, who was Belichick's player personnel director handling the draft for the Patriots at the time, said that good fortune more than football acumen led the Patriots to snagging Brady when they did. But to Belichick's credit, once he had Brady on the team, he sensed his promise very quickly.

In addition to Brady, Belichick would make many excellent draft choices and build a team of relatively selfless players, but many who are well known to football fans.

Deion Branch

Deion Branch was a second round draft pick for the Patriots in 2002. A superb wide receiver, Branch played for the Patriots for four seasons and he was named 2004 Super Bowl MVP. He was traded to the Seattle Seahawks where he played for four seasons before he returned to the Patriots where he played through 2012

Kevin Faulk

Kevin Faulk was a second round draft choice of the Patriots in 1999. A veteran of 13 NFL seasons in New England, he was a solid running back and excellent receiver who also contributed as a punt and kick returner.

Matt Light

Offensive tackle Matt Light was a dependable and tough player on the Patriots' line for 11 seasons. Light was a second round draft choice out of Purdue.

Matt Slater

Premier special teams player and multi-year special teams captain Matt Slater helped the Patriots win games on kick returns and kick coverage. Slater served as a kick returner as well as a "gunner"—a speedy player who runs down the sideline on kickoffs and punts to tackle the returner.

Mike Vrabel

Linebacker Mike Vrabel played for eight seasons in New England under Belichick. At 6-foot-4, 261 pounds, and very athletic, Vrabel occasionally played receiver in critical goal-line situations.

Rob Gronkowski

Tight ends are once more a significant offensive threat in many NFL offenses. Rob Gronkowski is a best-of-breed tight end with versatility and power.

Tedy Bruschi

Tedy Bruschi was one of the Patriots' most inspirational players who returned to play after suffering a stroke. Bruschi was a relentless pass rusher and tackler who helped provide some bite on the defensive side of the ball for 13 seasons.

Tom Brady

Tom Brady is considered one of the best quarterbacks in NFL history. He also serves as a team leader who does not disappoint his coach or fans. Brady plays big in the clutch, but he does not let down at any time. He is a tactical player who can perform a game plan with precision and masterfully ad lib.

Troy Brown

Veteran wide receiver Troy Brown played 7 years before Belichick's arrival in New England and played another 8 years during Belichick's tenure. Brown also served as a punt and kick returner and he was given a much more active role in the offense under Belichick.

Vince Wilfork

Vince Wilfork is one of the best defensive tackles in the NFL. A first round pick in 2004, Wilfork is a powerful lineman with surprisingly good movement for his size. He has the ability to clog holes while drawing a double team.

Wes Welker

Wes Welker was a steady receiver and punt-returner for the Patriots for six seasons. He had 100-plus receptions for over 1,000 yards in five of six seasons with the Patriots. He was one of Brady's most reliable targets. At 5-foot-9, Welker is short, but powerfully built and durable.

2000 Season

The first Patriots' season under Belichick was a poor one. Initially, Belichick was upset with the condition of his players. When they reported to camp, he grumbled:

> *We've got too many people who are overweight, too many guys who are out of shape, and too many guys who just haven't paid the price they need to pay at this time of the season. You can't win with 40 good players while the other team has 53.[15]*

The Patriots finished last in the AFC East with a 5–11 mark.

2001 Season

The Patriots had a good quarterback in Drew Bledsoe who was in his eighth season when Belichick took over. Bledsoe had a completion percentage of 58.8% and a quarterback rating of 77.3 in 2000.[16] However, he played poorly in the 2001 preseason and the Patriots struggled as the season got underway. After losing to the Bengals, 23–17, in the season opener, they faced the Jets in the second game. Bledsoe was injured when a hit he took sheared a blood vessel in his chest. No one knew the nature of the injury at the time. Bledsoe toughed it out—he continued to play until the pain became intolerable. Brady replaced Bledsoe. Bledsoe was 18 for 28, but he had two interceptions. Brady went 5 for 10. The Patriots lost the game 10–3.

Bledsoe was hospitalized and out of action for several weeks. Traditional football protocol dictates that an injury is not a reason for someone to lose their starting position. Bledsoe expected to have his job back when he was able to return in late November. It did not happen. Belichick had decided that Brady was the better quarterback and he thought he was a better fit for his system. He liked Brady's leadership qualities, his knowledge of the playbook, his practice habits, and most everything else about him. Bledsoe stewed, but to his great credit, he kept relatively quiet. He continued to work hard to become a better, stronger player, and he waited for his next opportunity.

In the third game of the season, Brady led the Patriots to a 44–13 clubbing of the Colts. Brady had modest numbers for the day, 13 completions in 23 attempts for 168 yards, but the Patriots used a balanced attack that took full advantage of the run. Antowain Smith rushed 22 times for 94 yards and two touchdowns while Kevin Faulk rushed 9 times for 48 yards and one touchdown. Adam Vinatieri chipped in three field goals. On the other side of the ball, Peyton Manning, who was in his third year with the Colts, was intercepted three times with two of those leading to Patriot touchdowns. After the Patriots lost 30–10 the following week to the Miami Dolphins, no one envisioned a dynasty in the making in New England. The Dolphins would play .500 football against the Patriots during the early Belichick era that coincided with Miami coach Dave Wannstedt's tenure from 2000-2004.

The next game was huge for the Patriots. They came from behind to take the San Diego Chargers into overtime and won the contest, 29–26, on a 44-

yard field goal by Adam Vinatieri. Tom Brady threw for 364 yards completing 33 of 54 passes. Terry Glenn had 6 catches for 110 yards and a touchdown.

On October 21, 2001, the Patriots defeated the Colts for the second time that season. It was David Patten who lit things up for the Patriots in the 38–17 victory. Patten became the first player since Walter Payton in 1979 to score touchdowns three different ways. Patten snagged a 91-yard touchdown pass from Brady, he passed to Troy Brown for a score, and he rushed for another touchdown from 29 yards out. It was a high-energy game for the Patriots.

Following the big win against the Colts, the Patriots fell back with a 31–20 loss to the Denver Broncos. Brady threw four interceptions in the game. He completed 25 of 38 passes for 203 yards and two touchdowns. As the season charged into November, the Patriots beat Atlanta, 24–10, and then Buffalo, 21–11, before losing to the Saint Louis Rams, 24–17. The Rams were known at the time as "The Greatest Show on Turf" for their high-octane offense devised by head coach Mike Martz. The Rams' offense was setting new standards in point and yardage production with a potent passing game featuring quarterback Kurt Warner and several first rate receivers as well as a superb running game featuring Marshall Faulk.

The Patriots got back on track with an impressive and unexpected string of wins against the Saints, Jets, Browns, Bills, and Dolphins. Brady was improving. He completed 19 of 26 passes for 258 yards and four touchdowns in a 34–17 win against the Saints. He completed 20 of 28 passes for 213 yards against the Jets, but the Patriots managed to eke out a 17–16 win with short yardage touchdown runs by Antowain Smith and Marc Edwards along with a late Vinatieri field goal.

Brady completed 19 of 28 passes for 218 yards against the Browns in a 27–16 win. He was also intercepted twice—one that was returned for a touchdown. The Patriots salvaged the day with a stingy defense that allowed no touchdowns by the Browns' offense and only three field goals. New England's special teams "kicked in" a score as well when Troy Brown ran a punt back for an 85-yard score. Vinatieri kicked two field goals.

Against the Bills, Brady completed 19 passes in 35 attempts for 237 yards with one interception. Vinatieri's four field goals, including one in overtime, gave the Patriots the win by a score of 12–9. Antowain Smith had another strong day with 20 rushes for 95 yards.

Brady had an anemic day against the Dolphins, who had a stingy, tough defense that gave the best teams in the league problems. Brady completed 11 of 19 passes for 108 yards and one touchdown. Antowain Smith had 26 rushes for 156 yards including a 2-yard touchdown run. Vinatieri kicked two field goals. It all added up to a Patriots' victory, 20–13.

Against the Panthers, Brady completed 17 of 29 passes for 198 yards, scoring one touchdown and throwing two interceptions. Ty Law snagged an interception that he ran back for 46 yards and a touchdown. Otis Smith had another Patriot interception that he returned for 76 yards and a touchdown.

Troy Brown ran a punt back for a 68-yard score. Vinatieri kicked a field goal. All phases of the game contributed in the 38–6 win over the Panthers.

Brady completed 32 of 52 pass attempts for 312 yards against the Oakland Raiders. He was intercepted once. Brady rushed for a 6-yard score. Once again, Vinatieri's performance was key—kicking three field goals including one in overtime for the 16–13 victory over the Oakland Raiders.

AFC Championship Game

Brady's and Bledsoe's combined efforts, a strong defense, and special teams won the AFC Championship game against the Steelers. Brady completed 12 of 18 pass attempts for 115 yards and had to leave the game with a sprained ankle. Bledsoe came in and completed 10 of 21 attempts for 102 yards and one touchdown. The Patriots scored on a Troy Brown 55-yard punt return for a touchdown and a blocked field goal that was returned by Antwan Harris for 49 yards. The Patriots beat the Steelers, 24–17.

Super Bowl XXXVI

Super Bowl XXXVI pitted the Patriots against the Rams. It was the first NFL championship that followed the September 11 attacks. Security was heightened and the game was pushed back a week into February. The Rams had beaten the Patriots, 24–17, in the regular season. It was the kind of challenge that Belichick relished.

The highly-talented explosive Rams were the favorite coming into the game. Rams' QB, Kurt Warner, had a completion percentage of 68.7% for the season and a 101.4 quarterback rating. Brady had a completion percentage of 63.9% and a quarterback rating of 86.5.

The Rams scored on a 50-yard field goal to take an early lead, 3–0, but missed a similar attempt early in the second quarter. Midway through the quarter, Ty Law intercepted a Kurt Warner pass and ran it back 47 yards for a Patriots' touchdown. Late in the half, Warner was driving again, but after a 15-yard reception close to midfield, Rams' receiver Ricky Proehl fumbled on the tackle. Terrell Buckley grabbed the loose ball and ran it back to the Rams 40-yard line. A couple of quick Brady strikes gave the Patriots another touchdown and a 14–3 lead at the half.

The Patriots struggled offensively in the second half and were stuffed by the Rams' defense for most of it while the Rams' offense was on the move. However, the Rams were making costly mistakes that the Patriots were avoiding. A third quarter interception of a Kurt Warner pass helped the Patriots move into field goal range. The ever-reliable Vinatieri kicked a 37-yard field goal that gave New England a 17–3 lead. The Rams followed with a long drive, but Warner almost lost the ball at the Patriots' 2-yard line on a fumble that was overturned because of a holding call. Warner scored on a quarterback sneak and the New England lead stood at 17–10.

Late in the game, the Rams got the ball with less than two minutes remaining. Warner threw three strikes including a 26-yard pass to Proehl for a score. After the extra point, the score was tied at 17–17.

With just 1:30 remaining in the game, Brady came of age in the NFL. He moved the ball up the field with three quick passes to running back J. R. Redmond. Completions to Troy Brown and Jermaine Wiggins gave Vinatieri a 48-yard field goal attempt with 7 seconds remaining on the clock. Vinatieri made the kick, the Patriots won the game, 20–17, and Brady was named MVP.

The 2001 season would be Bledsoe's last with the Patriots. Bledsoe moved on to Buffalo where he played three seasons and then on to Dallas for two more.

2002 Season

Belichick is a team builder and his team is always under construction. He is always looking ahead. Even when he has a Super Bowl team, he is looking ahead to next year. He runs his team like a business—one that keeps improving and moving forward affordably. He hates to overpay; it leaves less for others.

The defending Super Bowl champion New England Patriots played the 2002 season in new Gillette Stadium. On offense, the Patriots were more creative than the previous season as Brady grew more confident. Receiver Deion Branch, acquired in the 2002 draft, was a huge addition to Belichick's offense. The Patriots rolled over the Steelers and the Jets in their first two games. Much more passing was featured and Brady turned in a tremendous game in week three against the Chiefs—passing for over 400 yards with Troy Brown catching 16 passes in this high-scoring game. It was another Vinatieri field goal in overtime that gave the Patriots a 41–38 win. In the fourth game, the Patriots hit a post Super Bowl wall. They lost four straight games. The Chargers, Dolphins, Packers, and Broncos beat the Super Bowl champions. The Patriots regrouped and beat Drew Bledsoe's Buffalo Bills, 38–7. The following week, Brady led a fourth quarter comeback against the Bears and pulled out a 33–30 victory. After losing to the Raiders, the Patriots beat the Vikings, Lions, and the Bills. As the season was winding down, a very good Titans team beat the Patriots 24-7. AFC East Division rival, the New York Jets, came to Gillette Stadium in Foxborough for the most critical contest of the season for both teams. The Jets prevailed 30-17.

In the last game of the season, the Patriots played the Dolphins and found themselves down, 24–13, with five minutes remaining. The Patriots made another comeback that included a Brady touchdown pass to Troy Brown and two Vinatieri field goals—the second one in overtime that gave the Patriots the win. The season ended with the Jets, Patriots, and Dolphins all atop the AFC East with identical 9–7 records, but tiebreaker rules awarded the AFC East to the Jets.

Bill Belichick and His Patriots

2003 Season

Belichick and his staff knew that 2002 was to some degree a Super Bowl hangover, but it was more than that. The season exposed critical needs. Belichick was poised to make many changes to his Super Bowl lineup.

Belichick signed safety Rodney Harrison and nose tackle Ted Washington. Harrison had been released by the San Diego Chargers. He replaced a popular New England player named Lawyer Milloy. Perhaps more than any other move made that season, releasing Lawyer Milloy was a move that would certainly cast Belichick in a certain no-nonsense win-at-all costs kind of coach for a great number of people. Milloy was a popular figure in New England, but he and the Patriots could not come to terms on a new contract.[17]

Washington was acquired by a trade from the Chicago Bears. Washington had been injured in the previous season, but he was a huge strong man in the middle who could stop the run. In another personnel move, the Patriots used a first round draft pick to select Ty Warren, a defensive tackle whom Belichick wanted badly enough to trade up in the draft for him. Also added via the draft were defensive back Eugene Wilson, wide receiver Bethel Johnson, defensive tackle Dan Klecko, defensive back Asante Samuel, and center Dan Koppen.

The Patriots' first game of the 2003 season was a crushing 31-0 loss to the Buffalo Bills who had picked up Lawyer Milloy and already had ex-Patriot Drew Bledsoe. Both played well in the season opener for the Bills. The Patriots regrouped quickly coming back strong to beat the Eagles, 31–10, in game two. They beat the Jets, 23–16, in game three. In game four, they lost to the Washington Redskins, 20–17; Brady threw three interceptions. The Patriots ran the table on the rest of the season finishing 14–2. They played a tight contest on October 19 against the Dolphins—winning 19–13 in overtime on Brady's 82-yard touchdown pass to Troy Brown. In their last regular game of the season, the Patriots gave the Bills a 31–0 drubbing paying back their AFC East rivals for the punishing season opener. The Patriots beat the Titans in the fourth quarter of their division playoff, 17–14, with a 46-yard Vinatieri field goal. In the conference championship game against Peyton Manning and the Colts, the Patriots limited the Indianapolis quarterback's passing game to one touchdown with four interceptions. Five Vinatieri field goals helped secure the 24–14 win.

Super Bowl XXXVIII

Super Bowl XXXVIII featured a match between the New England Patriots and the Carolina Panthers in Houston. The game started out as a defensive struggle that went scoreless well into the second quarter and then progressed into a wild high-scoring contest that was won in the last nine seconds.

The first scoring opportunities were Vinatieri field goal attempts—one that missed and one that was blocked. The first break of the game came when Patriots' linebacker Mike Vrabel chopped at Carolina QB Jake Delhomme's throwing arm as he was about to pass causing a fumble that was recovered by New England's Richard Seymour on the Carolina 20-yard line. Brady went to work, but the Patriots netted only 3 yards on two plays. On third down, Brady had a nifty 12-yard run. Next play, he threw a 5-yard touchdown pass to Deion Branch to go ahead. After the extra point, it was New England 7–Panthers 0.

When Carolina got the ball back, its offense came to life. In a quick drive, Delhomme hit Ricky Proehl for a 13-yard gain and then went to Muhsin Muhammad for 23 more. Delhomme finished the drive off with a 39-yard touchdown pass to Steve Smith. Brady came right back with a 78-yard drive that took less than a minute. The Patriots moved downfield quickly when Branch leaped up for a 52-yard pass and held on. Brady finished off the drive with a short 5-yard pass to David Givens in the end zone. With 18 seconds remaining in the half, Belichick called for a squib kick on the kickoff, but the Panthers were able to return the ball to midfield. Coach John Fox of the Panthers then called for a running play when everyone in the stadium was expecting a pass. Stephen Davis's nifty running play put the Panthers in field goal range. John Kasay kicked a 50-yard field goal to bring the Panthers back. When the half ended, it was Patriots 14—Panthers 10.

After the half, once again the game settled into a defensive battle with neither team scoring. In the first minute of the fourth quarter, New England was finishing up a touchdown drive that included a 33-yard reception by Daniel Graham and ended with a short run by Antowain Smith. New England was up, 21–10.

In the next series, Delhomme sped things up with a no-huddle offense that featured a one-two punch: Steve Smith pass receptions and a monster 33-yard touchdown run by DeShaun Foster. After the Panthers' two point conversion failed, New England was up 21–16. When New England got the ball back they drove all the way to the Panther 9-yard line and just when it looked like the Patriots were going to seal the game, Brady threw an interception to Reggie Howard.

After the turnover, the Panthers faced a third and ten on their next drive when Delhomme led Mohammed perfectly on an 85-yard touchdown pass. Once again, the Panthers missed a 2-point conversion. The Panthers were up, 22–21. When the Patriots got the ball, Brady took them down the field with two big passes to David Givens. The Patriots finished the drive off with a pass to Mike Vrabel who was put into the game for added muscle on a play that would normally call for a run. Next, the Patriots did what the Panthers could not on two previous tries, make a two point conversion. The Patriots moved ahead, 29–22.

Delhomme responded with a super drive of his own that included another strike to Mohammed and two more to Proehl including a 12-yard touchdown pass. With a successful point after touchdown, the game was tied 29–29.

Unfortunately for the Panthers, Kasay punched the ball out of bounds on the kickoff giving the Patriots excellent field position with 1:08 to go. Brady drove the Patriots downfield on two 13-yard completions to Brown. He followed with a short pass to Daniel Graham and called time out for Vinatieri to come out for a field goal attempt. With the season on the line and seconds on the clock, Vinatieri kicked a 41-yard field goal to win the game, 32–29.

2004 Season

Remarkably enough, 2004 would look very much like 2003 for the Patriots. They finished the regular season once again with a 14–2 mark. Belichick did everything he could to keep the team from getting a big head after the previous season and he had to work especially hard to remind them of how much work they needed.

They opened the season against the Indianapolis Colts on a Thursday night with lots of fanfare as the reigning Super Bowl champions, but found themselves losing 17–13 at the half. The Patriots fought back with two passing touchdowns in the second half while the Colts could just muster up one more TD. With seconds remaining in the second half, the Colts missed a field goal that would have tied the game. It was the 16th win in a row for New England. The final score was Patriots 27–Colts 24. Following the opener, the Patriots rolled past the Cardinals, the Bills, and the Dolphins. Beating the Dolphins gave them 19 wins in a row and the record for most consecutive wins in the NFL. After they beat the Seahawks and the Jets, they had an astounding 21 consecutive wins.

The Patriots' first loss came at the hands of the Steelers by a score of 34–20 in the seventh game of the season. Brady threw two interceptions and the Steelers recovered two New England fumbles. The Patriots put their running game on the shelf that day with only 6 rushes for a total of 5 yards. The Steelers' rookie quarterback, Ben Rothlisberger, played an excellent game connecting on 18 of 24 passes for 196 yards and two touchdowns.

Troy Brown, a veteran receiver, was asked to fill in at defensive back. Against the Rams, Brown played cornerback after Asante Samuel was injured in the first few minutes of the game. Brown played well on defense, caught three balls as a receiver, and caught another one on a fake field goal to win the game.

After a six-game winning streak, the Patriots lost to the Dolphins, 29–28, in the 14th game of the season. The Dolphins intercepted four Brady passes that day.

The Patriots faced the Colts in the division playoff. In a bend-don't-break defensive performance, the Patriots allowed Manning to connect on 27 of 42 pass attempts for 238 yards, but no touchdowns. Manning was intercepted once and the Colts also turned the ball over on two fumbles. The Colts gained 46 yards on the ground. Brady had a relatively quiet day. He connected on 18 of 27 attempts for 144 yards. He passed for one touchdown and he ran for one touchdown as well. But unlike the Colts, the Patriots' running game was good for over 200 yards. Corey Dillon had 144 yards on 23 attempts. The Patriots beat Indianapolis, 20–3, limiting Manning's Colts to one Mike Vanderjagt field goal.

AFC Championship Game

In the conference championship game, the Patriots faced the Steelers, the team that had beaten them earlier in the season to break their winning streak. The Steelers came into the championship game with a 15-1 regular season record and the team was undergoing a renaissance with their rookie quarterback, Ben Roethlisberger. The Steelers had a great coaching staff that included Bill Cowher as head coach, Dick LeBeau as defensive coordinator, and Ken Whisenhunt as offensive coordinator. Cowher had been head coach in Pittsburgh since 1992, but in 2004 he had one of the league's premier quarterbacks.

The Patriots were able to knock the Steelers off balance right from the start. After a 48-yard Vinatieri field goal, Brady connected with Branch on a 60-yard touchdown pass. Jeff Reed broke the ice for the Steelers on a 43-yard field goal before the quarter ended. The Patriots led, 10–3.

In the second quarter, Brady hit Givens on a 9-yard touchdown pass to extend the lead. Before the Steelers could score again, Patriots' safety Rodney Harrison intercepted a Roethlisberger pass and ran it back 85 yards for another score. The Patriots led 24–3 at halftime.

In the third quarter when Jerome "the Bus" Bettis scored on a 5-yard plunge, the Patriots responded with a drive of their own and a Corey Dillon 25-yard touchdown run. Hines Ward caught a touchdown pass at the end of the third quarter, and then early in the fourth, Reed kicked another field goal. The Steelers had cut the Patriots' lead to 11 points; it was Patriots 31–Steelers 20. When Vinatieri kicked another field goal, the Patriots lead swelled to 14—not an insurmountable amount, but the Steelers were running out of time. However, when Brady hit Branch for another score, it was pretty much over with the Patriots leading, 41-20. Plaxico Burress caught a Roethlisberger pass for another Steelers' score late in the quarter, but the Patriots prevailed, 41–27.

Brady was 14-of-21 for 207 yards and two touchdowns with no interceptions. Roethlisberger was 14-of-24 for 226 yards and two touchdowns with three interceptions. Corey Dillon of the Patriots was the leading rusher with 24 attempts for 73 yards.

Super Bowl XXXIX

The New England Patriots faced the Philadelphia Eagles in Super Bowl XXXIX. Both the Eagles and the Patriots set out to put extra pressure on the opposing quarterbacks. The Eagles received the opening kickoff and Roderick Hood returned the ball all the way to the Eagles' 39-yard line. When the Eagles' quarterback, Donovan McNabb, was sacked by Bruschi for a 10-yard loss on third down, the Eagles punted the ball to the Patriots. Neither team could advance the ball until midway through the quarter. On the Eagles' possession, McNabb drove downfield on short passes to Westbrook and Smith. McNabb hit Terrell Owens on a 30-yard pass and the Eagles picked up more on an unnecessary roughness call. With first and goal at the 8-yard line, McNabb dropped back and was sacked at the 24-yard line. The Eagles' quarterback threw a pass that was intercepted by Asante Samuel, but the play was called back on a penalty. McNabb followed with another pass and it was intercepted by Rodney Harrison. The Eagles' threat was dead. The first quarter played out without any score.

In the second quarter, Todd Pinkston made a phenomenal catch on third down for a 17-yard gain that kept an Eagles' drive alive. After extending his drive downfield, McNabb threw a strike to L. J. Smith in the end zone. It was Eagles 7–Patriots 0. Brady moved the Patriots down to the Eagles' 4-yard line, but he was sacked and he fumbled the ball to the Eagles. The Eagles could not advance the ball. A poor punt gave the Patriots the ball back at the Eagles' 37-yard line. On the Patriots' series, Brady moved the ball around to different receivers; he hit Graham, Branch, Brown, and Givens. He went to Givens again on a 4-yard touchdown pass. At the half, the score was tied, 7–7.

The Eagles blitzed Brady as the second half got started, but he was able to avoid the sack and pick the defense apart. When the Patriots got down to the 2-yard line, they inserted linebacker Mike Vrabel as an eligible receiver. Brady tossed a pass to Vrabel who was able to tip it up and catch the ball for a touchdown. After the extra point, the Patriots led, 14–7. When the Eagles had the ball, McNabb threw frequently to Terrell Owens but he also responded to the Patriot' pressure by throwing to his running back, Brian Westbrook. Westbrook caught a 10-yard touchdown pass that McNabb rocketed between two Patriot defenders. After the extra point, the score was tied, 14–14.

The Patriots answered with a drive that featured a mix of different pass plays and runs that made frequent use of their running backs, Faulk and Dillon. The Patriots finished off the drive with a short touchdown run by Dillon. The Patriots were ahead 21–14. After holding down the Eagles' offense again, the Patriots took over and moved the ball downfield for a Vinatieri field goal that gave the Patriots a seemingly insurmountable 24–14 lead in the fourth quarter. On the Eagles' possession, McNabb connected with Owens who looked unstoppable. But McNabb turned the ball over on an errant pass right into the hands of linebacker Tedy Bruschi.

The Eagles stopped the Patriots from scoring and had the ball with five minutes to go. McNabb led the Eagles on a drive that took about three minutes and included a number of short passes. With a little less than two minutes remaining, the Eagles scored on a 30-yard pass from McNabb to Greg Lewis. The Patriots led, 24–21. An onside kick by Philadelphia failed and the Patriots were able to burn down the clock to just 17 seconds when McNabb took over. McNabb threw a desperate pass that was intercepted by Harrison with seconds remaining. The Patriots won 24–21. It was Belichick's third Super Bowl victory in 4 years.

2005 Season

In 2005, the Patriots ended the season with a 10–6 record, good enough to win the AFC East and go to a Wild Card game where they easily defeated the Jacksonville Jaguars 28–3. They faced the Broncos in the Divisional playoff. The Patriots suffered through five turnovers: three fumbles and two interceptions. Vinatieri kicked two field goals and Brady passed for one touchdown. Denver scored three touchdowns and two field goals to win 27–13. Denver lost the AFC Championship to the Pittsburgh Steelers who would go on to win Super Bowl XL.

2006 Season

Belichick once again demonstrated his strong-willed management style making decisions he believed were best for the Patriots' overall financial health regardless of the public relations outcomes.

The Patriots could not come to terms with Adam Vinatieri on a new contract and the clutch kicker left for the Indianapolis Colts. Vinatieri had 19 game-winning kicks in his 10 seasons in New England. Belichick drafted another excellent kicker, Stephen Gostkowski, in the fourth round of the 2006 draft. The Patriots finished the regular 2006 season with a 12–4 record and an AFC East title. After winning their Wild Card match with the Jets, they beat the San Diego Chargers in the divisional playoff. In the AFC Championship game, the Patriots jumped out ahead of the Colts. On their first scoring drive, a Tom Brady handoff to Kevin Faulk in the red zone was muffed. As Indianapolis fans sat in horror, the ball passed through several Indianapolis players' hands on a miraculous 5-yard journey into the end zone where Patriots' guard Logan Makins fell on it for the score. The Colts were able to get on the board with Adam Vinatieri's 42-yard field goal. New England responded with an excellent Tom Brady led drive that included a few risky fourth-down conversions. The drive was finished off with a Corey Dillon 7-yard scamper into the end zone. When the Colts tried to get back on track on offense, Assante Samuel stepped in front of a Colts' receiver and intercepted a Peyton Manning pass, which he ran in for a touchdown. It looked like lights out for Indy: New England 21—Indianapolis 3.

New England had knocked the Colts out of the playoffs for the last two seasons and Peyton Manning was determined to turn the tables. The Colts stuffed the next New England drive and then drove the ball into Patriots' territory and kicked a field goal. A short time later, the Colts followed with a touchdown drive that Manning himself finished off with a quarterback sneak. It was New England 21—Indianapolis 13.

Once again the Colts were able to stop the Patriots' offense, but the Patriots were unable to return the favor. Manning was in a zone. Another drive was engineered by Manning and a blatant pass interference foul gave the Colts the ball on the 1-yard line. The Colts brought in 275 pound defensive tackle Dan Klecko who came out of the backfield to catch a touchdown pass. It was reminiscent of the Patriots' use of Mike Vrabel on goal line situations. After making a 2-point conversion, the score was 21–21.

On the ensuing kickoff, Ellis Hobbs brought the Patriots back to life in a hurry with a sideline dash all the way down to the Colts' 16-yard line. In a

New England minute, Brady threw a strike to Jabar Gaffney in the end zone. After the extra point, it was New England 28—Indianapolis 21. The Colts came right back with a combination of strong running and accurate passing. In the red zone, Dominic Rhodes got the call to run the ball in, but he fumbled. However, this time the Colts center Jeff Saturday beat the Patriots to the ball and recovered it in the end zone for an Indianapolis touchdown. The Colts had caught-up to the Patriots once again; the score was 28–28. New England recovered quickly to drive down for another field goal to give them a 31–28 lead. The Colts responded with a clutch Vinatieri field goal that was matched by yet another from the Patriot's Steve Gostkowski. The score stood at 34–31 with just under four minutes to play.

When the Colts took possession, Manning proceeded to thread the ball through the New England defense—throwing passes in tight places that few other quarterbacks could do successfully. In another dramatic play, as the Colts drove the ball downfield, wide receiver Reggie Wayne snagged a pass and then bobbled the ball with three Patriot defenders swatting at it. Wayne was able to bring the ball back into his grasp. The drive was finished off by Joseph Addai who took a handoff from Manning and ran through the center of the New England line for a score. After the extra point, the Colts were ahead, 38–34.

But the Colts and other NFL teams know that you can't count Belichick and Brady out until the game ends. When Brady got back on the field, the Patriots, had one minute remaining to play and 80 yards between them and victory. Marlin Jackson stepped out in front of a Brady pass to make an interception that sealed the Colts' victory. Two weeks later, the Colts went on to beat the Bears, 29–17, in Super Bowl XLI.

2007 Season

Belichick's Patriots suffered during the offseason from their painful 38–34 loss to the Indianapolis Colts in the 2006 Conference Championship game. It wasn't that they had lost to a poor team, after all, the Colts went on to win the Super Bowl; it was painful because they seemed to have the game in hand when they led, 21–6, at the half and then collapsed. Belichick went to work shoring up weaknesses almost immediately. Free agents Adalius Thomas, Kyle Brady, and Sammy Morris were signed. Wide receiver Donte Stallworth came over from Philadelphia as a free agent and headline receiver Randy Moss arrived from Oakland in a trade. Wes Welker, who would serve as one of Brady's favorite targets for six seasons, was acquired through a trade with the Dolphins.

The Patriots opened up strong and beat the Jets, Chargers, Bills, Bengals, and Browns. In week six, the Cowboys gave the Patriots a tough first half, but the Patriots turned things around to beat them soundly, 48–27. The Patriots handled the Dolphins and Redskins without much trouble, but had their hands full when they faced Peyton Manning and the Colts. Belichick's team came from behind in the fourth quarter to win 24–20. Brady threw for two touchdowns in the last 8 minutes of the game while the Patriots' defense sacked Manning twice and forced two fumbles. The second half of the season was more difficult than the first. The Patriots blasted the Bills, 56–10, but had to fight past the Eagles, 31–28, and the Ravens, 27–24. After beating the Jets, Steelers, and Dolphins handily, they wrestled with the Giants to maintain their unblemished record in the last game of the regular season. Both Tom Brady and Giants' quarterback Eli Manning played well. With less than five minutes to go, the Giants had the ball trailing by 10 points. Manning surgically brought the ball downfield with short passes and he hit Plexico Burress for the score with a little over one minute remaining. Trailing 38–35, the Giants tried an onside kick, but Mike Vrabel recovered the ball for the Patriots and Brady closed out the last minute for the win.

When the Patriots faced the Jacksonville Jaguars in the divisional playoff game, Brady played a superb game, hitting 22 of 26 passes for a new NFL completion record. The Jaguars focused on Moss and defending the big play so Brady played ball control with short strikes to his other receivers. At the half, the teams were tied at 14 all. In the third quarter, the Patriots pulled ahead and kept the Jaguars out of the end zone. New England won, 31-20.

The San Diego Chargers had fought past the Colts in their divisional match to face the Patriots in the Conference Championship game. LaDanian Tomlinson, who was good for 1,949 yards of offense in 2007, crossed onto the field briefly and had to sit out the balance of the game with an injury. The Chargers were able to put together some solid drives, but they lacked the offensive punch to get the ball into the end zone. Nate Keading kicked four field goals that accounted for all of the Chargers' 12 points. Patriots' running back Laurence Maroney rushed for 122 yards for the second playoff game in a row. Brady had another conservative day with 22 completions on 33 attempts for 209 yards and two touchdowns. He also tossed three troubling interceptions in the game, but the 21–12 win was the Patriots 18th victory in a row and one that set a new record for 16 consecutive wins in a season.

Super Bowl XLII

The "perfect" 16–0 Patriots faced the "nothing-to-lose" 10–6 New York Giants who had come into the playoffs as a Wild Card team. In the Giants' first series of the game, they held the ball for over nine minutes, scored 3 points on a Lawrence Tynes 32-yard field goal, and perhaps most importantly, they kept the ball out of Tom Brady's hands. On the kickoff, the Giants' special teams did not maintain their lanes and allowed an easy return to midfield by Maroney. Starting in excellent field position, Brady passed his way toward the goal. When the Giants were called for pass interference in the end zone, the Patriots had a first down on the 1-yard line. Maroney ran the ball in and after the extra point, the score was Patriots 7—Giants 3.

The rest of the first half played out as a series of mistakes by both the Giants and the Patriots followed by tenacious defenses that kept both teams from scoring. The Giants were able to put tremendous pressure on Brady.

After a scoreless third quarter, Eli Manning linked up with Kevin Boss for 45 yards. A few plays later, Manning hit David Tyre for a touchdown. After the extra point, the Giants led, 10–7. A few possessions later, Brady and the Patriots came back to life. Brady skillfully called on Moss, Welker, and Faulk to move downfield. On the final play of the drive, Brady tossed Moss a 7-yard pass in the end zone after cornerback Corey Webster lost his footing. With the point after touchdown, the Patriots had the lead, 14–10.

New York took over with 2:39 to go. Manning showed incredible poise and determination. After a couple of successful passes to Amoni Toomer, the Giants stalled and found themselves with a fourth down and inches. A successful lunge by Brandon Jacobs provided new life. On the Giants' 44-yard line, Manning dropped back on a third down with 5 yards to go for the first. The Patriots swarmed all over Manning, but he twisted and turned to pull himself away from what looked like a sure sack. Once clear, Manning threw a high bullet towards David Tyre. Fully extended and arm in arm with defensive back Rodney Harrison, Tyre trapped the ball against his helmet in midair and then grabbed it with both hands as he fell to the ground. It was the most incredible catch in Super Bowl history. With 35 seconds to go, Plexico Burress was able to get behind the Patriot defenders in the end zone for a Manning pass and score. After the extra point, the Giants led 17–14. In the waning seconds, Brady tried to drive the ball down for one last score, but failed on a couple of desperate bombs. For the game, Manning completed 19 of 34 passes for 255 yards and two touchdowns while throwing two interceptions. Brady was 29 of 48 for 266 yards and one touchdown with no interceptions. Super Bowl XLII was Belichick's fourth appearance in the championship game.

2008-2010 Seasons

In 2008, quarterback Matt Cassel replaced Brady who suffered a season-ending knee injury in the opening game. Despite an impressive 11–5 season, the Patriots were nosed out of the playoffs by the Miami Dolphins. Under Cassel, the Patriots were a good football team, but they were not a great one.

In 2009, the Patriots ended the season with a 10–6 record and the AFC East title. Their postseason was short. They lost to the Ravens in a Wild Card game. After the Ravens took the opening kickoff, on their first play from scrimmage, Ray Rice rushed for 83 yards and a touchdown. The players took their first sip of Gatorade when Billy Cundiff kicked the extra point. On the Patriots' first series, Brady was sacked by Terrell Suggs on third down and fumbled the ball, which Suggs himself recovered at the Patriots' 17-yard line. The Ravens' Willis McGahee and Ray Rice drove the ball down to the 1-yard-line on short runs. From there, 260-pound fullback, LeRon McClain, got the last tough yard with a 1-yard plunge. Things did not improve much for the Patriots on the day and the Ravens brought home a 33–14 victory.

In 2010, the Patriots looked to be in very good form again when they finished the season 14–2. What followed was a disappointing 28–21 loss to their bitter rivals, the New York Jets, in the divisional round of the playoffs. Brady threw for 299 yards and two touchdowns with one interception, but he was sacked five times by the Jets' defense. The Jets' Mark Sanchez did not roll up the same yardage numbers as Brady, but he threw for three touchdowns with no interceptions. Early in the season, the Jets beat the Patriots by a score of 28–14, at the New Meadowlands Stadium, but New England embarrassed the Jets in a 45–3 blowout before a national audience on Monday Night Football on December 6 in Foxborough.[18]

2011 Season

In their excellent 2011 season, the Patriots lost to the Bills, the Steelers, and the Giants—and won every other game to end the season with a 13-3 record, the best in the AFC. They lost to the Bills in the early season and beat them in the last game. After falling behind 21–0 at the end of the first quarter, the Patriots' offense caught fire scoring 49 unanswered points and crushing the Bills 49–21.

Tebow and the Divisional Match

Tim Tebow created a lot of excitement in Denver in 2011 when he came off the bench to lead the Broncos to 6 wins in a row including 2 in overtime. But when the Broncos faced Brady and the Patriots on December 18, the Denver season crumbled. The Patriots beat back the Broncos, 43–23. The Broncos finished out their season with losses to the Bills and the Chiefs. When the Broncos 8-8 record was good enough to get them into a WildCard game, they managed to beat the Steelers 29–23 only to face the Patriots in a divisional game. In the divisional game, Brady threw six touchdown passes and Gronkowski caught three of them in the Patriots' 45–10 win against the Tim Tebow led Denver Broncos.

AFC Championship Game

The AFC Championship Game against the Baltimore Ravens proved to be a much tougher contest for the Patriots. Defense and field position played a critical role in this game that featured five field goals and four touchdowns. Towards the end of regulation, a scoreboard error required a rushed attempt at a 32-yard field goal that was missed by Billy Cundiff of the Ravens. The Patriots won the game, 23–20.

Oddly enough, both quarterbacks were 22 for 36. The Ravens' Joe Flacco passed for 306 yards and two touchdowns while tossing one interception. Brady had a rough day by his standards. He passed for 239 yards without a touchdown throw although he did rush for one of the Patriots' two touchdowns from 1 yard out. BenJarvus Green-Ellis rushed for the other Patriots' touchdown, while Gostkowski kicked three field goals. Flacco hit Dennis Pitta from 6 yards out for the Ravens first touchdown. Their second came in the third quarter when Torrey Smith caught a 29-yard pass from Flacco. Cundiff chipped in two field goals in the Ravens' 20-point effort.

Brady was visibly distraught over his performance in interviews after the game, although the 23–20 win moved the Patriots into another Super Bowl. Plus Brady tied Joe Montana's 16 career post season wins record and it also put him in position to match John Elway's record as the only quarterback to start five Super Bowls. Belichick's mind may have been on what he was going to do to fix the Patriots' shortcomings for the Super Bowl, but he took a few minutes to gush about his quarterback:

Anything that's associated with winning, I'm proud of. I mean, I'm proud -- there's no quarterback I'd rather have than Tom Brady. He's the best. He does so much for us in so many ways on so many different levels. I'm really fortunate that he's our quarterback and for what he's able to do for this team. It's good to win with him and all the rest of our players.[19]

Super Bowl XLVI

Super Bowl XLVI pitted the New England Patriots against the New York Giants. The Giants held a lowly 9–7 regular season record, they allowed more points than they scored, and they lost four games in a row in the middle of the season. But they beat the Falcons, Packers, and 49ers in the post season.

Almost immediately, the Patriots dug themselves into a hole. After the Giants received the kickoff, they advanced to midfield and punted the ball deep into the Patriots' territory. With Brady throwing from the end zone on the Patriots' first play from scrimmage, he tossed one down the middle with no player in the area. Charged with intentional grounding in the end zone, the play was ruled a safety with two points awarded to the Giants. After Zolton Mesko's 62-yard punt following the safety and a 4-yard return, quarterback Eli Manning started at his own 22-yard line. The Giants looked like they had planned for the Patriots all season long. Manning's first three plays netted 45 yards with short passes to Henry Hynosk and DJ Ware followed by a 24-yard run by Ahmad Bradshaw. Manning drove the Giants to the Patriots' 16-yard line and on third down, Victor Cruz caught a short pass but he fumbled. The Patriots recovered the ball, but they had 12 men on the field so the ball went back to the Giants at the 6-yard line. After Bradshaw gained a few more yards, Manning hit Cruz for a touchdown.

Early in the second quarter, Brady drove the Patriots down to the Giants' 11-yard line where the drive stalled and Gostkowski kicked a field goal. The Giants' careful offense stalled out on a few series and with a little over four minutes to play in the half, Steve Weatherford executed a flawless punt that went out of bounds on the Patriots' 4-yard line. From there Brady began a long drive to recapture the lead. Overcoming a false start and a holding penalty along the way, the Patriots drove downfield on 16 plays. With 15 seconds on the clock, Brady hit Danny Woodhead from 4 yards out for the score. After the point after, the Patriots led 10–9.

Brady started the second half where he had left off in the first. He drove the Patriots downfield for a touchdown on the first offensive series of the second half. An opening pass to Chad "Ochocinco" Johnson net 21 yards and demonstrated the need for the Giants to protect for the deeper throws. The Patriots mixed in some runs and short passes to move up towards the goal, and Brady hit his big tight end Aaron Hernandez from 12 yards out for another score. After the extra point, the Patriots led 17-9. Manning responded with a solid drive, but a few incomplete passes brought in the field goal unit at the New England 24. The Giants closed to 17-12 with a Lawrence Tynes 38-yard field goal.

The Giants' defense tightened. After a Patriots 3 and out, Manning drove the ball again for another Tynes' field goal—this one from the 33-yard line. It was now Patriots 17–Giants 15 as the third quarter wound down. Both the Patriots and the Giants trolled the bottom of NFL defensive stats for the year, but the Giants mustered a defensive stand that kept the Patriots from scoring in the final quarter.

Brady was intercepted on the Patriots' next possession, but the Giants failed to capitalize. The Patriots' next drive stalled outside of field goal range and after a Mesko punt, the Giants took over on their own 12-yard line. On first down, Manning gave the Patriots' defense a scare when he hit Mario Manningham for 38 yards. Manning went right back to another deep pass to Manningham that missed, but he switched over to short passes and a few Bradshaw runs to move the ball towards the goal. From the 6-yard line Bradshaw ran up the middle for a Giants' score. A two point conversion was tried, but failed. The Giants led 21-17.

The dramatic game was coming to an end as Brady started out on his own 20-yard line with 57 seconds to go after the Tynes' kickoff resulted in a touchback. The Giants' defense was up to the task and after three downs, Brady needed 16 yards for a first down. Remarkably, Brady hit Branch for 19 yards and a new lease on life with just 39 seconds remaining. He hit Hernandez for 11 yards, but with no time outs, Brady spiked the ball to stop the clock with 19 seconds on the New England 44-yard line. Two incomplete passes and a penalty on the Giants, put the ball on the Patriots' 49-yard line with just enough time for one more play. Brady hoisted the ball into the end zone towards a cluster of players and the game ended with a tipped ball that fell a couple feet away from a hobbled Rob Grankowski. The Giants won 21-17.

2012 Season

In 2012, the Patriots' won the AFC East title and made another run at the Super Bowl. The Patriots ended the season with a 12–4 record. After the first six games, the Patriots looked like they might be in for a struggle. They lost by a single point to the Baltimore Ravens and the Seattle Seahawks, both contending teams, but they were surprised by the Arizona Cardinals in a 20–18 loss. After just getting by in a week seven overtime win against the Jets, the Patriots won six in a row. After losing to a rising San Francisco 49ers team, they won their last two regular season matches.

Belichick's Patriots beat an excellent Houston Texans team in the divisional playoff in which Tom Brady outgunned Texans quarterback Matt Schaub by 1 yard in total passing—344 to 343. The Patriots lost to the Baltimore Ravens in the Conference Championship game. Tight end Rob Gronkowski had a broken forearm and was not available for that game. The Ravens went on to win Super Bowl XLVII.

2013 Season

In 2013, the Patriots' regular season ended like so many under Belichick with an AFC East title and another playoff appearance.

In the first half of the season, the Patriots rolled out four wins before losing to the Cincinnati Bengals, 13-6, in game five. The Bengals defense, one of the best in the NFL, harassed Brady with four sacks and they provided excellent coverage of Patriot receivers. Former Patriots' running back, BenJarvus Green-Ellis of the Bengals, scored the only touchdown of the game on a 1-yard plunge. Towards the end of the game, the Patriots looked like they were poised for a Brady led come-from-behind score, but the Bengals prevailed. The Patriots were held to two field goals and no touchdowns—a feat no defense had been able to manage since the Jets did it in the 2009 season. The loss also ended a remarkable Tom Brady 52-game touchdown pass streak—a mark that is second only to Drew Breese's record of 54.

After beating the Saints, the Patriots fell to the Jets, 30-27. A Nick Folk field goal in overtime won it for New York. Following a loss to a very good Carolina Panthers team, 24-20, the Patriots got past Peyton Manning's Broncos, 34-31, in overtime on a Gostkowski field goal. New England struggled to beat the Texans and the Browns, two teams that were doing poorly. Post season hopes started to fade when the Patriots lost, 24–20, to the Dolphins. But their 41–7 thrashing of the Baltimore Ravens and a 34–20 win over the Bills gave Belichick something to build on as the Patriots headed into the playoffs atop the AFC East.

Chuck Pagano's Indianapolis Colts led by quarterback Andrew Luck stood in New England's path in the playoffs. Luck had just come off a 45–44 come-from-behind Wild Card win against the Chiefs when he lined up his team against the mighty Patriots at Gillette Stadium for the divisional playoff on January 11, 2014. Surprising many football fans and the media, Belichick's game plan called on a rigorous ground game that was led by LeGarrette Blount who rushed for 166 yards and four touchdowns. The Patriots sailed past the Colts, 43-22, on their way to the AFC Championship game against the Denver Broncos at Sports Authority Field in Mile High Stadium.

AFC Championship Game

Belichick's skill at finding and exploiting weaknesses in his opponents is legendary. In past matches that featured two of the greatest quarterbacks in football history, Tom Brady and Peyton Manning, Belichick's game plans often seemed invincible, Tom Brady's performance near flawless.

On an absolutely balmy day in Denver on January 19, a very mature, self assured Peyton Manning, with a superb supporting cast on offense and an inspired defense, defeated the Patriots, 26-16. Manning performed with cold calculated precision and the Broncos defense played with an inspired emotional edge.

On Denver's second possession, four completions by Manning brought the Broncos close enough for a Matt Prater field goal. Early in the second quarter, running backs Knowshon Moreno and Montee Ball softened up the Patriots' defense with some gains on the ground. Manning succeeded to drive the ball downfield with completions. A short pass to Jacob Tamme gave the Broncos a touchdown.

Brady struggled to establish scoring drives in the first half. Blount got next to nothing on the ground and Brady passed 17 times to eight different receivers trying to find some success. The best the Patriots could do was a Gostkowski field goal.

After Gostkowski's field goal, Manning brought the Broncos downfield on short passes and Prater kicked his second field goal of the game. Trailing 13–3 at the half, the key for the Patriots would be to improve passing accuracy and scoring. Holding Manning to 13 points in a half was encouraging as long as the Patriots' offense could step up and hit their stride. When the Broncos got the ball to lead off the second half, Manning led a time-consuming carefully-calibrated drive that ate up about half the quarter and ended in a short pass to Demaryius Thomas for a score. The Patriots running back Stevan Ridley was able to gain some yards on the ground in the next series, but Brady had trouble hitting his receivers for substantial gains. When Belichick called for a passing play on fourth down at the Denver 29-yard line, defensive tackle Terrance Knighton sacked the Patriots' quarterback to end the drive. Again, Manning carefully directed the Broncos' attack on the next series and got close enough for another Prater field goal. Time was running out for the Patriots; the Broncos were leading 23–3 with a little more than 12 minutes to go. Brady used up less than 3 minutes to take the Patriots downfield and score—making good use of several receivers, but favoring Julian Edelman. Edelman is a gifted receiver in the mold of Wes Welker—one of Brady's former favorite targets. The Broncos chewed up another 2 minutes on their next drive and Prater kicked a 53-yard field goal to make the score, 26–10. The Broncos defense was not giving anything away too deep on the Patriots next drive so Brady's drive featured mostly short passes. Brady carried the ball up the middle from the 5-yard line for another score—the series using up about 4 precious minutes. A 2-point conversion failed as did an onside kick attempt and the ball was in Denver's hands with 3:06 to go. Manning played it cautious, but managed a few first downs and the game ended with Denver winning, 26–16.

Manning completed 32 of 43 passes for 400 yards and two touchdowns. Brady completed 24 of 38 passes for 277 yards and one touchdown. Some in the media expressed the view that the Patriots have a relatively young corps of receivers who need more experience. The excellent running game that the Patriots displayed against the Colts was not present in Denver. The Patriots rushed for 64 yards.

In Belichick's press conference to discuss the game, he described the playoff loss as a "crash-landing" for the season and looked forward to working towards the next season. He praised the play and coaching of the Broncos and praised his own players for their efforts. As in other seasons, he expressed his plans to look carefully at players, coaches, and the other aspects of the Patriots' program.

Long Live Belichickism

At one time, football was a game where men suited up, put on their cleats, and faced off for an hour of brutal sport that was all running, pushing, shoving, tackling, diving, blocking, grabbing, and leaping. But the NFL game today is a mix of physicality and strategic planning and implementation. Professional football includes heady plans and preparations that put a premium on brain power. There are preseason strategies, pregame strategies, second half "adjustments," and postseason strategies. For Bill Belichick every game is a new beginning. When a team plays a Belichick team, most anything is possible because new wrinkles can be added from week to week.

Belichick sees potential in players that are overlooked by other teams. He selects players who can have a complete commitment to the team and the game. When he selects such players, he has complete confidence that his players will do all they can to stay on the field and perform. He can motivate his players by allowing them to work, to play, to succeed.

It was Scott Pioli who developed with Belichick a philosophy of team building by team need and fit, selecting character first–talent next. It was Belichick's family "waste not-want not" roots that taught him that wasted salaries in one player would lead to unmet needs in another. It was Steve Belichick's scouting and judgment of men that gave his son a desire to keep digging for potential and keep demanding performance in everyone around him. It was defensive coach Romeo Crennel who helped Belichick communicate game plans that build over game week and peak at the right time.

It was Charlie Weis who shared Belichick's passion for teaching and creating play calling. It was Bill Parcells who gave Belichick an example of a tough coach who garnered the respect of his players.

Belichick is a head coach who has worked hard to have a complete understanding of the game at every phase. He understands offense, defense, and special teams. This well-rounded understanding serves coaches well in the NFL. At the same time, Belichick is not afraid to hire strong coordinators and listen to opinions that are contrary to his own.

Belichick is a coach who strives to insure that his players have the skills and techniques that are necessary to counter the strengths of the opposition and maximize the strengths of his system. While other coaches may collect the best players, Belichick obtains the best players for his system.

Belichick is a coach who believes in the team concept in an age of the superstar. He has been able to consistently mold a group of men to perform at a very high level as a team with unselfish players who can spell each other when injuries occur. This does not just happen. In order to maintain a team of unselfish players, the team has to use discretion when drafting and signing free agents. Occasionally, the Patriots have added players that do not fit the Belichick system. These are often stop-gap moves to bolster a critical need for a short period of time.

Belichick and his staff work endlessly to successfully predict the opposition moves—not just what they will do, but why they do it. Belichick demonstrates a duty to move personnel that overrides any emotional attachment he has to his players. If a tough move needs to be made, he consistently makes it. Belichick is a task master who works hard to be a consistent manager of men, but he is not so self-righteous that he injures his team by being inflexible.

Final Measure Unknown

Belichick's contributions to football continue. His final measure in unknown. He has been at the helm of New England for over 13 seasons. In that time, he has won three Super Bowl titles, five Conference Championships, and 11 Division titles.[20] In 2007, Belichick coached the Patriots to a perfect 16-0 regular season. His winning percentage with New England is over 70%. His winning percentage as a head coach is among the elite of the sport. Belichick has been named Associated Press Coach of the Year three times.

Bill Belichick has made his mark in football by demanding that all the players and coaches involved with his team are dedicated and committed to a maximum effort. Belichick's organization is like military service—a call to duty is made and everyone is expected to be a comrade in arms. There are no stars. There are no celebrities. There are just soldiers and officers—the players are the soldiers, the coaches are the officers. No one talks out of turn because "loose lips sink ships." His success formula is out there for everyone to see and mimic, but the effort required to duplicate his success is rare.

Belichick is a coach who has created a team culture where all its members strive on a fundamental level to do their job and focus on their responsibilities. His players understand that performing under pressure is simply performing. In Belichick's system, one game is simply like every other game, but every game requires maximum effort.

Bill Belichick Timeline

1952

● April 16, 1952, William Stephen Belichick is born in Nashville, Tennessee.

1967-1971

● Belichick attends Annapolis High School and plays football and lacrosse, graduating in 1970. He finishes off another year of prep school education at Phillips Academy in 1971.

1972-1975

● Belichick attends Wesleyan University in Middletown, Connecticut, where he plays football and lacrosse. He graduates in 1975.
● Belichick begins pro career as special assistant on Ted Marchibroda's Baltimore Colts staff.

1976-1977

● Belichick works as personal assistant to Rick Forzano of the Detroit Lions.

1978

● Belichick works as assistant to special teams for Denver Broncos defensive coordinator, Joe Collier.

1979-1990

● Belichick works on staff of the New York Giants. He works with special teams, then linebackers, and in 1985 he takes over as defensive coordinator. He works under head coach Ray Perkins and then Bill Parcells who took over as head coach in 1983.

1991-1995

● On February 5, 1991, Belichick is hired as head coach of the Cleveland Browns.

1994

● Belichick has his best year with the Browns—the team ends the season, 12–4. The Steelers eliminate the Browns in the divisional playoff, 29–9.

1996

● Belichick joins Parcells staff of the New England Patriots as an assistant head coach and defensive backs coach for the 1996 season. The Patriots advance to the Super Bowl, but lose to the Packers and Bret Favre, 35–21.

1997-1999

● Belichick follows Parcells to the Jets in 1997 and stays through 1999 as defensive coordinator.
● After Parcells announces his retirement from coaching following the 1999 season, Belichick assumes the title of Jets' head coach by contract, but one day later, resigns the position.

2000

● Belichick takes over as head coach of the New England Patriots.
● Belichick drafts Tom Brady in the sixth round of the 2000 draft, pick number 199.

2002

● January 27, 2002, the 2001 New England Patriots defeat the Pittsburgh Steelers, 24–17, in the

AFC Championship game.

- February 3, 2002, the 2001 New England Patriots defeat the St. Louis Rams, 20–17, in Super Bowl XXXVI.
- The 2002 Patriots finish in a tie with the Jets and the Dolphins atop the AFC East Division. The Jets head into the post season based on tie-breaker rules.

2003

- Belichick is named AP, Sporting News, and Pro Football Weekly NFL Coach of the Year for 2003.

2004

- January 18, 2004, the 2003 New England Patriots defeat Peyton Manning and the Colts, 24–14, in the AFC Championship game.
- February 1, 2004, the 2003 New England Patriots defeat the Carolina Panthers, 32–29, in Super Bowl XXXVIII.

2005

- January 23, 2005, the 2004 New England Patriots defeat the Pittsburgh Steelers, 41–27, in the AFC Championship game.
- February 6, 2005, the 2004 New England Patriots defeat the Philadelphia Eagles, 24–21, in Super Bowl XXXIX.

2007

- January 21, 2007, the 2006 Indianapolis Colts defeat the 2006 New England Patriots, 38–34, in the NFC Championship game.
- Belichick is named AP, Sporting News, and Pro Football Weekly NFL Coach of the Year for 2007. He is

also given the Earle "Greasy" Neale Award for Professional Coach of the Year for 2007.

2008

- January 20, 2008, the 2007 New England Patriots defeat the San Diego Chargers, 21–12, in the AFC Championship game.
- February 3, 2008, the New York Giants defeat the New England Patriots, 17–14, in Super Bowl XLII.
- The 2008 Patriots finish in a tie with the Dolphins atop the AFC East Division. The Dolphins head into the post season based on tie-breaker rules.

2010

- Belichick is named AP NFL Coach of the Year for 2010.

2011-2012

- January 22, 2012, the 2011 New England Patriots defeat the Baltimore Ravens, 23–20, in the AFC Championship game.
- February 5, 2012, the New York Giants defeat the 2012 New England Patriots, 21–17, in Super Bowl XLVI.

2013

- January 20, 2013, the Baltimore Ravens defeat the 2012 New England Patriots, 28–13, in the AFC Championship game.
- The New England Patriots finish the regular 2013 season at the top spot in the AFC East for the 13th time in a row.
- January 19, 2014, the Denver Broncos defeat the 2013 New England Patriots in the AFC Championship game, 26–16.

Highlights

Bill Belichick brings military discipline into his coaching program to build teams that are consistently among the top in the NFL. His overall NFL record is 218–114–0 through the 2013 season. Through 2013, he has three NFL Championships to his credit— winning Super Bowl XXXVI, Super Bowl XXXVIII, and Super Bowl XXXIX—and he has five AFC Championships. The Patriots have come out on top of the AFC East Division for 13 consecutive seasons. Belichick's coaching decisions demonstrate a complete understanding of the game at every phase. His program consistently develops player skills that counter opposition strengths. Players predict opposition moves and understand the reasoning behind them. Unselfish players "do their job" and fill in for others. The right personnel move overrides any emotional attachments.

Endnotes

[1] Rick Morrissey, *In the Wake of the News* Column, "Staid Belichick Often Gets Last Laugh: Patriots Coach's Favorite Punch Line: Winning," *Chicago Tribune*, January 30, 2008, 4.1.

[2] David Halberstam, *The Education of a Coach*, (NY: Hyperion, 2005) 16.

[3] "In Their Own Words," NFL Films, 2004, Show #19, 2006, Bill Belichick.

[4] *Football Scouting Methods* is now available in a reprint edition published by Martino Fine Books (http://www.martinopublishing.com/).

[5] Michael Holley, *Patriot Reign: Bill Belichick, the Coaches and the Players Who Built a Championship*, (NY: HarperCollins, 2004) 11.

[6] Halberstam, *The Education of a Coach*, 109-111.

[7] Vic Carucci, "Despite Appearances, There Is No Mystery to Belichick's Winning Ways," NFL.com. Viewed at http://www.nfl.com/superbowl/story/09000d5d8064cdbd/article/despite-appearances-theres-no-mystery-to-belichicks-winning-ways on 12/6/13.

[8] Bill Belichick Press Conference, September 21, 2012, viewed at Patriots home page at http://www.patriots.com/news/article-1/Bill-Belichick-Press-Conference-Transcript/779ac9e9-eaab-4377-b657-5c461c45fd76 on November 5, 2013.

[9] Halberstam, *The Education of a Coach*, 129.

[10] Carlo DeVito, *Parcells: A Biography* (Chicago, Triumph Books, 2011).

[11] A small number of players are listed here to give readers some sense of the team—it's not meant to be inclusive.

[12] All purpose yards include yardage for rushing, receiving, kick returns, and punt returns.

[13] NFL Films, *"Cleveland '95: A Football Life,"* examines the move itself and includes interviews from many of the coaches, fans, and staff involved.

[14] Rick Harrow, *When the Game is on the Line: From the Man Who Brought the Heat to Miami and the Browns Back to Cleveland*, (Cambridge, MA, Da Capo Press, 2003) 169.

[15] Mike Freeman, "Belichick Has Patriots Ears, Now the Hard Part," *New York Times*, July 26, 2000, viewed at http://www.nytimes.com/2000/07/26/sports/pro-football-belichick-has-patriots-ears-now-the-hard-part.html on September 26, 2013.

[16] The Quarterback rating is the official NFL statistical analysis of the passing aspects of quarterbacking—it does not rate anything outside of passing, but it does reflect additional yards gained after the catch. It takes into account percentage of completions and interceptions, average yards gained, and percentage of touchdown passes.

[17] AP, NFL Roundup, "Patriots Cut Captain Lawyer Milloy," *Desert News*, September 3, 2003, viewed at http://www.deseretnews.com/article/510051541/Patriots-cut-captain-Lawyer-Milloy.html?pg=all on November 6, 2013.

[18] The New Meadowsland Stadium was renamed the MetLife Stadium in August 2011.

[19] Chris Forsberg, "Tom Brady Better than He Thinks," ESPN Boston, January 23, 2012, viewed at http://espn.go.com/boston/nfl/story/_/id/7491526/tom-brady-not-best-back-super-bowl on September 25, 2013.

[20] Belichick's Patriots finished 13 consecutive seasons on top of the AFC East based on win-loss record, but they were tied with the Jets and Dolphins in 2002 and they were tied with the Dolphins in 2008. Tie breaker rules gave the division crown to the Jets in 2002 and the Dolphins in 2008. Thus while the Patriots have finished atop their division for 13 seasons in a row, they have 11 division titles.

NFL Champions

1920	Akron Pros	Elgie Tobin
1921	Chicago Staleys	George Halas Dutch Sternaman
1922	Canton Bulldogs	Guy Chamberlin
1923	Canton Bulldogs	Guy Chamberlin
1924	Cleveland Bulldogs	Guy Chamberlin
1925	Chicago Cardinals	Norman Barry
1926	Frankford Yellow Jackets	Guy Chamberlin
1927	New York Giants	Earl Petteiger
1928	Providence Steamroller	Jimmy Conzelman
1929	Green Bay Packers	Curly Lambeau
1930	Green Bay Packers	Curly Lambeau
1931	Green Bay Packers	Curly Lambeau
1932	Chicago Bears	Ralph Jones
1933	Chicago Bears	George Halas
1934	New York Giants	Steve Owen
1935	Detroit Lions	Potsy Clark
1936	Green Bay Packers	Curly Lambeau
1937	Washington Redskins	Ray Flaherty
1938	New York Giants	Steve Owen
1939	Green Bay Packers	Curly Lambeau
1940	Chicago Bears	George Halas
1941	Chicago Bears	George Halas
1942	Washington Redskins	Ray Flaherty
1943	Chicago Bears	Hunk Anderson Luke Johnsos
1944	Green Bay Packers	Curly Lambeau
1945	Cleveland Rams	Adam Walsh
1946	Chicago Bears	George Halas
1947	Chicago Cardinals	Jimmy Conzelman
1948	Philadelphia Eagles	Greasy Neale
1949	Philadelphia Eagles	Greasy Neale
1950	Cleveland Browns	Paul Brown
1951	Los Angeles Rams	Joe Stydahar
1952	Detroit Lions	Buddy Parker
1953	Detroit Lions	Buddy Parker
1954	Cleveland Browns	Paul Brown
1955	Cleveland Browns	Paul Brown
1956	New York Giants	Jim Lee Howell
1957	Detroit Lions	George Wilson
1958	Baltimore Colts	Weeb Ewbank
1959	Baltimore Colts	Weeb Ewbank
1960	Philadelphia Eagles	Buck Shaw

1961	Green Bay Packers	Vince Lombardi
1962	Green Bay Packers	Vince Lombardi
1963	Chicago Bears	George Halas
1964	Cleveland Browns	Blanton Collier
1965	Green Bay Packers	Vince Lombardi
1966	Green Bay Packers	Vince Lombardi
1967	Green Bay Packers	Vince Lombardi
1968	New York Jets	Weeb Ewbank
1969	Kansas City Chiefs	Hank Stram
1970	Baltimore Colts	Don McCafferty
1971	Dallas Cowboys	Tom Landry
1972	Miami Dolphins	Don Shula
1973	Miami Dolphins	Don Shula
1974	Pittsburgh Steelers	Chuck Noll
1975	Pittsburgh Steelers	Chuck Noll
1976	Oakland Raiders	John Madden
1977	Dallas Cowboys	Tom Landry
1978	Pittsburgh Steelers	Chuck Noll
1979	Pittsburgh Steelers	Chuck Noll
1980	Oakland Raiders	Tom Flores
1981	San Francisco 49ers	Bill Walsh
1982	Washington Redskins	Joe Gibbs
1983	Los Angeles Raiders	Tom Flores
1984	San Francisco 49ers	Bill Walsh
1985	Chicago Bears	Mike Ditka
1986	New York Giants	Bill Parcells
1987	Washington Redskins	Joe Gibbs
1988	San Francisco 49ers	Bill Walsh
1989	San Francisco 49ers	George Seifert
1990	New York Giants	Bill Parcells
1991	Washington Redskins	Joe Gibbs
1992	Dallas Cowboys	Jimmy Johnson
1993	Dallas Cowboys	Jimmy Johnson
1994	San Francisco 49ers	George Seifert
1995	Dallas Cowboys	Barry Switzer
1996	Green Bay Packers	Mike Holmgren
1997	Denver Broncos	Mike Shanahan
1998	Denver Broncos	Mike Shanahan
1999	Saint Louis Rams	Dick Vermeil
2000	Baltimore Ravens	Brian Billick
2001	New England Patriots	Bill Belichick
2002	Tampa Bay Buccaneers	Jon Gruden
2003	New England Patriots	Bill Belichick
2004	New England Patriots	Bill Belichick

2005	Pittsburgh Steelers	Bill Cowher
2006	Indianapolis Colts	Tony Dungy
2007	New York Giants	Tom Coughlin
2008	Pittsburgh Steelers	Mike Tomlin
2009	New Orleans Saints	Sean Payton
2010	Green Bay Packers	Mike McCarthy
2011	New York Giants	Tom Coughlin
2012	Baltimore Ravens	John Harbaugh
2013	Seattle Seahawks	Pete Carroll

Championship Teams and Years

Green Bay Packers (13)	1929 1930 1931 1936 1939 1944 1961 1962 1965 1966 1967 1996 2010
Chicago Bears (9)	1921 1932 1933 1940 1941 1943 1946 1963 1985
New York Giants (8)	1927 1934 1938 1956 1986 1990 2007 2011
Pittsburgh Steelers (6)	1974 1975 1978 1979 2005 2008
Dallas Cowboys (5)	1971 1977 1992 1993 1995
San Francisco 49ers (5)	1981 1984 1988 1989 1994
Washington Redskins (5)	1937 1942 1982 1987 1991
Cleveland Browns (4)	1950 1954 1955 1964
Detroit Lions (4)	1935 1952 1953 1957
Baltimore/Indianapolis Colts (4)	1958 1959 1970 2006
Cleveland/LA/SL Rams (3)	1945 1951 1999
Oakland/LA Raiders (3)	1976 1980 1983
Philadelphia Eagles (3)	1948 1949 1960
New England Patriots (3)	2001 2003 2004
Canton Bulldogs (2)	1922 1923
Chicago Cardinals (2)	1925 1947
Denver Broncos (2)	1997 1998
Miami Dolphins (2)	1972 1973
Baltimore Ravens (2)	2000 2012
Akron Pros (1)	1920
Cleveland Bulldogs (1)	1924
Frankford Yellow Jackets (1)	1926
Kansas City Chiefs (1)	1969
New York Jets (1)	1968
Providence Steamroller (1)	1928
Tampa Bay Buccaneers (1)	2002
New Orleans Saints (1)	2009
Seattle Seahawks (1)	2013

Championship Total: 94

NFL Championship Coaches

Ten NFL Coaches are responsible for 40 Championships

1. **George Halas** (6)
    Chicago Staleys.............. 1921
    Chicago Bears .... 1933 1940 1941 1946 1963............HOF 1963
      He had an additional two as an owner 1932 1943

2. **Curly Lambeau** (6)
    Green Bay Packers .... 1929 1930 1931 1936 1939 1944...HOF 1963

3. **Vince Lombardi** (5)
    Green Bay Packers .... 1961 1962 1965 1966 1967............HOF 1971

4. **Guy Chamberlin** (4)
    Canton Bulldogs............. 1922 1923
    Cleveland Bulldogs 1924
    Frankford Yellow Jackets.. 1926..HOF 1965

5. **Chuck Noll** (4)
    Pittsburgh Steelers.......... 1974 1975 1978 1979.....................HOF 1993

6. **Paul Brown** (3)
    Cleveland Browns .... 1950 1954 1955.............................HOF 1967

7. **Weeb Ewbank** (3)
    Baltimore Colts 1958 1959
    New York Jets................. 1968..HOF 1978

8. **Bill Walsh** (3)
    San Francisco 49ers........ 1981 1984 1988.............................HOF 1993

9. **Joe Gibbs** (3)
    Washington Redskins ..... 1982 1987 1991.............................HOF 1996

10. **Bill Belichick** (3)
    New England Patriots..... 2001 2003 2004

13 NFL Coaches are responsible for 26 Championships

1. **Steve Owen** (2)
   New York Giants .... 1934 1938 .... HOF 1966

2. **Jimmy Conzelman** (2)
   Providence Steamroller 1928
   Chicago Cardinals .... 1947 .... HOF 1964

3. **Ray Flaherty** (2)
   Washington Redskins .... 1937 1942 .... HOF 1976

4. **Greasy Neale** (2)
   Philadelphia Eagles .... 1948 1949 .... HOF 1969

5. **Buddy Parker** (2)
   Detroit Lions 1952 1953

6. **Tom Landry** (2)
   Dallas Cowboys......................... 1971 1977 .... HOF 1990

7. **Don Shula** (2)
   Miami Dolphins......................... 1972 1973 .... HOF 1997

8. **Tom Flores** (2)
   Oakland/Los Angeles Raiders 1980 1983

9. **Bill Parcells** (2)
   New York Giants .... 1986 1990 .... HOF 2013

10. **Jimmy Johnson** (2)
    Dallas Cowboys......................... 1992 1993

11. **George Seifert** (2)
    San Francisco 49ers................... 1989 1994

12. **Mike Shanahan** (2)
    Denver Broncos......................... 1997 1998

13. **Tom Coughlin** (2)
    New York Giants 2007 2011

28* NFL Coaches are responsible for 28 Championships.

1)	Elgie Tobin	(1)	Akron Pros	1920
2)	Norman Barry	(1)	Chicago Cardinals	1925
3)	Earl Potteiger	(1)	New York Giants	1927
4)	Ralph Jones	(1)	Chicago Bears	1932
5)	Potsy Clark	(1)	Detroit Lions	1935
6)	Hunk Anderson	(1)	Chicago Bears	1943
	Luke Johnsos			
7)	Adam Walsh	(1)	Cleveland Rams	1945
8)	Joe Stydahar	(1)	Los Angeles Rams	1951	HOF 1967
9)	Jim Lee Howell	(1)	New York Giants	1956
10)	George Wilson	(1)	Detroit Lions	1957
11)	Buck Shaw	(1)	Philadelphia Eagles	1960
12)	Blanton Collier	(1)	Cleveland Browns	1964
13)	Hank Stram	(1)	Kansas City Chiefs	1969	HOF 2003
14)	Don McCafferty	(1)	Baltimore Colts	1970
15)	John Madden	(1)	Oakland Raiders	1976	HOF 2006
16)	Mike Ditka	(1)	Chicago Bears	1985	HOF 1988
17)	Barry Switzer	(1)	Dallas Cowboys	1995
18)	Mike Holmgren	(1)	Green Bay Packers	1996
19)	Dick Vermeil	(1)	Saint Louis Rams	1999
20)	Brian Billick	(1)	Baltimore Ravens	2000
21)	Jon Gruden	(1)	Tampa Bay Buccaneers	2002
22)	Bill Cowher	(1)	Pittsburgh Steelers	2005
23)	Tony Dungy	(1)	Indianapolis Colts	2006
24)	Mike Tomlin	(1)	Pittsburgh Steelers	2008
25)	Sean Payton	(1)	New Orleans Saints	2009
26)	Mike McCarthy	(1)	Green Bay Packers	2010
27)	John Harbaugh	(1)	Baltimore Ravens	2012
28)	Pete Carroll	(1)	Seattle Seahawks	2013

* Hunk Anderson and Luke Johnsos served as co-coaches for 1943 Chicago Bears.

Photographs and Illustrations Credits

All photos and illustrations are reproduced with permission
from the sources shown below.

Page	Description	Source
Cover	Pillars of the NFL cover	Don Torres
xvi	George Halas Illustration	© William Potter
26	George Halas and Bears on Snowy Practice Field.	Chicago History Museum
38	Bill Wade Throwing	McCaskey Family
44	George Halas Goal Line Card by Gary Thomas	© Goal Line Art, Inc.
52	Guy Chamberlin Illustration	© William Potter
54	Guy Chamberlin, Nebraska Wesleyan Track	Rob Sherwood, Chamberlin Family
56	University of Nebraska v. Notre Dame, 1915	Rob Sherwood, Chamberlin Family
58	Guy Chamberlin Letterman, 1915 University of Nebraska	Rob Sherwood, Chamberlin Family
62	Guy Chamberlin at University of Nebraska Ready to Play	Rob Sherwood, Chamberlin Family
66	1922 Canton Bulldogs	Rob Sherwood, Chamberlin Family
72	Guy Chamberlin, Second Lieutenant	Rob Sherwood, Chamberlin Family
78	Curly Lambeau Illustration	© William Potter
82	Four Horsemen of Football at Notre Dame	Library of Congress
112	Paul Brown Illustration	© William Potter
116	Paul Brown Miami Player	From the Walter Havighurst Special Collections, Miami University Libraries, Oxford, Ohio
126	Paul Brown in the Classroom	Michael Schwartz Library, Cleveland State University
154	Paul Brown signing Autographs	Michael Schwartz Library Cleveland State University
162	Weeb Ewbank Illustration	© William Potter
164	Weeb Ewbank Miami Player	From the Walter Havighurst Special Collections, Miami University Libraries, Oxford, Ohio
166	Miami University Football Team	From the Walter Havighurst Special Collections, Miami University Libraries, Oxford, Ohio
198	Vince Lombardi Illustration	© William Potter

Page	Description	Source
202	Vince Lombardi at Fordham University	Archives and Special Collections of Fordham University Library, Bronx, NY
222	"Fabulous Green Bay Packers," *Milwaukee Journal* Publication Commemorating the Green Bay Packers of 1967. Drawing by Gregg Klees of Packers' No. 84, Carroll Dale, blocking Bears No. 26, Bennie McRae.	Wisconsin Historical Society
230	Fr. Dennis Burke (President of St. Norbert Collete), Bishop Aloysius Wycislo, and Vince Lombardi at the Graduation Ceremony at St. Norbert College in 1968.	St. Norbert College
238	Chuck Noll Illustration	© William Potter
248	Chuck Noll Moments after Immaculate Reception Win	Pittsburgh Post-Gazette, Copyright © Pittsburgh Post-Gazette, 2014, all rights reserved. Reprinted with Permission.
268	Chuck Noll Closeup	Pittsburgh Post-Gazette, Copyright © Pittsburgh Post-Gazette, 2014, all rights reserved. Reprinted with Permission.
276	Bill Walsh Illustration	© William Potter
280	Bill Walsh at San Jose State	San Jose State University Athletics
308	Joe Gibbs Illustration	© William Potter
342	Joe Gibbs	U.S. Air Force Staff Sgt. D. Myles Cullen, Source: Wikipedia Commons
348	Bill Belichick Illustration	© William Potter
364	Belichick on sidelines.	Keith Allison

Index